PRACTICAL ELECTRICAL PROJECT ENGINEERING

PRACTICAL ELECTRICAL PROJECT ENGINEERING

LIONEL B. ROE

Managing Director
L. B. Roe (Consultants), Ltd.
Anaheim, California,
and Blackpool, England

Senior Member
Institute of Electrical and Electronics Engineers

McGraw-Hill Book Company

New York St. Louis San Francisco Auckland Bogotá Düsseldorf Johannesburg London Madrid Mexico Montreal New Delhi Panama Paris São Paulo Singapore Sydney Tokyo Toronto

Dedicated to my sister Nadia and S. H.

Library of Congress Cataloging in Publication Data

Roe, L. B., date.
Practical electrical project engineering.

Includes index.
1. Electric engineering – Handbooks, manuals, etc.
I. Title.
TK151.R69 621.31 77-18534
ISBN 0-07-053392-X

234567890 FGRFGR 765432109

The editors for this book were Tyler G. Hicks and Joseph Williams, the designer was Elliot Epstein, and the production supervisor was Frank Bellantoni. It was set in Baskerville by The Kingsport Press.

Printed and bound by Fairfield Graphics.

CONTENTS

PREFACE

This book is written for the whole of the engineering profession and the contractors and constructors who are engaged in the "designing and building" of industrial projects.

The book is primarily aimed at senior electrical engineers—and also designers who are hoping to move into a position of more responsibility (as "lead men") and project electrical engineers. It will also be of valuable assistance to senior engineers of other disciplines who have some project responsibility requiring coordination with the electrical department.

There are two basic parts to a project: conception and production. The second part is the routine production of a set of drawings to be issued for construction by designers working under a fairly rigid set of guidelines, instructions, and supervision. This, incidently, was covered in my first book "Practices and Procedures of Industrial Electrical Design" (McGraw-Hill, 1972).

In contrast, the first part of the project (which this book deals with) involves an imaginary view into the future to try and determine in advance how the production will progress under different situations of labor, economics, deliveries, time lapse, codes, and regulations, including possible client and management changes of decisions in midstream.

In addition, there are technical decisions to be made—also in advance. The individuals responsible for these decisions must consider alternate technical choices, such as system types and performance, and must know the possible problems beforehand, considering various vagaries in the performance of individual components and variations in manufacturers' designs and deliveries which will affect the project cost and completion date.

To cover all the initial project decisions in a single book is an impossibility; a book can be written on any single chapter. This book, then, is an extension of my first book. It assumes that the individual is experienced in technical procedures and mathematics up to the level presented there.

The book is not intended to be an application engineering book giving finite answers to specific problems. It is intended to present a broad range of general possibilities for consideration with guidelines on how to approach a situation, evaluate the alternatives, and make a decision in a selective manner. Once this point is reached, the problem of application engineering is turned over to the "production" part of the team, i.e., the "designer."

Codes and regulations have been specifically omitted as much as possible because enforcement codes differ with location and periodic issue. In any event it should be unnecessary to repeatedly stress the use of the correct and up-to-date codes.

In this book we have presented a chapter on *symmetrical components*. It is only an introduction to the subject; however, it is a natural extension to the section on mathematics presented in my first book and should present no problems to readers who have studied the mathematics section or reached this level by conventional schooling. The same applies to the mathematical logic that is used; a change of signs and symbols should present no problems to anyone who has studied the mathematics section in my first book.

The author gives acknowledgment to General Electric, Westinghouse, Square D, and Electrical Machinery Mfg. Co. for specific information. And also to all electrical companies who have researched, developed, and disseminated their information to the industry over many years, resulting in much more predictable and reliable designs. Without their pioneering efforts we could still be using candles and windmills for lighting and power.

L. B. Roe

Part One
PROJECT PRELIMINARIES

1 BASIC DESIGN CRITERIA

1.1 PREPARATORY DESIGN REQUIREMENTS

The mandatory minimum requirements before actively using design personnel are:

1. Customer specification
2. Plot plan of applicable area
3. Current electrical code in authority
4. Agreement with customer on design standards and symbols

These items are production tools but cannot be utilized unless a design plan is available. Therefore, before personnel can be effectively utilized, the senior design engineer must spend some time compiling preparatory design information.

This is where a combination of skill, imagination, guesswork, and assessment are necessary. It is mandatory to establish a scope of the complete project: how many drawings are required, how many employees, what is the estimated completion date, what is the required completion date, what specific and/or unique problems could affect the design production, what liaison problems exist, who has what information, etc.

In this chapter we will discuss specific documents and methods of acquiring the necessary information preparatory to using personnel. Again, there may be alternate ways, depending on individuals and companies, but generally the net result must be the same before a design can commence.

1.2 THE JOB FILE

The first requirement is to establish a *job file*. This may be a file folder or preferably a three-ring looseleaf binder. Throughout the project, notes, sketches, comments, messages, instructions, and "guesstimates" will accumulate. Inevitably, at some later point in the project a question will be raised; many times the answer is in the previous information considered in the early days of the project. The rule, then, is never to discard information no matter how insignificant it may seem at the time; also, date each document either with a date stamp or by writing on the date. The *job file* will be the history of the project design. In the event a change is made in senior engineers (design production supervisor), it is a simple matter for the new individual to peruse the *job file* and assess the existing situation. If a problem existed with the design production, the new responsible individual can determine from the procedure outlined in the job file whether the problem was technical or political.

1.3 THE PLOT PLAN

One of the first essential documents necessary for evaluation of the scope or size of a project is the *plot plan.* This drawing is generally supplied by the customer and outlines the property boundaries. It will usually show the entrance point for the utility-company electrical service. In addition, it will possibly show a "not to scale" approximate layout of the areas and buildings. In the case of a project having hazardous areas, it may (or may not) show the area classifications. Whatever information is presented on the customer's document (i.e., large drawing or $8\frac{1}{2}'' \times 11''$ sketch), it is necessary to *redline* (add in red pencil) any omitted information in order to have a complete picture of the project.

Try to imagine an aerial photograph of the final project that shows roof lines, large equipment, substation(s), switchracks, and motor control centers. If information is not available, then a "best guess" should be made, and noted with "HOLD."

This redlined plot plan will be the source of information for the designer who will eventually produce the *electrical plot plan.* It will also be the source of information for the design of the power-distribution single line. It will delineate the blocks of power necessary for the project and will also be used for the preliminary assessment of underground conduit banks. It is, in fact, a valuable record document.

1.4 CLIENT SPECIFICATION AND CONTRACT

The client specification is a document outlining the client's (customer's) intentions. The specification may be very specific and detailed, or it may be imprecise. In the case of the detailed presentation, only careful perusal is needed to extract the pertinent information. In the imprecise presentation it is necessary to annotate the specification. This will result in a list of questions that must be answered by the client in order to confirm the interpretation of the specification.

The specification is an extremely important document. The senior design engineer should be completely familiar with all sections of it, and should also be completely confident in the interpretation of it. Sometimes the specification will include or define a contractual obligation. This portion must be thoroughly understood and confirmed. Eventually an electrical specification must be written for the contractor (constructor) and some of the information will be derived from the client specification.

The "contracts" portion of a specification is usually limited to an outline of how the client desires the general contracts and subcontracts to be let. Other detailed contract information is invariably "restricted and confidential," with limited publication.

1.5 FLOW SHEETS (P&ID)

The *flow sheet* is exactly as it describes itself; it is a diagram of the process flow. It shows the flow and treatment of the raw material through pumps, pressure vessels, mixers, and various other pieces of equipment. Superimposed on this flow diagram is the instrumentation, which is indicated in symbolic form. The flow diagram identifies electrical interlocks (this will be covered in more detail later in the book).

With the flow and instrumentation being shown on the same diagram, this results in an alternate name for this drawing (or set of drawings); this is P&ID (*process and instrumentation diagram*). This is an essential source of information. The probability is that, in the early stages of a project, the P&ID will be issued in preliminary form.

Throughout the duration of the project, changes will constantly be made. This, of course, is normal; however, provision must be made to ensure that the electrical design supervisor is on the distribution list for new issues of revised P&IDs.

One problem exists with information flow. When the process or instrumentation engineer makes a change to a P&ID, it is usually redlined on his own personal reference print, which is then retained for a period of time in case he changes his mind or in anticipation of more changes. In the meantime the electrical department may be designing with obsolete information.

Economics plays a major part in this transmittal of information. If new prints were issued for every small revision, then nothing would be accomplished because everyone would be producing prints. The suggestion is that the electrical supervisor notify the process and instrumentation engineers to issue a simple handwritten memo to the electrical department, briefly stating the changes as they are made. This will serve a dual purpose. The electrical design can be changed to accommodate the revision, and when the drawings are finally distributed, a check of the memos against the revision will confirm that the change was not rescinded.

1.6 PRELIMINARY DRAWINGS

In some cases the client has preliminary drawings which were utilized for study prior to contracting with an engineering company. Where buildings are involved, the drawings are probably architectural, indicating the type of structure intended. When a refinery or process plant is involved, the drawings are usually layouts indicating major areas and the location of key equipment and offices.

These drawings can be used to advantage in the early stages for estimating design hours. Buildings and structures on these preliminary drawings may not change drastically in size; however, the arrangement and location within the site perimeter may change. The significance of change with regard to the estimating of design hours is not too drastic at this point.

Similarly, the preliminary drawings can be used for a preliminary study of a probable distribution system. It is not advisable to rely too heavily on these preliminary drawings for power loads, but they can be used for an approximation of lighting loads. Buildings and specific areas can be assessed for lighting on a "watts per square foot" basis. These lighting loads then move with the buildings and areas in event of relocation. The same applies to the outdoor lighting. This can also be estimated the same way. The amount of outdoor lighting is going to be the net difference between the total building and/or specific area lighting and the total site area, regardless of where the buildings and specific areas are finally located.

In summation then, the preliminary drawings issued by the client can be a useful source of information but should be used very judiciously.

1.7 MOTOR LIST

An essential part of the early design is a guess at the amount of power required at the service entrance. The largest portion of load in any industrial or process plant is usually the motor load. At initial meetings and conferences basic parameters will have been established for production outputs. During this early period the probability is that a rough list of motor requirements was made. The various mechanical engineers would have taken their best guess at what they may possibly require. This initial motor list is usually adequate to estimate the probable size of service required. Usually the standard-size-transformer break point is the dictating factor. If the total motor load was 1250 hp, the next highest transformer would be 1500 kVA. The next one above that is 2000 kVA. The probability is that the 1500 kVA would be selected with a "HOLD" until further information was forthcoming. However, the 1250 hp plus the estimated lighting load would give an approximate selection so that discussion with the power company can commence.

The final motor list can only be compiled from the actual purchase orders. At any other time up to this point motors are subject to possible change in size and quantity.

It is obvious that it is not possible to wait for a "final" motor list before commencing a design; therefore, the early motor list is used as a base and is constantly changed and updated throughout the duration of the project.

The P&ID will usually show most of the motors; this is for the purpose of indicating interlocks. The P&ID will also show the identification number of the equipment being operated by the motor. This number and description, that is, "pump P101," should be used on the motor list. Eventually this identification will also be used on the single line.

Some P&IDs also show the horsepower rating of the motor, but this is by no means the rule. This is an area where the process engineers, for reasons known to themselves, decide whether or not to show horsepowers on the P&ID or to issue and continually update a motor list.

The problem with the latter approach is that usually the engineer is working on an actual drawing and is involved in evaluating a motor/pump size; once completed, it is redlined on his drawing. Transferring it to a motor list becomes a clerical chore which he intends to do. By the time it is entered on the motor list and the revised motor list issued, it could have changed again. The conclusion then is that the design supervisor should establish some specific procedure with the process and mechanical department for transmitting information which will result in a constantly up-to-date motor list.

1.8 SUMMATION OF CRITERIA

In these early stages the design supervisor is trying to develop a "feel" for the size and type of project. He may not have had the benefit of attending early-stage conferences, and therefore must work with the preliminary information available. The following is a list of information which may be available:

- Plot plan (mandatory)
- Client specification (mandatory)
- Motor list (mandatory, probable rough estimate)
- P&ID (may or may not be available)
- Previous drawings of similar project (sometimes available)

Beyond this, any more information would probably be in the form of notes, sketches, or verbal comments from individuals who were in the early conferences. By perusing all this information, an experienced individual will gradually develop a mental picture of the size of the design group required, a fairly rough approximation of the duration of the project, and an isolation of peculiar and critical problems. For example, installing multiple 20,000-hp motors for a wind tunnel presents no problem with regard to installing wire and conduit. The obvious problem, however, is "how do you start them?" and "what effect will starting them have on the power system?" The immediate consideration then is additional time for a study of this problem plus the requirement for an experienced individual to whom this study can be assigned.

With this mental picture established, the supervisor can now decide what the next steps should be and what personnel should be assigned initially.

1.9 MODEL OR NO MODEL

This is the question. The increasing trend on major projects is to produce a scale model of the project. This model is produced in lieu of some mechanical drawings. The intention is that, with a model, the total design can be monitored by all departments by the simple procedure of going to the model department and examining the model. A further "selling" feature of using a model is that the assumption is made that by use of a model certain drawings become unnecessary. The subject of models will be discussed later in the book (Sec. 3.4); therefore, in this section the only intention is to point out that models do exist, they are becoming a major factor in design procedure, and they should be taken into consideration when evaluating the design requirements of a new project.

1.10 LOGIC DIAGRAM REQUIREMENT

Another design trend which is being seen more and more is the use of *logic diagrams*. These are drawings which originate in process and instrumentation. They indicate the sequence of operation of equipment. They will also be discussed later in the book, but again, it must be established initially whether logic diagrams are to be produced as part of the process and instrumentation design. This must then be taken into consideration with regard to electrical design group personnel.

The logic diagrams will be used for designing the control schematics; therefore, the individuals considered for the control design should have experience with this type of logic diagram. There are two reasons for experience being mandatory.

First, and most important, an individual trained in "logic" can recognize an error in the issued logic diagrams; he can then question it and correct it. Second, an individual learning "on-the-job" without the mathematical background would require excessive supervision and would require more time than can reasonably be allowed, and furthermore, an error in understanding can be carried throughout many drawings, resulting in expensive rework.

1.11 LOOP DIAGRAM REQUIREMENT

This is another type of diagram/drawing that may or may not be issued as part of a design package. It is essentially an "instrumentation" diagram. As self-described, it is a complete instrument loop showing the origin of the instrument circuit, progressing to the various areas and accounting for all the components associated with that particular circuit. It is necessary to establish whether loop diagrams are intended to be issued because in most cases the electrical department will be involved to some degree with these loop diagrams. Accordingly, time and labor must be made available. This must then be included in the design estimate for total hours contemplated.

1.12 SCHEDULES AND PROGRESS CHART REQUIREMENT

Schedules and progress charts can be simple or complex, depending on the detailed breakdown required. If it is a simple matter of scheduling electrical department manpower loading, then this is fairly simple. Alternatively, if a detailed "total project" schedule and analysis is required, detailing drawing issues and expected deliveries of equipment, and is coordinated with other departments, then this is a subject for careful consideration. It involves periodic reviews, updating, slipdates, discussions with other personnel, and constant attention if it is going to have meaningful results. It should be established specifically exactly what is required; the hours must then be adjusted accordingly.

1.13 CONCLUSION

It must be repeatedly stressed that the correct, up-to-date enforcing codes be used from the project's inception. These are the electrical and OSHA codes in effect and as used by the local inspectors at the location of construction.

Other code enforcement may be introduced depending on the project; therefore check with all involved authorities regarding these codes.

2 DESIGN PACKAGE "GUESSTIMATE"

2.1 THE DRAWING LIST

Essentially, an electrical design package consists of a set of drawings, a specification, and a bill of material. Additional items, such as instruction books, start-up procedures, field engineering, construction supervision, and construction cost estimates are possible items to be added to the basic three items.

If a drawing list is prepared and unit hours assigned to each drawing, the majority of hours will be accounted for. The remainder will be a small portion for the specification and bill of material.

Preparing the drawing list requires a combination of experience and imagination. The imagination is not of the daydreaming type, it is an instant method of creating a mental picture of a building or area that does not yet exist. It is mentally created in seconds and is demolished as fast. The only thing necessary to provide fuel for this imagination is the information discussed in the preceding chapters. Unless the essential information is available, that is, plot plan, client specification, and motor list, the imagination has no information to draw on from the memory banks of the brain. The effectiveness and accuracy of an imaginary picture is a function of how much preliminary information the mind has absorbed.

Certain drawings are mandatory and require no imagination, for example, symbol sheet, electrical plot plan, single line, grounding, schematics. The electrical plans which deal specifically with installation of raceways are the drawings which require careful consideration. The number of sheets required will depend on the total area plus specific areas that will be congested, requiring larger scale detail.

In this chapter we will consider a routine for producing a drawing list, applying unit hours, and estimating manloading.

2.2 DRAWING INDEX

The first drawing or sheet in a design package should be the *drawing index*. This should show all the drawings in the package by actual number and title as it appears on the specific drawing. When compiling the drawing list, we are only reserving space; because the drawing is assigned as the first sheet, it does not mean it must be the first one to be worked on. In fact the drawing index will be the last to be completed.

Assign one full sheet (assuming a 24″ × 36″ sheet). If the whole sheet is not used, the remaining part of the sheet can be used for some general notes.

2.3 PLOT-PLAN LAYOUT

This drawing should be the second sheet in the package. This drawing is intended to give an overall impression of the size and complexity of the project. It should show the perimeter fence and some coordinates that will identify the exact location in the township. Usually two adjacent streets, identified by name and at right angles to each other, will serve this purpose. This will be necessary for discussions with the electric utility company. All major areas and buildings should be shown and identified. All "inplant" roads and traffic areas should be shown. A north arrow should be shown, and the plan should be oriented so the north arrow points to the top of the sheet (if possible), although the orientation may already have been established by the client's plot plan, in which case this should be followed. The "scale" selected for this drawing will be whatever scale will allow it to fit on one sheet. Any other information relating to a specific location address can also be shown.

2.4 HAZARDOUS AREA IDENTIFICATION DRAWING

For projects having areas where explosive gases, vapors, or dusts are present, area classification is necessary. How to classify the areas will be discussed in Chapters 4 and 5, but for now it is only necessary to know that a drawing must be made which will identify these areas. This will be the third sheet in the package (or combined with the plot plan). The mechanics of producing this drawing allow two choices. First, produce (by drafting) a plan similar to the plot plan with the various areas cross-hatched and a legend identifying the cross-hatching. Alternatively, have the local blueprint company produce another "tracing" of the plot plan with the title block blocked out (i.e., empty). This can then be used as a background; the draftsman/designer can then add the area classifications.

2.5 SYMBOL SHEET

This drawing would be next in the package. It is self-explanatory; however, a word of caution is necessary. The design supervisor should confirm (in writing if necessary) whether the client's symbols, engineering company symbols, U.S. standard symbols, or international standard symbols should be used. It is time-consuming and "error-generating" to have to change symbols when a design is partially completed. Notes should also be added to the symbol sheet with regard to whether metric measurements should be used instead of or in addition to the English feet and inches. Allow one full sheet.

2.6 SINGLE-LINE DIAGRAM

Sometime referred to as a "one-line" diagram. Like the plot plan, the first single line in the package should show the overall plant-distribution system. The intent of this drawing is to present a picture so that the observer can assess the blocks of power required, can rapidly identify a particular feeder, and can also ascertain the main protective devices responsible for plant outages. A special effort should be made to try and present this single line on one sheet. If it is necessary to use more than one sheet, the break should be by voltage levels rather than by splitting a *bus*.

The title blocks would read accordingly, for example, "Single Line 69 kV and 13.8 kV," "Single line 4160 V—Power Distribution Center," "Single Line 460 V Motor Control Center A."

In some cases it is possible to show all voltage levels down to the motor control centers. At this point it is advisable to use other sheets for showing single lines of specific motor control centers. The only concern at this point in time is "how many sheets should be used for single lines?"

If it is obvious that a single sheet is adequate for distribution with feeders terminating at motor control centers, allow one sheet plus a sheet for each motor control center. If there are a predominant amount of size one and two starters (up to 25 hp), allow one sheet to every three or four vertical sections of motor control center, assuming of course the standard 460-V three-phase 60-Hz system.

A memory trick for assigning starter size to horsepower for estimating purposes is remembering that the United States coins are 10, 25, 50, and 100 cents (one dollar); these numbers are also maximum horsepowers for 460-V motor starters (size 1—10 hp max; size 2—25 hp max; size 3—50 hp max; size 4—100 hp max). Above this requires size 5 with a maximum of 200 hp at 460 V.

By using the motor list, a rough guess of how many sections of motor control center can be ascertained. This then defines the approximate sheets required for single-line drawings. If it is marginal, then add an extra sheet; that is, reserve a drawing number and identify it as a "spare."

2.7 THE PARTIAL PACKAGE

At this point the basic reference drawings are accounted for: Drawing Index, Plot Plan, Area Classification, Symbol Sheet, Power Distribution Single Line, Motor Control Center Single Line. These are drawings that can be started early. The drawings in preliminary form are necessary for discussion with the electric utility company.

The motor-control-center single lines are not too essential in early discussions, but the approximate loads are necessary for transformer sizing on the power-distribution single line. These loads will be assessed by the power company along with the geographical location and layout of the plant from the plot plan. They will then advise where the service entrance will be and provide the necessary instructions for compliance with their requirements.

In this chapter we are concerned only with estimating a design package which is essentially the drawings, specification, and bill of material. The problem is that the senior design engineer rarely has the luxury of doing only one thing at once. The probability is that during this estimating period preliminary engineering will be required; therefore these initial drawings can be assigned in a partial package to a senior designer who can produce the drawings from verbal instructions. This then allows the senior design engineer to return to his estimating.

2.8 BELOW-GRADE DRAWINGS

These are the next drawings in order of importance and priority. As excavating and trenching are initial phases of construction, the contractor usually cannot get these drawings too soon. The problem of course is evaluating how many drawings and how complex the below-grade design will be. To evaluate this, it is necessary to have a print of the plot plan. Prior instructions will have been outlined by the client with regard to the below-grade requirements. If instructions have not been given, it becomes a standard engineering assessment problem. In either case detailed knowledge is not necessary at this stage.

With a print of the plot plan available and a red pencil, draw straight lines between all points requiring below-grade installations of raceway or tunnels. It is immaterial whether we are considering a single conduit or a large bank of conduits; the concern is how many sheets are required. If the "scale" of the plot plan is not too small, it may be possible to utilize the "background" of the plot plan for the below-grade trenching, in which case, with one plot plan, only one below-grade drawing is necessary.

If the plot plan is a very small "scale," then a "scale" must be selected and an area established that can be accommodated on a standard-size sheet. If the sheet is 24 in. × 36 in., allowing a 5-in. margin for notes, etc., gives 31 in. in length. Allow an inch top and bottom for possible match lines, which gives 22 in. in height. If the selected scale is 1 in. equals 20 ft, the area is 620 ft long by 420 ft wide. It is now only necessary to block off 620 × 420 ft sections on the plot plan to arrive at the sheets required.

It is also necessary to know the contents and arrangement of the below-grade installations. This is done by "cutting sections." The sections are identified on the trenching plan by letter and symbol and should all be "cut" in the same direction, that is, "inward" or "outward." It is necessary to "cut a section" each time the contents of the trench change; a "cut" should also be made whenever a trench leaves or enters a building, motor control center, switchrack, etc. In some cases the information in the section precludes the necessity of making a "stub up" arrangement. When all the "cuts" have been redlined on the plot-plan print, they can be counted. An estimate is then made of the number of additional sheets required to accommodate these sections. Fifteen to twenty per standard sheet is a good guide. Allow an additional two or three sheets as spares.

2.9 ELECTRICAL PLANS

The electrical plans show all the above-grade electrical installations (e.g., Electrical Power Plan). The title block usually identifies the building or area and sometimes the specific location, such as "Machine Room, Basement, S.E. Corner." A complete title might be "Electrical Power Plan, Machine Room Basement."

The scale of an electrical plan, excluding lighting plans, is usually $\frac{1}{4}$ in. equals 1 ft. Sometimes $\frac{1}{8}$ in. equals 1 ft is used, but the use of the $\frac{1}{8}''$ scale can result in congested and often incomprehensible detail. Using the smaller $\frac{1}{8}''$ scale results in fewer drawings (i.e., sheets of paper). It does not reduce the amount of information that must be presented on the paper.

If we assume the amount of information is the same for either scale, then the only cost saving is the value of the paper. Furthermore, the drafting time will probably be longer using the smaller scale because more care is required. In addition any areas such as an electric room with numerous conduits will require "blowing up" in scale, probably to $\frac{1}{4}''$ with minimum details and sections or $\frac{1}{8}''$ with excessive details and sections.

If in doubt, select the $\frac{1}{4}''$ scale. In fact for estimating purposes it is probably better to use the $\frac{1}{4}''$ scale. After reviewing the final budget figure, it may be required to conduct a budget reduction exercise. The $\frac{1}{8}''$ scale can be considered at this time.

The approach to evaluating the quantity of above-grade drawings (sheets) required is similar to the below-grade procedure. Take a plot plan and redline the area that can be covered by a drawing using $\frac{1}{4}''$ scale. At this point in time it is not known where or how the electrical installation will develop; therefore, we make an assumption that all areas not already covered by below-grade drawings will require an above-grade drawing. Each floor or platform in each building must be completely covered by drawing allocation. Any rooms which might require extensive details should have a separate drawing allocated. The total is then added to the drawing list by title. After ensuring that all areas are covered, allow two or three spare numbers for areas which may develop due to additions. Probably, some of these drawings will never be used, in which case the title is changed to *spare* on the drawing list. This will not be known, however, until more detailed information is available. This we will cover in a later paragraph.

2.10 DETAILS AND SECTIONS

Additional drawings must be allocated on the drawing list for sections and details. The below-grade sections are fairly simple to estimate and are accounted for by some drawing-number allocations immediately following the below-grade drawings. The above-grade, however, is not as clear-cut. Here we must rely on experience for a calculated guess. Keep in mind that a drawing list is like the chapters in a book. Groups of numbers are expected to be complete. If we see that a drawing list allocates the numbers E20, 21, 22, 23, 24, 25, as details, we would not normally expect to find an additional one belonging to the same group with the number E203. This is what happens if you underestimate. Therefore, it is better to overestimate the number allocation and not use them than to underestimate. On the smallest project allocate three spare numbers for details and sections. On the larger projects allocate 5 to 10%.

2.11 LIGHTING DRAWINGS

These drawings are usually $\frac{1}{8}''$ scale for indoor or equipment areas (outdoor). These can be estimated on the same basis as the electrical plans. Floodlighting and outdoor lighting, such as parking areas and fence (security) lighting, must be evaluated by an examination of the plot plan and a probable guess as to whether they can be shown on an already existing drawing (i.e., a below-grade drawing showing all fencing) or whether separate drawings are required.

An additional one or two drawings will probably be required for a lighting-fixture schedule; this will list the various types of lighting fixtures and lamp sizes with the designated symbol.

2.12 GROUNDING

The grounding drawings should be a separate and complete group of drawings. The set of drawings should show the below-grade grounding, such as a "ground grid."

Next the above-grade grounding should be shown in plan form, indicating which steel columns or specific equipment require bonding. The remainder is usually covered by detail sheets showing standard methods for grounding all conducting enclosures and equipment.

Again, the plot plan is probably the only drawing available that gives some kind of feel for the possible magnitude of the grounding installation. Add three sheets for details and add additional drawings as the evaluation of the plot plan indicates.

2.13 SCHEMATICS/ELEMENTARIES

The schematic or alternately designed "elementary" drawing is, of course, the control relays and devices drawing. This drawing shows the function and sequence of operation of the various components without regard to the physical arrangement of the items. Any reader requiring further explanation must review the previous book.[1] Estimating the quantity of drawings and the amount of detail at the initial outset is purely a guess. Experience will help some; however, the time spent on schematics is a function of project size and clarity of communication with instrument and mechanical department.

If the intended automatic sequence of equipment operation is defined accurately and precisely on paper, either in words or in "logic diagram" form, then the schematic design is fairly straightforward. However, if the information is inaccurate, imprecise, and changing constantly, then the time required extends accordingly, but the number of sheets will probably remain the same. There are then two unknown quantities to estimate: first, the quantity of sheets; and second, a "time factor."

In the early stages, such as we are now considering, we must assume that information will be received "normally." "Normally" is defined as "fairly accurate but with minor changes." A more precise evaluation of time will be considered later under budget reduction. The main problem now is to produce an estimate for the number of sheets required and to assign numbers and titles. Referring to the motor list and equipment list will give some clues. Break the schematics down into groups, such as "machine room area," "offloading area," "packaging area," and "pumping area." Alternatively, if enough information is available the schematics can be designated "freshwater system," "chemical pumps system," "offloading system," etc. The latter is probably the best approach but requires more detailed knowledge than breaking up by area. Keep in mind that this is only a preliminary estimate and that the whole drawing list will be revised at some later date with possible, and probably, different allocations of scale, areas, titles, etc., but before this can be done a base must be established; therefore, if all else fails, take your best guess and assign a block of numbers for schematics. They can be reduced in quantity at a later date; the unused ones becoming spare.

2.14 INTERCONNECTION DIAGRAMS

These are sometimes referred to as wiring diagrams. They show the specific components and the component terminals. They also show the wire and wire number connecting to the terminals. From this drawing the electrician can make the connections and can also determine the "wire bundles" that are required for a specific raceway.

Estimating the quantity of sheets is fraught with the same problems as the schematics and should therefore be approached in the same manner.

2.15 INSTRUMENTATION

These drawings fall into the same category as the schematics and interconnection diagrams. The only difference being that this group of drawings

[1] L. B. Roe, *Practices and Procedures of Industrial Electrical Design,* McGraw-Hill Book Company, New York, 1972.

is concerned with instruments, display panels, readouts, transducers, etc.

The line of demarcation between the work required from the electrical department and the information provided by the instrument department is always an unknown quantity on each project. It will rarely be the same. Presentation may change, allocation of work to vendors may vary, and quantity of work assigned to the electrical department will change.

It is necessary then (in the early stages) to discuss this with the instrument department or the individual assigned this responsibility. Try and define the line of demarcation. Once this is done, based on the information a guess must be made on the quantity of drawings required to show both the schematic part and the interconnection part of the instrument installation. The same procedure can be used as mentioned in the preceding two paragraphs and adding some spares for "detail sheets."

2.16 MISCELLANEOUS DRAWINGS

Additional groups of drawings will be necessary depending on the project requirements: telephone, paging (loud-hailer) system, corrosion protection system, pipe heating systems, emergency power and/or lighting systems, etc.

These must all be listed on the preliminary drawing list. The quantity of drawings must be estimated, but usually the specialized systems don't require many sheets. If nothing at all is known about a system, but the specifications require one, then allocate five or ten drawing numbers, depending on a "best guess" at the time.

2.17 SUMMATION AND "GUESSTIMATE"

At this early stage we have a drawing list which is a compilation of the probable groups of drawings required for the project. Titles have been assigned to specific drawings, and in some cases titles have been assigned to groups of drawings such as *schematics.* This list will now become the basis of compiling an estimate. The list in itself is only a "guess"; however, it is an educated guess and as such is accurate up to a point. We will differentiate between an estimate and a guesstimate by defining the latter as "a collection of groups of drawings with an arbitrary hourly unit assigned per sheet." The former (estimate) we will define as "a firm drawing list with hours assigned to each specific drawing (or group of drawings) whose total hours will be translated into money and entered into the project estimate."

2.18 UNIT HOURS PER DRAWING

With this preliminary drawing list complete and checked for omissions, we total the number of drawings required. We then apply a unit figure of "hours per drawing" to the total. This unit figure can vary from 45 to 120 hours. The 45 hours should not be used unless an exceptional team exists and is repeating an established procedure with acceptable results. The 120 hours should be considered where predictable slowness is anticipated due to bureaucracy, inexperienced personnel, anticipated slowness of information from other departments, stringent or inconclusive specifications, or other anticipated problems which would result in inefficiency and low morale. Where a project "appears" to be average and tight, a fair and nominal figure is approximately 80 hours per drawing. True, it can be shown that some drawings may only require 10 hours, but others may require 150 hours before the project is completed. In any case, we are only trying to establish a base that we can add to or subtract from.

2.19 UNIT HOUR MONEY

The next guess is an average money figure against the hourly rate. The best person to establish this is generally the individual who is responsible for the technical interview with a prospective employee, which is generally a local resident and knows others in the industry outside the company. This person is aware of what the "local going rate" is and also is generally aware of the rate necessary to attract a new employee.

For the purpose of the guesstimate it is only necessary to work with the *direct labor cost,* which is the amount actually paid (gross) to the employee. This figure is then multiplied by the number of total hours to complete the drawings. For example, 100 drawings at 80 hours per drawing is 8000 hours. At the established hourly rate, 8000 × rate per hour = direct cost.

We now have a guideline as to the size and investment into the electrical design. This figure is now presented to the project manager (via normal channels), who then applies other multipliers which cover overhead G&A (general and administrative), etc., and adds the figure to the total project estimate.

An experienced project manager will then compare the electrical guesstimate with the total project cost and evaluate the percentage assigned to electrical design. If the percentage is lower than expected, it will be questioned whether anything has been accidentally omitted. If the percentage is high, the project manager will naturally question the applied figures of unit hours and unit money. This then leads to the first "meeting of the minds."

2.20 BUDGET ASSESSMENT

During this first meeting, the project manager will have a preliminary budget figure previously considered as adequate for the electrical design and probably based on statistical methods accrued from previous similar projects. The difference between this statistical budget figure and the guesstimate will enable the project manager to assess the electrical design approach. The project manager will make comments like: "Don't bother with pipe heating, this will be done by vendor." "Don't bother with instrumentation except for power supplies." These comments when applied to the drawing list will then narrow down the margin of error. The remaining areas requiring more specific information will then be more obvious.

In the interest of budget accuracy, the project manager will probably advise other departments that the electrical department requires further information. If not, he will probably instruct the electrical department to meet with other departments to provide further information on expected scope. If neither of these instructions appears, then the senior electrical designer should institute the proceedings to obtain further information.

Before going on to a final estimate and final drawing list, all possible information with regard to scope should be collected and applied to the preliminary drawing list.

The result should be a trimmed-down list with suspect or guessed areas flagged with a "HOLD." The individual compiling the guesstimate should feel completely familiar with the project scope, the size of the electrical design, and the intended method of design for the various parts. With this point reached, it becomes a natural "break" point where discussion can now be made with other senior electrical designers. Decisions can be made with regard to design considerations, methods, and procedures, using the guesstimate and preliminary drawing list as a basis for discussion.

3 INITIAL DESIGN DECISIONS

3.1 THE FINAL DRAWING LIST

After evaluating the preliminary drawing list, considering all the alternate procedures, methods, etc., the electrical design approach should be fairly well established. The actual drawing numbers to be used on the project have been assigned to the electrical department. It is now time to produce the probable final drawing list. The word "final" refers to a final estimated drawing list on which the design will be based. The ultimate drawing list will of course only be concluded after the design is complete and issued. Up to this time it will be constantly changed and modified.

This final drawing list will be used throughout the duration of the project; therefore, select the paper carefully. It should be multicolumn, beginning with space for the number then space for the title. The remaining columns will be used for scheduling and revision information.

To produce the final drawing list, a careful analysis of the preliminary drawing list is required. Initially a guess was made as to area covered and scale used. Now the decision must be made with finality. All problem areas must be accounted for and a firm decision made with regard to numbering and designating of wires and relays, panels, etc. Grounding and distribution systems should be selected. The quantity of schematics should be more critically evaluated along with the wiring diagrams.

In essence, then, the final drawing list is a list of decisions. These will be transmitted to paper by a designer. If the decisions are good ones, modifications to the list will be minimal. If the decisions are mediocre, then changes will be many and will be reflected in a poor discontinuous design with loose ends and errors predominating.

3.2 SCHEDULING REQUIREMENTS

With the final drawing list established, it is now necessary to complete the project within the allotted time. In order to do this the projected hours will be spread over the allotted time period. The problem then becomes the prediction of information availability. Initially, only a few designers have enough information to do meaningful work. Later on there is usually more information than designers; after a period of time, as designers complete their assignments, the project is back to a few designers again.

By referring back to the final drawing list, we can now utilize the additional columns allowed on the drawing list sheets. After considering each drawing, a date can be entered against that drawing. This date would be the estimated start date. The estimated finish date can also be entered. The total hours assigned to that particular drawing can also be listed. Assign another column for "hours used" and another column for "revision." A further column should be assigned "Issued for construction."

This list will become the means of evaluating progress during the project. It should be accurately maintained. Hours can be monitored weekly by entering time from time cards. The other columns are maintained by entering the dates of issue and changing the revision number.

On major projects there is usually a master schedule for the whole project. This is probably updated weekly or even daily in some cases. The information groups entered on the master schedule are sometimes segregated in inconvenient sets. It is therefore important that, when the final drawing list and electrical design schedule is completed, a copy is immediately passed to the master scheduling department. This enables the schedulers to group the electrical design sets with projected target dates that have significant value. Without this coordination we sometimes find that on the master schedule we are required to order switchgear and high-voltage cable before the single-line drawing is firmed up.

3.3 MASTER SCHEDULE DEFINITION

The master schedule is a set of target dates for all critical and semicritical items. The target dates are set to coordinate equipment deliveries and drawing issues with construction. To maintain construction costs at reasonable levels, it is essential that it progresses without serious interruption. Long-lead items are important especially when they are associated with below-grade excavating.

Excavating machinery is expensive; therefore, the intent of the contractor is to complete all the excavating and return most of the equipment to the leasing company or to other projects, retaining only a smaller versatile, general-purpose excavating machine. Then, rebar and concrete deliveries have to be scheduled so that uninterrupted pouring can be accomplished.

If all below-grade materials are available to the subtrades on schedule and the subtrades installations are on schedule, then the lag time between excavating and pouring concrete is minimal. If materials are not available to subtrades when scheduled, the concrete pouring will be delayed; the concrete that was available may now not be available as readily. In addition, in seasonal areas, weather factors are always a necessary consideration.

The electrical design then is not necessarily an independent element. The drawing issues should be scheduled to coordinate with the anticipated construction progress. In fact, the only reason for the existence of the design group is to collect information and present it on paper in a form that will result in more efficient construction. This statement will become more significant and awakening when we discuss "model making."

3.4 MODEL MAKING

Model making is not new, models of industrial plants and process plants have been made for years. There is, however, a change in the trend and intent of a model. In the past, models were generally constructed from issued drawings. The reason for the models or intent of the models were to assist in future expansion studies or to sit in magnificent view in the entrance to the head office as a three-dimensional picture of progress.

The purpose of model making has now changed. A model is now built with the intent of providing a three-dimensional design and eliminating the requirement for some drawings.

The models are exact-scale models. A new type of designer is now emerging. Instead of using a pencil and drafting machine, the designer uses plastic miniatures of motors, valves, tanks, stairs, platforms, wide-flange beams, etc. The model maker designer is intended to replace the "drafting board" designer in some instances. This then eliminates the need for certain drawings. Model making is by no means a "cut and dried" operation.

As far as the electrical design is concerned, it is recommended that a final drawing list of a conventional nature is prepared. The hypothesis should be made that this is the necessary minimum information required for construction. This drawing list must then be reviewed by the project engineer (overall) and the model-making supervisor in conjunction with the responsible senior electrical designer. There are three sources where a design responsibility must originate: engineering, model making, contractor engineering. The responsibility for all the items of information on the final drawing list must be allocated.

It may be decided that all "above-grade electrical plans" will show equipment only. Major raceway banks will be shown on the model. The contractor will engineer and install his own individual raceway installations. This then requires an alteration to the final drawing list. If we assume that there were 20 drawings allocated at $\frac{1}{4}''$ scale for above-grade electrical plans at 80 hours each, it can now probably be changed to 10 drawings at $\frac{1}{8}''$ scale and 20 to 40 hours per drawing. This does not necessarily mean that the overall project is saving money; it only means that the model makers and the contractor have to design the omitted portion.

What then is the advantage of the model? Its main advantage is that various alternate schemes can be considered in minutes instead of hours. Other departments and trades become aware of conflicting installations. The accidental problem of vertical conduits being installed in the middle of a doorway is eliminated. An object appearing in a catalog becomes apparently too large or problematical when shown on the model.

The discussion on the merits of model making over conventional drawing presentation is beyond the scope of this book. As far as the electrical design is concerned, the decision will be handed down that a model will be used. It is therefore the responsibility of the senior electrical designer to add a model-making electrical designer(s) to the group and define the lines of demarcation of design responsibility.

3.5 COMPUTER PROGRAMS

Computer programs are available as another aid to compiling design information and removing the drudgery of repetitive calculations. Like model making, the evaluation of using computer programming over conventional techniques is beyond the scope of this book. We will, however, make some comments on the subject.

The senior electrical designer will be advised that a computer program is available, or alternatively, "the computer *will* be used." It is therefore necessary that the senior electrical designer obtain the instruction book on the program available and a sample of a printout of a previous project. The program instruction book will explain which codes the program is based on. It will indicate the flexibility and adaptability to accept additional instruction to comply with local codes.

The program will also indicate how the information should be compiled to be acceptable to the computer.

Schematics may have to be numbered a certain way. Single lines may require a modified presentation and equipment numbers; relay and control component numbers may all require precise presentation.

Once the program is fully understood and information presentation is formalized, it is necessary to review the printout. The contractor must be instructed on how to "read" the printout. Any comments may indicate the advisability of using the computer or abandoning its use for that particular project.

The senior designer then must once again review his final drawing list. Each drawing must be considered, and where the drawing is required for computer information, it should be identified as such. Sample methods of presentation must then be drawn, with copies going to the designers so that precise drawings can be made which are acceptable as computer information.

Programs exist in various forms. The printouts can indicate conduit sizes, wire sizes, conduit fill, wire bundles, termination and interconnection points, overcurrent protection, and many other design factors.

One rule with computers to remember always: The information printed out by the computer is only as good as the accuracy of the information fed into it.

3.6 MANPOWER LOADING

The previous three chapters have been concerned with the mundane problems creating the necessary background facilities and creating a "base line" or starting point for the new project. The preceding paragraphs indicate that, with the final drawing list established, the schedule worked out, and decisions on model making and computer programs solidified, it is now time to start producing.

Obviously, at this stage the senior design engineer has a very good "feel" for the size and duration of the project. The schedule has already outlined the required completion date. The only variable in manpower loading that can be manipulated is group size, that is, a large group on an 8-hour day or a smaller group on an 8-hour day plus overtime. This is assuming experienced personnel in both cases.

A large group becomes unwieldy after a certain point; therefore it must be split into subgroups, each with its own senior design engineer, all reporting to an overall electrical project engineer.

A small group working overtime as required is easier to handle; also, when the flow of information slows up, it is only necessary to cut back on the overtime until it begins to flow again. With the larger group, when information slows up, the personnel become unproductive and use up valuable hours or they must be "laid off," with the possibility of losing them permanently. Overtime requires premium rates of pay but the overtime can be regulated. When this is compared to carrying unproductive personnel, it is probably better to try for a small compact group with the decision to work overtime "as required." There are many other factors that will affect this decision and opinions obviously will vary, but a small compact group with flexible working hours should be the initial objective.

3.7 MANPOWER EXPERIENCE OUTLINE

The senior design engineer has already spent considerable time evaluating the project and is therefore best qualified to outline the types of individuals required. This outline should be based on the drawing list. The senior design engineer knows the quantity of drawings required and also knows the type of drawings required; therefore the outline should be "tied" to the intended assignments.

The outline description should indicate the type of experience by technical experience rather than "project type."

EXAMPLE Designer capable of original design of control circuits from flow sheets and logic diagrams.

Alternatively, this is sometimes written as: Designer minimum 7 years experience for control circuits in chemical plants.

The first outline will obtain "all" designers with control experience. They can then be interviewed for selection. The second outline will eliminate all individuals with less than 7 years' experience. This could include an individual that has only 3 years' experience, but the experience has been total immersion in control circuits. Compare this with the individual with 7 years' experience but only 6 months' experience on controls. In the first outline both individuals can be considered. In the second outline only one may be considered; the individual with the 3 years' experience may not apply. Therefore consider the outline description carefully.

3.8 MANPOWER ACQUISITION

The routine for acquiring personnel for a new project varies with different companies. Some companies have a personnel department. This department will use the outlines as a guide and will begin to procure applicants. The employees in the personnel department are not technical experts, they can only interview in general terms within the scope of the outline. The problem here is if the outline says "degree required" all applicants without degrees will be excluded, even the individuals with heavy experience that is more than equivalent to a degree. This is not the fault of the personnel department; they can only grade applicants on the outlines presented by the design department. Ensure then that the instructions to personnel are broad enough yet specific enough to acquire the exact experience required.

After grading, the personnel department will forward the applicant to the electrical department for interview. The electrical department will then approve or reject the applicant.

In some companies there is no personnel department. The probability here is that the chief engineer (electrical) assumes this responsibility. In this case the senior design engineer will probably get what the chief engineer decides he needs. The problem here is that the chief engineer is probably busy with many other duties and possible other projects. He will also be interviewing in general terms, whereas the senior design engineer would be interviewing in specific terms. For example, the chief engineer will generally only ask "What have you done?" whereas the senior design engineer can ask "Can you produce a drawing like this from this information?" The ideal then is to have the senior design engineer select his own people. In many cases this is not done. The senior design engineer is usually given the responsibility to produce a design package, but unfortunately he is sometimes not given the authority to allow him to arrange and control his decisions whether they be design decisions or personnel control decisions.

3.9 CONTRACT AND TEMPORARY HELP

The engineering business, as most companies know, is a "feast or famine" life cycle. This is due to the fact that engineering companies work on projects funded by investment capital. When national and international economic situations change, the allocation of investment capital changes. What is generally good for one company is usually good for other similar companies; therefore, if there is a surplus of chemical products, new plants will probably be curtailed. A shortage of chemical products may result in many companies hurriedly trying to build chemical plants. This then creates an overall industry manpower loading problem. Companies always try to retain a group of key personnel at senior levels. The remaining manpower force is acquired as needed. The majority of new hires are employed on a "permanent" basis. This means that they are permanently employed as long as work is available. These individuals are the major work force. In addition to this normal work force it is necessary to have additional personnel for short peak periods. Here we have available a large work force of contract or temporary personnel.

The contract-type personnel is generally known in slang terms as a "job shopper," whose duration of "assignment" to a project can be anywhere from one day to more than 1 or 2 years. The average assignment is probably 3 to 6 months.

With the constant changing of assignments, the job shopper is usually versatile and requires a minimum of phasing in time and explanations. Whereas permanent employees may "resist" working overtime, the job shopper will probably desire it. The mechanics of hiring contract personnel is simple. Various companies specialize in maintaining a work force on file cards. On file is a résumé of the background and type of work the individual has experienced. When a prospective customer phones in a requirement, all the résumés in the required category are pulled from the files. They are then sorted to find the experience to match the submitted outline.

After the sorting is completed, the individuals are contacted to determine availability. If they are available and the negotiated terms are agreeable, they are sent to the prospective customer for a technical interview. This can sometimes be done by telephone. If acceptable, the "job shop" is notified. They in turn notify the individual to report to a specific person at a time and date at a certain address. The designer then goes to work as though a permanent employee, subject to the same regulations as the permanent employee. The difference being that the pay for this person is provided by the job shop company. He is in fact employed by the job shop. He is only "assigned" to the customer.

The customer's benefit is derived from having a supply of a mobile and easily expendable work force. Administration and payroll is reduced to paying a single invoice whether it is one individual or fifty. Cash flow, taxes, disability, insurance, hospitalization, and other factors all enter into considerations for utilizing temporary help. In some cases, the temporary help eventually becomes permanent staff. Whether the use of this type of help is justified or not depends on the specific situation. It is discussed here to point out that it is an available viable and useful work force.

3.10 SUMMATION

The first three chapters have outlined the considerations and preliminary requirements (with available options) necessary for preparation of a new project. It is difficult to be precise and specific because projects vary in size. The responsibility assigned to senior design engineers is also extremely variable, as is the assigned authority. The intent then was to introduce the subject, discuss it in general terms, and allow for the good judgment of the reader to utilize the information most beneficial. Obviously many readers will be familiar with some subjects, but other readers may be just "emerging" to this level.

Part Two
TECHNICAL CONSIDERATIONS

4 HAZARDOUS AREAS AND DEFINITIONS

4.1 HAZARDOUS AREA–DEFINITION

A hazardous area in the electrical sense is an area where the atmosphere could be ignited as a result of the proximity of electric equipment.

Throughout this book we will make comments and references pertaining to hazardous areas. It must be understood that the information presented in this book is purely for guidance and is in fact an interpretation. It is intended to guide and assist, and not replace, sound engineering procedure based on the recognized code applicable to that project.

The National Electrical Code, Articles 500 to 517, deals with hazardous areas in detail. Therefore, we will not duplicate this effort. We will, however, outline some of the code guidelines and comment on their intent.

4.2 HAZARDOUS AREA IDENTIFICATION (CLASS)

Hazardous locations are identified by Class, Division, and Group. The Class segregates atmospheres into three types.

CLASS I Gases and vapors
This usually includes liquids which either create a vapor/mist when sprayed or a liquid which emits a vapor/gas when exposed to the atmosphere.

CLASS II Combustible dusts.

CLASS III Easily ignitable fibers and flyings. This is qualified by an additional statement: "*which are not likely to be in suspension in the air in quantities sufficient to produce ignitable mixtures.*"

This is the first part of a hazardous area identification.

4.3 HAZARDOUS AREA IDENTIFICATION (DIVISION)

The second part allows two degrees of hazard. These are identified as Division 1 and Division 2.

- Division 1 is the most hazardous condition.
- Division 2 is the less hazardous condition.

The precise definition is stated in the National Electrical Code. For preliminary consideration, Division 1 locations are all locations where hazardous atmospheres can be predictable. This may be due to temporary maintenance situations, or in fact any situation under normal operating conditions which may (by design, or intermittently or periodically) produce a hazardous atmosphere.

Division 2 locations are generally areas where an "abnormal" and "not anticipated" accident could produce a hazardous atmosphere.

For example, a tank containing gasoline may have its vents identified as Division 1 and the area surrounding the tank as Division 2, even if the Division 2 area includes a pipe connection with a blind flange. Normal and predictable is the condition in which vapors will be vented periodically, but it would be unpredictable and abnormal if the blind flange burst due to rusty bolts.

4.4 HAZARDOUS AREA IDENTIFICATION (GROUP)

The third part of the identification is the Group. Atmospheres are categorized into Groups, which are identified by a capital letter.

GROUPS A, B, C, AND D	Gases and Vapors
GROUP E, F, AND G	Dusts

The Groups identify the particular type(s) of hazardous material in the atmosphere, as listed in the National Electrical Code. For example,

GROUP A	Acetylene
GROUP B	Butadiene, ethylene oxide, hydrogen, manufactured gases containing more than 30% hydrogen (by volume), propylene oxide
GROUP C	Acetaldehyde, cyclopropane, diethyl ether, ethylene, unsymmetrical dimethyl hydrazine (UDMH1, 1-dimethyl hydrazine)

For group classification of unlisted chemicals it will be necessary to refer to NFPA No. 325M[1] for the characteristics.

These, then, are the three parts of a hazardous area identification: Class,

[1] Fire-Hazard Properties of Flammable Liquids, Gases, Volatile Solids, by National Fire Protection Association.

Division, and Group. For example, a gasoline station would be Class 1, Group D, with Division 1 and Division 2 locations.

4.5 IGNITION TEMPERATURES

In order to understand the conditions which can cause a (hazardous) potentially explosive/flammable atmosphere, it is necessary to know the terminology and the effect of ignition sources on vapors and gases. We do not intend to present a course in physics, but will briefly outline some conditions. The *ignition temperature* of a substance is the minimum temperature at which it will ignite, causing self-sustained combustion. This temperature is not very indicative unless all other conditions were known about the test conducted to produce the ignition temperature.

4.6 FLASH POINT

The *flash point* of a liquid is the temperature at which it gives off enough vapor to form an ignitable mixture with the air near the surface of the liquid being used. Again, the conditions of the determining test should be known.

4.7 FLAMMABLE AND EXPLOSIVE LIMITS

Certain vapors or gases, when mixed with air, can form mixtures which are ignitable on contact with an adequate energy source of ignition. For ignition to occur, the mixture must be correct. A minimum amount of the flammable portion determines the *lower limit.* Below this "minimum" amount, the mixture will be too lean and will not ignite, as for example, when starting a car in winter without "choke."

A "maximum" amount also affects ignition. If the mixture is too rich, it will not ignite (for example, starting a car when it is "flooded"). This is termed the *upper limit.*

The percentage mixture required for minimum and maximum additions of flammable portions determines the lower and upper flammable or explosive limits.

4.8 FLAMMABLE RANGE

The flammable range of atmospheric mixtures is the vapor or gas/air mixtures between the lower and upper limits (Sec. 4.7). This is sometimes called the *explosive range.* In order to visualize the components of igniting an atmosphere, we will consider the ordinary 100 octane gasoline. The flash point is −36°F, the ignition temperature is 853°F, the lower limit is 1.4% by volume (with air), and the upper limit is 7.4% by volume (with air). To consider the significance of these figures, we see that at −36°F (a very cold winter day) vapor will be given off which is sufficient to form an ignitable mixture near the surface of the gasoline. The term *sufficient to form* refers to the *ability to produce* a component part of an ignitable mixture. As this vapor is being produced, if mixing with air, it will not form an explosive mixture until a unit volume of the mixture is 1.4% gasoline vapor and 98.6% air (totaling 100% volume). This mixture will remain explosive with the addition of more gasoline vapor until a ratio of 7.4% gasoline vapor and 92.6% air is reached. The addition of more gasoline vapor in excess of the 7.4%, will take the mixture above the *upper* limit of flammability and it will lose its explosive capability.

The problem with relying on the *upper* limit for safety is that the mixture must go through the flammable range first. Also, pockets of flammable mixture can be present even though the main bulk of the mixture is above the upper limit.

4.9 VAPOR DENSITY

The *vapor density* is the relative density of a vapor or gas when referred to air, assuming no air is present in the vapor/gas sample.

In tables listing vapor densities, it will show a number. If this number is less than 1 (air = 1), the vapor or gas is lighter than air and will rise in a normal atmosphere. If the number is more than 1, the vapor or gas will descend in a normal atmosphere. For example, a balloon filled with hydrogen would rise in the atmosphere, while the same balloon filled with butane gas would sink to the floor. The vapor density for hydrogen is 0.1, while the vapor density for butane is 2.0.

The latter (butane) could be considered possibly more treacherous than the hydrogen. It can sink to floor level and flow like water from a hazardous area into a nonclassified area. It is invisible and the odors can easily be masked by other odors; therefore, this should be a consideration when pits and depressions are evident.

4.10 INCENDIVE SPARK

In Sec. 4.5 we define ignition temperature, and in Sec. 4.8 it was noted that gasoline has an ignition temperature of 853°F. For ignition to occur, three factors must be present.

1. A mixture in the flammable range
2. A heat source with a temperature equal to or higher than the ignition temperature
3. An ignition source whose thermal output is higher than the thermal losses of the ignitable mixture.

Items 2 and 3 can be combined and by definition be termed an *incendive spark*. This means a spark has enough energy to ignite a flammable/explosive mixture. A *nonincendive spark* has insufficient energy to initiate ignition in a flammable/explosive mixture, even if the spark occurred in the mixture.

The ignition temperature is an important figure. Although it was pointed out in Sec. 4.5 that this figure is not very indicative unless the test conditions were known, as far as electrical design is concerned, we must use the ignition temperatures specified in the code having jurisdiction. This of course can then be related to the identification number indicating maximum surface temperatures of electrical products. This list will also be included in the code.

If the required code does not contain this information, then it is recommended that the National Electrical Code be adopted (officially) to supplement the jurisdictional code.

4.11 IGNITION SOURCES

Ignition can be from many sources—a worker smoking, a welding torch, a friction spark, etc. We are concerned only with the ignition sources created by the installation of an electric system. There are only two basic sources:

1. Sparks (arcs)
2. Surface temperatures

Sparks are caused by the ionization of the air between two conducting points. Ionization is essentially a flow of electrons between positive- and negative-charged points. When the potential difference is low, the electrons flow fairly slow. As the potential is increased, the electrons flow faster. Eventually, a critical point is reached. The friction or collision between electrons produces an avalanche effect, and for the same applied potential an increase in ionization will occur. Since an ionized arc is a good electrical conductor, a continuous arc can be produced, provided that the impedance of the circuit maintains the current at a level below the rating of the overcurrent protection. Hence we have the equivalent of an electric welding arc, an obvious source of ignition.

The second source of ignition is the surface temperature of an electrical product. This is created by I^2R losses (watt losses) (heating effect) and contributed to by the ambient temperature and hysteresis (magnetic molecule agitation) where iron cores are used in the products. The heat from a product is dissipated over the surface area of the enclosure. For a specific heat source, an increase in surface area will result in a lower surface temperature (all other factors assumed equal). This principle is used when designing a product requiring approval for use in hazardous areas.

4.12 STATIC ELECTRICITY

The source of the initial ignition potential can be either the electrical power installation or from a nonelectrical installation which generates *static electricity*. This paragraph deals with the latter.

Static electricity is produced by "friction" or "the expenditure of mechanical work." When two materials are brought into contact or close proximity, a transfer of electrons will take place until a stabilization point is reached. The electron bond between the two materials can be weak or strong, depending on the type of materials. If the materials are mechanically separated, energy must be expended to overcome the attractive force of the electrons. This then appears as a "tension," or electrical potential, between the two materials. When this potential exceeds the dielectric strength of the air, a discharge will occur and the electrons will return back to their original bodies.

5 HAZARDOUS AREA CLASSIFICATION

5.1 AREA CLASSIFICATION DRAWING

To define hazardous areas, it is necessary to have a firm plot plan of the final plant arrangement (see Sec. 2.4). All buildings and areas must be identified, and the process or partial process must be defined. This latter information may have to be obtained from the process department.

A new drawing or reproduced background of the plot plan is necessary. The title of the drawing will be "Hazardous Area Classification." All hazardous areas will have to be accounted for on this drawing. Any buildings which

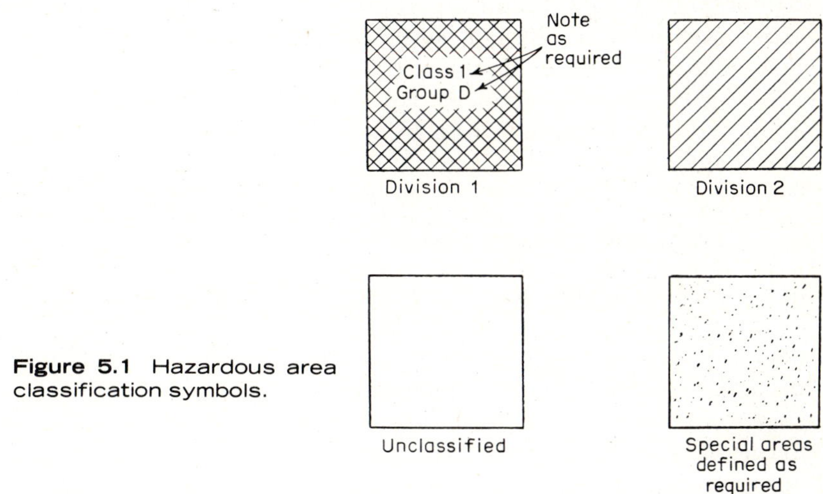

Figure 5.1 Hazardous area classification symbols.

are multiple floor or platform will have to have "hazardous area" levels extracted and shown as a "detail" and/or "section." The symbol list should show the *cross-hatch* symbols for area classification. If not, the symbols shown in Fig. 5.1 can be adopted. The Class and Group should be printed on the drawing in the shaded areas.

A plant may have multiple classes and multiple groups in the same plant. Therefore, it is necessary to print the Class and Group in each cross-hatched area. If there is only a single Class and Group, this can be covered by a note on the drawing: e.g. "All hazardous areas are Class I, Group D, except as noted."

Before making the final drawing, a print of the plot plan can be utilized with *redlined* sketching.

5.2 SPECIFIC CLASSIFICATIONS CLASS I

Articles 510 through 517 of the National Electrical Code deal with some specific locations. The Code defines the distances and direction necessary to outline the Division 1 and 2 areas. It also specifies the Class; however, this can also be obtained from the earlier part of Article 500.

Since the National Electrical Code and other codes are constantly changing, any specific detailed presentation of area classification would probably be obsolete before publication of this book. We can therefore only deal in generalities[1] and insist that the up-to-date code of the enforcing authority be used for classification.

5.3 GARAGES

Most industrial plants will have their own garage and repair facilities for trucks. This is covered by Article 511 of the NEC, which "includes locations used for service and repair operations in connection with self-propelled vehicles (including passenger automobiles, buses, trucks, tractors, etc.) in which volatile flammable liquids are used for fuel or power."

This article is only intended for truck maintenance type installations and not for "truck operational installations," such as gasoline loading racks for tanker trucks.

5.4 GASOLINE DISPENSING

Many industrial plants have their own gasoline pumps for company trucks and cars. This is covered by Article 514 in NEC, which defines the area specifically with the boundaries for Class 1, Division 1 and 2 limitations. As the gas pump location can sometimes be adjacent to nonhazardous office facilities, it is necessary to precisely define the hazardous locations. A doorway into the office within 20 ft of the gasoline dispenser would be Class 1, Division 2, up to 18 in. above the driveway or ground level. If the secretary was using an electric fire on the floor, the fire bar and the receptacle plug would both constitute a hazard and probable violation of the Code.

[1] API (American Petroleum Institute) publications can also be used for guidance.

5.5 LOADING RACKS

Loading racks are the platforms and high-output dispensers for loading truck- and train-tank transporters. They are covered by Article 515 (Bulk Storage Plants) of the NEC. This article defines the distances from nozzles, domes, and platforms for the Division 1 and 2 areas. Generally the location of these loading racks (platforms) is in the center of a yard to allow for truck mobility. The problem of overlapping into office areas is not usually a major problem but must be considered.

5.6 TANK STORAGE

Tank storage of flammable liquids is also covered by Article 515 of the NEC. The distances from the tanks for the Division 1 and 2 areas are specified; however, some tanks are required to be contained by a wall or dike. This shall be high enough to contain all the liquid within the tank if it bursts. In this case, the top of the dike shall be classified as Class 1, Division 2. The classification of Division 2 finishes at the "top of the dike." In actual practice, the tops of a dike are used as walkways and for the installation of switchracks for motor and pump control. Although they are technically nonhazardous areas, the practice is to use explosionproof equipment. This is generally dictated by customer specification.

5.7 SUMPS, PITS, AND DEPRESSIONS

Since most hydrocarbon products are heavier than air, they tend to collect and remain in pits, sumps, and depressions unless adequately ventilated. Installations where this is possible should be treated as Class 1, Division 1, unless special ventilation is present. Even then they would require a Division 2 classification, based on a specific exemption, such as NEC 515–2(e)(3), or abnormal operation, NEC 500–4(b)(2).

Whether the ventilation is adequate or not requires further criteria. This must be obtained from the code authorities having jurisdiction. If this is not available, then reference to the Flammable and Combustible Liquids Code (NFPA No. 30–) will provide some guidelines which can then be submitted to the enforcing code authorities for acceptance.

5.8 PUMPS, METERS, AND DEVICES

The classifications for these items are detailed in NEC 515–2(a)(1), (2), (3). They are fairly specific and should present no problems. The resulting difference requiring consideration whether to ventilate or not could depend on the size and quantity of motors. In Division 2 areas a standard open-type three-phase motor can be used. In a Division 1 location the motor must be explosionproof and approved for that location's Class and Group. This may present problems in delivery, cost, and maintenance. A repair to an *explosionproof motor* can only be performed by someone approved for explosionproof work. Therefore, when classifying enclosed pumping areas, the mechanical department should be notified of the options and the significance of ventilation.

5.9 VENTS

All vents from tanks containing flammable liquids should be considered Class 1, Division 1. The distance dictated as Class 1 varies with the section of the code. For instance, when a tanker truck is loaded from the top through an open dome, the space extending 3 ft in all directions from the dome is required to be Class 1, Division 1. Whereas for the vent from an above-ground tank in a bulk storage plant requires that 5 ft of space in all directions be Class 1, Division 1.

This means that any motors used in or near (within 3 ft) a vent pipe must be explosionproof and approved for the Class and Group. This includes the fan blades, which should also be made of a "nonarcing material."

5.10 FINISHING PROCESSES

The term *finishing processes* refers to the spraying and coating of articles or component parts. Specific details with drawings and precise information are given in Article 516 of the NEC. Ingenuity can be used to design and locate most of the equipment outside the hazardous areas. Particularly, the design of lighting can preclude the use of expensive explosionproof fixtures by complying with Article 516–3(c).

It need not be pointed out that spray painting or atomizing a flammable liquid creates an extremely hazardous atmosphere. Although ingenuity is recommended for the design layout, the first requirement is a safe installation.

5.11 AIRCRAFT AND AEROSPACE

In general an aircraft or aerospace production facility is a nonhazardous location. The primary work done there is with metals, plastics, and standard nonflammable materials. The only hazardous areas involved are "special" areas, such as hangars and filling platforms, where a production item is transformed into an operational vehicle.

Article 513 of the NEC specifies the requirements for aircraft hangars. Although this is defined it is limited to the inside of a hangar. There is the possibility that other parts of an aircraft plant will have areas which are governed by other articles (for example, bulk storage and gasoline dispensing areas).

5.12 PETROCHEMICAL PROCESSES

Petrochemical plants and processes are unique in that no two plants are ever the same. Even a plant that is to be "repeated" will probably have modifications from the previous one. Chemical process technology is fast-moving and generally proprietary (secret). Fertilizer is made by chemical process, small iron-ore reduction plants now function with chemical process, and plastics and liquid products are all produced in petrochemical plants. For the area classification of these types of plants, it is necessary to consult the process department for detailed information. The probability is that a total process area will be classified.

Another possibility is that the classified process area is surrounded by roads. The guidance for classifying this type of plant would be customer specifications and the general articles of Chapter 5 of the National Electrical Code.

This, of course, assumes that other codes and requirements are less comprehensive. When the classification drawing is complete, it should be checked with the process department and then sent to the enforcing authority for approval.

5.13 CLASSIFICATION OF CLASS II AND III AREAS

Most of the classification problems fall into a Class I category. The classification of Class II and Class III areas is not as specific as the Class I areas.

For Class II areas, the guiding paragraph is NEC 500–5, with general articles on equipment in NEC 502–1 through 502–16.

For class III areas, the guiding paragraph is NEC 500–6, with general articles in NEC 503–1 through 503–16.

If it is necessary to know the location of particular areas that may be hazardous, a decision based on the code outline must be made. Alternately, the customer's specification may have already outlined the areas that require classifying based on previous experience in other plants.

It is essential to know the characteristics of the types of dusts and materials. Some are conductive and some are nonconductive; however, they may be potentially explosive whether they are conductive or not. Dried egg and milk powders are seemingly harmless products, but in dust form they can become combustible. Magnesium dust is extremely hazardous.

Rayon, cotton, hemp, and sisal are good examples of Class III fibers which are easily ignitable. Since designers of the electrical department are not intended to be expert in chemical compositions, the expertise of the process department should be used to obtain the required understanding of the characteristics of the materials.

5.14 SUMMATION

Classifying hazardous areas should not be too difficult. Most of the guidelines for classification are spelled out in the specific locations in the National

Electrical Code. Other areas can be classified by reference to other paragraphs in Chapter 5 of the National Electrical Code. The essential point is to have some understanding of the hazardous substance. Does it rise? Does it sink? Is it highly volatile?

Don't do what some forgotten designer did and design an installation complete with large sign stating "Helium Gas Danger—No Smoking." Helium is an inert, nonexplosive gas.

6 POWER DISTRIBUTION

6.1 THE SINGLE LINE

The first electrical drawing is the *power-distribution single-line diagram.* This outlines, in a shorthand form, the components, component arrangement, and component size.

The three-phase system is represented by a *single line* rather than three lines. The single lines are arranged in any convenient method, without regard to geographical location. The primary intent in arrangement is to avoid line crossovers and confusing arrangements. It is important to show the complete system on a single sheet if possible. If not, the *single line* should be divided by voltage level, rather than by showing the complete system with half on one sheet and half on another sheet.

The symbol sheet will already have a listing of symbols that have previously been approved for use. Redundant and duplicate information should be avoided. The word *transformer* is unnecessary next to the symbol, as is the case with the designations "CT" and "PT." These will be identified by the symbols; writing the term contributes nothing to drawing clarity.

6.2 PRELIMINARY SINGLE LINE

A single-line drawing does not suddenly exist. The designer begins with a blank sheet. He then makes certain assumptions and decisions, and a system begins to emerge. Usually the only information available early in a new project is the "plot plan," and even this may be only in preliminary form. The first single-line drawing to be produced, then, is for the purpose of collecting information and having a visual representation of ideas and intended approaches to designing an efficient power-distribution system for the project. This drawing may be changed many times, which is its purpose; it is a "thinking" drawing. Hence the term *preliminary single line.* Among office supplies are rubber stamps, such as a "PRELIMINARY" stamp. By using this stamp on all prints of the *single line,* along with a date stamp, it is simple to determine what changes have been made.

6.3 PRELIMINARY INFORMATION (POWER COMPANY)

The first essential information required for the single-line diagram is the "available electric power." The probability is that an approximate value can be determined for the final plant loading. This can be obtained from the customer's other plants of a similar type. Alternately, major electrical equipment manufacturers have technical brochures or experts who can assist with this preliminary estimate of power consumption. The power company will also have records of the power consumption in similar plants. Another source of information is the mechanical department. They probably have figures of total horsepower requirements. If a preliminary motor list is available, this can be totaled and added to lighting-load estimates and other miscellaneous loads. When this load estimate and the electrical plot plan are ready, a meeting with the power company should be set up. The following information should be obtained from the power company.

1. A power billing rate schedule
2. Location of incoming service on plot plan
3. Service incoming voltage
4. Power company requirements for service entrance
5. Power company "short-circuit availability"
6. Yearly "outage" rate, that is, reliability
7. Approximate date of intended service installation
8. Power company transformer impedance
9. System grounding information
10. Temporary power availability for construction
11. "Special" points, such as the system stability being affected by extremely heavy loading, for example, wind tunnels; alternate feeder availability; etc.

6.4 PRELIMINARY SYSTEM INFORMATION

The power company feeder voltage will have some bearing on the plant's power-distribution systems. If the incoming feeder is high voltage (above 15,000 V), a transformer will be required. This means that the power company will require their own substation on plant property. The plant will probably be required to provide some portion of the installation. In any case, the power company will issue instructions for their requirements. With the installation of a substation transformer, the design engineer has an option on the incoming service voltage. The more common options in the United States are 2.4, 4.16, 6.9, and 13.8 kV, and are all classed as a medium-voltage range. The factors affecting this selection will be covered in Sec. 6.10.

If the incoming power company feeder happens to be at one of these medium voltages, the decision is already made. It is usually uneconomical to change voltages when this is the situation.

The other necessary decision, as far as the power company is concerned, is the number of kilowatt-hour meter(s) to be used. In some cases more than one meter may be required, for billing purposes. This would require incoming service sections for each meter.

6.5 CIRCUIT TYPE (RADIAL)

When considering which type of circuit to use in a plant, an evaluation should be made of load centers. A plant will have load concentrations and areas which can be circled (red-lined) on a plot-plan print. The intention, then, is to place a source of low voltage (460 V) power in the center. The problem is to supply a low voltage to these load-center areas with a minimum of losses and at an economical cost.

A rule to remember is that by doubling a system voltage it is possible to go four times the distance for the same losses, that is, IR and I^2R losses.

An evaluation of the possible feeder distances will show whether one or more load concentrations or areas can be picked up with a single high-voltage feeder. This high-voltage feeder can then be "tapped" and a transformer installed in these load areas, preferably in the approximate center (see Fig. 6.1).

This circuit arrangement then is classified as a *radial circuit arrangement* with *load-center* distribution. It is very simple and probably the most economical type of circuit arrangement. Its reliability is good, and it is probably used more extensively than any other type of circuit arrangement.

Technically, the high-voltage feeders could have been low-voltage radial feeders. This would have eliminated the transformers but would have increased the transformer capacity at the source. Additional problems are that the feeders would be large in copper content, the distance would be limited, and multiple feeders would be required to feed individual areas. The low-voltage radial-feeder arrangement is virtually obsolete and would only be considered for use as a special-case installation where the load concentrations happen to be unusually close.

The drawback to the radial system is that a failure in one high-voltage feeder can shut down one or more areas. When comparing this with initial capital outlay for a more reliable system, the following argument can be made;

> In a continuous process plant operation, any failure can probably cause an interruption in the process, requiring a shutdown and startup sequence. The difference in downtime, then, is a function of the time it takes to repair the fault.

This then is considered against the construction budget.

6.6 CIRCUIT TYPE (SECONDARY SELECTIVE)

Secondary selective refers to the secondary side of the load-center transformers. The *selective* means that an optional source of power is available and that the *secondary*, or low-voltage, side can select one or the other source of power. The OR is the logic "exclusive" definition of "one or the other but not both."

Consider two radial feeders of the type shown in Fig. 6.1. If the secondary

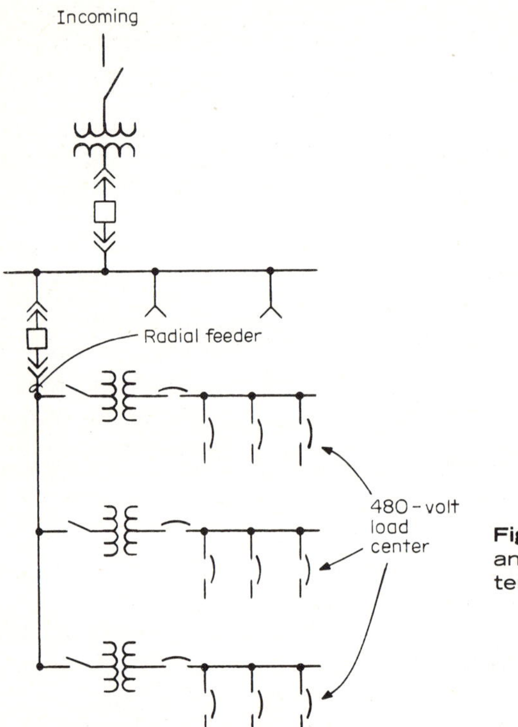

Figure 6.1 Radial feeder and low-voltage load centers.

distribution bus of one load center is connected (through a circuit breaker) to the secondary distribution bus of a load center on the other radial feeder, the closing of this breaker will allow both load centers to be supplied by one alternate feed. Hence the term *secondary selective* (see Fig. 6.2).

The secondary-selective system is operated with the interconnecting, or "tie," breaker(s) in the open position. By using a key interlock on the main breaker of the transformer secondary and the *tie* breaker, the selective system becomes logically "exclusive." This limits the alternate selection of feeders to "one or the other but not both." Since the alternate radial feeders originate from the same original source bus, closing the tie breaker while both transformer secondary breakers are closed results in parallel operation of the load center(s). A problem then occurs because of the increased short-circuit duty on the load-center circuit breakers. They are usually operating close to maximum short-circuit duty and would most probably be dangerously underrated.

The reliability of the secondary-selective system is of course better than the radial system, owing to the option of alternate supplies. The initial installation cost is higher, however. Apart from the cost of the tie breaker, the size

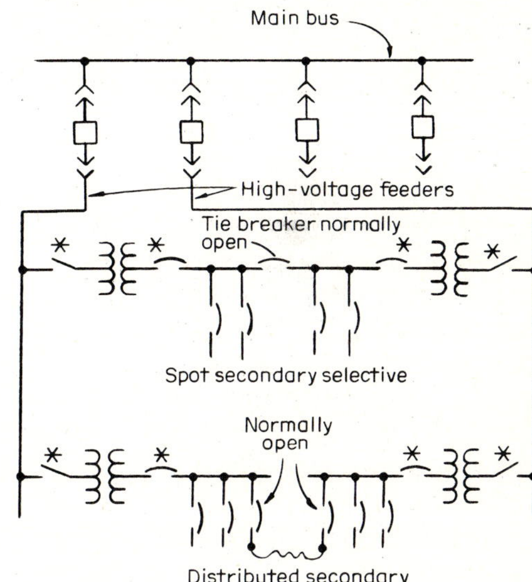

Figure 6.2 Secondary-selective-system arrangements.

of the transformers and radial-feeder conductor must be considered. If a failure occurs on one radial feeder, the other radial feeder must carry the load previously carried by two radial feeders. This is assuming that 100% operation is maintained. In actual practice, however, only essential supplies are maintained. This then brings up the following point. If only essential supplies can be maintained, then this means a probable shutdown and startup sequence anyway; this could also happen with a radial system. Therefore, what is the advantage of the secondary-selective system?

Here then we come down to the specific point of the argument what is "essential."

1. If an accidental shutdown can "damage equipment, then it is "essential" to have a controlled shutdown for which power is necessary.
2. If an accidental shutdown can create a "hazardous" situation, then power is mandatory.
3. If an accidental shutdown affects only production output loss, then it is not "essential." This is in the sense that average output and pricing of products considers a percentage of "downtime" as inevitable and acceptable.

When the *essential* loads are defined, the designer can then ascertain whether increased conductor and transformer capacity are necessary.

The secondary-selective system is the next most popular to the radial system. Between them they account for the largest percentage of industrial installations.

6.7 CIRCUIT TYPE (PRIMARY SELECTIVE)

The primary-selective system is similar to the secondary selective except that the transfer from one radial feeder to the other is done at the primary side of the load-center transformer. Another difference is that the feeders are sized so that a single feeder can carry the combined load of both feeders. The normal operating situation is with an *exclusive* OR arrangement of the primary-selective switches (or power circuit breakers).

By using power circuit breakers instead of the lower-cost selective switches, reliability is increased. This is because of the ability to switch loads while the feeders are energized. Normally, the transfer is done by opening the circuit breaker on the required feeder, making the transfer, and then reenergizing the feeder by closing the feeder circuit breaker. Figure 6.3 shows an arrangement for a primary-selective system.

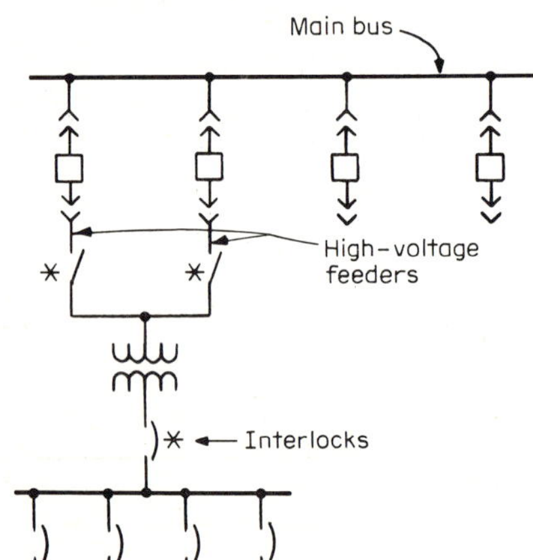

Figure 6.3 Primary-selective-system arrangement.

The reliability of this system is approximately the same as that of the secondary-selective system if circuit breakers are used in both cases. Transferring power from one feeder to the other can be potentially hazardous unless the transfer switches are key interlocked with the main feeder breakers, ensuring that the feeders are deenergized when transfer is made.

Unless specific conditions point to use of the primary-selective system, it is probably better to go with the secondary-selective system instead.

6.8 CIRCUIT TYPE (SECONDARY NETWORK)

The secondary-network system is similar in respects to the secondary selective. The difference is that the secondaries of the transformers are "tied" and therefore operate in parallel. In addition, the secondary main circuit breaker is replaced with a network protector. The operational sequence of this type of system is dependent on the complexity of the relaying associated with the network protectors. If a fault (i.e., short circuit) occurs on a primary feeder or on a transformer, the relays associated with the network protectors will automatically cause the circuit-breaker portion of the network protector to open on the transformer secondary. This immediately isolates the load from the faulty feeder (or transformer) without interruption. Power to the load is maintained because of the parallel "ties." In the meantime the circuit breaker protecting the faulty feeder also trips because of the overcurrent due to the fault.

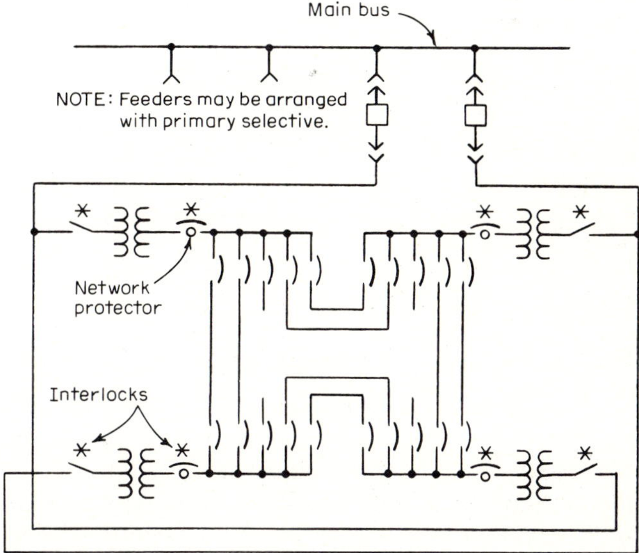

Figure 6.4a Secondary-network arrangement.

When the repairs to the faulty feeder are completed, and the feeder breaker is closed, the relays will sense the availability of additional power and will automatically cause the network protector circuit breaker to close, returning the system back to normal.

This description is by no means complete and is only intended to indicate that a system capable of maintaining power to all loads while dumping faulty feeders exists, and is available for approximately 150% of the cost of a secondary-selective system. The reliability over the radial and secondary-selective systems is very marginal. Its main advantage over the other two systems lies in its ability to maintain power to loads when a fault occurs on a feeder or transformer.

The difference between the secondary and the "spot" network is that the spot-network transformers are connected to the same bus installation.

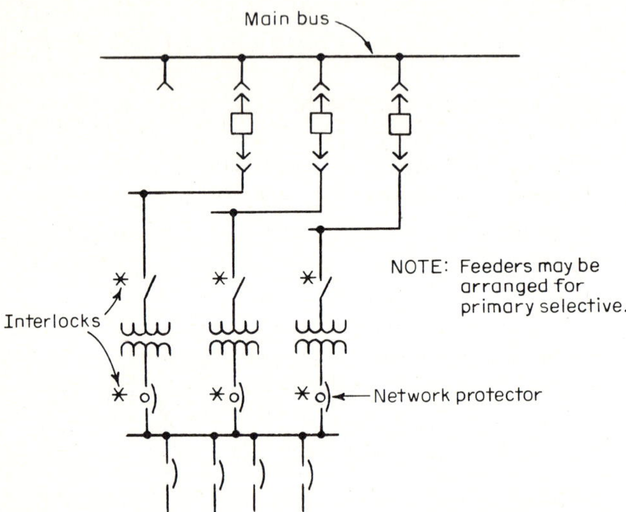

Figure 6.4b Simple spot secondary-network arrangement.

6.9 CIRCUIT TYPE (OTHER SYSTEMS)

Other systems and variations are possible. The only limiting factors are ingenuity and money. Since most systems are radial or secondary selective, the decision to use a more sophisticated system revolves around special requirements. The fact that special requirements exist means that a study of the requirements is necessary before a system selection is recommended. This study will investigate the need for emergency power, an uninterruptible power supply, essential load supplies, and critical load supplies. All these factors will have a bearing on the selection of a particular type of basic power-distribution system.

The selection of a system is largely dictated by cost. The client will probably have figured some previous cost projections when deciding whether to build a new plant or not. This will mean that most probably a system has already been selected, based on the client's assessment of the cost/reliability ratio. The downtime will have been evaluated based on past experience in other plants. Therefore, it isn't really a case of sitting down and saying "right, let's pick a system"; it is more a case of a system emerging as preliminary information is compiled and the plot plan studied.

The final problem, of course, is to obtain the approval to spend additional money if the system is anything other than the standard radial, which accounts for 90% of plant systems. The additional cost for a secondary-selective system is a smaller part of the total electrical budget as the projects get larger; therefore, the objection to cost is less likely to be raised. This is one contributing part to the fact that most secondary-selective systems are installed in the larger kVA loaded plants.

6.10 PRIMARY-VOLTAGE SELECTION

The primary-voltage selection for the power-distribution system will be between 2.4 and 13.8 kV. The use of voltages higher than this results in exceeding the 15-kV class limitation for buildings. The selection then is limited to the standard voltage levels between these two ratings. There are two voltage designations. One is the *nominal* system voltage, the other is the *actual* voltage, rating of equipment. We have "old" standards and "new" standards. Foreign standards also vary from United States standards. This means that nothing can be taken for granted. When equipment is ordered and voltages are specified, it should be defined with the prefix *nominal voltage* or *rated voltage.* For the purpose of selecting a voltage class for the power system, we will use the prefix *nominal voltage.* The understanding is that the actual voltage levels associated with that system can vary within a certain bandwidth. The nominal rating, then, is more like an identification label rather than an actual voltage setting.

The nominal voltages available for consideration are **2.4, 4.16, 4.8, 6.9, 12, 13.2, 13.8** kV. The selection is then further limited to four alternates. The use of the other nonpreferred voltages would generally be dictated by the need to utilize existing systems, owing to a plant expansion or to the utility company providing a service which is a direct tap off an existing feeder.

Selecting a system voltage requires two immediate estimates:

1. Immediate plant load and possible expansion on the same service
2. Distance of inplant feeders, that is, long or short

The trend in selecting system voltages is to use as high a voltage as is economically feasible. If we group the four alternate selections into two groups, we have:

1. 2.4 kV and 4.16 kV
2. 6.9 kV and 13.8 kV

Major electrical equipment manufacturers have done many exhaustive studies on the relative cost comparisons of the four system voltages. The general results of these studies indicates that if a free choice is allowable, it should be made between the use of a 4.16-kV system or a 13.8-kV system. The reasons for these ultimate selections and recommendations are many and a book could be written about this subject alone. Some obvious reasons are:

1. Higher kVA transmission for the same amount of copper
2. Longer circuits for the same power transmission with the same losses
3. Higher interrupting rating of circuit breakers

These items, of course, compare the 2.4-kV and the 4.16-kV systems, and the 6.9-kV and the 13.8-kV systems.

If we accept the information compiled by manufacturers, a choice is left between installing either the 4.16-kV system or the 13.8-kV system. Drawing further on published data, the general recommendation is that up to a 10,000-kVA service (generally the utility-company transformer), the 4.16-kV system is recommended as the most economic installation. When the supply (service) is 20,000 kVA and higher, the 13.8-kV system is recommended. For a service supply above 10,000 kVA but less than 20,000 kVA, either system could be used.

When considering both systems (for the 10,000 to 20,000 kVA range), the first consideration is possible future expansion. If it can be determined that future expansion is possible, this would be a major factor in considering the use of the 13.8-kV system. Trying to obtain information on possible expansion may be difficult for many reasons but briefly and bluntly, a business cannot remain static. If it does not grow, then it generally goes out of business. If it is successful, it must grow. If land is available for plant expansion, a successful company will inevitably use it.

6.11 SECONDARY-VOLTAGE SELECTION (POWER)

In industrial plants in the United States the *nominal* power-distribution system at the secondary level is 460 V, three-phase, 60 Hz. Any plants using other voltages such as 240 V or 208/120 V are either "commercial" or light manufacturing installations rather than heavy industrial, or the installed equipment is such that its availability is limited to these voltages. All motors of 200 hp and below would be supplied by the 460-V system. Even fractional-horsepower motors, if used in production, should be the three-phase, 460-V squirrel-cage type. They are more rugged than the single-phase, they can be supplied from standard starters, and the familiar three conductors are installed. In effect, although a process motor is a fractional horsepower, it should be treated as an integral size. The fractional-horsepower motors for toilet vents or other nonprocess/nonproduction duty can be supplied from lighting panels and be single phase, light duty.

6.12 SECONDARY-VOLTAGE SELECTION (SUBSYSTEMS)

The subsystems in an industrial plant consist of lighting, convenience receptacles, welding systems, small machines, heating and ventilating, material handling, maintenance machines, hand tools, etc. The selection of a subsystem voltage requires more detailed information than the selection of the primary voltage. This information may be difficult to obtain in the very early stages. It may be necessary to delay this decision until the distinctive load information is available from the other departments.

It is mandatory to have 120 V; therefore, one decision to be made is whether to use a single-phase 240/120-V three-wire system or the 208Y/120-V four-wire system. Both are versatile systems. Both 240/120 and 208/120 V can both be used for lighting circuits. A slight advantage of the 208Y/120-V system is the availability of three-phase at 208 V, although this is of marginal significance. The 208 V may be detrimental in that most single-phase dual-voltage products are rated 230/115 V for use on the 240/120-V system.

Another option is the 480Y/277-V nominal system, with the rating of lighting products at 265 V. The 277-V line-to-neutral voltage supplies single-phase for lighting circuits exclusively. The 120-V loads are supplied by 460-240/120-V transformers.

This can be summarized by comparing three basic systems supplying a similar-size load.

1. A unit substation for a 208Y/120-V system to supply the whole of the plant subsystems.
2. A 240/120-V three-wire system using 460-V feeders to supply small 25-kVA transformers located as required.
3. A 480Y/277-V system from a delta-star-connected plant substation with three-phase four-wire feeders supplying the lighting areas and single-phase supplied by 25-kVA 460-240/120-V transformers as in system 2.

The first system probably has the highest installed cost, but should be considered if the 120-V load is large. That is over 50% of the secondary total load.

The next most expensive system would be the second system outlined. It is approximately 25 to 30% less expensive than the 208Y/120-V system. In a plant where the miscellaneous loads are less than 50%, this system would be considered.

The least expensive system is the combination of the 480Y/277 V for mercury and fluorescent lighting and the 240/120 V for the miscellaneous loads. The installed cost of this system is approximately 40% less than for the 208Y/120-V system and 20% less than for the 240/120-V system.

The short-circuit current is highest in the 208Y/120-V system and lowest in the 480Y/277-V (and 240/120-V) system, and in between both these systems for the 240/120-V system.

The grounding regulations must be considered and applied when using the 480Y/277-V system, whereas the other systems have the voltage to ground limited to below 150 V. These comments on alternate systems are assuming similar size installations and cost comparisons on a "per kVA" basis.

6.13 SUMMATION

With this limited information and use of a plot-plan print, a fairly good guess can be made at the probable type of primary and secondary systems preferred. The reasons will be established and considered and a preliminary single line can be "roughed out" on the back of an obsolete print. Using an obsolete print for roughing out gives an indication of whether the draftsman will have trouble showing the system on a single sheet. All component parts of the system should be shown, but at this stage accurate sizes need not be considered. The important point is to develop the intended philosophy that will be adhered to during the final design.

With the roughed-out single line at hand, preliminary estimated-load calculations can be made on standard calculation sheets. These will be retained in the job file and will be added to and modified as more information is received. When it is apparent that most of the loads are beginning to firm up and power-distribution transformers can be approximately sized and selected as to type, the single line can be turned over to a draftsman, who will produce the actual-system single-line drawing complete with title block and drawing number. Feeders and circuit breakers should not be sized because precise calculations are necessary at a later date for the job file. Since these calculations require firm load information, it is better to leave this until later.

The transformers are available in standard sizes and the selection of a probable size is fairly simple. For instance, if the estimated load is 600 kVA for a three-phase transformer, the choice is a standard 500 or 750 kVA. Since the actual loads tend to be larger, rather than smaller, than the estimated loads, the first choice would be the 750 kVA. All selections on a preliminary single line should be marked with "HOLD." In any event, its whole purpose as a "preliminary" is to be changed and modified until loads are firm.

The time to issue the final single line is when the specifications and bills of material are required for ordering the equipment. Once these are issued, the single line should be issued. This "fixes" the power-system design. Any changes after this must be as a result of unavoidable revisions to loads. Changes after issue should only be made as a result of "official" notification, in the form of an interoffice communication memo, or an issue of a revised drawing by the other departments, resulting in the necessary changes. Issuing revisions is expensive and should only be done when absolutely necessary.

7 POWER-DISTRIBUTION-EQUIPMENT SELECTION

7.1 SERVICE-ENTRANCE EQUIPMENT

The power company will have detailed instructions with regard to the necessary requirements for the service-entrance equipment and its arrangement. The minimum equipment required in an industrial plant are a main disconnect device with overcurrent protection, a metering section, and usually a transition section.

Switchgear ratings up to and including 13.8 kV are available in oilless types for indoor or outdoor applications. For outdoor applications above 14.4 kV the oil-type switchgear is generally used.

The National Electrical Code requires that a means shall be provided to disconnect all conductors in a building or other structure from the service-entrance conductors. It shall be identified as a service disconnect, and it should be "approved" for "service equipment." Each disconnecting means shall simultaneously disconnect all ungrounded conductors. It must also be operable by hand (in the event of a power failure). More information is given in the Code with regard to the options for the service disconnect. The major manufacturers of electric equipment have approved service-entrance equipment available. It should, however, be written in the purchase order that the service-entrance equipment shall meet the requirements of the specific local code and of the local power company.

7.2 METERING

Metering, and instrumentation, is located in its own section of the "lineup." The instrumentation requires current transformers and potential transformers, which usually take a full section. The meters can be installed in various combinations: voltmeter, ammeter, wattmeter, varmeter, power factor meter, watthour meter, demand meter, frequency meter. Sometimes an additional "transition" section is required to connect the incoming service section with the plant equipment. The service equipment is sealed by the power company to prevent tampering with the metering, which of course is used for billing purposes.

For power factor and demand meter requirements, it is necessary to obtain a rate schedule that will be applicable to the plant when it is in operation. Billing is made by measuring energy, that is, watt-hours. In an alternating-current system, "watts" does not define the total power; it only defines the "used" power. The power to supply magnetic circuits, such as the magnetic flux in motors, transformers, and ballasts (lighting), does not register on a watthour meter. The power company supplies a service in kVA (kilovolt-amperes). Assume a hypothetical size of 100 kVA for the service. If the plant has a power factor of 80%, the watts would be 1000 kVA × 0.80 = 800 kW. The power company is supplying 1000 kVA but only getting paid for 800. To prevent excessive "giveaway" of power, the power company will usually have a power-factor penalty clause in the billing schedule.

7.3 POWER-DISTRIBUTION CENTER (PDC)

The term *power-distribution center* is an accurate self-description. When the power is available at the service-entrance lineup, it consists of a single three-phase power supply. It must now be broken down into multiple smaller units of power. This is accomplished by connecting the incoming service to a long continuous busbar. Circuit breakers are then attached to the busbar giving multiple smaller units of power.

These circuit breakers then provide protection for high-voltage feeders which supply power to the approximate center of a load area. Here, the power is transformed down to the utilizing voltage. In some cases, it provides power for high-voltage motors, in which event it connects to another busbar without transformation. The motor starters then obtain their power from this new bus.

When we talk about connecting to busbars, the circuit-breaker lineup and motor-starter lineup are actually purchased with the busbar connected as an integral unit and no connecting is actually required except for the feeder connection.

7.4 LOAD-CENTER DISTRIBUTION

Load-center distribution is the name given to a concept. This concept is that when a system has medium/high incoming voltage, that is, 2.4 to 15 kV, it is transmitted through metal-clad switchgear or master unit substations via medium-voltage/high-voltage feeders to the various areas of load concentration. Here the feeder supplies a small *load center* consisting of the transformer and switchgear in a packaged unit. This unit substation and switchgear provide the low-voltage utilization power. This, combined with using the correct distribution-circuit arrangement, will provide a low-cost, reliable, flexible system, with low line losses.

Load centers are compact centrally located units, usually located in special "electric rooms" or "vaults." Equipment is all *deadfront,* meaning that operators (nonskilled electrical) can have access to starting motors under limited conditions. No exposed live conductors are accessible without opening doors. The equipment is usually interlocked so that power is shut off if the door is opened.

7.5 UNIT SUBSTATIONS

The unit substation is a complete package. It is supplied by the manufacturer in accordance with the purchase-order specification. It generally consists of three sections integrated into a single load-center substation. The basic parts are (1) the incoming line section, (2) transformer section, and (3) low-voltage feeder section. Various combinations and arrangements can be specified, depending on the designer's requirements.

The kVA rating of nominal 460-V three-phase unit substations is between 500 and 1500 kVA, with the lowest economic size at 750 kVA. In the case of a 208Y/120-V three-phase system the economic range is 300 to 750 kVA, with the 300 kVA and 500 kVA being the most economical units.

For estimating and preliminary selection purposes it is necessary to determine the total plant kVA required. In order to produce a starting figure for consideration, the plant can be grouped into load areas. Manufacturing areas can be assigned 15 volt-amperes per square foot. Light manufacturing and assembly areas can be assigned half this amount ($7\frac{1}{2}$ volt-amperes/square foot). Outdoor lighting can be assessed at 200 W per lineal 100 ft of fence and/or exterior building walls. The indoor lighting can be estimated by using 2 W per square foot for 50 fc when using fluorescent and mercury vapor and by using 5 W per square foot if incandescent lighting is contemplated.

With the plot-plan print marked off in areas and load-estimate figures, it can be subdivided into 750-kVA unit areas. A load-center unit substation can then be located in the center of the areas. This will then provide a "first consideration layout."

7.6 UNIT SUBLOAD ESTIMATE

In Sec. 6.3 some load information had already been acquired; this was necessary for discussion with the power company. This should be reviewed and compared with the new total figure. The former load figure was probably obtained by a different method than this second figure.

The difference between the two figures for total plant loading should not be too wide; otherwise, a gross error has been made in one or the other. In this case both estimates should be reviewed to see if significant loads have been "missed." For instance a boiler house which is relatively lightly loaded could have a large single motor for driving a compressor. It is possible that the mechanical department did not get around to designing this and omitted to tell the electrical department.

Many times a complete system can be omitted because the mechanical department has not yet hired the individual to design this particular part of the process. It is essential then, when estimating the loads, that all mechanical departments are contacted and questioned with regard to total contemplated loads.

With the areas approximately loaded to 750 kVA, it may be found that 2000 kVA or more is required for a particular highly concentrated load area. In this case consideration should be given to using multiple 750-kVA units or two 1000-kVA units instead of a single "oversize" unit.

If transformers can be standardized to a single size throughout the plant, one spare can be carried. If various sizes are used, that is, 500, 750, and 1000-kVA, multiple spares must be carried or no spares, relying on fast service work to repair the faulty unit.

7.7 LOAD-CENTER ENCLOSURES

The majority of load-center unit substations are metal-clad indoor-unit enclosures. They are usually installed inside the plant; furthermore, as previously mentioned, they are installed in their own rooms, or vaults, or elevated on platforms. It is only necessary then to provide a general-purpose enclosure that meets the code safety regulations. In the case of outdoor installations, the general-purpose enclosure is still the most common. It is installed in a weatherproof metal enclosure or building and can be ordered in this form complete from the manufacturer. In some cases it may be more economical to build an outdoor building, but in any event the load center is still basically a general-purpose enclosure.

If a plant has hazardous areas, the load centers are usually located in nonhazardous areas of the plant; however, hazardous-area design requires different considerations, which will be covered in later chapters.

7.8 TRANSFORMER ENCLOSURES

Since the load center is inherently an indoor-type unit, to maintain the economy and ease of installation and maintenance, the transformers are usually either the *dry type* or *askarel filled* (inert liquid). The oil-filled transformers should be reserved for outdoor use. The first choice for overall general application is the askarel-filled type. It is equivalent in all respects to the oil-filled type except that its weight is approximately 20 to 25% more. The disadvantages are that disposing of askarel liquid is a problem and local waste-disposing regulations must be checked. Also, askarel may affect sensitive skin; therefore, the liquid should be carefully handled. Apart from these two maintenance-type problems, the askarel type of transformer is very acceptable.

The second choice available is the dry-type transformer. These can be supplied as a *sealed* unit or as a normally open ventilated type, which is more common. The open ventilated type has only 50% of the impulse strength of the askarel-filled type, making it susceptible to lightning. It requires frequent cleaning to remove dust. Its temperature and sound rating are higher than the equivalent askarel. The advantages are that its cost is approximately 10% less and its weight is approximately 35% less than for the equivalent askarel-filled type.

In general, dry-type transformers would be selected only for installations with no air contaminants, that is, dust, moisture, acid, oil, or corrosive and/or hazardous vapors, and where the weight advantage is a consideration. Reliability should be the first consideration in an industrial plant.

7.9 INCOMING LINE SECTION

The incoming feeder to a load center is already protected by the feeder circuit breaker at the power-distribution center. Therefore, it is unnecessary to terminate the feeder into another circuit breaker. The load center, however, consists of a transformer and secondary circuit breakers. The incoming-line-section switchgear must be selected in accordance with the code requirements for a transformer. This is dictated by the local governing code, which in some cases may require overcurrent protection in the primary regardless of the protection in the secondary. According to the National Electrical Code, if the transformer has an overcurrent device in the secondary (as a main overcurrent device) and the settings of the overcurrent devices of the secondary *and* the primary feeder (in the PDC) comply with the code exceptions, an individual primary overcurrent device is not required.

This means that various alternates exist. In any case a primary disconnect should be installed whether required by code or not. This is necessary for maintenance and isolating purposes.

If a primary disconnect device is used instead of a primary circuit breaker, it should be key interlocked with the secondary main circuit breaker so that it cannot be opened under load. Once the secondary circuit breaker is opened, the disconnect has only to interrupt the magnetizing current of the transformer. Without the key interlock it is possible for an individual under "panic" conditions of overload to open the primary disconnect instead of the secondary main circuit breaker. This may be hazardous or not depending on the selection and quality of the primary disconnect; in any event, it is not good practice unless it happens to be a correctly sized circuit breaker used in lieu of a load disconnect switch.

7.10 SECONDARY SWITCHGEAR SECTION

This section is the low-voltage (nominal 460 V) power section. It is recommended that a main circuit breaker be installed in the secondary as the preferred arrangement, rather than in the primary section. It is required by code anyway if the overcurrent protection is not installed in the primary side.

The main circuit breaker will then supply the low-voltage switchgear. The selection of low-voltage switchgear is limited to three types:

1. Large drawout-type air circuit breakers
2. Fixed-molded-case light-duty circuit breakers
3. Motor control center

7.11 POWER CIRCUIT BREAKERS

The large, heavy-duty power air circuit breakers would be selected where a low-voltage feeder is required or where a large-size branch circuit is required, that is, 4/0 copper. The available range of these circuit breakers is 15 to 4000 A continuous and 15,000 to 100,000 A interrupting (asymmetrical). The metal-clad enclosure allows stacking of approximately four high in the large-frame size.

Where more than one vertical section of metalclad is used, all the sections are joined by a horizontal bus which is supplied by the main circuit breakers. This horizontal bus then supplies the drawout breakers with power.

7.12 MOLDED-CASE CIRCUIT BREAKERS

Where many light-duty loads exist, a *power panel* is usually installed. This power panel contains *molded-case* circuit breakers. These are light, compact, and low cost, compared with the heavy-duty power circuit breaker. Various electrical manufacturers produce this type of circuit breaker. The range varies with manufacturer and consequently the available trip and interrupting ranges. Technology is constantly improving and extending the range. At present, molded-case circuit breakers are available from 15 to 2000 A and 15,000 to 85,000 A symmetrical interrupting ratings. This does not mean that the molded-case types can be substituted for the heavy-duty drawout types, because the "spread" of continuous rating to interrupting rating may not be identical in both lines; also, the tripping characteristics are different. The life (repeated operations) of molded-case circuit breakers is also shorter than for power circuit breakers. In effect, where a circuit is an isolated circuit requiring only protection for its own conductor and repeated switching operations are not needed, the molded-case circuit breaker can be used. Where the circuit requires coordinated tripping with other circuits, repeated operations, and selective tripping, the power circuit breaker must be considered.

7.13 MOTOR CONTROL CENTER

A natural location for a motor control center is next to the source of power. Instead of using individual motor starters located all over the plant, it is generally preferred to have them all centrally located. This reduces the cost of interconnecting controls and also allows a flexibility of interchange and modification.

The motor control center (MCC) is purchased in a prepackaged unit with the correct-size starters already installed. The power is supplied to a horizontal bus (in the MCC) connecting all the vertical sections. A vertical bus in each section provides continuous power for that particular section; the circuit breaker and motor starter are then connected to this vertical bus. The motor control center is usually supplied by a power circuit breaker connected by a short run of cable or bus to the motor-control-center horizontal bus.

7.14 SECONDARY EQUIPMENT ARRANGEMENT

The secondary-distribution switchgear can be any one of the three previously mentioned arrangements or it can be a combination of all three. Electrical manufacturers all have their own designs for metal-clad gear and the component parts; it is therefore necessary to consider all the various manufacturers' catalogs. Some things to consider are customer service, technical assistance backup, wide or limited range of products, speed of delivery, reliability, warrantee policy, and credibility of promises.

When selecting a load center, it is better to purchase complete primary, transformer, and secondary equipment from the same manufacturer as a package. This means that any problems with installation or performance become a single source responsibility directly back to the manufacturer. Many times, manufacturers will accept a moral obligation to correct a problem with equipment that is not a warrantee commitment; however, if another manufacturer's equipment is intermixed, this service could be restricted.

Since load centers are long-delivery items, it is essential that they be ordered as soon as possible. This can only be done when the loads are firmed up, but don't wait until the last piece of load information is in before ordering. The metal-clad unit can be ordered with spare compartments only; later on, if extra circuits are required, the circuit breakers can be ordered. These are an off-the-shelf item and are essentially a short-delivery item.

8 TRANSFORMERS

8.1 TRANSFORMERS

Transformers are available in many types, sizes, construction, and output characteristics. They can, however, be grouped into usage types.

1. Utility-company power-transmission type
2. Utility-company poleline-distribution type
3. Utility-company industrial-service type
4. Plant-substation type (interchangeable with 3)
5. "In-plant" unit-substation type
6. "In-plant" distribution type
7. Lighting transformers
8. Control power transformers
9. Metering transformers
10. Relaying transformers
11. Speciality types

The first three types are of no concern in this book. They are beyond the scope of the electrical designers involved in industrial plants. In addition, the utility companies are not covered by the National Electrical Code requirements. The remaining types can be further classified by rating, cooling, winding type, impedance, sound level, and core types. In this chapter we will discuss the various effects of all these variables. The designer must then try to find a manufacturer who can supply the transformer with the variables as specified.

8.2 TRANSFORMER CHARACTERISTICS

To discuss or specify a transformer intelligently, it is necessary to know the optional characteristics over which the designer/purchaser has some control. Its specification must consider the following points.

1. Three-phase or single-phase type
2. Winding type (two-winding, three-winding, or autotransformer)
3. Winding connection (delta/delta, star/delta, delta/star, star/star, star/delta–tertiary/star, or special connection
4. kVA rating
5. Voltage ratings and ratios
6. Primary and/or secondary taps
7. Impulse levels (lightning susceptibility)
8. Type of cooling and enclosure (oil, askarel, air-open type, air-sealed type, forced cooling, other)
9. Insulation class (standard or high temperature)
10. Sound level
11. Impedance (standard, special high impedance)
12. Delivery and availability
13. Terminal types (exposed bushings, pothead, or enclosed-throat connection)
14. Bushing transformers (yes or no, and rating)
15. Accessories (gas relay, thermometer, etc.)

8.3 SELECTION (SINGLE-PHASE OR THREE-PHASE)

Considering item 1, the trend in industrial plants is predominantly with the three-phase transformer. The reliability and simplicity of installation of the three-phase unit far outweighs the one advantage of using three single-phase units. If one transformer fails in a bank of three single-phase transformers, they can be connected *open delta* and still provide 57.7% of the total kVA for the three transformers, which is 86% of the total output of the two transformer nameplate kVA ratings. If one phase fails in a three-phase transformer, the whole transformer is shut down.

More floor space is required for the single-phase transformers than for the equivalent three-phase. The transformers must be interconnected, and if the wiring is exposed, a protective fence must be installed. The installation cost then would be less for the three-phase transformer than the equivalent size in three single-phase transformers.

8.4 WINDING TYPE (TWO-WINDING)

The winding types available in power transformers are the two-winding, three-winding, and autotransformer. In the two-winding transformer there is no electrical connection between the primary and secondary. Power is transferred between the two windings by electromagnetic induction; therefore, the windings must use a common core, but the actual wire of each winding is separated from the core and the other winding by carefully calculated and installed insulation.

The two-winding transformer is by far the most popular, and in fact the only one that should be used for general industrial installations.

8.5 WINDING TYPE (THREE-WINDING)

The three-winding transformer has one primary winding and two separate secondary windings at different voltages. This type is limited to special applications in light industrial plants. For example, plants which have large areas of distribution and a possible 208Y/120-V secondary system and a boiler/compressor with large loads requiring 460 V. The three-winding transformer could then have the primary at 2300 or 4160 V, with one secondary for the 208Y/120-V load-center distribution and the other secondary winding to supply the boiler/compressor house with 460 V. The transformer would probably be located near the boiler house (in an adjacent building), allowing short runs on 460-V circuits.

The three-winding transformer is a rare selection, and though there is no "technical" objection to using this type, because the construction and reliability are similar to the two winding, special conditions must exist for this type to show advantages over the conventional installation. See Fig. 8.1.

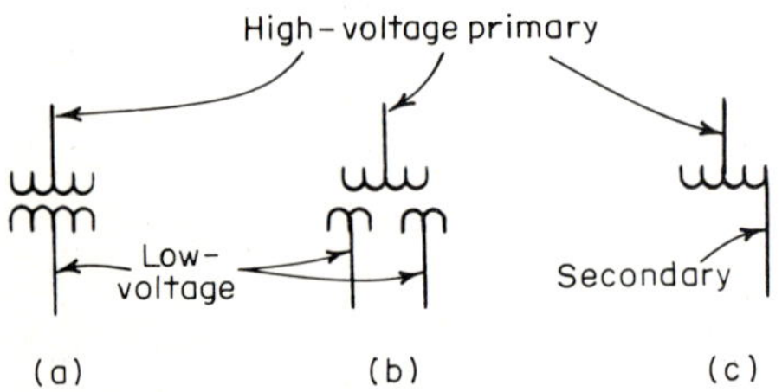

Figure 8.1 Single-line representation of transformer windings: (a) two-winding transformer; (b) three-winding transformer; (c) autotransformer.

8.6 WINDING TYPE (AUTOTRANSFORMER)

The autotransformer is a transformer which has parts of the primary and secondary windings in common. This means that the primary and secondary windings are "electrically" connected. It has only a single winding; the primary (high voltage) is connected to the ends of the winding, while the secondary is connected only to one end with a "tap" connection at some portion of the winding. If the primary voltage is 100 V and the winding has

100 turns, a secondary tap at 40 turns would produce voltages of 40 and 60 V, respectively, when measured between the ends of the winding and the tap.

This type of transformer is economical when the voltage ratios between the primary and secondary are limited to about 2:1. Utility companies sometimes use them for high-voltage transmission, for example, 345 to 172 kV, which is actually a nominal 169 kV. The 2:1 ratio allows much further distance for high-voltage transmission. Autotransformers can be used or considered for special distribution problems involving the 208Y/120-V system where an occasional 460 V may be required. They can also be used in speciality applications, such as reduced-voltage motor starting. Because the primary and secondary windings are electrically connected, safety becomes a problem. It is therefore essential that the local enforcing codes be checked with regard to the use of autotransformers. An understanding of the autotransformer design characteristics and system grounding is also necessary.

8.7 WINDING CONNECTIONS

The actual connection diagrams are readily available from manufacturer catalogs. Here we will discuss the merits of the various connection arrangements, limited to the general industrial plant three-phase system.

The type of system, that is, grounded or ungrounded, may have been specified in the customer's specification; however, it should still be evaluated for specific advantages and disadvantages that may arise when considering the peculiarities of a particular plant.

8.8 DELTA CONNECTION

This connection is formed by connecting the ends of each phase winding directly to the phase conductors. For example,

- Winding 1 would connect between phase conductors A and B.
- Winding 2 would connect between phase conductors B and C.
- Winding 3 would connect between phase conductors C and A.

With this arrangement each winding would receive full line voltage E, but the current in the winding would only be $I/1.73$. This means that the power rating of the three windings would be 3 $EI/1.73$. Since 3 is approximately equal to $(1.73)^2$, we can rewrite the three-phase output as
$1.73 \times 1.73EI/1.73 = 1.73EI$.

8.9 STAR CONNECTION

The star connection is sometimes referred to as a *wye* connection because of its similarity in vector form to the capital Y. This connection is formed by connecting one end of the three windings together and then connecting the other three ends to each phase. This means that there are two windings in series between any two phase conductors. The voltage on any single winding then becomes $E/1.73$. Since the current is the same in the series-connected windings, it remains as I. The power rating of each winding is $IE/1.73$, and the rating of the three windings is $3IE/1.73$. This also reduces to $1.73EI$ for total output.

We see then that the delta and wye connections are equivalent as far as power output is concerned. This is of course assuming that everything is balanced and equal in both connections.

8.10 DELTA-DELTA CONNECTION

The delta-delta connection is permissible for three-phase balanced power loads. If a neutral is required for any reason, this connection should not be used. Balanced three-phase delta-delta arrangements will not introduce harmonics into the line, that is, 3rd and the multiples. In situations where the load has a very high current but relatively low voltage, the delta connection produces only $I/1.73$, or 58% of line current in the winding; this of course requires less copper. In transformers that have a slight turn-ratio difference between phases, a circulating current will be produced which will circulate in both the primary and secondary windings contributing to elevated temperatures. The delta-delta connection is adaptable to using three single-phase transformers of different size and impedance, although the division of currents and loads between units requires some special analysis. The delta-delta connection will not introduce a phase shift between the primary and secondary, which makes it particularly attractive in metering and relaying.

8.11 STAR-DELTA CONNECTION

If loads are balanced and all other things are equal, the star-delta connection is nearly equivalent to the delta-delta. The star-delta connection will provide a neutral point; however, when on the primary, it should not be grounded. The star-delta connection produces a phase shift of 30° between the primary and secondary, but in cases where the primary voltage is high and the current low, it reduces the insulation requirement for the winding to $E/1.73$, or 58% of line voltage. A star-delta-connected three-phase transformer can be applied to an ungrounded delta-delta system to produce a grounded system. In this case, the neutral "may" be grounded, but problems can arise if one phase on the primary becomes open. For example, the flux in the core can be distorted and circulate in surrounding iron or steel components, such as supporting webs and tie rods. This flux will in effect act like an induction heater on these components and possibly destroy the transformer. The star-delta connection then produces an ungrounded system and where grounding is required, grounding transformers should be used on the secondary side.

The star-delta connection overcomes most of the objections of delta-delta connections because it has characteristics of both the delta and the star. The delta eliminates the third- and multiple-harmonic problems associated with the star connection while also stabilizing the neutral. The star connection determines the division of current between phases, regardless of variations in impedance. The problem of excessive circulating currents is virtually eliminated by the inability of the star connection to reproduce them. For an ungrounded system the star-delta connection should be considered over the delta-delta.

8.12 DELTA-STAR CONNECTION

This connection is by far the most popular and the only one that should be used with a three-phase four-wire secondary system. It is, of course, a "mirror" of the star-delta and has all the same benefits attributed to the combination of a delta and star. Its greatest attribute is the ability to supply three-phase and single-phase loads simultaneously, while retaining reasonable regulation. Its second major benefit is its fault-protection feature. With the grounded neutral, faults and fault currents can be monitored and cause an immediate shutdown of the faulty circuit. Ground faults can be limited in magnitude by inserting an impedance in the neutral. Transient overvoltages are reduced in magnitude, and voltage to ground is limited to $E/1.73$, or 58% of line voltage. It is a safe, reliable connection with a low plant-maintenance cost. It should be the first choice for any industrial plant, with the star-delta and delta-delta as second and third choices, respectively.

8.13 STAR-STAR CONNECTION

This connection should never be used in an industrial plant. Apart from being interesting it has no productive contribution to industrial-plant design. We could go into a highly technical analysis of why it should not be used but briefly, the star-star connection is high in harmonic content, which can affect telephone systems; regulation is a problem and varies with the construction of the transformer; and neutral inversion is possible, resulting in higher than normal voltages. All considered, this connection has too many potential problems. Autotransformers are a special case and should be considered as required.

8.14 STAR-DELTA-STAR CONNECTION

Introducing an intermediate delta winding into the star-star connection brings us back to the advantages of the star-delta and delta-star connections; repeating some of these that are applicable to the star-delta-star:

1. The neutral can be grounded on both star points.
2. Both star connections would have normal regulation with single-phase loads, that is, line to neutral.
3. The primary and secondary connections have no phase shift between them.
4. Third harmonics are negligible.
5. The tertiary (intermediate) delta winding can be used to provide a different impedance to three-phase faults than it does to line-to-ground faults. This connection is probably more useful to a utility company with their own special problems than to an industrial plant.

8.15 CONNECTIONS (CONCLUSIONS)

The system type may have already been established. If not, either a grounded or ungrounded system will be selected. With the former the choice would be the delta-star connection; for the three-phase transformer(s), and in the latter case, it would be a selection of the star-delta or the delta-delta connection. Of these two, the star-delta would be considered first. Most of the other connections, such as open delta, open star, and specialized types, including parallel operations, are all operational-type connections made in the field or instrument and metering connections and not purchase-order-type connections, which we are concerned with at this time.

8.16 kVA RATING

All transformers are rated in kVA at a specified temperature rise, except in the very small control-power types, which are rated in VA. The three-phase transformers are rated in total output; that is, a 1500-kVA transformer would be equivalent to three single-phase transformers at 500 kVA formed into a three-phase bank. Single-phase transformers are rated by the single-phase output. Autotransformers are rated by their designed output and not by their physical equivalent size. A 1000-kVA autotransformer could be physically equivalent, approximately, to a 500-kVA two-winding transformer.

The kVA output can be increased by use of forced ventilating; therefore, the kVA rating may be in multiples and "tied" to the cooling method. For instance, a self-cooled 1000-kVA transformer can be rated 1150-kVA with forced-air cooling. (See Sec. 8.19, Transformer Cooling.)

8.17 VOLTAGE-RATING TAPS

The voltage rating of the transformer is the correct voltage desired at the terminals of the primary and secondary. The supply voltage or incoming voltage is generally the same as the nominal voltage. This, however, should not be taken for granted. Confirmation from the power company should be obtained, specifically stating the voltage at the service point. Once this voltage is known, the transformer primary voltage can be specified. In order to adjust slight variations in the incoming voltage, the transformer can be ordered with *primary taps.* These taps are generally specified as (2) at $2\frac{1}{2}\%$ above and (2) at $2\frac{1}{2}\%$ below the specified voltage. These are *no-load* taps and are changed when the transformer is deenergized. They are not intended to compensate for poor regulation. The function of the taps is to change the turns ratio between the primary and secondary. In the delta-delta-connection arrangement, odd ratios in transformers in three-phase banks can produce circulating currents.

Consideration must also be given to the particular location in the system of the transformer and the load it is serving. A nominal 460-V system is generally 480 V at the transformer and 440 V at the motor. A word of caution: Check the desired incoming bus voltages carefully, and specify the taps so that they are not wasted by the incoming voltage not being centered between the high and low taps.

8.18 IMPULSE LEVELS

The designation "BIL" is the abbreviation for *basic impulse level.* Transient voltages from lightning, switching surges, and circuit phenomena can blow a hole in insulation. Insulation is rated with a dielectric stress capability of "volts per mil"; when this stress is exceeded, a breakdown occurs. The BIL, then, is a rating of the peak voltage which can be impressed on the insulation without causing damage. The ANSI-NEMA standard for basic impulse levels is given in Table 8.1.

TABLE 8.1 Basic Impulse Levels

Voltage class	*Standard ANSI–NEMA*
600 V	10 kV
2400 V	20 kV
5000 V	25 kV
8660 V	35 kV
15,000 V	50 kV

8.19 TRANSFORMER COOLING

Transformers are rated with a kVA output at a specific temperature. This specific temperature is calculated using a number of factors. One factor is

TABLE 8.2 Classes of Transformer Cooling

Type letters	*Cooling method*
OA	Oil-immersed, self-cooled
OW	Oil-immersed, water-cooled
OW/A	Oil-immersed, water-cooled/self-cooled
OA/FA	Oil-immersed, self-cooled/forced-air-cooled (above 500 kVA)
OA/FA/FA	Oil-immersed, self-cooled/forced-air-cooled/forced-air-cooled (10,000 kVA and up)
OA/FOA/FOA	Oil-immersed, self-cooled/forced-air-forced-oil-cooled/forced air–forced-oil-cooled (10,000 kVA and up)
FOA	Oil-immersed, forced-oil-cooled with forced-air-cooled (10,000 kVA and up)
FOW	Oil-immersed, forced-oil cooled with forced-water-cooled (10,000 kVA and up)
AA	Dry-type, self-cooled
AFA	Dry-type, forced-air-cooled
AA/FA	Dry-type, self-cooled/forced-air-cooled (above 500 kVA)

TABLE 8.3 Transformer Rating with Forced Cooling

	Self-cooled rated kVA		*% increase of self-cooled kVA with auxiliary cooling*	
Type of cooling	*Single-phase*	*Three-phase*	*First stage*	*Second stage*
OA/FA	501–2499	501–2499	115	
	2500–9999	2500–11,999	125	
	10,000 and larger	12,000 and larger	133.33	
OA/FA/FA	10,000 and larger	12,000 and larger	133.33	166.66
AA/FA*	501	501	133.33	

* Not applicable to sealed dry-type transformers

the ambient air temperature. If this is lower than what is normally specified as "standard," that is, 40°C, the kVA output can be increased. If we consider this process in reverse, we can have a transformer running at full load and rated temperature. If we require an overload on the transformer, it must compensate for the extra heat generated by equivalent cooling. This can be done by blowing with fans (automatically started) and/or by using forced liquid circulation or by other methods.

The cooling method and the overload allowable is dictated by ANSI and NEMA standards. These are shown in Tables 8.2 and 8.3.

8.20 INSULATION CLASS

The transformer temperature rating is a function of the type of insulation used. If the insulation is a type that can withstand higher temperatures, the kVA output can be increased; or alternately, for the same output the transformer can be operated with less cooling capability.

This is particularly applicable in the air-cooled or ventilated types of transformers, that is, dry-type transformers.

Class A insulation is limited to transformers designed for a continuous full-load temperature rise not exceeding 55°C above a 40°C ambient. This also allows for a *hot-spot* temperature of 10°C, which means that the hottest spot in the winding should be no more than 105°C. This type of insulation is generally limited to oil-filled transformers.

Class B insulation requires a temperature rise not exceeding 80°C over a 40°C ambient. The hot-spot temperature is limited to a maximum of 150°C.

Class F insulation limits the temperature rise to a maximum of 115°C over a 40°C ambient with a maximum hot-spot temperature of 185°C in the winding.

Class H insulation has an allowance of a 150°C rise over a 40°C ambient. The hot-spot temperature in the winding is limited to 220°C.

Insulation life is inversely related to temperature. The higher the temperature, the shorter the life. It is essential, when a transformer temperature is stated by a manufacturer, that the life expectancy also be confirmed for that temperature. The ANSI and NEMA standards specify life versus temperature figures for a given insulation, but like the Code, these are minimum standards and are not always acceptable when viewed from plant operational requirements. For example, the 20,000 hours required to qualify for Class H is not a long life, by industry standards, for continuous plant operation.

8.21 SOUND LEVEL

The noise from a transformer is caused by *magnetostriction.* The steel in the core is magnetized, but because the current is alternating in polarity, the orientation of the steel molecules is reversed with each cycle. This generates both heat and noise. By good engineering the sound levels can be reduced.

There are NEMA standards outlining sound levels, but unless some specific reason for special acoustic requirements exists, as in a film theatre, most industrial plants use standard sound levels transformers.

8.22 IMPEDANCE

The impedance of a transformer is $Z = \sqrt{R^2 + X^2} = E/I$ and is by definition the *total* opposition to an electric current. In short-circuit calculations it is sometimes defined as X, but this is only because the R is neglected for purposes of the calculation. The transformer impedance is specified in $\%Z$. This is the figure used in short-circuit calculations. Standard impedances are listed in Table 8.4 and sizes in Table 8.5.

If a transformer is ordered with the standard impedance, the nameplate on the actual transformer may not be exactly as specified; however, it will be acceptably close. It is not possible to design a production-line type of transformer with the exact impedance; for example, a 5.5% may be delivered as a 5.4 or 5.6%.

If short-circuit currents are expected to be high, then a nonstandard transformer can be ordered, with a higher impedance to limit the short-circuit current in that circuit. The problem with this is that spares become a problem. If the transformer fails and it has to be temporarily replaced with a standard-impedance model, the short-circuit currents on the circuit breakers

TABLE 8.4 Approximate Transformer Impedances

POWER TRANSFORMERS

High-voltage rating	*Low voltage at 480 V*	*Low voltage at 2400 V and up*
2400–22,900	5.75%	5.5%
26,400–34,400	6.25%	6.0%
43,800	6.75%	6.5%
67,000		7.0%

SECONDARY UNIT SUBSTATION TRANSFORMERS

Rated kVA	*Design impedances*
112.5–225	Not less than 2% (use 3% for estimate)
300–500	Not less than 4.5% (use 5% for estimate)
Above 500	Use power-transformer impedances, or (use 5.5% for estimate 750 to 2000)

NOTE: Forced-oil-cooling transformers will have higher impedance values than self-cooled or water-cooled transformers; therefore, check with the manufacturer. Alternatively, estimate 122% increase for 15 kV and lower and 150% increase in impedance for higher voltages.

TABLE 8.5 Standard Transformer kVA Sizes

Single-phase kVA				*Three-phase kVA*			
3	75	1,250	10,000	9	225	2,500	20,000
5	100	1,667	12,500	15	300	3,750	25,000
10	167	2,500	16,667	30	500	5,000	30,000
15	250	3,333	20,000	45	750	7,500	37,500
25	333	5,000	25,000	75	1000	10,000	50,000
37.5	500	6,667	33,300	112.5	1500	12,000	60,000
50	833	8,333		150	2000	15,000	75,000
							100,000

would be excessive. If this were not a problem, the high-impedance transformer would not have been ordered in the first place.

8.23 TERMINAL TYPES

Termination at transformers is to a conductor mounted on an insulator. If the insulators are exposed, some kind of protective enclosure is necessary and therefore we get into the subject of *special enclosures.* An alternative to this is to order the transformer with a *throat* connection. Here the insulator and connection lug are mounted in a metal-enclosed compartment. After the connection is made, the cover is installed, and no exposed conductors are evident. This type of terminal connection is dead front and no special precautions are necessary because of possible termination exposure. Most load-center unit substations are throat-connected.

8.24 BUSHING TRANSFORMERS

The insulator on a transformer extends inside the transformer tank. Sometimes the current at the transformer terminals must be measured. In this case a current transformer is installed on the bushing. The current transformer (CT) is of the toroidal (doughnut) shape and is slipped over the conductor inside the tank. The CT must be specified as to burden and accuracy required. This can be spelled out in the specification, and the manufacturer can submit available types with the accuracies specified as recommendations which can be accepted or rejected.

8.25 TRANSFORMER ACCESSORIES

A transformer has various accessories that can be installed as required, such as temperature detectors, thermometers, and gas relays. The manufacturer will have a list of available accessories, and they should be included in the purchase specification as desired.

8.26 TRANSFORMER DELIVERIES

Large transformers, although standard types, are not generally sitting there waiting for a purchaser. More often than not they are built on demand. It is of the utmost importance that the main substation transformers are selected and ordered early in the project. The transformer must also be checked for damage on receipt at the site.

Sometimes transformers are shipped *liquid-filled*. Many times, however, they are shipped without liquid but sealed with an inert-gas filler under low pressure, for example, 4 to 5 lb. When shipped in this manner, the pressure should be checked and witnessed on receipt. Liquid-filled equipment should be available, and the tank must be specified as to whether it can be filled under vacuum or not.

In this case the purchase-order specification should include filling at the site by the manufacturer; alternatively, an experienced individual should be in charge of requisitioning the filling equipment and supervising the filling.

9 AC MOTOR RATINGS

9.1 AC MOTORS

In industrial plants the most widely used piece of equipment is the electric motor, with the most common being the *squirrel-cage* motor (named after the type of rotor design. See Figure 9.1). They come in all sizes, shapes, and designs; the characteristics vary over a wide range and the enclosures are also variable in design.

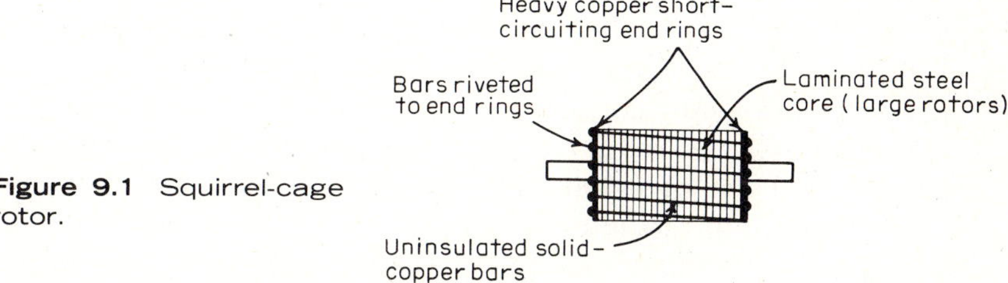

Figure 9.1 Squirrel-cage rotor.

It is impossible in one chapter to do justice to the characteristics of motors; therefore, we will concentrate on the points most useful to the electrical designer. We will discuss basic groups rather than specific motors. We will also discuss the ratings applicable to a motor and the characteristics that must be specified when ordering.

9.2 HORSEPOWER

The horsepower rating of a motor is the usable power at the shaft; therefore, it does not include the losses which occur in the motor. Since the output is pure working power, it has an equivalent rating in watts, that is, 746 watts equals one horsepower. By measuring with a *Prony brake test,* the power output can be determined by the formula

$$hp = \frac{2\pi NT}{33{,}000}$$

where N is the motor speed in rpm and T is the torque developed by the motor and measured along a moment arm in lb-ft.

For the purpose of designing branch circuits and electrical design functions, the Code makes it mandatory, by the word "shall," to use the tables in the National Electrical Code rather than nameplate ratings. This is generally a redundant statement because during design the motors have probably not been purchased or even allocated to a specific manufacturer. For estimating purposes for transformer loading, allow 1 kVA of power for each horsepower; for example 100 hp requires 100 kVA.

9.3 INDUCTION-MOTOR POWER FACTOR

The induction motor has two basic sets of losses;[1] these are mechanical and electrical. The electrical losses can be represented by a ratio known as the *power factor.* It is represented by the equation watts/voltamps = cos ϕ. In an induction motor it will vary with the load. At light loads it will be poor (losses high); at full load the losses will be as low as the design permits. In order to determine the full-load amperes of a motor, we must have a figure for the value of the power factor. This must be obtained from the manufacturer or by an educated guess. The power factor will also vary with speed; a slower-speed motor will have a lower (worse) power factor. As the Code requires that the tables be used for full-load currents for motors, the problem of selecting a power factor only occurs with large motors not listed.

As the motors get larger, the power factors get better. The electrical designer is usually informed that "we are adding a 1500-hp motor." This is usually the extent of the information received; the speed may not be fixed and the percent loading may not be known. However, a wire size must be selected and the power factor must be guessed. Large induction motors will have a power factor of around 0.92, depending on speed, loading, and horsepower. Luckily, conductor sizes are graded by ampacity, and also, the ampacity required must be the "next highest." This means that the power-factor figure selected will only create a problem when it results in a borderline selection of conductor size. If this occurs, time can be spent checking out the power factor, efficiency, etc., but in the long term it is usually better to use the next larger conductor and be safe. A larger conductor also serves the additional purpose of longer life, owing to its lower temperature, better short-circuit duty capability, and improved starting due to less IR loss.

[1] There are many types of losses which the motor designer has to contend with, but from a "user's" point of view the only interest is with reference to the "power required."

9.4 SYNCHRONOUS-MOTOR POWER FACTOR

The synchronous motor is usually limited to large sizes. There are two reasons for considering this type of motor. First, it is a true constant-speed motor at all loads. Second, it can serve a second purpose, by also being a *reactive-power* generator. As we already know, induction motors have a poor power factor (0.65 to 0.90) in the 5- to 200-hp range. This affects the whole plant system, causing a low power factor on the system. This can sometimes result in a penalty payment to the utility company. One of the methods used to contribute to a better power factor is to purchase a synchronous motor which has a *leading power factor.* This leading power factor will cancel out some of the poor, or "lagging," power factor, resulting in an improved plant power factor. A synchronous motor is higher in cost than the equivalent induction motor; therefore, an economic study must be conducted before selection. Sometimes, customers' specifications dictate when to purchase synchronous motors.

9.5 MOTOR EFFICIENCY

Of the two losses mentioned in the paragraph on power factor, the efficiency is concerned with the mechanical losses. These are caused by friction and windage. Like the power factor the efficiency is a figure that will probably have to be guessed. In the larger sizes it will be nearly the same as the power factor, that is, 0.9, 0.91, 0.92, etc. Again, the problem is conductor sizing. The product of the efficiency and power factor must be applied to the output power in order to determine the input power. The output power is 746 watts per horsepower; therefore if we have a 100-hp motor (output) at 0.9 efficiency and 0.91 power factor, an input requirement of $100 \times 746/0.9 \times 0.91$ (=91.09 kVA) is required. If we compare this with the output of 100×746 kW, we see that is is only $74.6/91.09 = 0.82$ of the input kVA. We can also see that we will have to provide an additional 18% more power for losses in order to get the 100-hp output.

9.6 MOTOR FULL-LOAD CURRENT

It is necessary to know the full-load current of a motor in order to design the correct branch and feeder circuits and select the required conductor sizes. We know the Code says it is mandatory that the tables in the National Electrical Code be used, rather than the nameplate ratings, and interpolated if necessary. We may, however, have an application where a motor is not listed in the Code, and special motors with a low speed or high torque require higher load currents. Here the Code allows a deviation to the nameplate amperes.

Since the horsepower of a motor is the "output," it must be adjusted to "input" requirements in order to determine the full-load current. This means including the mechanical losses (efficiency) and the electrical losses (power factor). The output then is divided by these two factors to give

$$\frac{\text{Output}}{\text{Efficiency} \times \text{power factor}} = \text{kVA}$$

For a three-phase system we can then obtain the full load:

$$\text{Full-load amps} = \frac{\text{hp} \times 746}{\sqrt{3} \times \text{volts} \times \text{efficiency} \times \text{PF}}$$

where hp is the horsepower and PF is the power factor in per units (for example, 0.9).

For a single-phase motor we use the same formula but delete the $\sqrt{3}$.

This full-load current is then used in conjunction with the Code requirements for determining conductor size.

9.7 MOTOR STARTING CURRENT

The starting current of an ac motor is different from the running current. When electric power is applied to a motor at standstill, for an instant, the effect is the same as if the rotor was locked. This locked rotor effect causes the required kVA to increase dramatically to provide the power necessary to overcome the inertia in the motor and the equipment it is driving. As the motor comes up to speed, the power requirement gradually reduces to its normal level. Here we encounter a problem which affects the electrical designer. The effect of this starting current is to imitate a short circuit when seen by the conductor overcurrent device. It can cause system disruptions, reducing

TABLE 9.1 Approximate Full-Voltage Starting-Inrush Factors for AC Motors

Type of motor	*Inrush current, approx %*
Induction motor—squirrel cage	600
Wound rotor—with full resistance	150
Synchronous motor:	
Low-speed low-torque	300
Low-speed high-torque	550
High-speed low-torque	400
High-speed high-torque	550

NOTE 1. High speed is over 500 rpm.

NOTE 2. Multiply values in NEC Table 430–150 by the above percentages to obtain approximate inrush current except where NEC Table 430–151 takes precedence.

voltage levels, and possible damage to the motor in cases where the resulting losses in the system cause the motor to come up to speed too slowly. It is essential, then, that an understanding of the dynamic conditions associated with startup be recognized.

The starting characteristics of a motor can be altered in two ways. First, by special design of the rotor, and second, by a special motor "starter." The former will be covered in more detail in Sec. 9.8 and the latter in the section on motor starters (Sec. 11.1).

For most design purposes Table 9.1 will be adequate for approximate starting inrush figures.

9.8 TORQUE AND STARTING TORQUE

The torque of a motor is a measure of its "turning effect." It is also a function of the rotor electrical characteristics and the applied voltage. The design of rotor characteristics is very complex and must include inertia torque, damping torque, load torque, and high or low starting current. The starting torque of the average induction motor is poor at initial starting. It does not have an instant increase like the starting current. In fact, the opposite occurs. We can make the statement that "the maximum torque varies inversely with the reactance and directly with the square of the applied voltage." The electrical designer has no control over the rotor reactance but does have control over the applied voltage.

When a motor is at standstill and the voltage is applied, we obtain a maximum voltage drop. Since the torque is directly proportional to the square of the applied voltage, we see that the maximum voltage drop (starting) gives the worse torque conditions. For example, using a reduced-voltage starter applying 60% voltage, we only obtain $(60\%)^2$, or 36% torque initially. If the driven equipment requires a 40% torque to start, the motor will never come up to speed and will burn out due to high current. If we review some of the curves in Fig. 9.2, we see that the kVA (current) curve starts high and reduces, while the torque curve starts low, slowly grows to a peak at about 80% synchronous speed, and then begins to drop rapidly to zero at 100% speed. As an induction motor runs at about 97% synchronous speed, we see that at approximately 100% torque is maintained at this speed.

Torque curves are more useful to the mechanical engineer selecting the equipment than to the electrical designer. However, there are times when the electrical designer must know the starting torque, for instance, when determining acceleration times in a centrifuge or in extremely large motors, which could affect the heating in cables.

In this case the peak of the torque curve should be used. This is approximately 200% on the average, regardless of starting method.

Synchronous motors are special motors and are generally in larger sizes. The required characteristics are usually "built in" to order; therefore, the electrical designer has more control than with the ordinary induction motor.

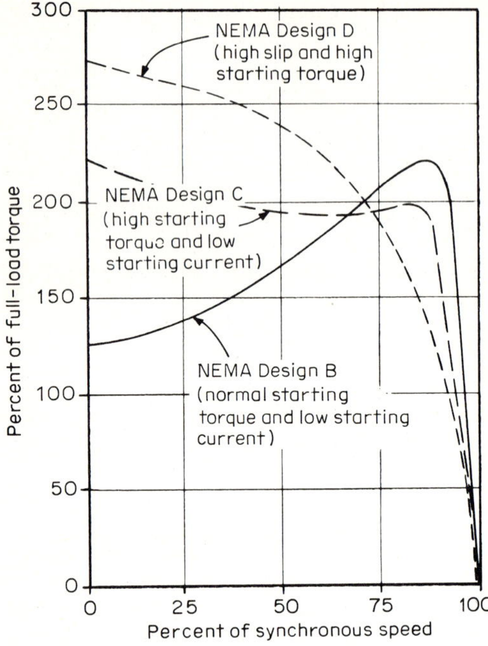

Figure 9.2 Typical torque curves for NEMA design B, C, and D induction motors.

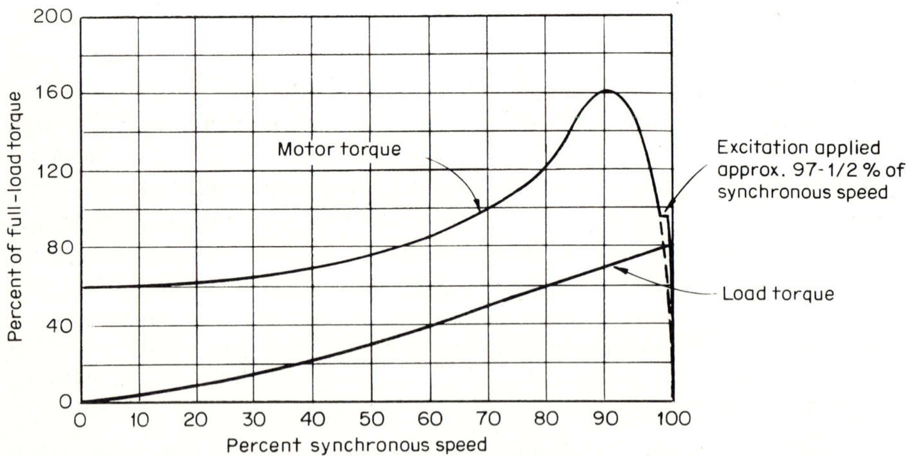

Figure 9.3 Typical starting torque for synchronous motor with high-inertia load.

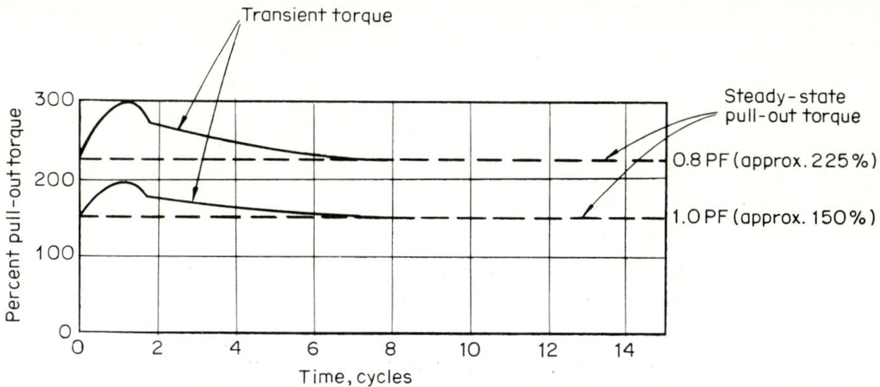

Figure 9.4 Transient pull-out torque of synchronous motor.

9.9 MOTOR CODE LETTERS

In Article 430 of the NEC, Table 430–7(b), there is a listing of *code letters.* This code letter identifies the starting conditions in "kVA per horsepower" when the motor is started on full voltage. It is a NEMA standard and is stamped on the motor nameplate. Unfortunately for the electrical designer, the motors are generally not purchased when the design information is required; therefore, the code letter may not be of too much assistance.

There is another letter associated with the design of a motor; it is also a NEMA designation and is sometimes confused with the code letter.

The NEMA *design letters* are A, B, C, D, and are limited to general-purpose motors up to 200 hp.

- Design A is normal starting torque and normal starting current.
- Design B is normal starting torque and low starting current.
- Design C is high starting torque and low starting current.
- Design D is high starting torque, low starting current, and high slip.

The NEMA code letters are not the same as the NEMA design letters. The NEMA design B motor is probably the most common general-purpose motor; this compares approximately with code letter F.

Some applications of NEMA designs are:

DESIGN A AND B	Machine tools, centrifugal pumps, line shafts, unloaded (starting) compressors, grinders, chippers, crushers, blowers, etc.
DESIGN C	Compressors (reciprocating and starting under load), pumps (reciprocating and displacement), conveyors and

	material-handling equipment (high breakaway required); loads with initial shock loading.
DESIGN D	Elevators, hoists, flywheel equipment.

A word of caution: Do not confuse the two designations of code letter and design letter.

9.10 MOTOR SPEED

The speed of an ac motor is a function of the frequency, poles, and slip. The stator of an ac motor contains the three-phase winding. When an alternating current is applied to the winding, a rotating magnetic field is produced. This is without the rotor being present. This can be verified by applying power to a stator only and placing a small steel ball bearing at the bottom of the stator. If the voltage is applied for a few seconds, the ball bearing will run around the stator, held in place by the magnetic forces. If it does not, a winding connection is improperly made. The speed of the rotating field is termed the *synchronous speed* and is dependent on the number of pole pairs and frequency. For a two-pole motor, that is, one pole pair, we have a maximum possible speed of 3600 rpm for a 60-Hz voltage. This is derived from the following equation:

$$\text{rpm} = \frac{\text{frequency} \times 60}{\text{poles}/2} = \frac{f \times 120}{P}$$

The speed, then, is derived from the winding in the stator which produces a rotating field traveling at synchronous speed.

We must now install a rotor. One type of rotor will rotate at exactly synchronous speed. This combination of stator and rotor is called a *synchronous motor.* The other (squirrel-cage) type of rotor lags behind the rotating field by a "slip" amount. This is called an *induction motor.* The former then will adhere to the first formula for speed. The squirrel-cage motor will require a modified formula for rotor speed which is

$$\text{rpm} = \frac{\text{frequency} \times 60}{\text{poles}/2} \times (1 - s)$$

where s is slip.

Consider the following example of a four-pole motor at 3% slip:

$$\begin{aligned}\text{rpm} &= \frac{60 \times 60 \times 2}{4}(1 - 0.03) \\ &= 1800 \times 0.97 \\ &= 1746 \text{ rpm}\end{aligned}$$

9.11 MOTOR TEMPERATURE

The temperature of a motor is given on the nameplate and indicates the *temperature rise* above an ambient temperature of 40°C. The limiting factor in temperature rise is the type of insulation used. Like the transformer, insulation is defined by class. However, the total temperature is calculated slightly differently. In the motor we have:

- Class A (105°C) total temperature for normal life
- Class B (130°C) total temperature for normal life
- Class F (155°C) total temperature for normal life
- Class H (180°C) total temperature for normal life

The calculation of temperature for a class A motor is as follows:

Ambient temperature	40°C	
Rise by thermometer	40°C	
Hot-spot allowance	15°C	
Service factor	10°C	
	105°C	Total temperature

Of course, the ambient temperature is of the surrounding air, which is assumed to be of a density corresponding to a maximum elevation of 3300 ft. The temperature rise is the temperature measured by a thermometer located at the hottest point externally, usually on the iron core (laminations). The hot-spot allowance is based on the premise that a point in the slots and possibly between the conductors will be up to 15°C hotter than the external temperature. The service factor is an overload allowance, which lets motors with a certain type of enclosure carry this overload continuously. If the service factor is 1.0, no overload is allowed.

If measuring the temperature of a running motor without special equipment, a rough indication will be a measurement of the rise which is added to the ambient, assuming that the thermometer is not located in the hottest external spot. This means that if the ambient temperature and temperature rise are at a maximum with this "loose" method, the probability is that the motor is running at too high a temperature. If this persists, the life of the insulation will be reduced significantly. The life-to-temperature ratio is an exponential function; therefore, a small increase in temperature can reduce the life by a large amount. An approximation can be used as follows: The "insulation life is inversely proportional to the square of the temperature"; for example, $1/(100\%)^2 = 1$ life span, whereas $1/(120\%)^2 = 0.7$ life span, where 100% is the normal temperature.

One other consideration must be made when specifying insulation (temperature) types. In tropical climates, insulation can be affected by moisture, corrosion, fungus, insects, and vermin, particularly termites. Tropical climates then must have the added appendage in the specification for special tropical treatment.

9.12 MOTOR VOLTAGE

This is a very simple designation on the nameplate and refers to the terminal voltage at the motor. In most cases actual voltage is not the same as the nominal system voltage.

The following table gives the three-phase preferred voltages.

Nominal system volts	*Transformer secondary volts*	*Motor terminal volts*
460	480/277	440
2,400	2,400	2,300
4,160	4,160Y/2,400	4,000
13,800	13,800Y/7,970	13,200

Other voltage systems will have different motor voltages when compared to the nominal system voltage. This then must be considered when working with unusual voltages.

9.13 MOTOR ENCLOSURES

Motor enclosures are defined by NEMA standards, which are very wordy; so we will not define the exact NEMA standards. We will, however, discuss a few types which are standard and in the greatest use.

The first type of enclosure is the *open type.* It is designed for indoor use. This type is further improved by protecting against water from above to 15° from the side which then becomes *dripproof.* If wire screens are added, it becomes *semi-enclosed.* This type is widely used, especially in hazardous (Class 1, Division 2) locations. A *totally enclosed* motor is generally *totally enclosed fan-cooled* (TEFC). The winding is completely enclosed by the motor housing and no access of any kind is evident. Cooling is provided by another housing which encloses the main housing (an air passage is left between housings); the external fan forces air between the two housings. Although this motor is totally enclosed, it is not suitable as an *explosionproof motor.* In fact, in Class 1, Division 2 locations it is preferable to use a dripproof enclosure with encapsulated winding rather than the totally enclosed. With the open type, gases are easily dispersed; with the totally enclosed, after the motor is shut down, the heat inside can suck in outside vapors as it cools.

These two types of motors are the most common in industrial plants. There are weather-protected motors with different types of enclosures, depending on whether the motor is vertical or horizontal. There are also machines which are *pipe-ventilated;* that is, air is sucked in or forced into pipe ducts for cooling.

Special construction is possible to meet specific requirements; therefore, anything other than the general types previously mentioned should be discussed with the manufacturer.

A few comments are necessary with regard to explosionproof motors. These motors have special long flanges on the end bells to provide a cooling path for exploding gases. The motor must be constructed to withstand and contain an explosion, the leads must be properly sealed, and the whole motor must be approved for the Class and Group specifically. When the motor is repaired, it must be repaired by an approved repair shop with explosionproof certification.

10 AC MOTOR TYPES

10.1 INDUCTION MOTOR

This motor is usually referred to as a *squirrel-cage* motor because of the design of the rotor-conducting bar arrangement. The motor consists of three basic parts: the rotor, stator core, and housing. The stator core (and winding) is fairly standard and limits the speed by providing the required number of poles. The rotor provides the performance variations by modifying the inductor design. The remaining part, the housing, has multiple variations as mentioned in Sec. 9.13.

A modified version is the *wound rotor;* see Sec. 10.10. As far as the electrical designer is concerned, most motors in an industrial plant will be of the induction (squirrel-cage) type. They will withstand far more abuse than ever intended. The main concern of the designer is the starting conditions. Starting large-size induction motors can cause a temporary but undesirable voltage drop in the system, can cause light flicker, and in extreme conditions can cause magnetic devices to drop out and synchronous motors to pull out of step. All these problems become imminent when the system or supply-bus voltage drop approaches 20 to 25%. Up to this point, the drop is tolerable, although undesirable. The other factor is that at 20% voltage drop the starting torque will be reduced to 64%; therefore, the mechanical designer must be sure that 64% is adequate for starting.

10.2 SYNCHRONOUS MOTOR

The synchronous motor is a true constant-speed motor. It also has the ability to provide leading reactive power to the electric system. These two points make it an alternate selection to the induction motor. The synchronous motor uses practically the same stator as the larger-size, lower-speed induction motor, although the winding design might be slightly different. The rotor of the synchronous motor, however, is significantly different and requires specific design. Since the rotor requires a dc source of power, it has special problems, including the need for some method of transmitting the direct current to the rotor winding. In addition, the amount of dc power to the rotor must be adjustable.

To further compound the problem, a synchronous motor is not self-starting; therefore, some method of starting is necessary. Two alternatives are available. One is the use of an auxiliary motor to bring the synchronous motor up to speed; the other is to install an additional squirrel-cage type of winding on the rotor. The second method is the most common; the first method is reserved for large motors, for example, 10,000 to 20,000 hp. The auxiliary winding is called an *amortisseur* winding and provides the starting and accelerating torque.

10.3 SYNCHRONOUS-MOTOR TORQUES

The synchronous motor has a number of different torques. The electrical designer should be familiar with these because they should be specified in the purchase order as minimum requirements. They can be described as:

1. *Starting torque.* The minimum breakaway torque required to move the rotor at the instant of starting regardless of the angular position.
2. *Accelerating torque.* The net available torque which exceeds the load torque at any given speed between standstill and pull-in.
3. *Pull-up torque.* The lowest torque available at some particular speed during acceleration. It is important when related to the load-torque requirements.
4. *Pull-in torque.* Torque required during the transition from acceleration to synchronized steady-state operation.
5. *Synchronous torque.* The torque developed during normal steady-state operation.
6. *Pull-out Torque.* The maximum torque developed during steady-state operation for one minute prior to pulling out of synchronism.

When ordering a synchronous motor, it is usually good practice to discuss it with the motor manufacturer before writing the purchase order specification. This will ensure that the motor requirements are technically possible. In most cases the motor manufacturer will run the requirements through a computer for confirmation of torques and accelerating times as related to temperature buildup in the amortisseur winding.

10.4 SYNCHRONOUS-MOTOR VAR GENERATOR

As previously mentioned, one of the main reasons for ordering a synchronous motor instead of an induction motor is its capability of assisting with power-factor correction.

The term *var* is an abbreviation of *voltamperes reactive.* The prefix "in" or "out" must be added to the var designation. The term *power factor* is synonymous with the term *var.* The former is a ratio of watts/voltamps, while the latter is a measure of the amount of reactive power. They can be used interchangeably as a descriptive means, but they are not the same thing mathematically. Therefore, when we define *leading power factor,* this also means *leading vars* are predominant.

A synchronous motor can be ordered, that is, specified, as a unity (1.0) PF (power factor), 0.9 PF, 0.8 PF, 0.7 PF, etc., with 1.0 and 0.8 standard. The power factor is always assumed to be *leading.* When we discuss power factor, we are generally talking about a total system or partial system. In a synchronous motor we are talking about two component outputs:

1. Horsepower, that is, watts, which is $EI \cos \phi$
2. Reactive power, that is, vars, which is $EI \sin \phi$ (leading)

We see then that it is in fact a *leading var* generator as well as a motor. If we require exactly 100 hp and the driven load requires 100 hp, a 1.0-PF motor

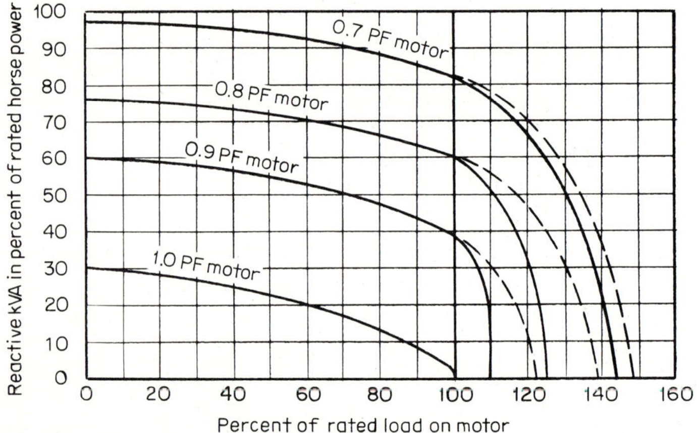

Figure 10.1 Leading reactive kVA in percent of motor horsepower for synchronous motors at various power factor ratings. (Solid lines are reduction in excitation at overload to maintain full-load amps. Dashed lines are for rated excitation to maintain rated pull-out torque.)

will not serve any useful purpose because the whole output is in horsepower. Consider the alternative and specify a 0.8-PF motor. At a load requirement of 100 hp, that is, 100% load on motor, 60% of the applied kVA would be in leading var's. We see then that the 100 hp is available to drive the load and approximately a 60-hp portion is available as leading vars to be injected into the electrical distribution system; for example, assuming hp as kVA, then $100 \times 0.8 = 80$ kW and

$$\text{kvar} = \sqrt{(\text{kVA})^2 - (\text{kW})^2}$$

$$\therefore \sqrt{100^2 - 80^2} = 60 \text{ kVA reactive}$$

10.5 SYNCHRONOUS-MOTOR EXCITATION

The synchronous motor with an amortisseur winding runs as an induction motor until it reaches approximately 2 to 3% of synchronous speed (i.e., rotating-field speed). When reaching synchronous speed, an extra "push" is required to "lock" it into synchronism with the rotating field.

This extra "push" or "pull-in" or torque is provided by applying direct current to the rotor. This creates "poles" of specific polarity in the rotor, which, when opposite, are attracted to the poles of the rotating field in the stator and are consequently dragged round by the rotating field. This is how rotation is effected. When we say "rotating field in the stator," we are referring to "magnetic field rotation," which of course is not visible until demonstrated by the ball-bearing experiment outlined in Sec. 9.10.

The excitation (dc power) is applied to the rotor by automatic controls when starting. During normal operation, for a particular synchronous motor there is a point, for each specific load, where the amount of excitation will

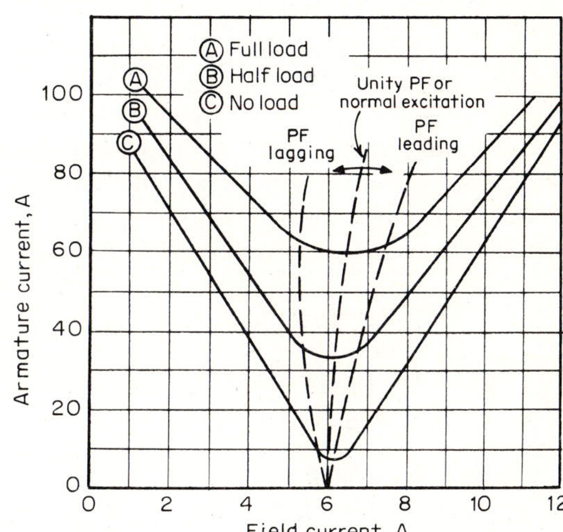

Figure 10.2 V curves for a synchronous motor.

produce a minimum stator or line current. Any increase or decrease in excitation from this point will "increase" the stator current. When these various conditions are plotted on graph paper, they appear as multiple curves in the shape of a letter "V"; therefore they are usually called V curves. If we consider a specific load, we are dealing with horsepower or watts. In a three-phase system it would be $P = \sqrt{3}EI \cos \phi$; $\cos \phi$ is the power factor. If we cross-multiply, we have $I = P/\sqrt{3}E \cos \phi$; if we fix $P/\sqrt{3}E$ at a constant, we see that I is proportional to $1/\cos \phi$. For example, at unity, or 100% power factor, $I = 100\%$; if the power factor is reduced to 0.8 (leading or lagging), $I/0.8 = 1.25I$, or 125% current. Hence the V curves, one for each load constant.

One rule to remember with excitation is that "overexciting" a synchronous motor will generate vars and push them into the system, improving the system power factor. Underexciting a synchronous motor will cause the motor to take vars from the system, contributing to a poor system power factor.

10.6 EXCITER POWER SUPPLY

The exciter must have a supply of dc power. Some synchronous motors use slip rings and carbon brushes to transfer the power to the rotor. More sophisticated developments eliminate the slip rings. In either case, conductors are necessary for supplying the rotor field power. In the former arrangement direct current is generally supplied direct to the rotor slip rings via carbon brushes from a dc source. In the brushless type, only single-phase alternating current is necessary. Here, it is important to exactly understand what type of controller is being supplied by the manufacturer and what the field (rotor) control portion consist of; also, how can field adjustments be made.

10.7 SYNCHRONOUS OR INDUCTION SELECTION

The decision to use a synchronous motor instead of an induction motor is not simple, except when constant speed at all loads is required; it then becomes mandatory. Other than this feature, the only other advantage is power-factor correction. Before considering this, we will list some advantages and disadvantages of synchronous motors which will require first consideration.

Advantages	*Disadvantages*
1. Better power factor	1. External field supply
2. Higher efficiency	2. Low starting torque/kVA
3. Low kVA inrush in low-torque applications	3. Higher maintenance
4. Adaptable to low speed, that is, large-frame applications	4. More complex controls
	5. Possible higher capital cost

If the advantages and disadvantages are acceptable, it comes down to a simple matter of economic justification. It is not possible to offer a general solution because each selection must be made on its own merits and against the allowable capital expenditure budget for the project. We can, however, offer some general guidelines for synchronous motor consideration.

1. All motors below 600 rpm and above 200 hp.
2. All motors 1200 rpm and lower; above 700 hp.
3. All motors above 2000 hp at 1800 rpm.
4. All motors above 3000 hp at 3600 rpm.
5. All high- (medium-) voltage motors 900 rpm and below.

As a general guideline, when the motor rating exceeds one horsepower per rpm, the synchronous motor and control will probably have a lower initial cost than a straight induction motor. The economic justification is based on three alternatives.

1. Pay the power-company penalty, which must be referred back to the accounting department for their evaluation.
2. Supply an induction motor with fixed capacitors.
3. Purchase a 0.8-PF synchronous motor (or other PF rating).

Some clients will have arbitrary instructions that all motors above a certain size will be synchronous; therefore, check the client specification.

10.8 MOTOR ACCELERATION

In both the synchronous and the induction motor it is sometimes necessary to know the approximate time required for the motor to come up to speed. For example, a centrifuge is notoriously slow. For this calculation it is necessary to know the inertia, torque, and speed. The inertia is WR^2, that is, weight × radius^2; however, since R stands for resistance in electrical calculations, it is usually presented as Wk^2.* This figure must be obtained for both the motor and the driven (load) equipment. The torque can be estimated or obtained from speed-torque curves for the specific type of motor. The motor rpm, of course, is established by the mechanical department. With these factors known, we can use the following accelerating time formula:

$$t = \frac{(Wk_1^2 + Wk_2^2) \times \text{rpm}}{308 \times T \times GR}$$

where t is time in seconds, Wk_1^2 is the inertia of motor, Wk_2^2 is the inertia of equipment. T is the torque at designated rpm, rpm is designated speed, and

* k is also a "radius of gyration" symbol which is *not* the radius of the rotating disk. Hence, Wk^2 is a unique complete symbol expressed in pound-feet squared.

GR is gear-reduction ratio to 1; that is, 50 : 5 = 10 : 1 = 10. The torque figure can be determined from the formula:

$$T = \frac{5252 \times \text{hp}}{\text{rpm}} \quad \text{in lb-ft}$$

This, however, is total torque. Since we are concerned with accelerating torque, we can only use the net available torque, which is the total torque minus the torque required by the load.

An exact determination must be done by plugging the net torque at a particular speed in small increments, that is, 10 or 20% increments, into the accelerating time formula. Adding all these times (seconds) will give the total time to come up to speed. For this it is necessary to have the equipment torque curves and the motor torque curves. Very often these are not available.

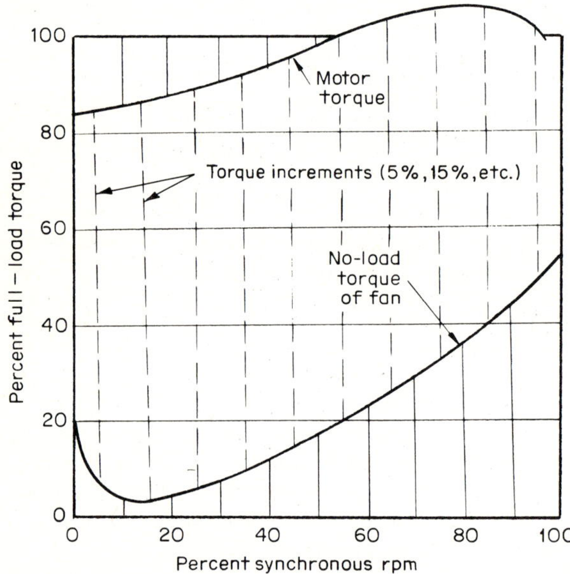

Figure 10.3 Motor and load torques for a centrifugal fan showing method for determining accelerating time of motor by increments of torque.

We can, however, obtain a minimum time by applying full torque. This assumes that the load requires zero torque, which is not possible; it will indicate that the motor cannot possibly come up to speed any faster than this, and furthermore, that it will definitely take additional time because of load (equipment torque requirements).

Consider a centrifugal fan and motor 600 hp at 900 rpm with fan and motor Wk^2 at 29,770 lb-ft.^{2}

$$\text{Full-load torque} = 600 \times 5250/900 = 3500 \text{ lb-ft}$$

$$t = \frac{29{,}770 \times 900}{308 \times 3500 \times 1} = 24.85 \text{ sec}$$

This is the least time possible. If we assume a 20% average load-torque requirement, this means that the available torque will only be 3500 × 0.8, or 2800. If this figure is plugged into the previous formula instead of 3500 a time of 31.06 sec. is produced, which is a more probable figure. The minimum time, however, serves a useful purpose when considering cable heating during startup or for voltage-drop and voltage-spread calculations. If a problem exists at minimum time, it will certainly be worse under normal conditions and therefore further investigation is required.

TABLE 10.1 Accelerating Time Using Increments of Torque (See Fig. 10.3)

% *rpm*	% *motor torque*	% *fan torque*	% *net torque*	*Torque lb-ft*	*Time, sec*
5	86	5	81	2840	1.46
15	88	3	85	2980	2.78
25	91	6	85	2980	2.78
35	93	10	83	2920	2.84
45	97	14	83	2920	2.84
55	99	19	80	2800	2.96
65	102	25	77	2700	3.08
75	104	32	72	2520	3.30
85	104	40	64	2240	3.80
95	100	50	50	1750	4.75
				Total seconds	30.59

10.9 ROTOR HEAT LOSS DURING STARTING

In a synchronous motor the amortisseur winding is very light and due to construction has little chance for good heat dissipation. In some cases it may be decided to use a self-starting synchronous motor; however, in the larger sizes, that is, the 10,000- to 20,000-hp range, there may be difficulty with heat buildup in the amortisseur winding.

In this case some alternative means of starting must be used. There are really only two alternatives in a case like this (excluding turbines); the wound-rotor induction motor and the solid-state variable-frequency power supply. In a such a situation the manufacturer is very involved in the early stages; however, it is helpful to be able to calculate the approximate heat loss so that the initial discussions can be intelligent and the electrical designer has some feel for why the motor manufacturer insists on supplying alternate starting means (at extra cost).

$$H = \frac{0.231 \times Wk^2 \times (\text{rpm})}{10^6}$$

where H is the heat energy in kW seconds, Wk^2 is the total inertia, and rpm is the speed point to which motor and load are accelerated. In the example used for torque calculations and assuming the required speed is 95% of synchronous speed, we have

$$H = \frac{0.231 \times 29770 \times (855)^2}{1{,}000{,}000}$$

$$= 5027 \text{ kilowatt-seconds}$$

If a gear reducer is used, this figure should be adjusted dividing by the *GR* (gear-reduction factor), which is the number of motor rpm to one rpm of equipment; that is, 50:5 is factor of 10:1; therefore, the *GR* is 10.

Note that the heat energy is caused by accelerating; because the amortisseur winding produces the starting torque, it must also absorb the energy. This takes place in the copper conductors first and is then partially dissipated in the laminations.

10.10 WOUND-ROTOR MOTOR

The wound-rotor motor is essentially an induction motor. Instead of a squirrel-cage winding on the rotor there is a phase-wound winding with the same number of poles as the stator. As the winding is three-phase, the three terminal points are brought out and connected to three slip rings mounted on the rotor shaft. By means of carbon brushes, the three slip rings (and phase points) are connected to a resistor bank, which is used during starting. These resistors are shorted out in increments until the rotor is running on its own resistance.

10.11 WOUND-ROTOR TORQUE

The torque in an induction motor is a function of the resistance and reactance of the rotor. The torque is maximum when the rotor resistance and inductive reactance X_L are equal. Since the reactance varies with frequency, and the frequency is the slip frequency, the torque will change with speed during acceleration. By changing the resistance in steps, it is possible to nearly match the resistance to the changing reactance. This means that the value of rotor resistance does not alter the value of maximum torque, because this is fixed by $R/X_L = 1$, but it effectively changes the slip at which the maximum torque occurs. This then provides an incremental number of maximum torques. The current is much less than in the conventional squirrel-cage motor and will very closely follow the torque curve, as shown in Fig. 10.4.

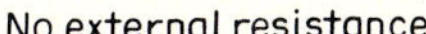

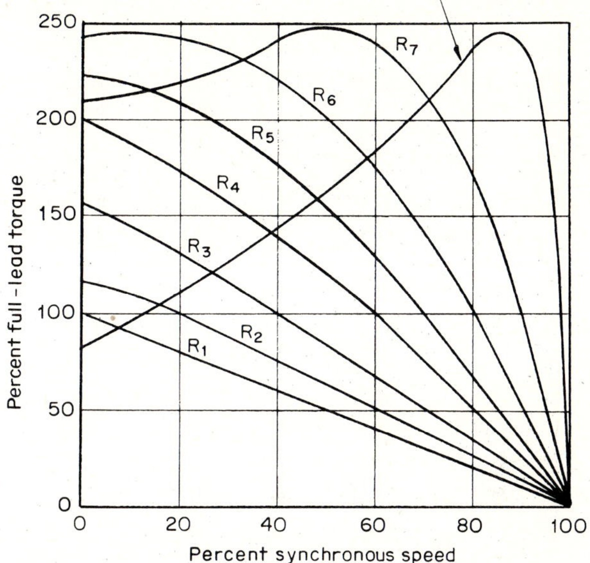

Figure 10.4a Torque curves of wound-rotor motor with seven steps of external resistance in the secondary circuit.

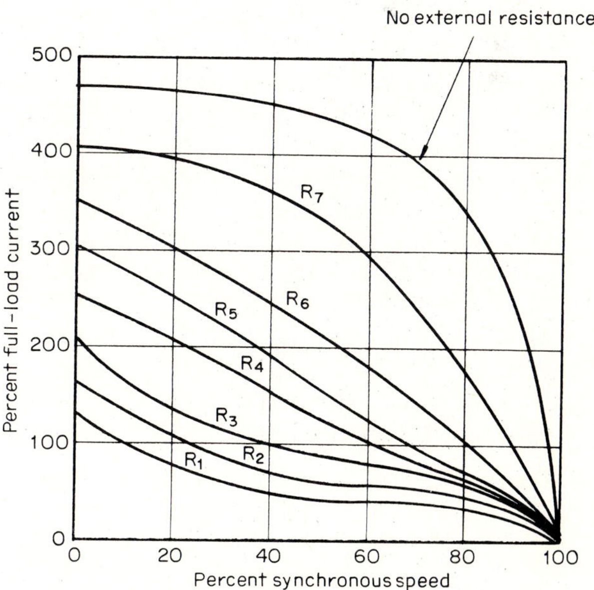

Figure 10.4b Starting curves of wound-rotor motor with seven resistance steps in secondary circuit.

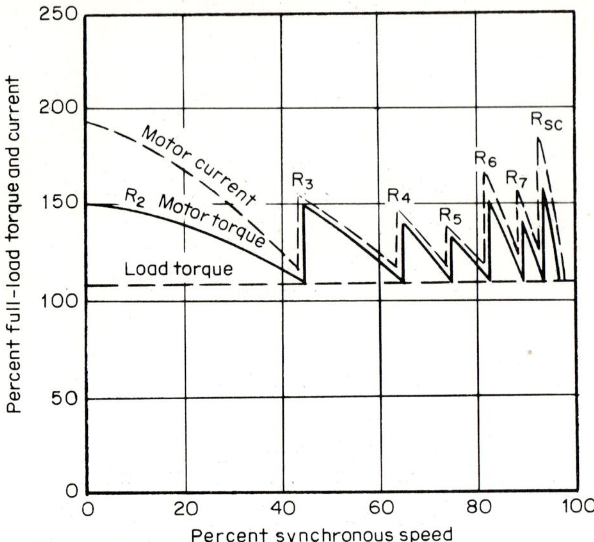

Figure 10.4c Wound-rotor increment starting torque and motor current curves.

These curves show that when a problem exists with high starting currents, but a loss in torque cannot be tolerated due to reduced voltage, then the wound-rotor motor can be considered.

10.12 WOUND-ROTOR MOTOR APPLICATIONS

Wound-rotor motors have two applications. One is for "problem starting," where high torque and low starting current is required. The other is where limited speed control is required. As previously mentioned, the changing value of resistance does not change the maximum torque, it only changes the slip at which maximum torque occurs. It follows, then, that if the resistance was left in the circuit and made adjustable, then the motor speed could be altered by changing from a higher slip to a lower slip. This slip control is good up to about 40 or 50% maximum; in addition, the speed regulation is not very good, and will vary with load. However for an application that can accept poor speed regulation, such as in cranes, boiler draft fans, and centrifugal pumps, it is far cheaper that the dc motor and probably comparable to other means of adjustable speed, such as variable pulleys.

On light systems, that is, systems with limited capacity, the wound-rotor motor is one of the alternate considerations available when starting large motors. The applications, advantages, and disadvantages are summarized in the following list:

1. *Applications*
   Adjustable speed requirements
   Minimum disturbance on system

High torque and low starting current
Starting on limited-size systems

2. *Advantages*
   Simple construction
   Low starting current
   Good load-starting capability (high-inertia loads)
   Adjustable speed within limits
   Simple maintenance

3. *Disadvantages*
   Controls (possible source of problems)
   Power factor (fair)
   Efficiency (fair to good)
   Limited areas (possible slip ring damage due to atmosphere)
   (not allowed in hazardous areas)

If the resistors applied to the rotor are used only for starting, they can be underrated because of the short time they are in use. When the resistors are used for speed control, they must be *continuous rated.* A wound-rotor motor should never be started without resistance in the rotor; therefore, for speed-control types the motor should be started with resistance first and controlled after the inrush has dissipated.

10.13 MAGNETIC CLUTCHES

The magnetic clutch is sometimes described as an "eddy-current" coupling. It is in fact a coupling connecting the motor with the load equipment. It could possibly be termed a hybrid between the synchronous motor and the induction motor. In the synchronous motor we have a rotor with field magnetic poles produced by an external dc power source applied to the winding. As the dc power is increased, the amp turns increase, which produces an increase in the magnetic flux emanating from the pole face. The rotor of the magnetic coupling is of similar design.

In order to explain the other half of the magnetic coupling, we will digress and explain about a conductor in a magnetic field. If a conductor is placed in a magnetic field, but without current flow in the conductor, the conductor will remain stationary. If a current is applied to the conductor while in the magnetic field, it will be deflected at right angles. If the conductor is on the surface of a rotor like a squirrel-cage winding, it will give a turning effect or torque. In the case of the magnetic clutch we have the magnetic field in the rotor, but the "ring" surrounding it has no winding. Therefore, how do we obtain a current-carrying conductor to produce the torque?

It is a well-known fact that eddy currents will be produced in steel if it is located in a magnetic field. If the *ring* of the coupling were made of steel, eddy currents would be induced into it by the rotor field. As soon as we have eddy currents, we have in effect "a current-carrying conductor in a magnetic field" and therefore torque will be produced. By varying the field current, the amount of slip between the rotor and ring can be controlled.

By use of a feedback circuit, obtaining a reference from a tachometer mounted on the load and related to operational functions of feedback transducers measuring pressure, temperature, levels, etc., an automatic control system with fairly good regulation can be produced.

The control procedure with a magnetic-clutch installation is to start the drive motor first and apply the field current second. The torque is nearly proportional to the applied excitation and is therefore a simple variable for electric circuits. Since magnetic clutches have high slip, sometimes they are provided with water cooling, which must also be controlled by the motor control circuit.

10.14 CONSEQUENT-POLE SQUIRREL-CAGE MOTOR

A squirrel-cage motor has its speed fixed by the number of poles connected in the stator winding and the frequency of the ac power. A change in speed

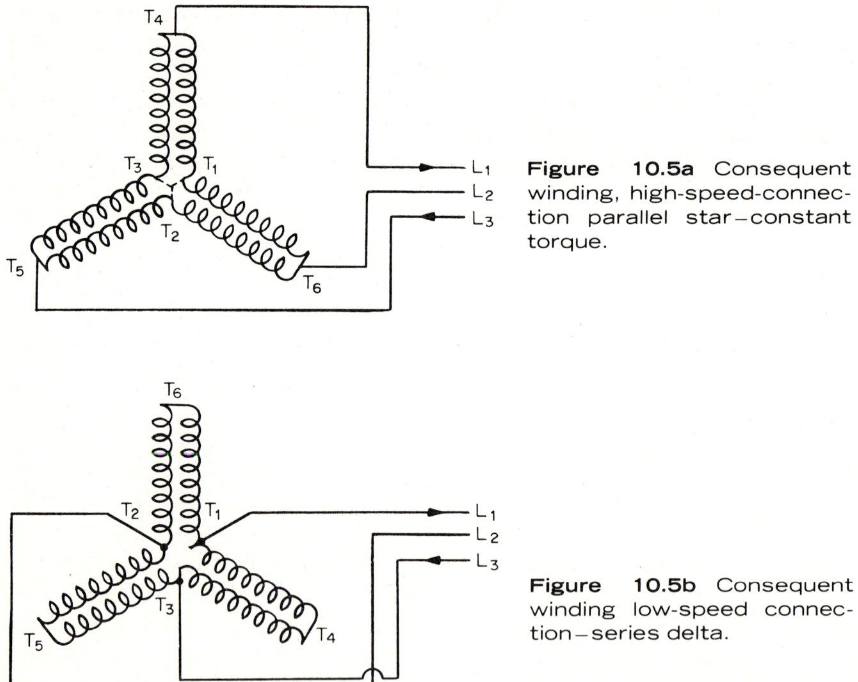

Figure 10.5a Consequent winding, high-speed-connection parallel star–constant torque.

Figure 10.5b Consequent winding low-speed connection–series delta.

then necessitates a reconnection of the winding to change the number of poles. By designing a single winding with the normal phase connections brought out from the center of each phase winding, we have a six-lead motor. Supplying power to the phase leads provides normal speed. Removing the power leads and reconnecting to the center-tap leads provides half of normal speed. This is accomplished by the current feeding two halves of a phase winding in different directions, creating twice the number of poles. This then reduces the speed by exactly half. This is known as a *consequent-pole* motor. This limits the practical possibilities of a single-winding consequent-pole multispeed motor to 2:1 ratios of speed. See Fig. 10.5.

10.15 POLE-AMPLITUDE-MODULATION (PAM) MOTORS

In the PAM motor, a single winding on the stator can be reconnected (or switched) to provide two speeds of ratios other than the 2:1 offered by the consequent-pole motor.

The single-winding reconnection can offer nearly any desired pole ratio. The difference between the consequent-pole reconnection and the PAM reconnection is shown in Figs. 10.5 and 10.6 but is of more interest to the manufacturer than the electrical designer. The main point of consideration to the designer is that the two-speed motor is available with other than 2:1 ratios. Motors with large horsepowers, (that is, 2,000 hp) are available, and for applications where the load torque varies as the square of the speed, the use of a PAM motor instead of a magnetic coupling or wound-rotor motor should be considered. An additional comment should be offered with regard to starting; starting inrush can be reduced by starting on slow speed and transferring to high speed. On ratios other than 2:1 a two-separate-winding stator is generally used. When switching from low speed to high speed with this motor, a large transient magnetic pull can be exerted if it

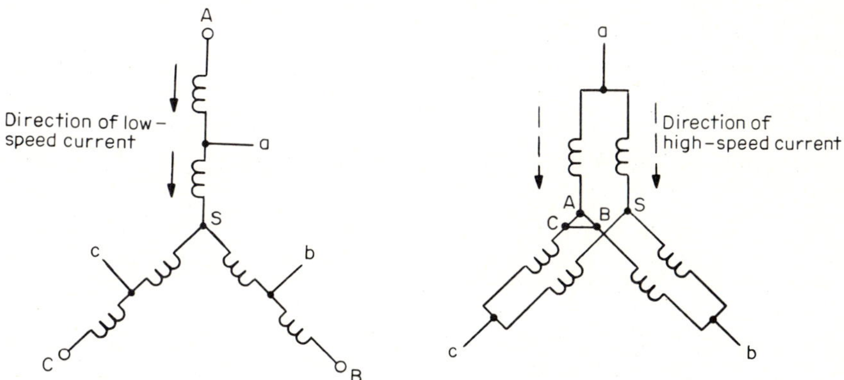

Figure 10.6 PAM connection: (a) low speed; (b) high speed.

is switched too fast, that is, in less than ½ second. By using a PAM motor, this switching time can be reduced to a few cycles, for example, 3 cycles, without the disturbing transient. Since the switching is done with relatively inexpensive magnetic starters (low voltage), the installed cost may be less than other alternatives. For high-voltage motors, high-voltage motor starters or switchgear breakers (properly rated) can be used.

10.16 MULTIWINDING SQUIRREL-CAGE MOTORS

To obtain two speeds in a ratio other than 2:1 or multiple selection of fixed speeds, it is necessary to install more than one winding in the same stator except for the PAM motors. The phase leads are then brought out into the terminal box with a diagram of connections for the various speeds. If two windings are installed in the motor and six leads per winding were brought out, it would be possible to obtain four speeds by connecting each winding with consequent pole. This then could produce speeds of 1800/900 and 1200/600, 1200/600 and 900/450, etc. Alternately, three speeds can be obtained by one winding in consequent pole and the other at a single speed. This would then require bringing out nine leads. Because horsepower is a function of speed and torque, we can see that for a reduction in speed we get a reduction in horsepower.

For example, if a motor has two speeds consequent pole 1800 and 900 rpm, the horsepower would be 100% at 1800 rpm, and 900/1800 would be 0.5, that is, 50% horsepower at the lower speed.

Both the consequent-pole motor and the multiple-winding motor can have speed changes by bringing all the leads to interlocked switches, allowing an operator to select speeds as required.

When specifying multispeed motors, note that they fall into three main categories: (1) constant horsepower, (2) constant torque, and (3) variable torque. The category must be specified to the motor manufacturer.

11 STARTING THREE-PHASE MOTORS

11.1 MOTOR STARTERS

Three-phase-motor starters are all designed to modify the starting conditions evidenced in the "across-the-line" starter. The main problem when starting an induction motor is the high inrush current, which is approximately six times normal. Since the starting current is proportional to line voltage, a reduction of line voltage reduces the starting current. The problem with this is that the starting torque reduces at a faster rate, that is, proportional to the square of the voltage. A 40% reduction in voltage means a 40% reduction in starting current, but a reduction of starting torque to $(100\% - 40\%)^2$, or 36%.

In general, most starters operate on the principle of changing the $I = E/Z$ components in the motor circuit. This provides a low-cost method of compromise in motor-starting characteristics. The more expensive variable-frequency and auxiliary-starting-wound-rotor motors are only considered when extra-large-horsepower motors are required.

11.2 ACROSS-THE-LINE STARTER

This is by far the most popular and commonly used starter. In modern industrial plants the power systems are usually "stiff" enough to handle the high starting kVA required. Also motors are mostly in the 5- to 75-hp range, with the next group in the 100- to 200-hp range (maximum for 460 V). Motors above this size are a small percentage of the total number of motors. In addition, all motors are not started simultaneously; therefore, starting surges are relatively small compared to the total system power. This is then the first choice for starting. Motors with high inertia loads or large horsepowers should be checked for starting ability to determine if an alternate consideration is necessary. If a plant is old or for some reason has a "light" power system, starting conditions must be analyzed to determine if a method other than the *across-the-line* method should be considered.

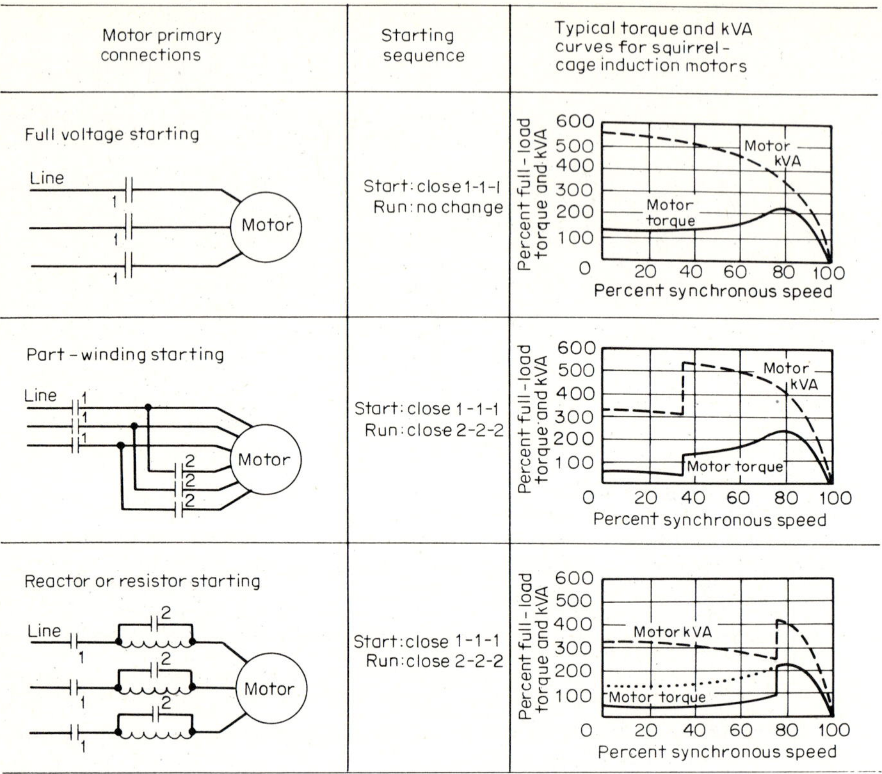

Figure 11.1 Induction motors—starting methods, connections, and torque curves.

11.3 REDUCED-VOLTAGE STARTER (AUTOTRANSFORMER)

The next most popular method of starting is probably the autotransformer starter. This is purchased as a complete unit to the specifications supplied by the electrical designer. The autotransformer usually has adjustable taps on the secondary to provide temporary reduced voltage. After reaching about 70% synchronous speed, the autotransformer is disconnected and the starter connects directly to the line. With this starter, the motor current will be reduced directly proportional to the reduction in voltage. The torque will be reduced by the square of the voltage, and the line current (primary side) will be reduced by the square of the voltage ratio of the autotransformer.

Taps are commonly 80, 65, and 50%, with the 80 and 65% taps most commonly used. If we consider an 80% tap reduced-voltage starter, we find that the "starting" line current is 64% of full-voltage starting line current. The starting torque is $(100\% - 20\%)^2$, or 64%.

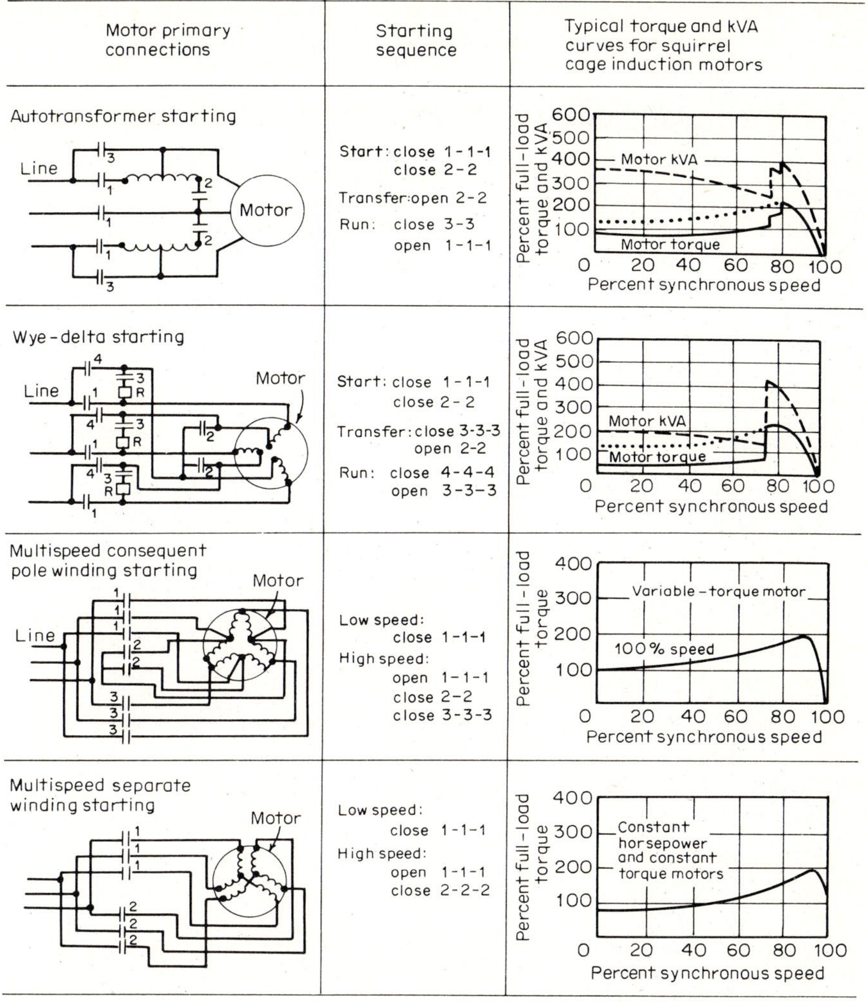

11.4 REDUCED-VOLTAGE STARTER (RESISTANCE TYPE)

Another method of reducing the voltage to a motor during startup is by adding resistance in series in the line. This produces an *IR,* that is, voltage drop so that the voltage appearing at the motor terminals is reduced in proportion to the added resistance. In this case its effect is the same as the autotransformer with the proportional reduction of starting current and torque reduction as the square of the voltage. The line current, however, is only reduced proportionally. For the same 80% reduction in voltage, the resistor start will only provide a reduction to 80% in line current instead of the 64% obtained with the autotransformer. The resistors must also be rated for full starting current but on a noncontinuous basis. After reaching approximately 70% speed, the resistors are shorted-out from the circuit. This method is not as popular as the autotransformer starter.

11.5 REDUCED-VOLTAGE STARTER (REACTOR TYPE)

The reactor starter is similar to the resistance starter except that the resistance is changed for impedance. This gives $I = E/Z$ instead of $I = E/R$. Since $Z = \sqrt{R^2 + X_L^2}$, we get a reactive component introduced which will affect the power factor; therefore, on startup the line current may be slightly higher than the equivalent resistance starter.

This type of starter generally has taps on 50, 65, and 80%. It is more economical than the equivalent autotransformer in the 2300- to 4800-V range.

11.6 PART-WINDING START

This starter consists of two contactors each connected to a part of the motor winding. In fact, by adding more contactors, incremental starting can be ob-

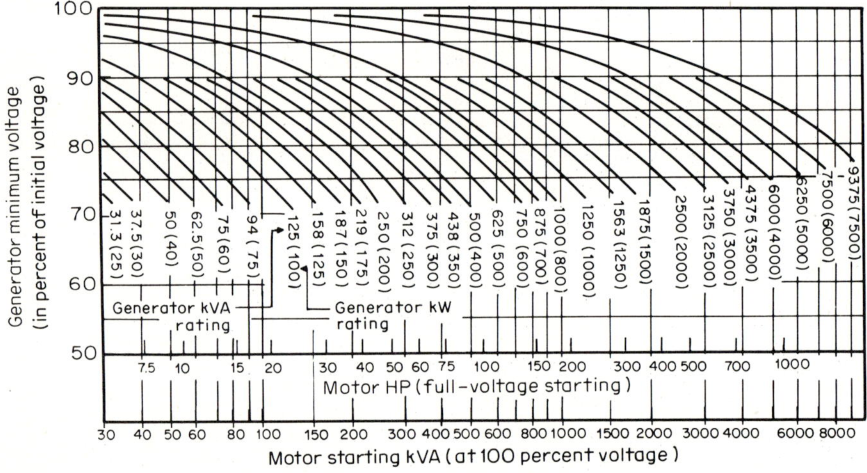

Notes:

1. Scale of motor-hp is based on starting current being equal to approximately 5.5 times normal
2. If there is no initial load, voltage regulator will restore voltage to 100 percent after dip to values given by curves
3. Initial load, if any, is assumed to be constant-current type
4. Generator characteristics assumed as follows:

   a. Generators rated 1000 kva or less
   Performance factor, $K = 1.0$
   Transient reactance, $X'_d = 25$ percent
   Synchronous reactance, $X_d = 120$ percent

   b. Generators rated above 1000 kVA; confirm with manufacturer regarding transient stability.

Figure 11.2 Starting large motors on the generator.

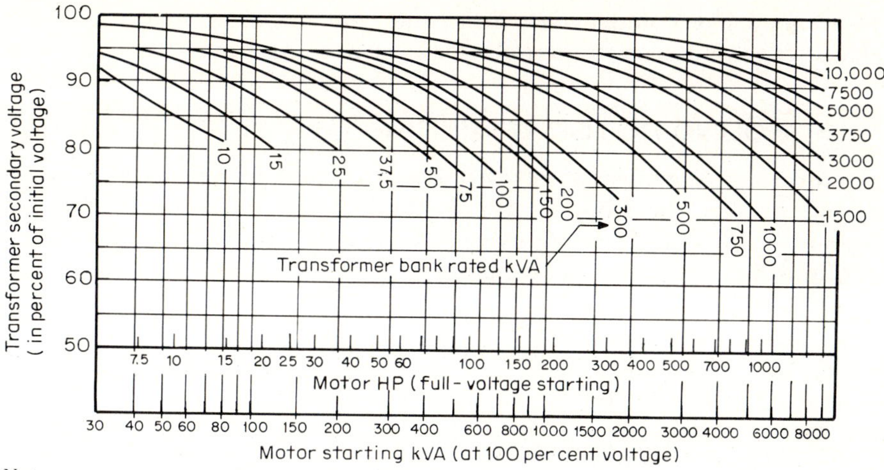

Notes:

1. Scale of motor hp based on starting current being equal to approximately 5.5 times normal.
2. Short-circuit kva of primary supply is assumed to be as follows:

Bank kVA	*Primary short-circuit kVA*
10–300	25,000
500–1000	50,000
1500–3000	100,000
3760–10,000	250,000

3. Transformer impedances are assumed to be as follows:

Bank kVA	*Bank impedance*
10–50	3%
75–150	4%
200–500	5%
750–2000	5.5%
3000–10,000	6.0%

4. Representative values of primary system voltage drop as a fraction of total drop are as follows, for the assumed conditions.

Bank kVA	*System drop/total drop*
100	0.09
1000	0.25
10000	0.44

Figure 11.3 Transformer voltage drops due to motor starting.

tained. This means that the starting equipment is low in first cost. The problem is that motor-winding taps are required for each starter added, and therefore a specially ordered motor is necessary. A good feature of the part-winding start is that the torque and starting current are reduced in proportion to the percentage of the winding. If 50% of the winding was used, then it would provide 50% torque, while requiring only 50% of the starting current. This type of starter is more effective on low-speed motors and specially designed equipment, like compressors, fans, and centrifugal pumps, where a motor can be manufactured in quantity for part-winding start.

11.7 WOUND-ROTOR STARTING

Wound-rotor starting has already been covered in Sec. 10.11, but we will point out that the wound-rotor method of starting provides low starting current, with high starting torques; its disadvantage, when compared to the autotransformer starter, is its higher cost.

11.8 VARIABLE-FREQUENCY STARTER

This method of starting is expensive. It is usually custom built for a specific installation and requires a lot of floor space. It is a solid-state piece of equipment and is only considered where motors have such a large size that rotor heating may become a problem on startup. If the requirement is for a bank of motors, the one starter could be used with a transfer scheme to normal power when full speed is attained, allowing the starter to be used for the other motors. This is a typical "extra-large" wind-tunnel application. This may not be the cheapest installation, but it should be considered along with the wound rotor or other alternatives.

11.9 AUXILIARY-MOTOR STARTING

Where extra-large motors are involved, they are generally of the synchronous type. With the small copper content of the amortisseur winding and difficult heat-dissipation problems, it may not be practical to build a self-starting motor. In this case an auxiliary motor is required to bring the synchronous motor up to 95% synchronous speed. The usual choice is the wound-rotor motor with its controlled starting current and high torque characteristics. This would have to be compared to the cost of the variable-frequency starter. With the wound-rotor starting, one motor would be required for each large motor, whereas with the variable-frequency starter, only a single unit for all the motors is required.

11.10 TURBINE STARTING

Another method of starting a large motor is by use of a turbine in place of the wound-rotor motor; however, turbines are not cheap and the installed cost is probably higher than the equivalent installation using a wound-rotor motor.

12 SINGLE-PHASE MOTORS

12.1 SINGLE-PHASE MOTORS

A single-phase motor has only two conductors supplying the stator instead of the three conductors required for the three-phase motors. These motors are cheap to manufacture, are mass-produced, and do a satisfactory job for most applications within their design range. A single-phase winding produces an alternating magnetic field but it does not rotate as in the three-phase motor. The squirrel-cage rotor acts as the secondary of a transformer, and therefore, currents are induced in the rotor conductors. As previously stated, a current-carrying conductor in a magnetic field is deflected at right angles; however, in the single-phase motor, the torque developed in one direction is cancelled out by an equal and opposite torque in the other direction. This means that no rotation is produced, owing to a lack of *net* torque. If the motor shaft is given a slight turn in one direction, enough net torque is provided to start the motor; once rotating at normal speed, the single-phase motor performs similar to a three-phase motor, but with a slight slip in speed.

12.2 SPLIT-PHASE MOTOR

The split-phase motor is probably the most simple of the single-phase motors. It consists of a coil for each pole which is inserted in the stator slots with the centerline of the coils separated by 360° ÷ poles; for example, a four-pole stator would have coils at 360°/4 = 90° spacing. To start the motor, another four coils are inserted with the same spacing but located between the main coils, that is, at 45°, 135°, 225°, and 315°. This winding is very light in copper content and will overheat in seconds. It is therefore necessary to disconnect this winding as soon as the motor comes up to speed. This is accomplished by mounting a centrifugal switch on the rotor shaft, which opens when the motor reaches a certain speed. This then disconnects the starting (auxiliary) winding. This split-phase motor has a fairly high starting current and the centrifugal switch can present maintenance problems, but the rotor is the simple squirrel-cage rotor centrifugally cast.

12.3 CAPACITOR START MOTORS

The capacitor start motor is also a split-phase type, but a capacitor is inserted in the start (auxiliary) winding. This winding is disconnected from the circuit when the motor has attained full speed.

12.4 CAPACITOR MOTOR

The capacitor motor is similar to the capacitor start motor except the auxiliary winding with series capacitor is left in the circuit under normal operation.

12.5 REACTOR START MOTOR

This motor is similar to the capacitor start motor except a reactor is placed in series with the auxiliary winding, which is disconnected when the motor has attained normal speed. A reactor provides a phase shift in the opposite direction to a capacitor.

12.6 RESISTOR START MOTOR

This motor has a resistor in series with the auxiliary winding, which is disconnected when the motor reaches the required speed.

12.7 STARTING TORQUES (SPLIT PHASE)

By modifying the phase angle between the starting winding and running winding, different starting torques can be produced. Therefore, the variation of reactance (both capacitive and inductive) and resistance of the start winding, all provide variable parameters for adjusting the starting torques.

12.8 REPULSION MOTOR

The repulsion motor is another single-phase-type motor with a single-phase stator winding. Instead of the squirrel-cage-type rotor it has a wound rotor with the coil ends connected to an end-mounted commutator (segmented conductors). This arrangement produces a field with poles of the same polarity as the stator. Since like poles repel, we get rotation and also the name (i.e., repulsion motor). When it reaches operating speed, the commutator is shorted out by a shorting disk, which effectively shorts out all the commutator segments. The motor then runs like an induction motor.

This motor has excellent starting characteristics, but is rarely used because of its higher manufacturing cost.

12.9 SERIES MOTOR

The series motor is essentially a dc motor adapted to a single-phase alternating-current supply. It is of course specially designed to minimize sparking of the commutator, but for all intents and purposes it is very much like the dc series motor. The characteristics are that it has high torque but a wide range of speed for different values of load. Very heavy loads will produce very low speeds, while light loads will produce high speeds. Most hand tools have series motors.

12.10 SHADED POLE MOTOR

This motor is a subfractional or instrument-type motor. The rotor is a "toothed," or induction type. The stator has the required number of poles, but by inserting a solid copper ring (offset from the main pole) in the stator, a small additional flux is set up off center which provides rotation. The torque in these motors is very light and application is limited to very small loads.

12.11 HYSTERESIS MOTOR

This motor is a miniature synchronous motor. By using a rotor which is magnetized (polarized) and a stator with a split-phase revolving field, the rotor will lock into synchronism and will hold in by virtue of the strength of the magnetized rotor field. Pull-in and pull-out torques are specified just as in large synchronous motors. This type of motor is used for timing devices and light drive trains.

13 DC MOTORS

13.1 DC MOTOR USE

DC motors are all "special" motors, in the sense that they are only used if ac motors cannot provide the desired characteristics. In fact if an ac motor can "nearly" provide the desired characteristics, it will generally be selected instead of the dc motor. The load or operating procedures will then be adapted to compensate for the marginal lack of performance of the ac motor. DC motors are excellent machines, but their cost and higher maintenance requirements limit their use to mandatory applications. These are predominantly applications which require wide ranges of speeds or torque, or both. They cannot be used in hazardous areas, and the commutators are susceptible to contaminated atmospheres. The control equipment is expensive, and it is not possible to start a dc motor across the line except for small motors.

There are two basic types of dc motor: the shunt and the series type. Modifications to the basic types produce a family of motors with varying characteristics.

13.2 DC SHUNT MOTOR

The basic shunt motor consists of a housing with four or more single projecting-type poles. These are wound with many turns of fine wire, producing a very concentrated magnetic field. By connecting each pole with alternate poles, an "alternate" field is provided; that is, the poles are north, south, north, south, etc. The rotating part of the dc motor is known as the *armature* and is constructed of multiple coils inserted into slots in the surface of the armature and banded with strong wire to prevent them flying out due to centrifugal force. The ends of these coils are connected to commutator (segmented conductors) segments. If a dc voltage is applied to two opposite segments on the commutator, a current will be circulated in that particular coil. We now know that if a current-carrying conductor is placed in a magnetic field, a right-angle deflection is produced.

This is the basic principle behind the dc motor. The commutator is necessary to change the polarity of the current in the armature coil with respect to the polarity of the main pole in the housing. In order to apply a voltage to the rotating commutator, carbon brushes are used. The incoming dc conductors are connected to the armature brushes and also to the two ends of the four (or more) poles which are connected in series. This provides a circuit in which the main poles in the housing are in parallel or *shunt-connected* to the armature. The reason for connecting the main poles in series is to obtain equal current in each pole. If the turns on each pole are equal, the flux is proportional to the amp turns and will be balanced in each pole.

This type of motor will maintain nearly constant speed regardless of the change in load, providing the applied voltage remains constant.[1] If we applied a dc voltage directly to an armature coil, a short circuit would exist; therefore, during starting a resistance must be inserted. This is done by using a stepped resistor which gradually cuts out the resistance as the speed is increased. This will reduce the current until a back emf is established, owing to the generating effect of conductors cutting the flux and opposing the incoming voltage.

By varying the incoming voltage or the strength of the field current, the speed can be controlled. Half voltage results in half speed. This characteristic is used for obtaining an adjustable-speed drive.

13.3 DC SERIES MOTOR

The dc series motor has a similar pole arrangement to the shunt-wound motor; the difference is in the copper wire around the pole. In the series motor the wire is very heavy, compared to the fine wire used in the shunt-wound motor. The poles are also all connected in series like those in the shunt-wound motor, but the two ends of the pole circuit are then connected between one incoming line and the armature. This effectively places the armature coil in series with the field coils. This means that the current in the field coils is the same as in the armature. If the flux in the field poles is proportional to the amp turns, an increase in load will produce an increase in armature current and consequently an increase in field current. As an increase in flux produces a decrease in speed, the speed will vary with the load. This also means that a series motor should never be run "unloaded." This could result in excessive high speed and destructive centrifugal forces. Loads driven by belts must be excluded.

The series motor finds application where high torques are required, but speed regulation is of no consequence. It is particularly suited to cranes and hoists.

[1] Speed regulation is about 5 to 10%, i.e., change in speed when full load is removed.

13.4 COMPOUND-WOUND MOTOR

The compound-wound motor is a combination of both the shunt and the series motor. A motor can be compounded or *overcompounded,* depending on the required characteristics. The addition of series-winding turns around the shunt-wound poles allows the variation of the two characteristics. The amount of compounding will be determined by the motor manufacturer, but the electrical designer should be familiar with the design in order to discuss it intelligently during pre-purchase communications.

13.5 INTERPOLES

Interpoles are auxiliary poles which are approximately half the physical size of the main poles and placed in between the main poles. The purpose of these interpoles is to give more even distribution of flux. They are located on the neutral axis of the flux distribution, and the winding is a small series winding. When a load is applied, the flux tends to distort. The function of the interpoles is to produce a flux which will oppose the distortion. This results in improved commutation and hopefully less sparking at the commutator brushes.

13.6 VARIABLE-SPEED CONTROL

By varying the voltage to a shunt motor, the speed can be reduced proportionally. By varying the current in the field winding, the amp turns and therefore the flux can be altered, resulting in a change of speed. If the flux is increased (amp turns increased), the motor will slow down. Alternately, if the flux is reduced (weakened), the motor will speed up. In the series-type motor, control of the armature current by inserting a series resistor will allow the speed to be varied for a fixed load, but once the speed is fixed, a change in load will produce a variation in the speed. Hence the term *variable speed.*

13.7 ADJUSTABLE-SPEED CONTROL

Adjustable-speed control means that once the speed is selected it will remain constant (within its design limits) for any load. If the motor is ordered for maximum speed at rated voltage, speed control is obtained by controlling the level of voltage to the armature. This is done by using a variable resistor. A reduction in voltage will produce a proportional reduction in speed; for example, if a motor is designed for 1200 rpm at 220 V and the voltage is reduced to 110 V, then the speed will be $(110/220) \times 1200 = 600$ rpm.

If a speed control is required where speeds higher than those supplied by the fixed voltage are necessary, field weakening is selected. This is done by inserting a rheostat (variable resistor) in series with the shunt winding on the main poles. By increasing the resistance, field strength is reduced and speed is increased.

13.8 ADJUSTABLE-SPEED DRIVES

An adjustable-speed drive is sometimes called a variable-speed drive. The former is the preferred terminology. The adjustable-speed drive is a complete system of motors and feedback signals which causes the drive system to maintain a constant speed regardless of load changes. The drive system should have good regulation. This means that the speed, once established, will not vary more than a designated amount from the desired speed. A drive system should also have good *speed of response* to load changes. This means that when a load change occurs, it will affect the drive speed; therefore, the feedback signals must identify this load change and call for compensating power to maintain the same speed at the new load. In order to identify a load change, the signals associated with the load change must have already occurred. The time elapsed between the signals occurring, being identified, and being compensated for is the *speed of response* time. Paper-machine drives run at speeds of around 4000 feet per minute with a series of rollers weighing thousands of pounds. A slight transient or "jerk" or "sag" in the speed control of these rollers will result in the partially formed paper being broken. At 4000 feet per minute, it will deposit 67 ft of waste every second if it breaks during operation. For a machine producing paper in rolls 10 to 15 ft wide; it doesn't take long to be engulfed in damaged paper.

13.9 ADJUSTABLE-DRIVE VENDOR DRAWINGS

Adjustable-speed drives are basic drives modified to suit a particular application. There are high-speed and low-speed drives. The high-speed drives are nearly all dc motors with a sophisticated closed-loop control system. The major manufacturers all have their own trade names which identify the basic approach to the control, that is, Amplidyne, Magamp, etc. As far as the electrical designer is concerned, the drive system will have been selected by the mechanical and process department. The contribution from the electrical design group will be to analyze the vendor drawings and produce drawings which the contractor can use to install the interconnecting wiring between the motors and the speed-control devices. Before doing this, the designer should ensure that the drawings are examined for acceptance. Any objections should be marked on the drawings and then returned to the vendor. When the final drawings are received and approved for construction, then work on the construction design drawings can commence. To try and hurry this production by using unapproved drawings usually results in redrawing, correcting, more checking, and an increase in errors in the final issued drawings.

13.10 DRIVE NAMES

We can give a brief list, which identifies some drives. However, because sophisticated solid-state equipment is constantly changing, it is useless to try and outline a typical drive system. New devices are constantly being integrated into these systems; therefore, we can only list a few basic names which are nearly generic in identification.

DC Drives

1. Ward Leonard adjustable voltage
2. Constant-potential direct current with field control
3. Amplidyne electronic speed regulator
4. Magamp (magnetic amplifier control)

AC Drives

5. Brush-shifting motor
6. Multispeed motor
7. Magnetic coupling
8. Wound-rotor motor
9. Variable-pitch sheaves
10. SCR (silicon controlled rectifier)

14 GENERATORS

14.1 AC GENERATORS

AC generators are sometimes called *alternators* to distinguish them from dc generators. Alternators are available in different sizes, shapes, and types. They are used as small, auxiliary generators for emergency use or they can be supplied in a large size generating at 6.9, 13.8, or 14.4 kV.

The small emergency-lighting generator is sometimes a single-phase unit, but the majority of generators are three-phase. The design of a generator is very similar to that of a synchronous motor. To generate a voltage, it is necessary to cut a magnetic field with a conductor. The voltage produced at the ends of the conductor will be proportional to the flux density, length of conductor, and relative speed of the conductor passing through the flux. If we recall, the synchronous motor consisted of a rotor which had a rotating dc field. The stator had a distributed three-phase winding. If we applied a turbine or engine to the rotor with the dc field energized, an alternating voltage would appear in the stator winding. This is due to the fact that the rotor poles are connected with alternate (north, south) polarity. For a given set of conductors in the stator; they are first "swept" by a north flux providing a voltage of positive-negative direction. As the next pole approaches the "same" conductors, a neutral point is reached where the north flux is decreasing and a south flux is beginning; here the voltage drops to zero. As the new south pole approaches the conductors another voltage begins to appear, however, this is now flowing in a negative-positive direction. If the rotor is four-pole and rotating at 1800 rpm, the changes will occur 60 times a second, with the speed establishing the frequency of change.

14.2 AC GENERATOR RATING

A generator is supplied with a nameplate giving the manufacturer's name, rated frequency, power factor, number of phases, rating in kVA and kW, normal volts and amperes corresponding to the rating, the speed in rpm, the insulation class, and ambient temperature rise with time rating.

The frequency is fixed by the speed of rotation and in the United States it is 60 cycles per second for normal power systems. The name *hertz* has been adopted as the designation for frequency, that is, 60 hertz is 60 cycles per second.

The rating of a generator is given in kilovoltamperes (kVA).[2] The reason for this is that if it was given in kW it would be identifying only the "real" power used and not the total power output by the generator. From our discussion on motors, we know that "real" power is "output" kW at the motor shaft and "reactive" power (kvar) for magnetic losses in the motor. By rating a generator in kVA it means that the total power output is identified. If we require a generator of a specific kW output to correspond with a connected motor load in horsepower, then we must estimate what the power factor of the load will be and order the generator accordingly. For example, if we require 1000 kW of revenue (billable) output power at the motors, then we must assume that the power factor will be approximately 80%. We therefore need a generator larger than the 1000 kW, because it must supply additional reactive power. In this case the generator is ordered for 1000 kW at 80% power factor; the nameplate will read 1000/0.8, or 1250 kVA.

The full-load current of the generator is determined from the kVA rating by $kVA/\sqrt{3}\,E$ for a three-phase system and kVA/E for a single-phase system. The insulation class and temperature rating will be determined by specific application.

14.3 SINGLE-PHASE GENERATOR

The single-phase generator is usually small and with an output voltage of 120/240 V giving a three-wire output. This type of generator is mostly limited to small portable and/or emergency generators. The generator is supplied with its own prime mover, automatic starter, and instrument panel. The output is generally picked up at a circuit breaker which is provided with the generator and correctly sized for the generator rating.

These small-size generators have varying degrees of stability, and therefore, when ordering, the application intended should be clearly defined. Some applications for generators are for computer uninterruptible power supplies. The term *uninterruptible* must also be defined. The time and voltage loss for a computer installation is far more critical than the response time for uninterruptible control circuits. The former might be critical within 3% voltage loss, whereas a control circuit does not get into trouble until it reaches around 20% voltage drop; at this point, magnetic devices begin to drop out.

[2] Generators usually have both the kVA and kW information because different users need different details. The installation designer and operators need to know the kVA. The utility companies work with kilowatts and megawatts because their revenue depends on the output not the input.

Regulation means controlling the voltage level to a predetermined bandwidth for all loads within the system design. The regulation required must also be specified. In the small emergency generators for lighting only, regulation is not too critical. With computers and computer-controlled plants, the regulation is significant both for speed (that is, frequency) and voltage. A change in frequency will cause a change in inductance, capacitance, and clock time base in circuits, while a raise in voltage will cause overheating of resistive components. The generator, then must be ordered with the correct regulator.

Another additional problem with the small generator is the output waveform. Where sophisticated equipment is being supplied, it may be necessary to provide line filters to protect the equipment from damaging transients and/or harmonics in the generator output.

14.4 THREE-PHASE GENERATORS

Three-phase generators range in size from small emergency types to massive slow-speed water-wheel units. Regardless of the size, they all work on the principle of the basic three-phase distributed winding with revolving dc field. The main differences are in the housing, bearings, regulators, cooling, and insulation. In the large types the form-wound coils are used for the winding, while in the small sizes the random-wound coils are adequate. The dc power is also supplied by various alternate methods. Sometimes the traditional shaft-mounted exciter provides the direct current; alternately, a central bus or static source of direct current is applied. This can be applied through slip rings or by the "brushless" method. All the points outlined for the single-phase generators also apply to the three-phase units.

14.5 PRIME MOVERS

A prime mover is the name given to the equipment which provides the driving power for the generator. These can be:

- Gasoline engine
- Gas turbine
- Water wheel
- Diesel engine
- Steam turbine
- Other alternates

In all cases, the prime mover must have good speed regulation; otherwise frequency becomes a problem. The speed is regulated by the governor. As the load changes, the governor senses the change and controls the fuel supply accordingly. The speed of response of the governor is important and where more than one generator is used, it must be with an adjustable "droop" characteristic. The *droop* of a governor is its ability to maintain speeds at certain loads. With zero droop the governor will have a flat *speed-to-load* curve, indicating no deviation. When droop is added, this means that the speed will drop slightly when load is applied. This characteristic is important when paralleling units, and many an electrical troubleshooter has been misled into investigating load dumping and swings as electrical problems when in fact they were caused by *droop* misadjustment.

In multiple units operating in parallel one engine must always be set with *droop;* otherwise, load division can never be maintained. It should also be noted that an air-breathing engine will lose approximately 2% efficiency per 1000 ft above sea level.

14.6 PARALLEL AC-GENERATOR OPERATION

Generators can be operated in parallel, providing certain conditions are fulfilled. There are certain characteristics regarding pulsating torques and critical frequencies between prime mover and generator which is the responsibility of the manufacturer to eliminate, therefore, a generator should be purchased as a unit, that is, generator and prime mover, and preferably on a single baseplate, making alignment problems minimal. The purchasing of a complete unit also gives the protection of a single source warrantee. The units may not be manufactured by the same company; however, the order placed with the generator manufacturer should be for a "generator complete with prime mover and necessary auxiliary equipment." It is then the responsibility of the electrical manufacturer to purchase the correct design of prime mover. Once installed, certain instruments and controls are necessary for the operator. The following list is a typical guide:

Common Bus Instruments

1. AC voltmeter[3]
2. Synchroscope[3]
3. Frequency meter[3]
4. Power-factor meter, or varmeter
5. Main ammeter
6. Wattmeter

General Instruments

1. Voltmeter
2. Ammeter
3. Wattmeter
4. Varmeter
5. Field rheostat
6. Exciter rheostat

[3] Mounted on swing brackets.

7. Frequency meter
8. Field/discharge switch, main circuit breaker
9. Associated instrument transformers, etc.

The selection of these instruments is purely a matter of desire and cost except for the "synchronizing" instruments. Some of these are mandatory as we will see.

To parallel generators, it is necessary to follow a set procedure. First, the prime movers should be started and allowed to run for the required warmup period. When two or more generators are to be paralleled, one unit should be selected as the *swing* generator. This will pick up all load changes. All units should have governors set with zero droop, except for the swing generator, which should have some droop. If manufacturer's instructions are not available, try 20%. Assuming two units, one running and carrying load and set with zero droop. Bring the incoming unit voltage up to bus voltage or slightly higher. Adjust the speed until the frequency is matching; close the synchroscope switch (it will now register "slow" or "fast"), adjust the speed until the synchroscope reads "0," or "12 o'clock." The instant this occurs close the generator circuit breaker. The swing unit will now be idling on the line. To pick up load, it is necessary to increase the speed of the prime mover, which means adjusting the governor. To adjust the reactive (kvar) load, it is necessary to adjust the generator field rheostat. The field effect on the kvars is the opposite to a synchronous motor; decreasing the field contributes vars to the system, improving the power factor.

14.7 GENERATOR STABILITY

If a plant is relying on a generator of limited size and it is required to start large motors, then it is necessary to ensure that the generator is large enough to accommodate the starting kVA. For example, to limit the voltage drop on starting to 10% and using *across-the-line* start, the maximum-size motor which could be started on a 2500-kVA generator would be 150 hp. See Fig. 11.2. With reduced-voltage start this could be improved, but a generator cannot start large motors without serious voltage-drop problems unless it is excessively oversized or unless the motor starting kVA is limited. Therefore, when a situation exists where a remote plant might be operating on generators of limited capacity, serious consideration must be given to generator oversizing and also to limiting the starting kVA of motors.

14.8 GENERATOR EXCITERS

Generator exciters have standard voltage ratings of 125 V dc for generators of up to approximately 10,000-kVA rating. Above this size they are usually rated at 250 V dc. The size of an exciter will vary inversely with the generator speed (but not necessarily proportional). The manufacturer will supply the correct-size exciter for the generator in order for it to meet the specification as ordered. Generally the size will vary from 1 to 5% of the generator output and is rated in kW. The exciter, or excitation, can be provided in many different ways; however, the designer has the option of selecting a "brushless" exciter when maintenance or other factors dictate. Other types require slip rings and carbon brushes, which require some maintenance and can be adversely affected by polluted atmospheres.

14.9 DC GENERATORS

There is very little to be discussed about dc generators because they are never used as conventional power system supplies and are usually only provided by the manufacturer for adjustable-speed drive systems. By connecting all the motors to a single generator and having the speed "voltage controlled," it is only necessary to vary the speed of the generator or generator voltage to cause all the motors to vary speed accordingly.

Since an adjustable-speed drive system is purchased as a package, the designer rarely has much to do other than follow the manufacturer's instructions with regard to the interconnecting wiring.

15 OVERCURRENT AND DISCONNECT DEVICES

15.1 OPENING CIRCUITS

Opening a circuit is more difficult than closing a circuit. An *open circuit* can be defined as a circuit in which the resistance has been increased until the current flow is reduced to an acceptable level. If we wish to go to ridiculous extremes, we can show that the normal switch or contactor, when opened, does not completely stop the electron flow through the air between two energized contacts. We will in fact have a slight ionization of the air, but for all "power" purposes this is acceptable. By closing the switch contacts, we decrease the resistance until we obtain the required current flow, which is not necessarily the maximum current flow because we still have resistance between the contacts. It is not possible to eliminate this resistance with practical means.

What we have then is two limits of compromise between maximum and minimum "practical" resistance which, when inserted in a circuit, is called *switching*. We will find that this resistance plus "ionization" determines how good or bad a switch performs. There is also another aspect to a switch. The mechanical design must be made to withstand electromagnetic forces as well as the physical closing actions. As these conditions and considerations multiply, so the switching equipment becomes more expensive and sophisticated. Here we begin to diversify into the many designs and variations of switchgear. By making the switchgear "self-sensing," it can be designed to determine its own "acceptable limits," above which it will refuse to carry any more current.

Here we define the component as an overcurrent device. This places the components in three categories:

1. Switch
2. Current-sensing switch
3. Melting-wire switch

These of course can be re-identified as:

1. Switch
2. Circuit breaker and variations
3. Fuse

In this chapter, then, we will discuss the general requirements, conditions, applications, and problems associated with the different devices. All manufacturers have their own ideas on specific designs; therefore, we can only discuss the general features rather than specific selections.

15.2 IONIZATION

In order to understand the problems associated with switching, we will briefly discuss ionization. If we accept the hypothesis that an electric current is in fact an electron flow, we can show by means of electrostatic instruments that it is virtually impossible to have nonionized air. If we further define ionization as the "ability to conduct," we can say that the air between any two masses will have an electron flow. The electron flow can be speeded up or slowed down by the difference in potential between the two masses. The potential can be electrostatic or a potential difference between two conductors. This is immaterial; it is still a voltage difference between two points. As the potential is increased, the "ions" travel from one point to the other with an increasing speed because of the increase in potential. When a certain acceleration point is reached, the "ions" bump each other and further acceleration is acquired by some ions which in turn bump others, etc. This then creates "ionization by collision" and an avalanche effect takes place. The air then changes in characteristic and becomes more conducting than insulating; hence, a flash or arc occurs. Unless the ionization is checked, or the potential difference reduced, the arc can be sustained indefinitely. This of course is how an electric welder operates, and is also one of the main problems in switching.

15.3 NON-LOAD-BREAK SWITCH (DISCONNECT)

Switches can be divided into two types: those with the ability to open under load and those that must be opened only after the load is removed. These non-load-break types of switches are generally classed as disconnects in the general sense but can have other names in the specialized sense, such as *no-load tap changer* and *distribution-line sectionalizer,* etc.

Many industrial circuits require isolating at one time or another for emergency or maintenance purposes. It may also be necessary to work on the transformers or circuit breakers themselves which are actually supplying the power to the circuit. In this case it is necessary to remove the power at some convenient point so that all the equipment can be worked on in perfect safety.

As this is only done on a planned basis or on rare occasions, a low-cost device is all that is required. If all the load is removed by opening the circuit breakers and load-break devices, the disconnect is carrying no discernible current. It can then be safely opened and locked in an open position. When the work is completed, it must first be closed before any of the load devices are closed. This type of switch is usually a copper-blade knife switch, and it is rated to carry continuous current.

These disconnects are available in nearly all voltage ratings, with indoor or outdoor design. They can also be fused or unfused.

15.4 LOAD-BREAK SWITCH (MEDIUM VOLTAGE)

The load-break switch is of course very similar to the non-load-break switch. The difference is that load-break switches can be opened when carrying full-rated current. They are designed to be safe when closing into a short circuit, and this is usually specified as to the maximum short-circuit rating. They can be ordered with or without fuses, and the fuses are generally the current-limiting type. This type of switch is for low-cost switching and circuit protection (when fused) where occasional and infrequent use is intended.

Specific applications are in service entrances, load centers for transformer primary and/or secondary switching, and power-center feeder circuits (sectionalized primary feeders). They are rated in voltages up to 13.8 kV and 1200-A continuous-current rating. The enclosures available are both indoor and outdoor.

The limitation of these switches is the inability to open overloads or short-circuit currents. Any attempt to do this could destroy the whole switch, and includes the possibility of an explosion. This, however, should rarely happen because other protective devices in the circuit(s) should have operated long before an operator is able to open the switch; however, it has happened, and with near-devastating results. In order to preclude this, these units should always be ordered fused.

15.5 SAFETY SWITCHES (LOW VOLTAGE)

The safety switch is the low-voltage version of the load-break disconnect, except it is intended for general use rather than occasional use. These are available in many sizes and ratings from 30 to 1200 A heavy-duty type. Enclosures are for indoor and outdoor applications, and either the fused or unfused design can be selected.

The safety switches are usually "horsepower rated," as well as rated for continuous load. They can be used as motor disconnect switches, although special versions of the safety switch are manufactured and designated as motor circuit switches. These are unfused switches and are intended to meet the code requirement for motor disconnecting means. In most industrial plants, motor control is accomplished by using motor control centers which meet the code requirements without the need for this type of switch.

The application for these switches is for nonprocess duty where auxiliary equipment such as vent fans, sump pumps, air-conditioning circuits, and maintenance machines require control.

15.6 OVERCURRENT PROTECTION DEVICES

Every circuit must have overcurrent protection. This means automatic opening of the circuit when the current exceeds a predetermined limit. There are only two devices capable of offering this protection: the *circuit breaker* and the *fuse.* The requirements for each of these devices is very severe. It must carry, open, and close the normal load current for which it is rated. It must open (interrupt) a short-circuit current. It must be able to be closed on a short circuit safely. In addition, it must do this many times within its life cycle without significant deterioration in performance or safety. A fuse, of course, would require renewal of the fusible element, but the important qualification is that the fuse body remain intact during the fusing period and also remain in its holder.

15.7 FUSES

A fuse is a single-phase device which opens a circuit by means of the heat generated by the current flow and the consequent melting of a metallic element. They are available in extremes of voltage, current ratings, and fusing-time characteristics. They are low-cost devices, require very little space, are simply manufactured, and are easily installed. They have the ability to limit fault currents, fast-acting consistent performance, and fail-safe operation.

The disadvantages of fuse protection are generally weighed against the cost of similar protection provided by a circuit breaker. One big disadvantage on motor circuits is that a fuse is a single-phase device. If only one fuse blows, a three-phase motor will still keep running but with reduced power output. This can cause overheating and it is always debatable whether the motor-running overcurrent protection will disconnect the motor in time to prevent damage. A further disadvantage is that fuses are not controllable by remote operation. Fuses with replacable elements sometimes have oversize replacements. The stocking of replacement fuses and elements is also an inconvenience along with the requirement for a qualified individual to replace the fuse without encountering a hazardous condition.

One last problem is the coordination of fuses into a protective scheme. Sometimes the "time-current" rating is inconsistent with its performance. Aging and partial fusing can result in prematurely open circuits.

Fuses, then, are not the best selection in all cases; they do, however, have specific applications where economy and probability of operation make them an obvious choice.

15.8 POWER FUSES

Power fuses are essentially high-voltage rated, that is, from 600 V to 34.5 kV; they have high interrupting ratings and are available for indoor and outdoor use, sometimes in conjunction with the previously mentioned load-break switch.

The application of these fuses would be in circuits which require protection but have a low probability of failure. Some typical applications are transformer circuits, that is, control power transformers, potential transformers, power transformers, banks of capacitors, and feeder circuits.

When specifying power fuses, it is necessary to provide the following information: current rating, voltage rating, frequency rating, interrupting rating, enclosure type, location, and mounting details. Also, a request for coordination time-current curves should be made.

The load-current rating of a fuse must be equal or higher than the maximum continuous load current, including possible temporary overloads. The code will dictate the size of the fuse for the specific application.

The voltage rating of a fuse is the *nominal* rating, equal to or more than the *nominal* system line-to-line voltage. The frequency must also be specified and is, of course, the standard 60 Hz for the United States.

The interrupting rating of a fuse should be in excess of the expected maximum short-circuit current at the point of installation. The rating can be given in short-circuit kVA or amperes asymmetrical, that is, including the dc component.

Inrush currents which occur during switching operations are caused by transformers having negligible impedance at the instant power is applied. This inrush is for a very short duration but can be many times the load current. Generally the normal selection of a fuse requires some oversizing for acceptable circuit performance. In most cases this oversizing will also adequately compensate for the transformer magnetizing inrush.

Coordination of fuses will be covered in later chapter(s) when coordination study procedures are outlined.

15.9 CURRENT-LIMITING FUSES

The current-limiting fuse is different from the normal, or *non-current-limiting*, fuse. The normal fuse carries the total fault current, and if the fault current exceeds the short-circuit rating of the fuse, it will explode. In contrast, the CLF (current-limiting fuse) responds within the first half cycle of the fault-current curve. This means that as the fault current begins to increase, it also begins to melt the fuse element. When the current reaches its "limiting" rating, the element melts completely, resulting in an arc which gradually decays. The fuse never has to consider the maximum fault current because this value is never reached. Typical applications for current-limiting fuses are in load-center unit substations, safety switches, lighting-circuit feeders, combination motor starters, and in some cases with a circuit breaker in the same package to improve its interrupting capability. They are finding more and more acceptance as power systems get stiffer, offering higher short-circuit currents to motor starters and circuits.

15.10 OIL-FUSE CUTOUTS

The oil-fuse cutout is a combination of a load interrupter switch and non-current-limiting fuse immersed in a tank filled with oil. These are small, compact units which find application in primary-selective switching and primary load-center protection. The oil can be the regular type or the askarel nonflammable type. The problems with this type of device are that the actual switch is not visible, changing fuses can be a messy job, and filtering of the oil is required periodically.

15.11 CIRCUIT BREAKERS

A circuit breaker is a pair of contacts designed to open a circuit automatically at a preselected current without damage to the circuit breaker under normal and abnormal conditions within its design limits.

Circuit breakers have such a wide range of designs and types that it is impossible to do justice to the subject in the limitations of a single chapter. We can therefore only cover the general aspects of circuit-breaker design and application.

A circuit breaker also doubles as a switch. It can be remotely operated; the tripping characteristics have wide flexibility when relaying is applied. They can be used as motor starters and can be supplied in single-, double-, or three-pole units; air-type or oil-immersed; and enclosed for indoor or outdoor operation. Sime circuit breakers are the draw-out type; that is, the whole unit slides out of its housing. Other types are so large that, after draining the oil, you can walk inside to inspect them.

15.12 OIL CIRCUIT BREAKER (OCB)

This type of circuit breaker is usually limited to the large substation type for outdoor operation. Indoor oil circuit breakers are available for small industrial applications, but because oilless types are available in adequate ratings, they are rarely used in general plant applications. Special atmospheres with dust or corrosive fumes may dictate the use of the oil type but they would be only selected as a "special" item. Thus, we will not go into further detail on these.

15.13 POWER CIRCUIT BREAKER

A power circuit breaker can be defined as a breaker in the medium- and high-voltage class for switching blocks of power. They can be oil or oilless, and since oilless ratings are getting higher, the use of the oil type is being reduced. We will then be referring only to the oilless type when we refer to power circuit breakers.

The power circuit breaker is a complex and precision piece of engineering production. It is generally taken for granted without the realization that extreme forces are constantly trying to tear it apart. It must be fast operating, repetitive, safe, and easily maintained.

The power circuit breaker consists of a three-pole set of contacts enclosed by *arc chutes.* These contacts are manipulated by a mechanical mechanism, which can be operated by hand or motor for closing and which also responds to opening by relay signals operating a stored energy system.

They are predominantly of the drawout type, meaning that a single spare breaker can be carried and periodically used to replace a faulty or suspect breaker.

Power circuit breakers in industrial plants are usually lined up in *load-center* areas. The lineup is then called a PDC, or *power-distribution center.* The purpose of the PDC is to supply high-voltage feeder circuits to small load-center unit substations. A pulp and paper mill or steel mill may have many power-distribution centers, supplying various localized areas of high power density.

A PDC would probably have a voltage of 13.8 kV and supply a unit substation with secondary breakers at 4.16 kV. Power circuit breakers would also be used as "tie" breakers, feeder breakers, motor starters (modified rating), and main shutdown breakers ahead of a lineup of high-voltage motor starters, including of course transformer protection.

15.14 POWER-CIRCUIT-BREAKER RATING

A power circuit breaker has to perform many functions; therefore, all these functions must be rated. The ratings are minimum, maximum, and rated voltage; impulse voltage; continuous, interrupting, momentary, and 4-second current; frequency; three-phase interrupting kVA (mVA); and interrupting time in cycles.

1. *Rated voltage* is the nominal system voltage for which the circuit breaker is to be applied.

2. *Minimum voltage* is the lowest voltage at which the circuit breaker will interrupt its rated mVA. Since mVA means $10^{-6} \times$ volts $\times$ amperes $\times \sqrt{3}$, a reduction in voltage would allow an increase in amperes for the same interrupting mVA. The minimum voltage, then, is intended to limit the increase in amperes by this method of calculation.

3. *Maximum voltage* is the allowable increase in voltage due to the difference in nominal system voltage and actual operating voltage. For example, regulation may normally increase the voltage at light load periods.

4. *Impulse voltage* is the impulse crest value of a lightning strike and the rating in kV is its ability to withstand a voltage of this magnitude.

5. *Insulation-withstand voltage* is a measure of the insulation ability to withstand rated-frequency high-potential voltages; rated in rms values.

6. *Frequency* is the rated frequency of the system and is 60 Hz in the United States.

7. *Continuous-current rating* is the normal current-carrying capacity on a continuous basis without exceeding the design temperature.

8. *Interrupting rating;* this is usually in three-phase mVA and is for all voltages between maximum and minimum ratings, and is obtained by $10^{-6} \times EI_{sc}\sqrt{3}$ where I_{sc} is the symmetrical short-circuit current to be interrupted.

9. *Interrupting current* is the rms value of the maximum amperes the circuit breaker is required to interrupt at rated voltage.

10. *Maximum interrupting current* is the maximum current the circuit breaker will interrupt regardless of how low the voltage is with reference to the mVA rating. This is a function of minimum voltage.

11. *Momentary rating* is the ability of the circuit breaker to contain the mechanical forces caused by a short circuit until the circuit breaker has time to interrupt. This is the asymmetrical current rating, including all sources of fault current. This rating is extremely critical; if it is exceeded, the circuit breaker can fly apart. This rating is usually about 1.6 to 1.7 times the maximum interrupting rating in amperes.

12. *4-second rating* is the maximum current that the breaker will support in a closed position for a period of 4 seconds. It is the same value as the maximum interrupting current.

13. *Interrupting time* this is the time in hertz on rated frequency basis (60 Hz) that elapses between the circuit-breaker trip coil energizing and the circuit breaker clearing the fault. For most power breakers in an industrial plant it is about 8 Hz.

The above ratings are based on installations not exceeding 3300 ft above sea level. Above this height the manufacturer should be contacted and the specific conditions outlined.

15.15 LARGE AIR CIRCUIT BREAKER (LOW VOLTAGE)

The low-voltage large air circuit breaker is similar in performance to the high-voltage power circuit breaker. It is heavy duty, rugged construction, carries high continuous currents and heavy interrupting currents, and can have various trip characteristics. It can be set up for remote-control operation or it can be obtained with manual or electrically operated control. Rated as high as 4000 A continuous current with interrupting ratings of 100,000 A asymmetrical at 460 and 600 V, these large breakers usually find application in load-center unit substations where large blocks of low-voltage power are utilized. The air circuit breaker can be fitted with auxiliary switches and many other signaling devices. They can be supplied for indoor and outdoor use, including explosionproof enclosures.

The usual installation is the indoor metal-clad enclosure with the circuit breakers stacked in vertical sections. The air circuit breaker can also be "cascaded." This allows it to be used for circuits with higher short-circuit currents than the breaker is rated for.

15.16 AIR-CIRCUIT-BREAKER RATINGS

The low-voltage air circuit breaker has slightly different ratings than the power circuit breaker. These are: rated voltage, maximum design voltage, rated maximum voltage, rated frequency, rated continuous current, rated short-time current, rated short-circuit current, and cascading interrupting current.

1. *Rated voltage* is the nominal system voltage line to line and should equal or exceed the nominal voltage.
2. *Rated maximum voltage* is the maximum voltage that may be applied to the circuit breaker (i.e., from regulation due to lightly loaded circuits, etc.)
3. *Rated frequency* is the system frequency (60 Hz in the United States).
4. *Rated continuous current* is the current which the breaker will carry continuously without exceeding its allowable temperature rise. This rating generally signifies the "frame" size. The current that a breaker will carry is a function of the overload trip rating; therefore, when selecting a circuit-breaker continuous-current rating, it should be selected with a frame size equal or in excess of the continuous current it has to carry. For example, a 600-A current requirement could be met in two ways: (1) using a 600-A frame maximum (adjustable trip of 40 to 600 A), or (2) using a 1600-A frame with adjustable trip to 200 to 1600 A.

   In the first instance it would be a poor selection because there is no guarantee that the current would be exactly 600 A maximum and could in fact exceed the circuit-breaker rating during service. In the second instance the breaker is larger than required, but with the advantage that the circuit rating could be increased by changing the trip.
5. *Short-time rating* is the highest rms current, including the dc component, which it will be required to carry for a limited short time. The short-time rating of a breaker is determined by test and consists of maintained rated short-time current for two periods of $\frac{1}{2}$ sec each, with a 15-sec interval of zero current between the $\frac{1}{2}$-sec periods. After the test, the circuit breaker must be capable of carrying its rated current without exceeding the design temperature rise and shall also be capable of interrupting its rated short-circuit current.

6. *Interrupting rating* is the maximum short-circuit current the breaker will interrupt with a *direct-acting trip* (i.e., instantaneous trip). This is rms symmetrical amperes at rated voltage. When under test, the symmetrical current is measured at an instant *one half cycle* after the short circuit occurs. The breaker shall also interrupt with every degree of asymmetry up to an X/R ratio of 6.6.

7. *Cascading interrupting rating* is the maximum short-circuit current which can be applied to the circuit breaker when the circuit breaker is arranged to meet the requirements for two-step cascade operation. This is the rms symmetrical rating.

8. *Other requirements,* any other special conditions, such as control-circuit voltage, trip types, special atmospheric conditions, and altitude and ambients other than normal should all be spelled out in the specifications when ordering.

15.17 MOLDED-CASE CIRCUIT BREAKERS

The molded-case circuit breaker is a low-cost light-service circuit breaker. It has a wide selective range of sizes and is very versatile. It is the economic answer to a device which has the advantages of a circuit breaker but the cost of an expensive fuse. It therefore eliminates the disadvantages of the fuse, but it cannot claim all the advantages of the large air circuit breaker. Although the interrupting ratings are quite good and the continuous-current ranges acceptable, that is, up to 2000 A, the breakers are not suitable for cascade operation. The trips are fixed or adjustable but lack the versatility of large air-circuit-breaker trips. The breakers can be supplied as single, two, or three pole. All breakers are "tripfree," meaning that if the toggle handle is held in the on position the circuit breaker will still trip on overload. They are a three-phase trip (three-pole breaker), which makes them ideal for motor circuits; a single-phase fault will open all three poles. They are extremely fast-acting, with both thermal and magnetic trip elements available. The thermal element monitors the continuous current, while the instantaneous magnetic trip senses the short-circuit current and gives fast opening by magnetically closing the trip circuit switch.

The specified ratings for a molded-case circuit breaker are rated voltage, maximum continuous-current rating (frame size), interrupting rating, and trip types.

15.18 MOLDED-CASE CIRCUIT-BREAKER RATINGS

The specified ratings of a molded-case circuit breaker are not as complex as the air circuit breakers.

1. *Rated voltage* is the maximum voltage the circuit breaker is designed for. This, however, takes into account variations due to regulation and

nominal systems of 460 V would use a 480-V circuit breaker; 575-V systems (Canada) would use the 600-V rating.

2. *Rated current* is the maximum continuous current it will carry without exceeding its temperature design limits.

3. The *interrupting rating* is the maximum rms symmetrical current the breaker will interrupt without damage to itself.

4. The number of poles must be specified.

5. The type of trip must also be specified, that is, thermal, magnetic, or both. The first is for sustained overloads, and the second is for short circuits. The breakers can be specified with single magnetic trips or with dual-element trips.

An additional comment is necessary on a special type of molded-case circuit breaker which is actually a current-limiting fuse in series with a circuit breaker, but installed in one integrated unit package.

The circuit-breaker portion handles the normal overloads and smaller short-circuit currents, while the current-limiting fuse protects against the extremely high short-circuit currents which could occur from high contribution or (under certain conditions) high single-phase fault. In the event that a single-phase fault blows out one fuse, a *shunt trip* actuates the circuit breaker, opening all three phases.

15.19 MOLDED-CASE CIRCUIT-BREAKER ACCESSORIES

There are a number of accessories which can be ordered with a molded-case circuit breaker. These supplement the basic unit, providing greater versatility. The following is a list of some of these components:

1. *Undervoltage protection.* This device will trip the circuit breaker when the line voltage drops to 30 to 60% of normal.

2. *Time delay unit for undervoltage relay.* This device prevents the undervoltage relay from operating during transient situations.

3. *Mechanical interlock.* This device enables two breakers to be interlocked so that only one can be energized at a time, although both can be in the off position at once.

4. *Auxiliary switch.* This is a switch with one to four SPDT (single-pole double-throw) contacts. The switches open and close with the breaker operation.

5. *Alarm switch.* This switch is actuated under overload or short-circuit trip conditions but is not actuated under normal on/off switching.

6. *Remote on/off push-button control.* This is a small motor-operated mechanism that mounts on to the circuit breaker and operates the toggle handle. Therefore, it can open, close, or reset the breaker by remote control. It

can also be lifted out of the way for normal hand operation of the circuit breaker.

7. *Shunt trip.* This device can be used to trip/open a breaker by remote control. When the breaker opens, the shunt trip is deenergized by an auxiliary switch.

8. *Three-phase shunt trip.* This trip is for the fused circuit-breaker combinations and eliminates single-phase trips by operating a three-phase trip.

9. *Enclosures.* These breakers can be mounted individually in general-purpose or special enclosures. Alternately, they can be panel-mounted in small multiple units.

15.20 MOLDED-CASE CIRCUIT-BREAKER APPLICATION

The applications for this type of breaker are mostly in branch circuits. Lighting panels, power panels, switchboards, and combination motor starters in motor control centers are the more obvious and traditional applications. They are very adaptable for use in plug-in bus ducts for both branch circuit and small panel-feeder applications. In single-phase panels they can be supplied in single-pole and two-pole units to provide 120/240-V circuits. Alternately, they can be installed in 120/208-V panels, providing 120/208-V, single-phase, and 208-V, three-phase. The economy of using this type of circuit breaker and the small space required for mounting make them a very attractive device. The availability of accessories increases their versatility and in some way compensates against the advantages of the large air circuit breaker. They can also be used as a disconnect switch by removing the trip element.

15.21 NETWORK PROTECTOR

The network protector is an electrically operated air circuit breaker whose tripping mechanism is operated by a control circuit and special relays. The amount of relaying required for the network protector depends on its application. A utility-type network with mutliple paths would require power directional relays, whereas in the industrial plant, the relaying need not be so sophisticated.

An automatic reclosing feature, which is integral in the utility-type network protector, can be optional in the industrial plant. The network protector, of course, is only applicable where the distribution system is set up as a "network" system.

15.22 LINE RECLOSER

A line recloser is actually a circuit breaker with an automatic-reclosing feature. It is predominantly used on pole-line distribution systems. Because of wind and weather conditions, as well as flying objects such as kites and birds, the phase conductors can develop temporary faults. These are self-clearing faults. By using a recloser, the problem of monitoring these can be overcome. The recloser can be programmed to automatically reclose after each fault, if the fault is still present, it will trip and reclose again. This can be repeated a preselected number of times (two or three), after which the recloser will open and remain open.

The recloser must interrupt a fault; therefore, it must have a fault-current rating or interrupting rating. These ratings are published by the manufacturers. The unit is specially designed as a pole-line recloser, although an ordinary air circuit breaker can be set up with relaying to provide the same function. In fact many main-distribution-line breakers are fitted with this feature.

15.23 LINE SECTIONALIZER

This device is very similar in operation to the recloser, except it does not have the ability to interrupt a fault current. They are a less-expensive unit than the recloser and can be coordinated with a recloser to try to locate a fault and isolate that faulty part of the line if the fault is permanent. If the sectionalizer is set up to count two outages from the recloser, and the recloser is set up for three "reclosures," after two "trips" of the recloser the sectionalizer will open on the second trip and remain open, isolating the line beyond the sectionalizer. On the third "try" at reclosing, the recloser will find that the fault has been removed and will remain "in." The sectionalizer will open during a trip or deenergized period of the recloser operation. As previously mentioned, they are not rated for interrupting.

16
REGULATORS

16.1 VOLTAGE REGULATION

The term *voltage regulation* means a measurement of the change in voltage between the full-load condition and the no-load condition at a single point. It is specified in "percent regulation," in terms of the full-load voltage. Defined mathematically, it is

$$\text{Percent regulation} = \frac{[(\text{no-load volts}) - (\text{full-load volts})] \times 100}{\text{full-load volts}}$$

For example, no-load volts of 480 V and full-load volts of 440 V would have a regulation of

$$\left(\frac{480 - 440}{440}\right) 100 = 9\% \text{ regulation}$$

This means that the voltage variation on some equipment can vary as much as 9%. This also means that some of the last motors to be started before full-load current is reached could have only about 83% of their rated starting torque for a 9% voltage drop below nameplate rating. Lighting output will be reduced by nearly 30% for incandescent and mercury vapor lamps; capacitor outputs will be reduced by approximately 19%, which is also the percentage loss for resistance heaters. If the voltage is set up so that the applied voltage is correct at full load, at light loads the voltage will be high and cause reduced life, higher starting currents in motors, reduction of life in some lighting types, and an increased stress on some insulation.

We see that the ideal situation is to have a device which monitors the voltage in a circuit and corrects for the voltage differences. These devices are called *regulators*. There are, however, other standard devices that are adaptable to regulation service. This chapter then will discuss the equipment and its effects on circuit regulation. We will also include line filters, because harmonics and transients are in effect voltage increases but at frequencies other than standard.

16.2 TAP-CHANGING TRANSFORMER

The adjustment of transformer taps by manual changing will only have significance on the regulation when a large static load has been added, such as an addition to an existing plant or the addition of a plant to an existing feeder. Under these conditions it may be possible to compensate for the additional average load by an increase in line voltage by tap adjustment. This will not work, however, if the plants are at extreme ends of the feeder, because the first one will have a higher than desired voltage while the farthest plant will have normal voltage. Alternately, the first plant could have normal voltage and the farthest one have a "too-low" voltage condition. The manual tap changer, then, has limited application as far as regulation is concerned.

16.3 AUTOMATIC TAP CHANGER

If the taps on a transformer were made automatic and "load-to-voltage sensitive," as the load increases the voltage could be increased to compensate. As the load is dropped, the voltage could be reduced to a reasonable level.

To accomplish this, it is necessary to order a transformer with an *automatic tap changer.* Since this additional tap changer is bulky and expensive, it is usually limited to applications where the power being brought into the plant is in excess of 15 kV and is being stepped down to the utilization voltage of 13.8 or 4.16 kV. The tap changer is designed to give 32 step changes of 5/8%, that is, less than 1% steps.

With the 32 changes it provides a range of (5 × 32)%/8, or 20% change. This gives the ability to control the voltage to plus or minus 10%. The economic value of this tap changer would depend on many factors, one of which is possible maintenance problems. When equipment has moving parts, failures must be considered. The return on investment by longer life and more consistent operation of equipment must also be considered. Unless the designer is familiar with this equipment by experience, he should investigate its suitability and economics with the various manufacturers.

16.4 STEP-VOLTAGE REGULATOR (THREE-PHASE)

The voltage regulator is a device built especially for regulation control. The *step-voltage regulator* is basically an autotransformer with an automatic tap changer. The unit is a three-phase unit, and like the automatic tap changer it has a range of plus or minus 10%.

This type of regulator would be used where the service voltage is at the utilizing voltage, that is 13.8 or 4.16 kV. The utility feeders supplying the service can vary quite significantly in voltage levels; therefore, if the variation is around 5%, the question of regulation arises and an evaluation of the problem should be conducted.

16.5 INDUCTION-VOLTAGE REGULATOR (OIL-FILLED STATION TYPE)

This type of regulator could be considered in place of the step-voltage regulator. They both have the same range of regulation. The induction-voltage regulator regulates by varying the induction instead of the turns ratio, as in the step-voltage regulator. They are available in single-phase, as well as three-phase, units and as such can be connected in open delta; however, a slight unbalance that could occur due to this connection would introduce problems with motor heating. Therefore, consider only the three-phase unit for normal service. The main advantage of the induction-voltage regulator over the step-voltage regulator is its ability to provide "stepless" regulation rather than regulation in 5/8% increments. Both the step- and induction-voltage regulator can be bypassed by cables for temporary removal for maintenance. This of course leaves a temporarily unregulated system.

16.6 INDUCTION-VOLTAGE REGULATOR (DRY TYPE)

This regulator is intended for localized applications at low voltage, that is, below 600 V. The units are operable on single-phase and three-phase circuits. The regulator consists of a transformer and a movable rotor. An exciting shunt winding is installed on the rotor, while the current-carrying series winding is on the stator. By varying the position of the rotor shunt winding with respect to the series-winding stator, a variation in flux occurs; this of course shows up as a change in the line voltage.

To determine whether this type of regulator is applicable, it is necessary to consider the specific requirements rather than the regulation of the available circuit. When the regulation requirements of the load equipment are established, a recording voltmeter can be installed to check the available voltage and its regulation. If the plant is being designed, then obviously recorders cannot be installed. If the design is new and good practices have been followed, regulation should not be a problem; however, some equipment requires much closer regulation than good practice provides; in this case the investment in a regulator is probably wise. The other alternative is to provide provision for future installation, if necessary, by installing a junction box where the regulator would be located. After the plant is built, recorders can be installed and the circuit regulation verified.

Typical applications for these regulators are lighting feeders, heat-treating systems, laboratories, computer installations, broadcasting stations, and communications systems. By using these small, relatively low-cost regulators, sized for the specific circuit, they provide the regulation exactly where it is needed.

16.7 AUTOTRANSFORMER REGULATION (BUCK AND BOOST)

In some cases, a low-voltage circuit (below 600-V) is consistently high or consistently low, which could cause problems. The information that a problem exists on the circuit would probably come from the maintenance crew. The repair cost and/or lamp replacements would cause suspicion. The next step is to install a voltage recorder and determine exactly what the regulation and spread of the voltage is. It may be determined that the regulation is fine but the level is wrong. Changing the tap on the main substation transformer may not correct the individual problem.

Here then is a typical application for a *buck/boost* transformer. A further obvious application is to the three-phase 120/208-V system where some load equipment may be rated at 230 V.

By taking an ordinary single-phase two-winding transformer and connecting one end of the secondary winding to one end of the primary winding, we have the equivalent of an autotransformer. We know that an autotransformer carries more load than the equivalent-size two-winding transformer; therefore, a transformer connected buck/boost would have a smaller nameplate kVA than the load. This can be shown mathematically by

$$\mathrm{kVA}_{1\mathrm{w}} = \mathrm{kVA}_{2\mathrm{w}} \frac{N-1}{N}$$

where $\mathrm{kVA}_{1\mathrm{w}}$ is one-winding-transformer size, $\mathrm{kVA}_{2\mathrm{w}}$ is two-winding-transformer size, and N is the transformer turns ratio (that is, HV/LV).
For example, boosting from 207 to 230 V would be calculated in the following manner:

$$\text{Percent voltage change} = \left(\frac{\text{high voltage} - \text{low voltage}}{\text{high voltage}}\right) 100$$

$$= \left(\frac{230 - 207}{230}\right) 100$$

$$= 10\% \text{ increase required}$$

It is now necessary to select a single-phase transformer with insulation levels of both windings within the correct voltage range. The nameplate kVA rating of the two-winding transformer will be incorrect and the transformer connected as an autotransformer will carry more load, in accordance with the previous equation. If we assume a load of 50 kVA for our previous example, we require a two-winding transformer of lower nameplate kVA rating:

$$\text{kVA as one winding connection} = 50\left(\frac{230 - 207}{230}\right)$$

$$= \text{5-kVA nameplate for two-winding transformer connected as an autotransformer}$$

16.8 SHUNT CAPACITORS

Shunt capacitors are essentially power-factor corrective devices; however, the voltage drop in a circuit is a function of IZ, where $Z = \sqrt{R^2 + X^2}$, which is the vector sum of the resistance and reactance in the circuit. If a circuit is highly reactive, two potential problems exist: excessive voltage drop and poor power factor. With voltage regulation we are concerned with the voltage levels rather than the power factor; however, in the case of shunt capacitors one must be considered with the other for an economical installation. As far as voltage levels are concerned, if a shunt capacitor is installed at the load, it will reduce the voltage drop by eliminating the drop due to reactance only. This has the effect of a permanent voltage rise and will still have the same "regulation" as before.

By fitting the capacitors with automatic switching, they can be applied only when the inductive load is applied. This arrangement will in effect contribute to better regulation by adding only the *IR* drop to the line rather than the expected *IZ* drop.

As mentioned before, shunt capacitors are power-factor correction devices, and although they can improve voltage regulation problems, they are not intended to replace the voltage regulator designed for the application.

16.9 SERIES CAPACITORS

Some regulation problems are essentially transient in nature. They are so fast-acting that a conventional regulator does not have time to respond. In effect we have a voltage "flicker" or "dip." A typical example is the electric welder with its very low power factor and constant restriking of an arc. As the voltage dip is due mostly to high lagging reactive power, it can be eliminated by inserting a reactance of high leading reactive power. We also require that the leading reactive power is only applied when needed; this rules out the shunt capacitor and leaves us with the series capacitor. As it must carry the full-load current, it is a much more expensive device than the shunt capacitor. The effect on the voltage regulation can be seen by examination of the approximate voltage-drop formula:

$$e = IR \cos \phi + I(X_L - X_C) \sin \phi$$

where e is the voltage drop in volts, I is the total current, R is the resistance, X_L is the inductive reactance in ohms, X_C is the capacitive reactance in ohms, and ϕ is the angular phase displacement. By factoring out the current in this equation, we obtain

$$e = I[R \cos \phi + (X_L - X_C) \sin \phi]$$

If the capacitive reactance in ohms (series capacitor) equals the inductive reactance in ohms (load reactance), the term $X_L - X_C$ becomes zero; this then cancels out the right-hand term of the sum, leaving $e = IR \cos \phi$. As there is no net reactive power, the power factor must be unity; therefore, $\cos \phi$ is equal to 1 and the equation reduces to $e = IR$.

We see then that the series capacitor is in effect matched against the inductive reactance. If we consider an excess of inductive reactance as providing voltage drop, we can also consider an excess of negative-capacitive reactance as producing a voltage rise. Therefore, we can say that the effect of capacitive reactance is as follows

$$e_C = IX_C \sin \phi$$

where sin ϕ is the reactive part of the load. By eliminating this part, we obtain the voltage across the series capacitor; that is, $E_C = IX_C$, where I is the load current.

The indiscriminate use of series capacitors can have possible detrimental effects on equipment. If the problem loads happen to be motors with pulsating loads or frequent starts, subsynchronous locking torques can be introduced, among other problems. Unless the electrical designer is experienced in the use of series capacitors, the assistance of the manufacturer should be obtained in analyzing the application. Keep in mind that it is the manufacturers' business to sell equipment and they will possibly tend to minimize some problems, but not usually to the extent where an incorrect application is made.

16.10 VOLTAGE STABILIZERS

The voltage stabilizer is a small unit designed for individual branch-circuit applications rather than for system correction. It consists of a packaged *RLC* circuit, that is, resistance, reactance, and capacitance. It is specially designed for the purpose of eliminating voltage transients which cause annoying flicker and dips. Its effect is to improve the regulation by taking an input voltage varying over a 20 to 25% range and giving an output which remains constant at different loads to within 1%. These are relatively inexpensive devices with no moving parts and very long life if used within their ratings.

16.11 LINE FILTERS

The line filter is another *RLC* circuit package. It is specifically designed to eliminate undesirable harmonics and transients from the circuit feeders. Some solid-state equipment, such as computers, guidance controllers, and sophisticated instruments, are susceptible to distortions in wave shape. One possible effect of harmonics is to introduce high-voltage spikes which are superimposed on the fundamental-frequency voltage wave. These spikes can damage solid-state devices by exceeding the dielectric strength of some materials. These spikes are so fast that they will not show up on a voltmeter; they can only be detected by an oscilloscope. By the time it is evident that a problem exists, it is usually too late and equipment is damaged.

When expensive solid-state equipment requires a power source, and possibly an emergency generator, the supplier (manufacturer) of the solid-state equipment should be contacted to determine whether the equipment has its own filters for self-protection or whether filters should be added in the line.

16.12 GENERATOR REGULATOR

One other piece of equipment should be mentioned, even though the average industrial designer will rarely come into contact with it. This is the voltage regulator supplied with a generator. There are different types by different manufacturers, each with their own advantages and disadvantages. For example, one manufacturer who produces both generators and regulators may elect to use a competitor's regulator for a particular reason. The possibility is that the designer may become involved with this type of regulator on plant startup. The effect of the regulator is to give fast recovery from a voltage dip due to motor starting or other large-load application. If on startup the voltage dips seem excessive, this regulator should be checked. An incorrect connection on the current transformers can result in compounding the voltage-dip problem. It should not be necessary to repeat the warning to obtain the correct instruction sheet and circuit for the particular regulator. This means "make and model."

A particular application of this could occur in long pipeline installations where each pumping station has its own generators.

17 INSTRUMENT AND CONTROL TRANSFORMERS

17.1 CONTROL POWER TRANSFORMERS

Control power transformers are simple dry-type two-winding single-phase transformers. The purpose of these transformers is to provide a safe working voltage, which is usually 120 V for control circuits. The sizes vary from 50 to around 5000 VA. The ratings of standard sizes are: 50, 75, 100, 150, 200, 250, 300, 350, 500, 750, 1000, 1500, 2000, 3000, and 5000 VA. Depending on the location, the intended regulation, and the use of the control power transformer the secondaries can be rated at 120, 115, or 110 V. The designation of the type of circuit is defined in Article 725 of the NEC for remote control, signaling, and power-limited circuits. The sizing and protection should comply with the code that has jurisdiction at the user location. A manufacturer may comply with the code in the location of his factory and yet violate the code when it is delivered to the customer. The loads on a control-circuit transformer, although small, must be computed and the inrush considered. The transformer can be specified to have better than normal regulation, probably at a slight increase in cost. They are usually open-type transformers with exposed terminals; therefore, they are intended only for use within a dead-front enclosure.

17.2 POTENTIAL TRANSFORMER

The potential transformer is a transformer specifically designed for metering and protective relaying. Its purpose is to accurately reduce a high voltage to a standard low voltage, that is, 115/120 V.

These transformers may be either the oil-filled or dry type. The load applied to these transformers must be within the limits of their design; otherwise, the accuracy of the output is affected. Since the output is intended to be proportional to the primary voltage, false readings can be given on the instruments. For protective relaying purposes, and where the load burden (voltamperes) is several loads connected in parallel, it is usually accurate enough to add the loads arithmetically. The inaccuracies in ratio and phase angle of a standard accuracy (ANSI)[1] class potential transformer can also usually be neglected for protective relaying schemes.

If a potential transformer is accurate at rated voltage, it is generally suitable up to 110% of its range. Above this, overheating could occur.

17.3 CURRENT TRANSFORMER

Whereas a potential transformer is simple to select, the current transformer requires much more consideration if it is to be selected properly. A current transformer (unlike a potential transformer) must go through extremes of performance over its design range. The accuracy required for metering and relaying are quite different. The current transformer consists of a primary and secondary winding. The secondary winding gives an output voltage proportional to the current in the primary; however, this is only true for a specific part of the range. Beyond this, saturation occurs and the accuracy is affected. In metering it is only necessary to know the currents at normal loads, but in protective relaying it is required to measure the currents under short-circuit conditions; here is where the problem can occur.

There are two basic types of current transformers: the *bushing* (doughnut) type which is slipped over the conductor, which also serves as the primary winding; and the *in-line* type, which is actually a short piece of bus bar with a distributed winding. This is then bolted into place, that is, in series, in the bus bar to be measured. The accuracy of the two types is slightly different.

17.4 TRANSFORMER BURDENS

The burden on a transformer is the load in voltamperes. Due to the possible saturation of a current transformer and distortion of load information, the load burdens are also given in ohms. The total burden Z_T consists of the transformer-secondary impedance, the interconnecting-lead impedance, and the impedance of the relays and other devices. Burdens are usually specified in voltamperes (VA) at a unit voltage or current base. For example, a relay is specified with a 5-A 60-Hz base. The burden is given as 0.24-Ω impedance. The actual load in voltamperes with 5-A base is equal to I^2Z; that is, $5^2 \times 0.24 = 6$ VA. The current transformer loads are generally given with a current base, whereas the potential transformer loads are given with a voltage base.

Consider a voltmeter with a burden of 3020 Ω impedance at 120-V 60-Hz base. The load in voltamperes would be $V^2/Z = (120)^2/3020 = 4.8$ VA.

If we wish to add loads of different base quantities in voltamperes, we use the following formula:

$$\mathrm{VA}_2 = \mathrm{VA}_1\,(I_2/I_1)^2 \qquad \text{or} \qquad \mathrm{VA}_1 = (V_2/V_1)^2$$

[1] American National Standards Institute.

We see then that the burdens vary as the square of the ratio of the base quantities.

To obtain the total burden, it is usually adequate to add the impedances arithmetically. If the performance depends on adding them vectorially, the calculation is too marginal and an alternate scheme should be considered.

17.5 TRANSFORMER ACCURACY

The accuracy of transformers of their specified range is very important. This is defined by ANSI for instrument transformers.

Instrument transformers are defined as *current* transformers or as *potential* (voltage) transformers. By further definition, an instrument transformer is a transformer in which the condition of current, voltage, or phase relations in the primary are faithfully reproduced in the secondary with acceptable accuracy. The question is "what is acceptable accuracy?" In order to ensure that everyone has the same idea of accuracy, ANSI has published definitions of accuracy. Broadly defined, it involves many definitions and subdefinitions; however, briefly explained, it is "the accuracy of an instrument transformer from its marked ratio and phase angle." It can be expressed as a percent deviation in ratio with phase angle also specified and related to specific input and burden conditions.

In order to understand accuracy classification, it is necessary to obtain definitions for some specific terms.

1. *True ratio.* This is the ratio of rms primary current or voltage to the rms secondary current or voltage under specific conditions.

2. *Marked ratio.* The ratio of primary current or voltage to the secondary current or voltage as specified on the nameplate.

3. *Ratio correction factor.* The factor by which the nameplate (marked) ratio is to be multiplied by to obtain the "true" ratio.

4. *Burden.* The property of the secondary circuit which determines the flow of true and reactive power from the transformer. It can be expressed in impedance (or voltamperes) and power factor. The former is usually used for current transformers, and the latter applied to potential transformers.

5. *Phase angle.* In a current transformer it is the angle between the primary-current vector and the secondary-current vector reversed. The angle is considered positive when the reversed-current vector leads the primary-vector. It is designated by the symbol β (beta).

6. *Phase angle.* Of a potential transformer this is the angle between the primary-voltage vector and the secondary-voltage vector reversed. It is considered positive when the reversed secondary leads the primary vector. It is designated by γ (gamma).

7. *Phase-angle correction factor.* This is essentially for wattmeters and watt-hour meters operated by one or more instrument transformers and it is "the factor by which the reading of a wattmeter or watt-hour meter must be multiplied to correct for errors in phase displacement due to the measuring apparatus." The factor equals the ratio of the true power factor to the apparent power factor.

8. *Instrument-transformer correction factor.* The factor by which a wattmeter reading must be multiplied to correct for the effect of the instrument-transformer ratio correction factor and phase angle.

The following abbreviations are also used: ratio correction factor (RCF), phase-angle correction factor (PACF), instrument-transformer correction factor (TCF), phase angle error (PAE). These terms are used when the accuracy "classes of transformers" are defined.

17.6 ACCURACY CLASS–POTENTIAL TRANSFORMERS

The potential transformer accuracy is defined by class. The accuracy of a transformer is a function of the burden. The *class* of accuracy is therefore related to a finite burden. The standard burdens are defined by letter and are shown in Table 17.1.

TABLE 17.1 ANSI Standard Burdens for Potential Transformers

Burden	*Voltamperes at 120 V*	*Burden power factor*
W	12.5	0.10
X	25.0	0.70
Y	75.0	0.85
Z	200.0	0.85
ZZ	400.0	0.85

NOTE: Standard burdens for potential transformers shall have the same voltampere and power-factor values for all frequencies.

The standard burdens are only a reference point by which other burdens can be related to. The accuracy class is defined in Table 17.2.

A potential transformer, then, can be rated by class and burden, giving a range of acceptable accuracies within limits. Some examples are:

- 0.3W, 0.3X, 0.6Y, 1.2Z,
- 0.3W, 0.6X, 1.2Y

TABLE 17.2 ANSI Accuracy Classes for Potential Transformers

Accuracy class	*Limits of ratio correction factor and transformer correction factor*	*Limits of power factor (lagging) of metered power load*
1.2	1.012–0.988	0.6–1.0
0.6	1.006–0.994	0.6–1.0
0.3	1.003–0.997	0.6–1.0

NOTE: The limits given for each accuracy class apply from 10% above rated voltage to 10% below rated voltage, at rated frequency, and from no burden on the potential transformer to the specified burden, maintaining the power factor of the specified burden.

If a class is omitted, as in the last example, this is an indication that the error for that burden was in excess of the poorest allowable.

This method only classifies transformers in groups of accuracy over a certain range. In order to determine the accuracy of an individual transformer specifically, it is necessary to test it or have it calibrated and certified.

17.7 ACCURACY CLASS–CURRENT TRANSFORMERS

The accuracy of current transformers is also related to the burden; therefore, in order to define accuracies, the burdens must be defined. These are given in Table 17.3, and the correction factors are given in Table 17.4.

TABLE 17.3 ANSI Standard Current-Transformer Burdens

	Burden characteristics		*Secondary burden at 60-Hz and 5-A secondary current*		
Designation of burden	*Resistance, Ω*	*Inductance, millihenrys*	*Impedance, Ω*	*Voltamperes*	*Power factor*
B-0.1	0.09	0.116	0.1	2.5	0.9
B-0.2	0.18	0.232	0.2	5.0	0.9
B-0.5	0.45	0.580	0.5	12.5	0.9
B-1	0.5	2.3	1.0	25.0	0.5
B-2	1.0	4.6	2.0	50.0	0.5
B-4	2.0	9.2	4.0	100.0	0.5
B-8	4.0	18.4	8.0	200.0	0.5

TABLE 17.4 ANSI Accuracy Classes for Metering Current Transformers

Accuracy class	*Limits of ratio correction factor and transformer correction factor*				*Limits of power factor (lagging) of metered power load*
	*100% rated current**		*10% rated current*		
	Min.	*Max.*	*Min.*	*Max.*	
1.2	0.988	1.012	0.976	1.024	0.6-1.0
0.6	0.994	1.006	0.988	1.012	0.6-1.0
0.3	0.997	1.003	0.994	1.006	0.6-1.0

* These limits also apply at the maximum continuous-thermal current, which is the product of rated current and the continuous-thermal-current rating factor.

By associating the class with the burden we have the following examples of a current transformer rating.

- 0.3B0.1, 0.3B0.2, 0.3B0.5, 0.3B2 or
- 0.3B0.1, 0.3B0.2, 0.6B0.5, 1.2B2
- 0.6B0.1, 0.6B0.2, 1.2B0.5

Note that the last part of the last example indicates that the accuracy at this burden is worse than the poorest allowable.

There is one other consideration with current transformers that potential transformers do not have to contend with. This is the sudden increase in primary current under short-circuit conditions. This must be faithfully reproduced in the secondary to provide the correct signals to the relays. Current transformers all have the secondaries rated at 5 A. The variation in turns ratio is referenced by the primary, that is, 100:5, 500:5, etc. Since power transformers are designed to limit short circuits to 20 to 25 times normal current, the expected current appearing at the secondary of a current transformer is based on "20 times normal" as a standard. This means that the secondary current would be considered up to $5 \times 20 = 100$ A. In actual fact the transformer does not "deliver a current," it "produces a voltage proportional to the current in the primary." These secondary voltages classes are 10, 20, 50, 100, 200, 400, and 800 V. The standard percent ratio-error classes are in two groups; these are 2.5% and 10%.

One other "two-group" classification is the accuracy of performance over the complete range of change in current, that is, from normal to 20 times normal. This is defined as H class or L class. The H-class transformer is accurate with a nearly constant percentage ratio error when delivering a

TABLE 17.5 Standard Accuracy Classes for H-Class Current Transformers for Relaying-Service High Internal Secondary Impedance

Standard accuracy class rating				*Secondary terminal voltage and burden limitations for overcurrent performance within the specified accuracy class*			
Standard accuracy class				*For 100- to 25-Amp secondary-current range*		*For 25- to 5-Amp secondary-current range*	
10% ratio error (1)	*2.5-% ratio error (2)*	*60-Hz standard burden (3)*	*Standard secondary terminal voltage at 100 amps, volts (4)*	*Secondary terminal voltage (5)*	*Burden impedance ohms§ (6)*	*Burden impedance ohms† (7)*	*Secondary terminal voltage‡ (8)*
10 H 10	2.5 H 10	B 0.1	10	10	10/amp	0.4	0.4 × amp
10 H 20	2.5 H 20	B 0.2	20	20	20/amp	0.8	0.8 × amp
10 H 50	2.5 H 50	B 0.5	50	50	50/amp	2	2 × amp
10 H 100	2.5 H 100	B 1.0	100	100	100/amp	4	4 × amp
10 H 200	2.5 H 200	B 2.0	200	200	200/amp	8	8 × amp
10 H 400	2.5 H 400	B 4.0	400	400	400/amp	16	16 × amp
10 H 800	2.5 H 800	B 8.0	800	800	800/amp	32	32 × amp

† Resistance and inductance values in each case are four times those for the corresponding standard burden given in column 3 of this table. See standard burdens.

§ The entries in column 6 indicate that the limiting value of the burden ohms is equal to the rated secondary terminal voltage, given in column 5, divided by the secondary current flowing. The resistance-inductance ratio of the burden thus determined is in each case the same as the resistance-inductance ratio of the corresponding standard burden listed in column 3 of this table. See Burdens.

‡ The entries in column 8 indicate that the limiting secondary terminal voltage is equal to the limiting burden ohms, given in column 7, multiplied by the secondary current flowing.

TABLE 17.6 Standard Accuracy Classes for L-Class Current Transformers For Relaying-Service Low Internal Secondary Impedance

Standard accuracy class rating				*Secondary terminal voltage and burden limitations for overcurrent performance within the specified accuracy class*	
Standard accuracy class				*For 5- to 100-A secondary-current range*	
10% ratio error (1)	*2.5% ratio error (2)*	*60-Hz standard burden (3)*	*Standard secondary terminal voltage at 100 A, volts (4)*	*Burden impedance ohms* (5)*	*Secondary terminal voltage† (6)*
10 L 10	2.5 L 10	B 0.1	10	0.1	0.1 × amp
10 L 20	2.5 L 20	B 0.2	20	0.2	0.2 × amp
10 L 50	2.5 L 50	B 0.5	50	0.5	0.5 × amp
10 L 100	2.5 L 100	B 1.0	100	1.0	1.0 × amp
10 L 200	2.5 L 200	B 2.0	200	2.0	2.0 × amp
10 L 400	2.5 L 400	B 4.0	400	4.0	4.0 × amp
10 L 800	2.5 L 800	B 8.0	800	8.0	8.0 × amp

* Resistance and inductance values are in each case the same as those for the corresponding standard burden given in column 3 of this table. See standard burdens.

† The entries in column 6 indicate that the limiting secondary terminal voltage is equal to the limiting burden ohms given in column 5, multiplied by the secondary current flowing.

fixed secondary voltage over a wide range of currents. See Tables 17.5 and 17.6.

In contrast, the L-class transformer has a nearly constant magnitude of error over its range. Grasping the significance of this might be a little awkward; therefore, we will explain a little further. As accuracy is related to burden, if we take the standard secondary current at maximum 20 times normal, we have 100 A. If we take the standard secondary voltage divided by the 100 A, we obtain the burden on the secondary in ohms, that is, $200/100 = 2\ \Omega$. If this is "tied" to a ratio error class as previously defined, we can give an example as 2.5(L)200. This means that the error will not exceed more than 2.5% error over its "20 times normal" range when the burden is 200/100 Ω (see Table 17.6).

Consider an H-class current transformer. In order to maintain its accuracy, the ratio of burden to multiples of normal load current must remain constant; for example, 10% error of a transformer rated 10H200 would only be maintained under these conditions:

- 10% at 2 Ω (20 times normal load current)
- 10% at 4 Ω (10 times normal load current)
- 10% at 8 Ω (5 times normal load current)

By contrast, considering a transformer rated 10L200; this essentially states that the transformer is capable of operating within its 10% accuracy range with all burdens up to that burden which will equal the specified voltage at 100 A, or 20 times normal. In this case $200/100 = 2\ \Omega$.

We see then that the H type must have the load impedance related to a portion of the multiples of load current whereas the L type is good up to 20 times normal load current for all burdens. See Tables 17.5 and 17.6 for the L and H class parameters.

17.8 BUSHING-TYPE CURRENT TRANSFORMERS

As briefly mentioned earlier, there are two basic types of current transformer. The bushing type is a toroid-wound secondary winding that is slipped over a conductor, which can be a copper bus or a single insulated conductor. It is the lower in cost of the two types of the same size and has a low-leakage reactance secondary; hence, these are designated L types.

Bushing transformers are used on switchgear; both small indoor metal-clad and large utility breakers. They are also available with multiple taps. If there is a problem with ratios, sometimes two can be installed on the one phase with the secondaries connected in series.

The bushing type of CT is also utilized as a possible test unit. It is designed to be split, placed around the conductor, reclosed, and used to measure current in existing installations.

17.9 THROUGH-TYPE (IN-LINE) CURRENT TRANSFORMER

This type of CT is built as a complete unit with a primary and a concentrated secondary winding. The installation is made by cutting the phase conductor and inserting the CT; then reconnecting the ends of the phase conductor to the ends of the CT primary. This CT has a high-leakage reactance and therefore is H class. Because of the added cost of including the primary in the construction, it would be a more expensive CT.

17.10 POLARITY

The polarity of an instrument transformer refers to the relative direction of current and voltage at a particular instant in time during the positive half cycle.

The standard method of identification of polarity is by use of a "dot" or an "X" on the identified terminal. This would be H_1 on the primary side and X_1 on the secondary side.

For a current transformer the current is considered to be "entering" at terminal H_1 and "coming out" of the secondary terminal X_1 and essentially "in phase" with the primary current.

For a potential transformer the identified terminals H_1 (primary) and X_1 (secondary) are both considered positive with respect to the unidentified terminals with the primary and secondary voltages essentially "in phase." See Fig. 17.1.

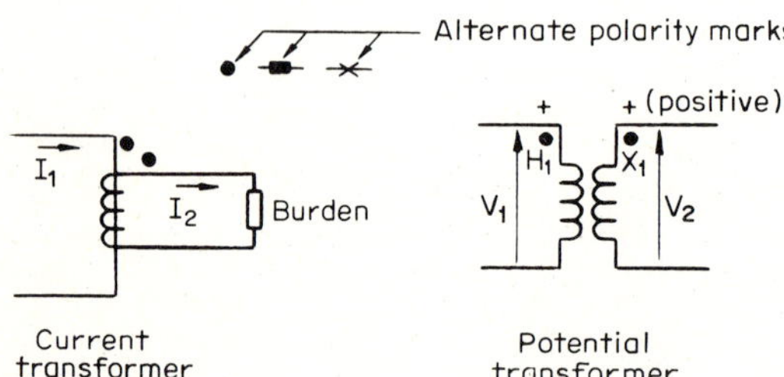

Figure 17.1 Instrument-transformer polarity identification.

17.11 CURRENT-TRANSFORMER SATURATION

The problem of current-transformer saturation is important enough to warrant some discussion. A current transformer will (nearly) faithfully reproduce a voltage in the secondary winding which is proportional to the current in the primary. This is true up to a point; as the current begins to increase, the magnetic core produces an increase in flux. Past a certain increase in current, the magnetic core becomes "saturated" and will not produce additional flux. The result is that further increase in current in the primary will not show up in the secondary. In actual fact, some slight increase will show in the secondary, but it will not be "proportional" to the input.

Saturation curves for a particular current transformer are made available by the transformer manufacturer and should be requested for the current transformers which are intended to be ordered. Figure 17.2 shows the saturation curves for a family of ratios for a *multitap* current transformer. It is also noticeable that as the ratios are increased and more magnetic core is introduced, the point at which the curve begins to flatten, or "saturate," becomes higher.

If the current transformer is to be used for metering, the operating point should be on the vertical linear portion of the curve. If the CT is used for relaying, it is desirable that the current coil on the relay not be subjected to higher currents than rated. If the maximum current rating of the relay is located on the flat part of the curve, the excess is limited. Here, the saturation phenomenon is advantageous. See Fig. 17.2.

17.12 MULTITAP CURRENT TRANSFORMERS

Current transformers can be purchased with multiple ratios on the primary, all related to a 5-A secondary. Although this may seem advantageous, sometimes a problem occurs because the lowest ratios provide too much current for the relays. The multitap current transformer cannot be ordered indiscriminately. Even though multitaps exist, the correct calculations should still be made and a specific ratio assigned for the duty expected. The multitap feature should be reserved for possible change to loads in the future.

17.13 INSTRUMENT-TRANSFORMER CONNECTIONS

Instrument-transformer connections make use of the star and delta connections. They also use the open star and open delta and the star-star. The connections then are not new or special. They are the standard connections that were described in the section on transformers. The point to keep in mind with instrument transformers is the significance of the phase shift when using a star-delta combination. There is a shift of 30° which occurs whenever this arrangement is used. This means that for delta-connected CTs, the current will be affected by the factor $\sqrt{3}$.

Potential transformers are rated for 120 V secondary for relaying which is the "line-to-line" transformer voltage of the primary, not "line to neutral," as with conventional secondary star connections. This means that if a protec-

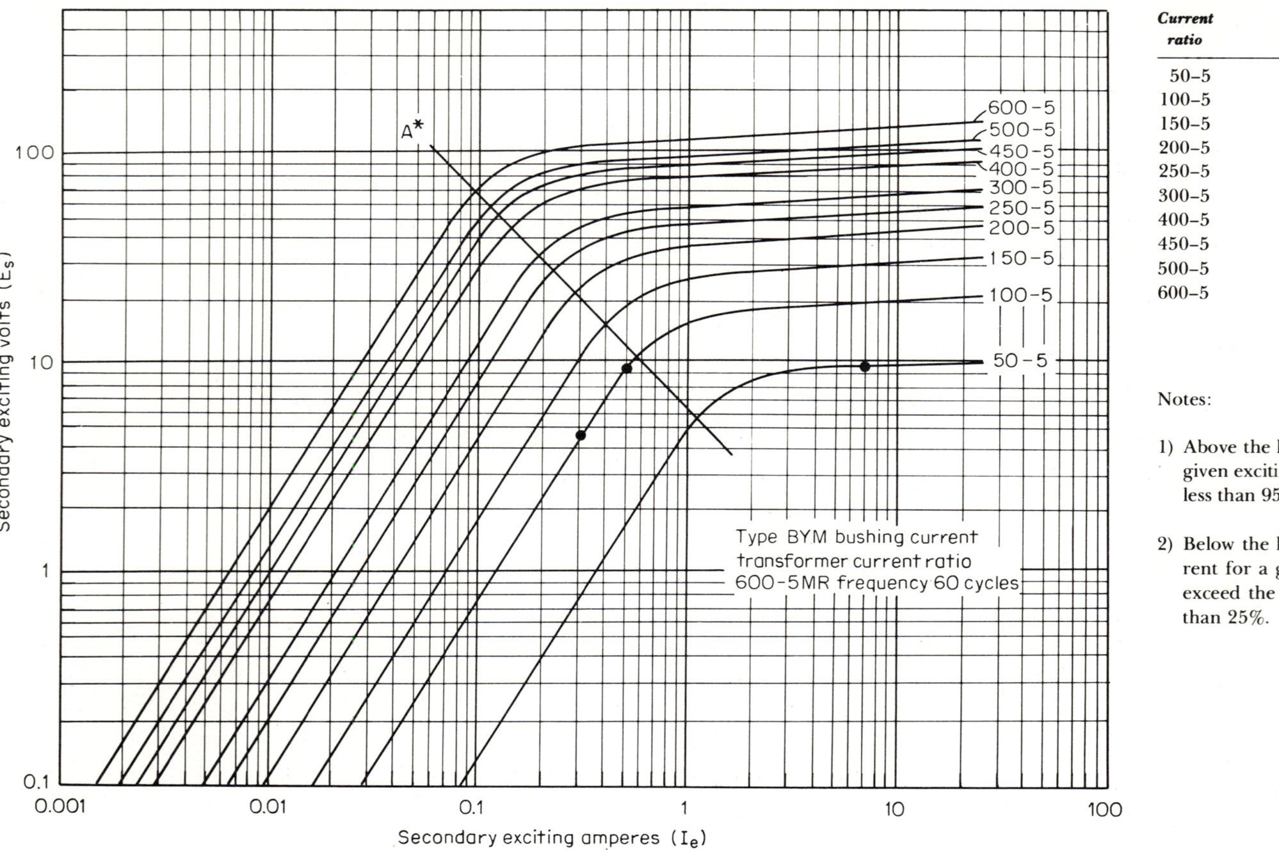

Current ratio	*Turn ratio*	*Sec. res.*
50–5	10–1	.061
100–5	20–1	.082
150–5	30–1	.104
200–5	40–1	.125
250–5	50–5	.146
300–5	60–1	.168
400–5	80–1	.211
450–5	90–1	.230
500–5	100–1	.242
600–5	120–1	.296

Notes:

1) Above the line, the voltage for a given exciting current will not be less than 95% of the curve value.

2) Below the line, the exciting current for a given voltage will not exceed the curve value by more than 25%.

Figure 17.2 Typical excitation curves for a multiratio bushing current transformer with an ANSI accuracy classification of 10L100.

tive relay or instrument is rated in line-to-neutral voltage, its coil is usually $120/\sqrt{3} = 60$ V.

By using the full range of transformer connections in relaying, phase angles in the ratio of 30° can be added to, subtracted from, or cancelled out in various relaying schemes.

18 CAPACITORS

18.1 CAPACITORS

Capacitors are essentially devices to contribute leading reactive power to a system. There are two basic types: the *shunt* capacitor and the *series* capacitor. The former type is used virtually exclusively for power-factor correction, while the second type finds limited use in problems associated with regulation. The average electrical designer will rarely have to consider the use of series capacitors and they have already been discussed in some detail in sec. 16.9; therefore, we will not discuss the series capacitor again in this chapter.

The shunt capacitor, however, has many applications in industrial power systems; therefore, the main topics will concern this equipment.

18.2 CAPACITORS AND POWER FACTOR

In the industrial plant there are many pieces of equipment which contribute to poor power factor. This equipment may run continuously or intermittently; either way can be a problem. By judicious use of the shunt capacitor, the lagging power factor attributed to these devices can be nullified or nearly cancelled out. As the power transmitted over a conductor (i.e., branch circuit or feeder) is the vector sum of the "real" current and "reactive" current, by locating capacitors at the load, the reactive current can be supplied direct from the capacitors. This means that the circuit conductors now only have to carry the real current.

This can be shown by the following equations:

$$\text{kVA} = \sqrt{\text{kW}^2 + \text{kvar}^2}$$

and

$$I_{\text{kVA}} = \sqrt{I_{\text{kW}}^2 + I_{\text{kvar}}^2}$$

Consider the example of a line current of 100 A and kW current of 80 A. By transposing the formula, we have:

$$I_{\text{kvar}} = \sqrt{I_{\text{kVA}}^2 - I_{\text{kW}}^2}$$
$$= \sqrt{100^2 - 80^2}$$
$$= 60 \text{ A}$$

Since the power factor is a ratio of kW/kVA, we can also use the ratio of $I_{\text{kW}}/I_{\text{kVA}} = 80/100 = 0.8$, or 80%. We see then that, if we apply capacitors of the correct size, we can make a reduction in circuit loading, which in turn means a reduction of heat in the conductor. Note that, although the reactive portion of the current was 60 A, we could not deduct this directly from the line current. We could only deduct it vectorially, which means that instead of carrying 100 A as indicated by a clip on ammeter, we would now be carrying 80 A, which is the amount of the real current. The savings, then, is about 20% in conductor loading but with the additional benefit of improving the system power factor. The amount of improvement to the system power factor would depend on the effect of these few kvars on the total system. This has to be considered when evaluating the cost of such an installation.

18.3 SHUNT CAPACITOR UNIT

The shunt capacitor unit is generally rated in three standard voltages: 240, 480, and 600 V. They are also available in single-phase and three-phase units. In turn, the units can be banked into a standard package of the correct kvar or (ckvar) as it is sometimes termed.

The standard sizes for 240 V are:

$2\frac{1}{2}$, 5, $7\frac{1}{2}$, 10, 15, 20, 25 ckvar

The standard sizes for 480 V are:

2, 3, 4, 5, 6, $7\frac{1}{2}$, 10, 15, 20, 25, 30, 35, 40, 45, 50, 60 ckvar.

The standard sizes for 600 V are:

5, $7\frac{1}{2}$, 10, 15, 20, 25, 30, 35, 40, 45, 50, 60 ckvar.

For other voltages which are nonstandard, such as 208 V, it is better to contact the manufacturer for specific details. Capacitors can be connected in parallel to provide more capacitance (ckvar), or they can be connected in series to reduce the voltage across a capacitor. For instance, on a 480-V circuit, two 240-V units in series would provide half the ckvar of a single unit, while two 480-V units on a 480-V circuit connected in parallel would provide twice the output of a single unit.

This problem generally does not occur because capacitor banks are purchased as package units for specific applications, but a designer should know the effect of connecting capacitors in parallel and series.

$$C_T = c_1 + c_2 + c_3 + \cdots \quad \text{for parallel connection}$$

$$C_T = \frac{1}{1/c_1 + 1/c_2 + 1/c_3 + \cdots} \quad \text{for series connection}$$

Each capacitor must be fitted with a discharge resistor across its terminals. This is required by code and it must discharge the capacitor in a certain period of time. The National Electric Code states that for capacitors under 600 V it must be reduced to 50 V within one minute. The Code allows for automatic-discharge equipment, but in general the fixed resistor is the usual method of discharge.

18.4 CAPACITOR SIZING (SYSTEM)

Although a capacitor is rated in the unit of capacitance (farad or "microfarad), for power-factor correction the units are rated in ckvar (capacitive reactive voltamperes). The units necessary for calculating capacitor sizes are: (power factor and kVA), or (kW and kVA). These can generally be obtained from the plant metering. Consider a very simplified example of a plant with a 1000-kVA load at a power factor of 0.6. It is desired to improve the power factor to 95% to avoid a penalty surcharge.

$$\begin{aligned} \text{kW} &= \text{kVA} \times \text{power factor} \\ &= 1000 \times 0.6 \\ &= 600 \text{ kW} \\ \text{kvar} &= \sqrt{\text{kVA}^2 - \text{kW}^2} \\ &= \sqrt{1000^2 - 600^2} \\ &= 800 \text{ kvar} \end{aligned}$$

To improve the power factor to 95%, the kW remains the same, but we must reduce the input power which is the kVA. This is done by taking the existing kW and dividing by the new power factor, or 600/0.95 = 632 kVA. If we now plug this into our standard equation, we have:

$$\begin{aligned} \text{kvar} &= \sqrt{632^2 - 600^2} \\ &= 199 \text{ ckvar} \end{aligned}$$

By subtracting the 199 ckvar from the existing 800 kvar, we find that we require 601 ckvar to correct to 95% power factor. This is approximately 100% of the kW load. The next question to determine is the cost of correcting compared with the cost of paying the penalty. An alternative may be to correct it to a lower figure. To simplify the calculations somewhat, the following equation is much simpler but "trig" tables are required. *Note:* For a power factor of 0.6, $\cos^{-1} 0.6$ is 53° and $\cos^{-1} 0.95$ is 18°.

Required ckvar = kW (tan ϕ_1 − tan ϕ_2)

For the previous example, we would have

$$\text{ckvar} = 600\ (1.327 - 0.3249)$$

$$= 601 \text{ ckvar}$$

We would therefore select the units providing the closest to 600 kvar, for example, twelve 50-ckvar units.

18.5 CAPACITOR SIZING (MOTORS)

The sizing of capacitors for a particular motor depends on some of the characteristics of the motor. Obviously, if the power factor of a motor varies with loading, we need to know the power factor of the particular motor under normal running conditions.

The National Electric Code limits the corrective ckvar allowed on the load side of a motor controller to a value which will raise the no-load power factor to unity. The no-load power factor is the "worse condition" power factor.

One other point to consider is that, if capacitors are added to a motor on the load side of the controller, the motor running overcurrent protection will only "see" the (kW) amps and not the (kVA) amps as originally expected; therefore, the "heaters" or overcurrent protection for the motor must be reduced in size.

Most designs are done before the motors are ordered, when the power factor of the motors is not known. If the motors are required to have capacitors installed, the motor should be ordered complete with capacitors to be switched on the load side of the motor controller. The manufacturer of the motor will then be able to match the capacitors to the exact characteristics of the motor and also specify the reduced value necessary for motor running overcurrent protection.

18.6 CAPACITOR EFFECT ON SWITCHGEAR

When we talk about capacitor switching, we must consider a capacitor-bank installation which has to be switched either manually or automatically, and also the alternative situation, in which capacitors are added to existing circuits as an extra piece of equipment to be switched by the circuit switchgear. According to the National Electric Code a disconnecting means shall be provided in each ungrounded conductor for each capacitor bank and it shall not be less than 135% of the rated current of the capacitor(s).

Due to possible harmonics producing overcurrents due to overvoltages, manufacturers recommend oversize current ratings for different types of switchgear.

- For fused and unfused safety switches, use 165%.
- For enclosed-type contactors, use 150%.

- For large air circuit breakers, use 135%.
- For open-type contactors, use 135%.
- For molded-case circuit breakers, use 150%.

The above recommendations are minimum oversizing; however, most capacitor manufacturers publish tables which are associated with their capacitors. These give more precise sizing according to the design characteristics of the switchgear.

If a capacitor bank is installed with an incomplete number of capacitors, the switchgear associated with that bank should be sized on the basis that the bank is completely filled.

Considering the capacitor banks which are essentially a systems power-factor-correction device, we will probably find that during periods of light loads the regulation of the line is affected. In this case automatic switching is usually employed to disconnect the capacitors if the voltage rise becomes excessive. There are two ways of accomplishing this. First, the switchgear used must have overcurrent protection for each ungrounded conductor. If an air circuit breaker is used, this is already provided for. Alternately, if a contactor is used for automatic switching, it is necessary to have a fused switch ahead of the contactor to provide the overcurrent protection. Either method will work, but economics will eventually dictate the preference.

The signal to control the automatic function can be provided by a current relay, voltage relay, or timer. A timer would be programmed to switch on when the plant starts and switch off when the plant shuts down. This is a simple installation, but the timer has to be reset to coincide with working hours or peak loading times. Of the current and voltage control signals, the current-sensitive is preferred over the voltage-sensitive signal.

Overvoltages can occur from sources other than capacitors, and the capacitors are required to be on during the busiest production period. Since the main function of a voltage relay is power-factor correction, it is possible that it could shut the capacitors off when they are in fact needed most.

The automatic switching should not be blindly selected; the problem must be studied and the alternates considered. The current signal is probably a good compromise between economy and performance.

The switching of capacitors on branch circuits and small feeders is usually done by the normal switching devices of the circuit conductors, with the capacitors being attached to the conductors by fuse-protected taps. The disconnecting means *is not* required to open all ungrounded conductors simultaneously; therefore, fuses are adequate. They are usually supplied as part of the capacitor and should be specified this way when ordered.

18.7 CAPACITOR EFFECT ON CONDUCTORS

When we consider capacitor circuit conductors, we must evaluate both the conductors connecting the capacitors to the line and the line conductors themselves. The conductors from the capacitor units must be a minimum 135% of the rated current of the capacitor. In addition, if the capacitors are connected to the motor-circuit conductors or motor terminals, they must be not less than one-third the ampacity of the motor branch-circuit conductors.

Another factor to keep in mind with circuit conductors is that capacitors are rated on a 40°C ambient, while the National Electric Code bases the ambient temperature for conductor ampacities on 30°C. Therefore, the conductors should be derated to 40°C ambient. This means that the most popular conductor, that is, 75°C rated THW, would be derated to 0.88 of its ampacity. Because the capacitor is a "fully loaded" device, it will have a 100% load current all the time.

Consider a capacitor load of 100 A. At 135% the conductor rating must be 135 A. According to the NEC, 1/0 at 75°C has an ampacity of 150 A. If this is derated to 0.88, as required for a 40°C ambient, it is rerated at 132 A. This means that the conductor is undersized and is in fact only 132% of the load current; therefore, a higher-amperage conductor must be used.

18.8 CAPACITOR EFFECT ON TRANSFORMERS

A transformer magnetizing current is a source of harmonics which are added to the fundamental frequency. A distortion to the 60-cycle sine wave means a change in the rms voltage. This change may be insignificant and therefore generally ignored; however, it can exist. A capacitor has the facility to amplify or smooth out these harmonics, depending on the particular circuit arrangement.

The reactance of a capacitor is a function of frequency, as shown in the formula $X_c = 10^6/2\pi fC$ in ohms. Since the current I_c varies with E/X, the current due to harmonics I_h will vary with the voltage due to harmonics E_h, or $I_h = E_h/X_c$. Since the reactance X_c is inversely proportional to the frequency, we see that harmonics added to the fundamental will increase the frequency, decrease the reactance, and therefore increase the current. If current increase is excessive or even transient in nature, the increase may be enough to blow the fuses. The ckvar of capacitors on a transformer bank should not exceed 65% of the transformer kVA rating unless sectionally switched as required.

18.9 CAPACITORS–VOLTAGE AND FREQUENCY

The voltage rise due to capacitors can be calculated. If a capacitor bank is installed at the secondary of a transformer, the voltage rise can be calculated by the equation

$$\text{Percent rise } V_c = \frac{\text{ckvar} \times \%Z \text{ (transformer)}}{\text{kVA (transformer)}}$$

On a distribution line with rise at capacitor bank

$$\text{Percent voltage rise} = \frac{\text{ckvar} \times d \times X}{(\text{kV})^2 \times 10}$$

where ckvar is three-phase rating, d is the distance in unit length, X is line reactance in ohms per unit length, and kV is line-to-line voltage.

The voltage drop in an existing circuit can be calculated from the formula:

$$e = RI \cos \phi \pm XI \sin \phi$$

where e is the voltage drop in volts and $\cos \phi$ is the power factor. It is a simple procedure to plug in the new values for $\cos \phi$ (and subsequently $\sin \phi$) which would reflect the new power factor as contributed by the selected capacitors; this will then indicate the voltage rise.

In some cases the line voltage will not be the same as the rated voltage of the capacitor and this will affect the ckvar output; therefore, a corrected figure can be determined by the following:

$$\text{Actual corrected ckvar} = \text{ckvar} \times \left(\frac{\text{measured voltage}}{\text{nameplate voltage}}\right)^2$$

The capacitors should be limited to a maximum voltage of 110% of nameplate rating.

Although the frequency will rarely change in an industrial plant, it may be necessary to consider another frequency if the project is in a foreign country. The change in ckvar can be calculated by the following:

$$\text{Actual corrected ckvar} = \frac{\text{rated ckvar} \times \text{new frequency}}{\text{nameplate frequency}}$$

18.10 CAPACITOR RATINGS

A capacitor must have a nameplate which gives the maker's name, rated voltage, frequency, ckvar or amperes, number of phases and, the amount and type of liquid in gallons and identified as flammable or nonflammable.

It should be noted that it is not required to show the capacitance in farads (microfarads). If the rating must be obtained in microfarads, the following method can be used.

$$I_c = E/X_c$$

where the I_c is the capacitor load current, E is the line voltage, and X_c is the capacitor reactance.

In order to determine the capacitance, we first obtain the reactance in ohms:

$$X_c = E/I_c$$

The E and I_c can be obtained from the capacitor nameplate, and give

$$X_c = 10^6/2\pi fC$$

By cross-multiplying, we can obtain the following:

$$C = 10^6/2\pi fX_c \qquad \text{in microfarads}$$

Since the frequency is also on the nameplate, it is a simple matter to substitute; we then only need to complete the necessary arithmetic.

19 CONTROL RELAYS AND DEVICES

19.1 INDUSTRIAL CONTROL

The automatic and/or remote control of industrial equipment is accomplished predominantly by simple relays and switches. This is not to be confused with "protective" relaying, which is far more sophisticated.

Before commencing design of a control circuit, it is necessary to select the control-system voltage. Relays are available up to a 600-V rating; however, the majority of control systems are designed for a nominal 120-V system. The 120-V ac circuit is advantageous for a number of reasons.

1. 120 V is readily available by use of a single-control power transformer or individual-control power transformers on motor starters.
2. 120 V is a fairly "safe" voltage, although any voltage over 50 V should be considered lethal.
3. 120 V is a high enough voltage to overcome insulating films which sometimes develop on contact faces.
4. 120 V can be picked up at any lighting panel circuit, although not recommended for control. See item 1.
5. 120 V provides reasonable distance without having to consider voltage drop.
6. Troubleshooting is sometimes done "live" even though circuits should be deenergized. In this case a 120-V pigtail socket and lamp is adequate to check circuits.
7. 300-V relays can be used.

Unless there is some reason to consider otherwise, the 120-V ac control circuit should be the first consideration.

19.2 CONTROL-CIRCUIT CONDUCTORS

In Class 1 circuits (remote-control and signalling circuits) conductors larger than No. 14 shall be protected against overcurrent in accordance with their rating as given in tables listing the conductor ampacities. For conductors No. 18, 16, and 14, they shall be considered as being protected by overcurrent devices of not over 20 A. However, always check the exact code requirement.

There are a number of factors to consider. First, a conductor must stand up to rough handling during construction. It is pulled through conduits more forcefully than gently. It must be terminated on relays and terminal blocks quickly and simply. Using No. 18 and/or No. 16 conductors would mean purchase of wire specifically for control; the wire would be lightweight and have higher voltage drop than the No. 14 or No. 12. It could possibly be damaged when pulled into conduits, and furthermore, the insulation must be 600 V.

Comparing these against No. 14 or No. 12, we find that No. 12 is usually the minimum size specified for lighting and small power loads; therefore it is purchased in bulk. If No. 14 is used, it must be ordered especially for control. Since the circuit protection is allowed to 20 A for the No. 14 or No. 12 (for Class 1 circuits), either is satisfactory. It is a little more difficult to terminate a No. 12 than a No. 14, owing to the stiffness of the wire, but the stiffness can be an advantage in preventing a wire loop opening when a screw is tightened down. Therefore, the terminating objections are self-cancelling.

From a "field" point of view a No. 12 means that the wire used for lighting and light power circuits can also be used for control, which eliminates another size. The voltage drop would be less than with the No. 14, and pulling No. 12 with larger-size conductors would lessen the possibility of damage because of its slightly heavier size. More current-carrying capacity is also an advantage, that is, 20 A against 15 A, or 33% more.

In some cases the client specification will outline the control-circuit parameters; if not, consider the 120-V circuit with No. 12 or 14 wire (600 V).

19.3 CONTROL RELAYS (GENERAL PURPOSE)

The general-purpose relay is a multicontact relay with a 300-V or 600-V standard insulation rating. It is available with various arrangements of contacts, with the general arrangement of the universal type, meaning that each contact can be wired for "normally open" or "normally closed." The contact ratings are generally 10 A for a noninductive load.

There are many other types of relays which can serve a general-purpose function, some of which are *plug-in* types. The only difference between these and the standard general-purpose types is that they are slightly lighter in construction and their contact ratings must be checked in the manufacturer's catalog. The fact that they are plug-in types makes them very attractive. Plug-in relays have a plastic or metal cover which excludes dust. This does not mean they are hermetically sealed, unless specified as such; moreover, they cannot be used in hazardous locations unless approved for Class and Group.

When ordering a relay, it is necessary to specify the coil voltage, the number of contacts, and the position of the contacts, for example, 4 N/O (normally open) and 4 N/C coil, 125 V, 300-V insulation class, panel mounting, 60 Hz.

To operate the relay, it is necessary to energize the coil; the solenoid then pulls in the armature, which in turn operates the contacts. In order for the contacts to remain closed, the power is maintained to the coil by a *seal-in* circuit. If the circuit is temporarily broken, the relay will drop out and remain open until reenergized.

19.4 LATCHING RELAY

The latching relay is a modified general-purpose relay. When energized, it closes the contacts and stays closed by a mechanical restraining mechanism. This means that only a pulse is necessary for it to close and remain closed. In order to open the relay contacts, it is necessary to apply a pulse to the "unlatching" coil. The advantage of the latching relay is that it will withstand shock loads, and in the case of an accidental shutdown it can ensure that, when the power is reapplied, a certain device is always the "first on."

19.5 TIMING RELAYS

A timing relay is designed to open or close a contact at a predetermined time after the power has been applied or removed. Timing relays always seem to cause some confusion, mainly in specifying the contact action and the relay itself.

A timing relay consists of two parts. The operating or (coil) part of the relay and the contact block part. The correct way to consider a timing relay

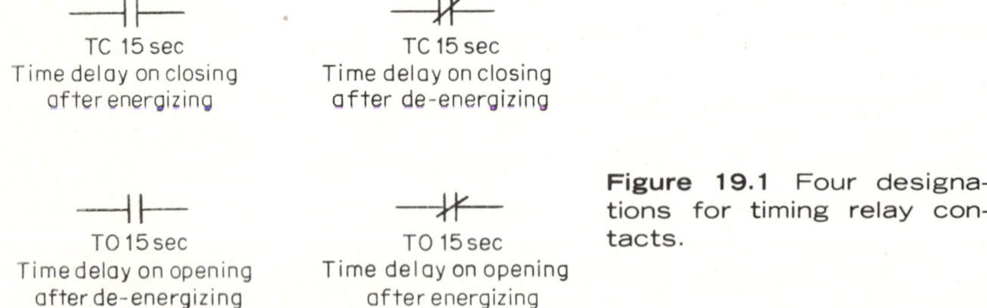

Figure 19.1 Four designations for timing relay contacts.

is to first consider the contact action required. This is simple. For a single-timed contact, there are only four possible ways it can be specified: open, closed, timed on energizing, timed on deenergizing. By using standard contact symbols, these can be simply shown. Note that contacts are always shown "off the shelf," that is, deenergized. See Fig. 19.1.

If a contact is shown normally closed and states "TC 15 sec," it should be obvious that it cannot close until it is first opened. Therefore, the symbol indicates "a normally closed contact which opens instantaneously and takes 15 seconds to close after deenergizing." No other explanations are necessary on the drawing. The same is true for the other designations. Standard symbols exist to identify timing contacts, but they are not absolutely necessary unless there is a strict policy of mandatory use of standard symbols.

The second part of selecting a timing relay should also be fairly simple. If the contacts have been decided upon, the *time-delay range* must have also been decided. In addition, the circuit function must also have been established to energize the (coil) part of the relay.

As far as the coil is concerned, this should be considered as having instantaneous action; that is, if power is applied, it instantly actuates the solenoid; if power is removed, the solenoid instantly drops out. The time delay, then, does not occur in the action of energizing the solenoid. So as far as the circuit is concerned, the designer shows a "coil" symbol and can summarize the circuit as follows, e.g.:

> When coil "A" energizes, the contact "A" will close after a 15-second delay.

The requirement for the timing relay has now been established. The next question is "can we find one to meet these requirements." First a number of details must be specified.

1. Voltage
2. Frequency
3. Number of timed contacts and type NC, NO, TC, TO
4. Time range (maximum)
5. Number of instantaneous contacts
6. Type of time-dial adjustments, that is, seconds, percent, etc.
7. Accuracy of timing
8. Repeatability of time operation (accuracy)
9. Interruptible or noninterruptible time sequence once timing has started
10. Type of mounting (plug-in or panel)
11. Type of enclosure
12. Temperature range

Timing relays fall into three basic groups

1. Gas- or liquid-displacement dashpot
2. Synchronous timing motor
3. Solid-state electronic timing

The dashpot or bellows-type timing device is about the oldest type of timing device, going back to the "sand bottle" or "sand egg timer" principle of controlled leakage. The modern version, however, is a precision device, rugged in construction and performance and a good general-purpose duty timing relay.

The synchronous-motor-type timer is in effect a counter. When the timing relay is energized, the synchronous motor provides a speed proportional to the frequency and therefore an accurate time base. By adjusting a clutch mechanism, the amount of revolutions or time can be made adjustable. This also is a good general-purpose relay with excellent timing accuracy. Compared with the dashpot type, the time delay can be affected by change in frequency, whereas the dashpot type is completely disassociated from the electrical vagaries.

The electronic timer is by far the most accurate with extreme preciseness not possible with mechanical means. The timing circuits are various combinations of the obvious *RLC* circuit (resistance, capacitance, reactance) with other circuits using magnetic cores, unijunction transistors, differential amplifiers, etc. The internal contents of the electronic timing relay are of no concern to the electrical designer. The wiring diagram supplied with the timing relay will show the connections which operate an imaginary (coil) and the timed and instantaneous contacts.

Timers, then, come in all shapes, sizes, and arrangements. The main consideration is the contact "time delays"; second is the coil signal. After that, the only concern beyond the operational portion are the qualifying specifications such as quality of performance and price.

19.6 THERMAL RELAYS

The thermal relay is mostly used in motor control and circuit-breaker operation. When current is increased, it produces a temperature rise proportional to I^2R. This shows that a 20% increase in current will produce a $(1.2)^2$, or 1.44 times temperature increase. The advantage or disadvantage, depending on the point of view, is the slow response time of this type of relay. The slow-acting feature is excellent for monitoring circuit currents for overloads because it will ignore transient increases and will only consider the rms value[1] of current increase, this being a more realistic measure of actual conductor temperatures. Since the current in the conductor is a measure of the current in a motor supplied by the conductor, by using the thermal relay on the branch-circuit conductors, we are in effect measuring the motor current. By sizing these thermal relays correctly, we can cause them to operate at a fixed percentage value of motor current. Because they are slow-acting, they will not operate during the transient "starting" period.

[1] The rms value is the root mean square value of the ac wave and the heating effect is proportional to the rms value.

19.7 MAGNETIC RELAY

The magnetic relay is not to be confused with the *solenoid*-operated control relay. The magnetic relay is used mainly in circuit-breaker trips and is overlapping into protective relaying. It can work in conjunction or separately with the thermal relay. The magnetic relay is basically a magnetic flux operating on a *reed*-type switch element. Because the flux is a function of current, a sudden increase in current will provide an increase in the magnetic flux. Unlike the thermal relay, there is no heat-loss compensation period; therefore, it is essentially nearly instantaneous acting. This means that it will act on all transients large enough to exceed the small inertia of the reed switch.

This is an ideal response for detecting short circuits. The problem is that when magnetic relays are used on motor circuits they will detect the inrush current during starting and trip the circuit. When using these magnetic relays, the trip must be set high enough so that they will not operate on motor starting (approximately 500% starting current). This means a setting of over 500% on the trip with a maximum of 700% as allowed by the NEC.

The main function of the magnetic trip relay is cable (conductor) short-circuit protection. It is essential to ascertain whether the short-circuit current is high enough to operate the relay above the 700% setting. Usually it is, but in some remote cases it could be marginal.

19.8 VIBRATION SWITCH

One device which falls in the category between a relay and a switch is the *vibration* switch. This is usually mounted on vertical pump motors. These pumps are very vulnerable to vibration. Since most of these pumps run unattended, a damaged impeller can cause vibration, which could seriously damage the bearings and possibly the winding of the motor. To preclude this type of failure, it is good practice to install these vibration switches on the motor. The switch contacts are then wired into the motor "running circuit."

The vibration switch is a simple device. It is essentially a pair of switch contacts set in an "inertia block" mount. When the amplitude of the vibration reaches a certain point, it overcomes the resistance offered by the inertia block; this in turn operates the contacts and signals the motor shutdown.

19.9 LIMIT SWITCH

The limit switch is a very simple device. It consists of a switch which is operated by a lever arm. Various arrangements of lever types, cams, and switch-contact arrangement offer a very versatile control component, without which the conveyor industry could barely exist. Like the timer, the limit switch requires proper specification as to its action relative to the contacts. It is necessary then to consider the following points:

1. Voltage
2. Current rating
3. Single-throw or double-throw action
4. Single-pole or multiple-pole switch
5. NO or NC contacts relative to operator position
6. Type of actuating arm (roller, yoke, push rod, etc.)
7. Spring-return lever
8. Non-spring-return lever
9. Snap-action switch or slow-action switch
10. Enclosure type

When shown on a schematic drawing the switch (and operating arm symbol) should be shown in the off-the-shelf position. If further explanation is necessary, regarding the action that takes place, it should be covered by adding "see note 1," (or other number) and explain the action in the note. There are standard symbols for limit switch presentation; these are shown in the symbol lists.

19.10 PHOTOCELL SWITCH

The photocell switch is basically a version of a limit switch. It is a simple device consisting of a light-actuated switch and a light source. This type of switch would be used where the product operating the switch cannot be touched by a lever arm. The light is set up in a location and "beamed" directly into the receiver. This operates the contacts, maintaining them open or closed. When the light beam is interrupted (broken) by an object passing through it, the contacts transfer to the other mode.

Sometimes a problem can exist by high ambient light operating the photocell switch. This can be eliminated by using an infrared filter over the light source, which also makes the beam invisible to the naked eye. By using a fairly sophisticated receiver, it is possible to reflect the light beam around corners by means of mirrors with a loss in light of about 8 to 10% per mirror. This, however, is a specialized installation and not the general industrial-control-type problem.

19.11 PRESSURE AND FLOW SWITCHES

These types of switches monitor mechanical conditions of liquid flow and pressures. Again, the electrical designer is not concerned with the method used by the switch manufacturer to operate the switch. The electrical designer's concern is that the switch is NC or NO when flow is present or not present. The same considerations apply as with the limit switches. The flow and pressure switches should be shown on a schematic in their off-the-shelf arrangement. The symbols are also fairly explanatory. If more explanation is necessary then it should be noted under the contact to "see note 1 (or other number)." Here a proper explanation can be given of the intended operation of the switch. These switches are generally used in conjunction with a timing relay. In order for the pressure or flow switch to function, it must have pressure or flow. Because the switch is usually a "shutdown switch," lack of flow or pressure would open the motor running circuit. This then must be temporarily closed when the motor/pump is started and pressure or flow has closed the switch. After that the timer opens the temporary bypass contacts.

19.12 THERMAL SWITCH

A thermal switch is a switch which actuates when a certain temperature is reached. It is essentially an on/off device for general-purpose use and not for temperature measurement. The intent is that the switch will actuate beyond a certain temperature. They are usually ordered as a fixed-temperature unit, with a single operating temperature.

19.13 LEVEL SWITCH

Level switches can become more complicated than is first imagined. Level switches are required for both liquids and solids. Consider the liquid level first. This is usually a float which rides on the surface of the liquid and as the level changes, the float changes; this in turn operates a switch. Although some very sophisticated float-switches with electronic amplifier and digital readout find application in refinery storage tank measuring, this is of course the simplest and oldest type of design. An alternative method is to insert two electrodes into the liquid; the conductivity between the electrodes due to the liquid operates a circuit, which in turn closes a relay, thereby completing the action. Both types have their problems. The float type is subject to mechanical interferences which prevent the float from rising. Leaky floats can also prevent operation. The electrode type is subject to the vagaries of the conductivity of the liquid and the cleanliness of the electrodes; both can cause poor operation.

Measuring the level of solids has always been a problem, mainly because solids tend to "pile" instead of forming a convenient flat surface, as is always maintained by liquids. The most accurate method, of course, is to meter the input and output and keep constant inventory. Alternately, a sonic doppler system can be used to measure the natural frequency of the storage tank when empty. If a liquid or a solid is added to the tank, the natural frequency will change. This can then be measured and can cause a relay to operate at a predetermined level.

19.14 DIFFERENTIAL SWITCHES

Differential switches are switches designed to sense two levels of operation. This is applicable to temperature or pressure, or even flow, etc. By use of the correct operating device, signals can maintain operation between a certain bandwidth. For example, a water level may be required to be maintained within 6 in. When the water level drops below the minimum, a switch closes and the pump begins to operate; when the level reaches 6 in. higher, another contact closes and shuts the pump off. This, then, is differential operation.

19.15 DRUM SWITCH

A drum switch is a multiple-contact switch which serves as an automatic-sequence operator. It is basically a drum with contact bars mounted on the surface. As the drum is rotated, the contact bars "wipe" and "jumper" two fixed contacts, completing the circuit.

The drum can be rotated by hand or can be motor-operated. A switching diagram displays which contacts are closed in a specific position. This is in essence the forerunner of the logic programmer.

19.16 SOLENOID-OPERATED VALVE

The solenoid-operated valve (SOV) is essentially a mechanical device and as such is generally ordered by the mechanical department; however, the electrical designer has the responsibility of wiring up the electrical circuit for the solenoid operation. The device is very simple and only requires a single-phase source of power and the necessary control-circuit functions. It is necessary to know the voltage and frequency of the solenoid coil. In addition the load (amperes) should be known. Although the load of a solenoid valve is small, sometimes many valves on a circuit can provide a marginal condition if they are all energized simultaneously. It should be considered as a process device with its own circuit(s). The controls would be part of the system control circuit. The SOV would not normally be supplied from the control-circuit power unless it happened to be an electro/pneumatic control device, in which case it could be considered as a type of relay.

19.17 TRANSDUCERS

A transducer is a device which translates a mechanical or dynamic function, such as temperature, into an electrical signal. The electrical-output signal may be proportional or exponential to the input function; in either case it can still be measured by electrical devices and also transmitted to a central control system where an operator or preprogrammed devices will determine the subsequent action. The electrical designer must be supplied with the necessary requirements for output wiring. Because the output signals are low voltage, it is necessary to know whether the wire should be shielded or twisted, or both, to prevent spurious signals from being picked up.

19.18 LOGIC PROGRAMMERS

This subject requires far more explanation than is possible here; therefore, we will introduce this subject only on the basis that we should make the designer aware that such devices exist. It is in essence a simplified computer with a keyboard. In a complex conveyor system all the drive and control functions are wired to terminals in the control panel. By use of the keyboard, it is possible to program the logic functions into the control panel for specific operation of all the circuits. If the operations require changing, it can be done through the use of the keyboard rather than by the rewiring or redesign of the control system. It must be understood that logic is in the sense of the "logic operators," which are AND, NEGATION, OR (inclusive), and OR (exclusive). By use of these logic operators, a device can be made to operate "with" or "instead of" or "only if" something else happens, etc.

As previously mentioned, this section is only intended to introduce the fact that these devices exist. More detailed information should be obtained from the various manufacturers about the scope, alternate devices, capability, and cost of their individual units. These facts then must be evaluated against designing the systems by conventional control-circuit methods.

19.19 COMPUTER-CONTROLLED SYSTEMS

In a large industrial complex, such as a refinery or large chemical plant, central control points are sometimes desirable. This enables systems to be monitored and controlled for optimum performance.

There are many levels of sophistication for these types of installations, but briefly, a simple system can consist of a *master terminal unit and minicomputer* at the central control point with *remote terminal units* at strategic points around the complex.

Basically, the remote-terminal unit is a microprocessor with the ability to "command" and monitor "status," the latter being in either digital or analog form. This means that temperatures and levels can be monitored. Likewise, the command signals can perform any function that a push button can perform. This means that all control and instrumentation wiring can be brought into the microprocessor at a nearby location.

In operation the master terminal unit is connected to all the remote terminal units by a simple telephone-line pair. On instructions from the minicomputer a coded signal is sent out which alerts a specific remote terminal unit. This terminal unit can then be scanned for information on "status" of all devices connected or a device can be "commanded" to operate or shut down.

This, then, is in essence a computer-controlled system. The description has been very brief and nothing has been said about cost, but obviously costs and performance will be related to the "performance requirements specification" and availability of standard and more sophisticated "building blocks" composing the system.

20 PROTECTIVE RELAYS

20.1 PROTECTIVE RELAYS

Protective relays are relays designed to sense and monitor system dynamics. As long as a system operates within specified limits, the relays will watch and wait. As soon as a dynamic function exceeds its design parameters, the relay comes into action and disconnects the offending circuit. There are many types of protective relays, with many combinations of characteristics. To know all the variations intimately requires experience. Furthermore, knowing relay characteristics is not much use without understanding the system dynamics to which the relays are to be applied. Add to this the necessary understanding of instrument transformers and time/operating characteristics of the circuit breakers the relays operate, and we see that protective relaying becomes more than a simple catalog selection of pieces. In fact the design of protective relaying systems is an "art." This is not to say that certain protective relays cannot be selected and specified; it means that a relay system of protection for networks and complex systems requires an experienced individual to obtain the best protection for the most economical installation.

20.2 DEFINITIONS

In order to discuss relaying intelligently, it is necessary to introduce the definitions used.

Relays can be listed in four basic groups:

1. *Auxiliary relays.* This relay is an intermediate relay whose function is to operate a device in response to a signal from another relay.
2. *Protective relay.* This relay is designed to detect a defect in a system which creates undesirable situations and consequently initiates corrective action by alarms or disconnecting circuits.

3. *Regulating relay.* This relay is designed to correct a variation in an operating parameter by initiating a signal to a supplementary device which corrects the variation to an acceptable level.

4. *Verification relay.* This relay is designed to signal that a system function has been verified and that some other function may be initiated as a consequence of this verification.

Relay operations must make other considerations; these can be defined as:

1. *Reliability.* This quality refers to the capability of the relay to perform repeated operations within its design limits accurately and with repeatability.

2. *Selectivity.* A relay must have the quality that ensures that the relay will operate only in the zones and sequence intended.

3. *Sensitivity.* This quality refers to the ability to detect the lowest possible variation in the system dynamic function which will initiate relay operation.

4. *Speed.* Speed in relaying refers to the initiating and corrective action taken. This means that the speed of an overcurrent relay must include the time required for the breaker to operate and open the circuit.

The parameters that can be monitored by relays can also be listed and defined:

1. *Current.* Positive, negative, and zero sequence quantities, algebraic sum of currents entering or leaving zones, vector sum of currents, direction of currents.

2. *Voltage.* Change in magnitude and phase relation.

3. *Impedance.* Change in magnitude and/or R and X ratio.

4. *Frequency.* Change in hertz.

5. *Neutral point.* Displacement of neutral point from its geometrical center.

6. *Pulse.* A repeated electrical omission or application of potential difference.

7. *Phase angle.* The measurement of the angle between the current and voltage wave in an alternating current circuit.

8. *Power factor.* Measurement of the ratio kW/kVA, which gives the cosine of the angle ($\cos \phi$) between the voltage and current wave.

9. *Reactive power.* Measurement of the reactive $EI \sin \phi$ portion of the total power supplied to a circuit.

10. *Other combinations.* Other combinations of the individual parameters to give specific desired parameters.

Relay systems can also be designed with two lines of defense. In the event a relay fails to operate a second one can take over. These are defined as:

1. *Primary relaying* is designed on the assumption that reliability of relays and supplementary equipment is 100%.
2. *Backup relaying* is based on the assumption that the reliability of relays and supplementary equipment is less than 100%.

20.3 RELAY APPLICATIONS

The consideration for relay requirements cannot be started too early in the design. When the preliminary single line is available, a spare print should be marked with contemplated relaying. This copy can then be sent to the selected vendors who will be supplying the switchgear for their comments. They may point out that for the basic system, as intended, relaying would be non-standard, and difficult or nearly impossible to provide as requested. It does not hurt, then, to obtain confirmation from the manufacturers that the relaying as intended is standard and economical.

Before considering relay applications certain design conditions must be established for the intended system. The following must be considered:

1. Adequate capacity of equipment to withstand load and fault conditions
2. Adequate interrupting capacity of circuit breakers and fuses
3. Versatile switching arrangement convenient for normal and abnormal situations
4. Desirable continuity of service regardless of cost
5. Desirable disconnection as fast as possible regardless of cost
6. Reclosing features for circuits
7. Reliability of service and/or equipment
8. Standard or nonstandard relay package
9. Primary and backup relaying (how much of each)
10. Economic limits of expenditure for protective relaying
11. Economic cost of equipment damage due to lack of relaying
12. Economic effect of production loss due to shutdown time

To assist in the evaluation of the previous items, the power system can be broken down into groups or zones.

ZONE 1 All generating equipment, including their transformers but not including the secondary switchgear.

ZONE 2 All distribution transformers, including their primary and secondary protective devices but excluding the generating transformers.

ZONE 3 All bus-bar and selective-switching groups.

ZONE 4 All distribution and transmission lines.

ZONE 5 All motor circuits, including the branch-circuit switchgear protective device.

ZONE 6 Special relaying not previously accounted for.

In some cases the client specification will already dictate the relaying he desires. This should not be accepted as final. During the relay study all aspects should be considered, and if the conclusions differ from the client specification, then the client should be notified about the differing opinion and the basis of the information on which the opinion was formed. He will then reply with a written (preferable) letter approving the deviation from the client specification or insisting the change is not allowed.

20.4 PREREQUISITES

The previous paragraphs have dealt with the consideration of general approach to system planning and possible relaying. Obviously the next step is to do some firm selecting. *Firm* selecting means the first choice in preliminary form. Once a selection has been made, it can be evaluated on the basis of its merit in that application. It may eventually be discarded, but until an item is selected, it cannot even be considered. At this stage the selection does not necessarily involve actual design calculations. For instance a large motor would have differential relaying red-lined in. Large important transformers may also have differential protection. Ground relaying must also be considered along with bus protection and reclosing for high-priority circuits.

The various protective devices are spotted in on the single line by showing the CTs and PTs and circles with the device number inscribed. The use of these device numbers indicates the "operational function" of the device.

These numbers are all listed in the Appendix (Table A-4) and specify the intent of the device rather than the actual catalog or characteristic details. For example, a "50" is an "instantaneous overcurrent," or rate-of-rise, relay.

This type of red-line layout on a *single-line* print is adequate for cost and analysis purposes. There is no point in calculating the numerous problem until it is decided that the relays will "stay."

A suggestion is that it is probably better to show all possible relay applications to give maximum protection with some backup relaying. A first round of elimination can be made on the basis of expected probability of operation; this will eliminate some. The next round of elimination would be on the basis of segregating mandatory or minimum relaying. The third elimination would be on the basis of economic return on capital investment for the balance of the relaying.

20.5 RELAY SELECTION

Once the type of protection has been established, each individual relay type must be selected from the vendor's catalog. As mentioned with respect to substations and switchgear, it is good practice to select relaying and circuit breakers from the same manufacturer. This means that warrantee problems become simpler. Contracting for a field engineer to set and coordinate all the relays is simple. Single responsibility for relay/breaker operation is always desirable.

If it is desirable to split the vendors into suppliers of circuit breakers and relays, then the specification should be written up so that the switchgear manufacturer will obtain the protective relaying and be responsible for its coordination ability.

The selection of relays to match the device number may result in a choice of more than one, each with slightly differing characteristics. These should all be listed as options. The eventual list will then have one or more relays available for possible use in a particular application.

Here, then, we come to the end of the line for general compiling and selection of relays. The next step is the application engineering for specific selection to meet the required design details.

20.6 TECHNICAL CALCULATIONS

In order to proceed with the necessary calculations, further information gathering is necessary. This should all be red-lined on a single-line print. The following parameters must be established.

1. All voltage levels must be marked at each distribution point.
2. All transformers must be sized (in kVA).
3. All transformer impedances must be established.
4. All transformer connections must be shown with details of neutral grounding method where applicable.
5. All motor loads must be marked with their respective reactances: X_d (synchronous reactance), X_d' (transient reactance), X_d'' (subtransient reactance). The subtransient is the most important because this gives the highest initial current value during a fault. Where there are many small motors, they can be lumped together as a single load with an approximate subtransient reactance of 25%. If the amount of motor load is not known, then it is generally considered as a percentage of the transformer size, which is usually 100% for a 460-V system unless part of the load can be segregated into lighting or other noncontributing load. For a 208-V system, assume 50% of transformer kVA.

6. Resistance and reactance of all main cables and feeders must be calculated, taking into account the raceway contribution, that is, magnetic or nonmagnetic raceway.

7. Other significant loads and impedances must be indicated.

When this single line is complete with all pertinent information, it is necessary to do a short-circuit study. Depending on the complexity of the system, an analytical (slide rule or pocket calculator accuracy) calculation can be carried out. A *network analyzer* can be used or (if available) a computer and short-circuit calculation program can simplify things. In any case a short-circuit study must be done. It is necessary to obtain one or more of the following:

<table>
<tr><td>1. Three-phase fault</td><td rowspan="2">Usually mandatory</td></tr>
<tr><td>2. Phase-to-ground fault</td></tr>
<tr><td>3. Two-phase to ground</td><td rowspan="2">Usually not required</td></tr>
<tr><td>4. Phase-to-phase fault</td></tr>
</table>

It is necessary to understand vectors, or in "electrical" terminology, *phasors.* This was covered in the previous book[1] on industrial electrical design expressing basic principles of manipulating vectors. Once this is understood then it is necessary to advance to symmetrical components (see Chap. 32).

This is essentially a method of reducing an unbalanced three-phase system into three separate balanced systems. Each one can then be solved independently by a standard outlined method. Both subjects, that is, short-circuit calculations and symmetrical components, are covered in other chapters, so we will just point out here that the calculations are required.

Instrument-transformer ratios must also be calculated and the burdens of the relays must also be obtained. The selection of the transformer ratios is based on the saturation curve; therefore, the correct curves must be obtained for the instrument transformers. Trip curves for breakers and melting curves for fuses must also be obtained. Finally it will be required to plot the various curves on paper to evaluate the coordination of the relaying, which will require some log-log paper. This is standardized and printed specifically for coordination with "time" as the ordinate and "current" as the abscissa.

20.7 RELAYING TYPES AND SCHEMES

The operating principle of protective relays falls into two basic categories: *electromagnetic attraction* and *electromagnetic induction.* The variations in relays, however, is never ending. The introduction of solid-state components into circuitry also provides another variable. The electrical designer should not be too concerned with how a relay works; his main concern is its operating

[1] L. B. Roe, *Practices and Procedures of Industrial Electrical Design,* McGraw-Hill Book Company, New York, 1972.

characteristics and pecularities. However, in order to give the electrical designer a broad visual picture of a relay, we will briefly describe the two basic principles.

The electromagnetic-attraction relay works on the solenoid principle with a plunger being drawn into a magnetic coil. Alternately it can operate a *beam balance* or *clapper* in various forms. These relays work satisfactorily on alternating or direct current and also fall into the category of auxiliary and control-type relays. When used for overcurrent protection, these relays sometimes are susceptible to transients. They act so fast that they trip on the dc offset or transient peak, rather than on the actual setting, which is much lower. This "transient overreach" should therefore be taken into consideration when setting fast-operating relays of this type.

The electromagnetic-induction-type relay only works on alternating current. This type of relay, however, is probably associated with more different protective relays than any other. The basic operation consists of magnetic fluxes acting on a disk of nonmagnetic material. If the flux arrangement produces out-of-phase components, then eddy currents will be set up in the disk; these will produce a torque and tend to rotate the disk (the same principle as an induction motor). When the disk has rotated a predetermined angle, it operates a trip mechanism. By varying the current and/or voltage signals and arranging the flux distribution and damping devices in numerous ways, many different types of operating characteristics can be produced.

The electromagnetic-induction-type relay is used for overcurrent, direction, distance relays, voltage-restrained overcurrent, differential relays, power relays, phase balance, and many others.

A comparison of the two basic types can be shown in the listing:

Attraction type	***Induction type***
Smaller	Larger
Cheaper	More expensive
AC, DC	AC only
Instantaneous only	High speed, inverse time, variable time
Low reset/pickup	High reset/pickup
Tend to vibrate	Smooth operation
Nondirectional	Directional
Transient overreach	Limited transient overreach

20.8 RELAY RATINGS

Relays have certain features which are fairly standard with regard to performance and should always be considered when specifying relays. The following list should be checked against the relay required.

1. Burden
2. Operating range
3. Continuous-time rating
4. Short-time rating
5. Contact rating
6. Seal-in rating
7. Target rating
8. Ambient rating (40°C)
9. Mounting type

The *burden* is the load offered to the instrument transformer by the relay. The *operating range* is the limits of adjustment of the pickup and reset specifications. The *continuous-time* rating specifies the limits of the relay under continuous operation at the specified ambient (40°C). The *short-time* rating is the length of time the current should be applied to a *current* coil in the relay. Current applied in excess of this time rating could damage the relay. *Seal-in* and *target rating* usually have control coils which operate these functions. The rating of these can vary, depending on whether the relay is tripping a circuit breaker directly or via an auxiliary relay, in which case it would probably have a lighter rating. The ambient rating is generally standardized at 40°C; therefore, a check should be made to confirm the relay rating and also the ambient temperature where it will be located.

The type of mounting refers to surface or recessed and also any unusual details of space, depth, etc.

Contact rating is generally not a problem because the relay only has to open control circuit loads; nevertheless it should be checked and confirmed.

20.9 INVERSE-TIME OVERCURRENT RELAY

This relay is about the most widely used of all protective relays. Since this relay is an *induction* type, it has a disk rotor and as such it has a natural time characteristic when plotted against the current. The operating time is approximately "inversely proportional to the current squared," giving the term *inverse-time overcurrent relay.* By modifying the operating time because of a change of location and size of some component parts, it is possible to obtain *very inverse* and *extremely inverse* characteristics. *Inverse* of course means "opposite in order," which in the case of the relay "as the current increases the tripping time decreases." See Fig. 20.1.

The inverse-time overcurrent relay finds application on transmission and distribution lines for phase and ground-fault applications. They are also utilized in differential protection arrangements applicable to bus, transformer, and machine protection. While the inverse and very inverse times are related to short-circuit-current behavior, the extremely inverse time is designed to match the fuse coordination curves with definite minimum time and moderately inverse time as the slowest.

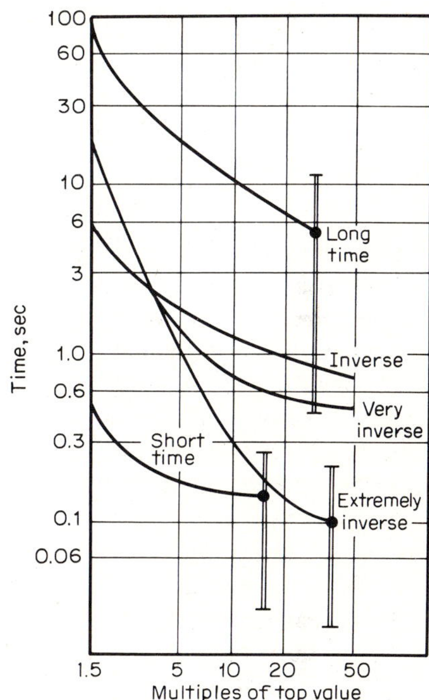

Figure 20.1 Inverse time overcurrent relay operating curves.

Note: Typical operating characteristics of Type IAC relays. Only the No. 5 time-dial setting is shown (see catalog for full family of curves) for each curve, and the range of time adjustment from 0.5 to 10 time-dial settings as shown for the extremely inverse, the short-time, and the long-time relays.

Time-dial setting of a relay changes the distance the disk must travel before tripping. The *tap setting* is the change of pickup strength or number of turns in the operating coil. See Fig. 20.2.

As we see in Fig. 20.2, there is a family of curves. These can be selected by changing the time-dial setting on the relay. The current is shown on the bottom scale and is in multiples of the minimum closing current (tap value). By varying these two alternates, the curve can be made to coordinate with other relays. For instance, if there are two circuit breakers on a line, the one closest to the load should trip first; if this one does not function, the next one will trip. The time lag between two relays should be around 0.4 sec. This is arrived at by allowing 0.13 sec for breaker opening time plus 0.1 sec for overtravel time and 0.17 sec for safety margin. See Fig. 20.3.

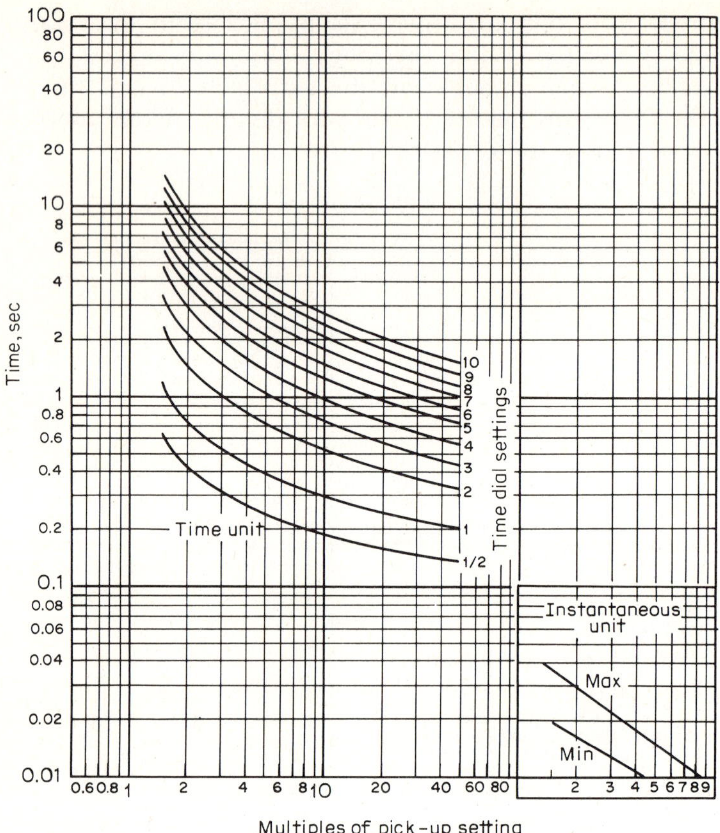

Figure 20.2 Multiples of minimum closing current (tap value) for type IAC relay, inverse-time characteristic curve.

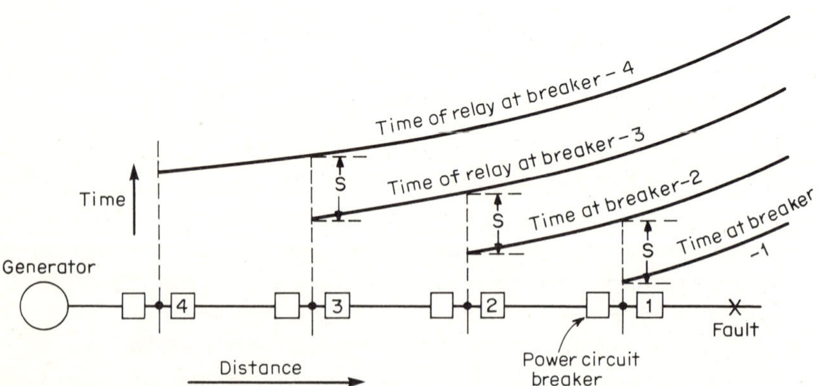

Figure 20.3 One-line diagram showing coordination of operating times for inverse overcurrent relays.

Further experience and/or more specific information can allow for more critical timing but during design the plant is not even built; therefore, a good guess is usually all the chance you get.

20.10 GROUND OVERCURRENT RELAYS

The inverse-time relay can also be used as a ground overcurrent sensor. There are two methods of ground relaying. The residual arrangement is the most common and is formed by installing the relay in the neutral of star-connected current transformers.

The neutral will not indicate any current under normal balanced conditions because the currents from each phase cancel out each other when 120° apart. During a ground fault an unbalanced situation is created and the relay "sees" the residual current. Hence it is termed *residually connected.* The residual connection will also see unbalanced currents caused by factors other than ground currents. Current-transformer characteristics might also differ in performance; therefore, the setting of these relays is not an easy problem.

High-accuracy current transformers should be used if possible. The ground fault current should be limited to a low fault level, and 0.5-A ground relays should be used. This will probably give slower operation than high ground-fault-current operation, but the choice is between possible damage caused by high fault current and fast clearing and damage caused by low fault current and slower clearing. In the case of solidly grounded neutrals there is no choice and the use of higher-current relays is probably better (i.e., in the 1.5/6.0 rating).

The other method of ground relaying is to connect a relay in the neutral of the transformer or generator. By using a CT with about one-fourth or one-third the neutral resistor rating, it will ensure adequate signal for operation. These relays are generally installed as a backup to the residual-connected relays and as such should be coordinated to trip slightly after the expected operating time of the circuit breaker operated by the residual relay.

20.11 DIRECTIONAL OVERCURRENT RELAYS

When a power system begins to take on the form of a network or modified network, protection by means of ordinary overcurrent relays can become a problem or nearly impossible. Since an ac circuit is nondirectional, some form of polarizing effect has to be introduced.

In the directional overcurrent relay a voltage is used to produce a polarizing signal. The operational signal (current) is then referred to the voltage. The phase angle between the two will dictate the direction of current flow under specific conditions. Under normal conditions the current will be in phase with the voltage, and under fault conditions the current will be out of phase.

These relays are available in single-phase and three-phase units; however, the single-phase unit is preferable for phase faults; it will also detect phase-to-ground faults at a lower level than the polyphase unit. The advantage of the polyphase unit is that it is probably less subject to misoperation than the single-phase units, but three single-phase units are more versatile.

The three most widely used connections for PT and CT connections on

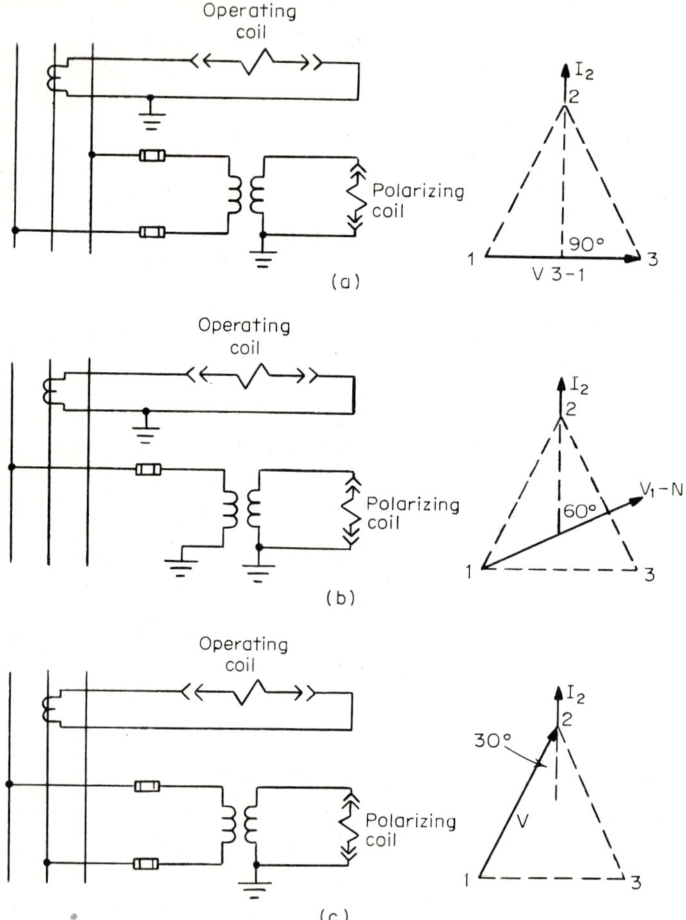

Figure 20.4 CT and PT connections for directional overcurrent relay. (a) Quadrature (90°) connection (recommended); (b) 60° connection; (c) 30° connection.

three-phase systems are the 90° (quadrature), 60°, and 30°. The quadrature connection is preferred, the 60° is a compromise, and the 30° is not recommended. In some cases where the CTs are star-connected, zero phase-sequence currents can sometimes cause false tripping, but this is not always the case and therefore only a mild possibility. See Fig. 20.4.

The directional overcurrent relay should not be confused with a *power-directional* relay. To all intents they are very similar relays; however, the *angle of maximum torque* between the two relays is different. In the overcurrent relay the maximum operating torque occurs when the primary currents lag the primary voltages by more than 45° for short-circuit protection under abnormal conditions.

The power-directional relay is arranged so that the maximum operating torque occurs when the voltage and current are in phase, that is, at maximum power. These relays are designed to protect against abnormal conditions, which is the opposite to the directional overcurrent relay. This explains why the two types should be selected carefully to avoid wrong application.

20.12 VOLTAGE RESTRAINT

The voltage-restraint feature allows discrimination between heavy overloads and fault conditions. The basic principle behind this feature is that when a fault occurs the "restraint" torque collapses, allowing the unit to trip.

During high but continuous overloads the phase voltage is still maintained and therefore produces a full restraining torque which prevents tripping.

20.13 DIRECTIONAL-OVERCURRENT-RELAY GROUND PROTECTION

The directional overcurrent relay can also be used for ground protection. It is applicable where systems are other than the straight radial. If the fault at the far end of a feeder produces less than twice the current of a reverse fault, the directional overcurrent relay could be considered instead of the straight overcurrent type.

20.14 DIFFERENTIAL RELAYING

In an industrial plant, differential relaying will inevitably be required when transformers or motors begin to become expensive in repair or replacement terms.

Differential relaying is not "a relay," it is a "scheme" whereby current transformers and a relay sense the difference in currents entering and leaving a piece of equipment. Having said that, we must now enter a word of caution. The principle is simple, but the selection of components can be critical to performance.

Differential relaying is applicable to various kinds of protective systems. In industrial plants it is predominantly "current" rather than voltage differential relaying. By installing a current transformer at the input terminal and a current transformer at the output terminal with the leads connected to a relay, we can connect the various leads so that the *input* current from the CT *into* the relay is cancelled out by the *output* current from the CT going *into* the relay. The algebraic or *net* current on the relay operating coil under normal conditions is zero. If a fault occurs within the "zone" between the CTs (including the equipment), the output current will *not* cancel out the input current. The difference between the input and output currents will cause the relay coil to operate.

We see that the only factor affecting the differential relay is the difference in current values between input and output. A change in voltage, frequency, or even load current will not affect the differential relay; it is generally immune from system dynamics. This means that it can operate at high speed because it is selective within the CT zones. It can be made extremely sensitive because it measures only fault-current quantities. In fact the operating (difference) current is proportional to the fault current.

Since the differential scheme is dependent on difference of currents for the CTs, we can readily see that inaccurate CTs can produce an "error" where none actually exists. It is extremely important then that CTs be high accuracy and "matched." It is very difficult to purchase matched CTs because CT accuracy depends on many factors which are not always economically controllable by the manufacturer. The approach then is to use standard high-accuracy CTs and a "modified" relay that will ignore transient signals from inconsistencies in the CTs.

20.15 PERCENTAGE DIFFERENTIAL RELAYING

Because CT errors are linear, that is, small with small through current and large with large through currents, a relay designed with restraining coils to oppose the main operating coil eliminates some of the problem of false tripping due to CT error currents. The result of the restraining coils on the operating coils is to produce a relay whose operating coils "pick up" can be "tied" to the through current as a fixed percentage. For example, a through current of 100 A with a 10% slope means that the pickup on the operating coil must be minimum of 10 A. See Figs. 20.5 and 20.6.

This by no means concludes the available types of relays which offer restrained tripping. Many other factors, such as transformer inrush currents, phase displacement in transformers between primary and secondary, and dynamic factors, must be considered. Therefore, the differential relaying should be ordered with the device it is intended to protect if possible (e.g., transformer complete with differential relaying).

20.16 CURRENT-BALANCE RELAYS

The phase-balance relay is a remote cousin to the differential relay. Whereas in the differential relay an input and output is required, in the phase-balance relay only the input currents are required. By comparing the currents in

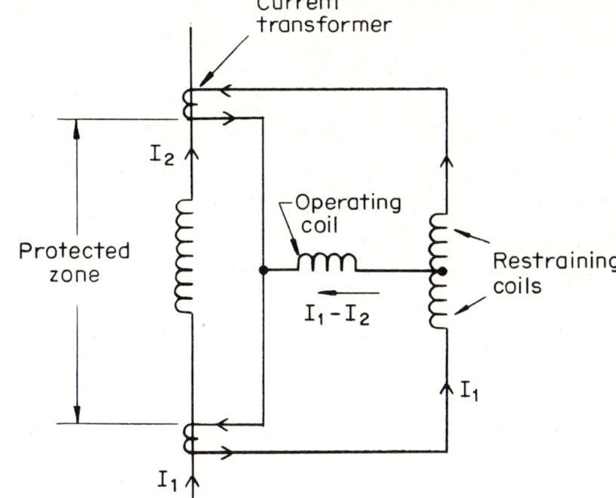

Figure 20.5 Differential relay scheme with restraint coils.

Note: On a star-delta connected transformer the CTs on the "star" side are connected in "delta" and the CTs on the "delta" side are connected "star."

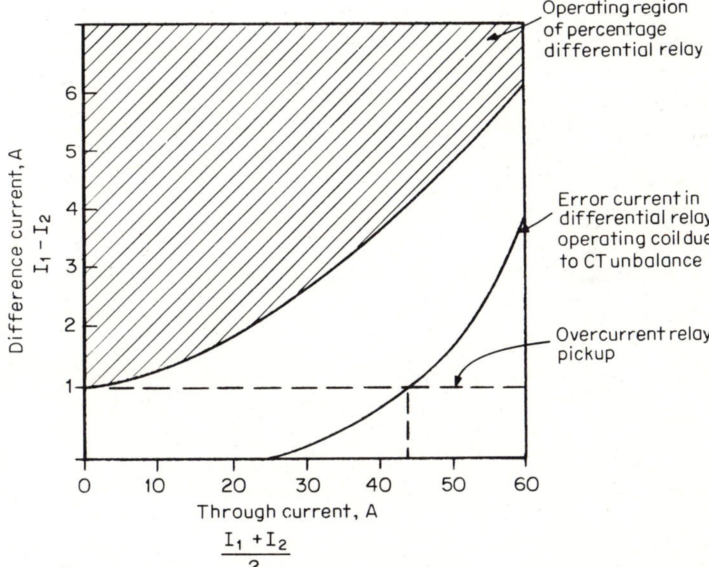

Figure 20.6 Curve showing advantage of percentage differential relay over differentially connected overcurrent relay.

each line of a balanced three-phase circuit, a fault in one line or two lines will cause an unbalance in the normally three balanced currents. This unbalance can be made to operate a relay. This will provide protection against a single-phase outage (fused), which would normally allow a three-phase motor to continue running with full differential protection.

20.17 PHASE-REVERSAL RELAY

The phase-reversal relay is a relay designed to prevent reverse rotation of a motor. If two leads of a three-phase motor are reversed, the direction of rotation will be changed. Sometimes during startup or after a maintenance shutdown it is possible to "switch" two conductors. If this happens on a main transformer, all the motors in the plant will reverse. If it is limited to a single circuit, then only the motors on that circuit are affected. Generally, experienced electricians are aware of this and motors are "phased" out for rotation during the pre-startup check and care is taken during maintenance. If the motor in question is expensive and if the cost to repair damage by reverse rotation is prohibitive, then a phase-reversal relay should be installed.

20.18 FREQUENCY RELAY

This relay is used more in the utility industry than in the industrial plant. Its function is to protect or signal a too-high or too-low frequency. As frequency is a function of generator speed, it is usually only applicable where some control is available over the prime movers. In some cases, highly specialized equipment can be damaged by operating at other than design frequency. In this case a frequency relay would be installed to disconnect the equipment beyond predetermined limits. One other application of a frequency relay is in the automatic synchronizing of generators which are to be run in parallel.

20.19 VOLTAGE RELAYS

Voltage relays vary considerably in type and application. A voltage relay can be the ordinary electromagnetic clapper type that gives undervoltage protection, which means that for a temporary loss of power a motor will not restart automatically. Low-voltage protection means that a motor can be running with low voltage, but due to the low-voltage condition its $EI \cos \phi$ output is reduced, which is in fact its effective horsepower. The result of low voltage is usually overheating. In order to prevent this, a relay can be installed to operate an alarm or shut down a motor at a predetermined low-voltage level. An ordinary relay (electromagnetic type) will not fall out until approximately 65% voltage and cannot be counted on to provide protection. The normal line-current heaters are relatively slow-acting, and although they will probably eventually shut down the motor, insulation damage could have already occurred.

High-voltage protection is also sometimes desirable but for slightly different reasons. Starting a motor on high voltage can produce excessive torque. This can sometimes damage the shaft and/or bearings of large machines of a specialized nature. It can also aggravate shaft currents, which may not be a problem at normal voltage but become threshold at abnormally high voltages, resulting in bearing damage.

Many other applications exist for voltage relays, particularly where computer installations are concerned, although computer manufacturers (if prudent) will protect their own equipment internally.

20.20 TEMPERATURE RELAYS

In large motors it is desirable to know the hot-spot temperature of the winding or the bearing temperatures. In both cases, RTDs (resistance-temperature detectors) are embedded in the winding and/or bearing; the leads are then brought out to a special relay which monitors the temperature. This can sometimes be in conjunction with a visual temperature readout with adjustable trip setting; however, this has the drawback that the operator may be tempted to raise it slightly if he is under pressure to maintain operations.

20.21 GAS RELAY

This relay is essentially a specialized relay for transformer protection. When a short circuit occurs in a liquid-filled transformer, gas is generated. Backup protection, which detects the gas pressure, is available for disconnecting the transformer from the power supply. It is not intended as a first line of protection and it is only applicable to some types of transformers. Its speed of operation is variable with its location to the fault and whether the fault is light or heavy.

20.22 OTHER RELAYS

There are many other types of relays of more sophisticated design and application. Generally these are more applicable to the utility company than to the industrial plant designer. Bus protection can utilize voltage differential schemes, with the alternates being the regular or percentage-current type with the use of specially designed reactors "linear couplers" in place of the conventional current transformer.

This gives three differential relaying alternates, each with its own characteristics which would have to be investigated for application to a particular installation.

Pilot-wire relays and distance-type relays are applicable to utility transmission-line problems. As such, they will not be considered here in detail. The understanding and application is specialized from a utility "viewpoint" to protection. Also, different problems exist than are faced in the average industrial plant.

21 MOTOR PROTECTION

21.1 PHILOSOPHY OF PROTECTION

The protection of an electric motor is dependent on a number of independent decisions. First, the enforcing code must be adhered to; this offers minimum protection. Second, the load or equipment being driven by the motor and whether running the motor to destruction is preferable to "instant" shutdown must be considered. Next, the anticipated areas of failure, that is, bearing failure, winding failure, ventilation failure, high- and low-voltage protection, phase-reversal protection, turn protection, vibration protection, field-failure protection, etc., must be considered. Last, but by no means least, is the cost of the protection. The intent then is to provide "optimum" protection. This would be a "break-even" point analysis where the consideration would be the cost of all charges involved in shutdown, loss of production, repairing, reinstalling, reconnecting, and recoupling. This would be plotted against the charges for various degrees of relaying which would offer some protection advantage over the minimum code requirement. At some point, relaying should show some protection at costs equal to shutdown costs, while further relaying would offer additional protection but at added cost. The use of additional relaying offers a possible saving in time on delivery schedules, etc., which would not show up in downtime costs.

These independent decisions will all be different, depending on who decides what. The chemical engineer may decide that the process could become unstable and that the motor should be run to destruction. An accountant might think that extra money is good insurance if it shortens downtime. An extra few seconds running time can provide valuable purging time for gas process systems where contamination of gas without the purging could involve costs which could have purchased many replacement motors. What we are saying in effect is that there is no easy answer. We can, however, make some general statements, which will be presented in the next few paragraphs.

21.2 OVERCURRENT PROTECTION

A motor branch circuit consists of a circuit supplied by a final circuit breaker (or fuses). This is the "last" circuit overcurrent device and therefore defines the motor circuit as a *branch circuit.* There are two types of protection for a motor circuit. The controller and conductors are protected against a short circuit by the *circuit breaker* which supplies the circuit. A short circuit by definition is an accidental connection between two points of differing potential by a conductor of zero impedance. This is one type of protection that is required. The other type of protection is required to prevent an increase in load from causing excessive current and, consequently, "heat" in the motor, conductors, and associated component parts. This "excessive" load may be a gradual increase caused by overloading, voltage drop, faulty bearings, or other reasons. In any case it is a slow-buildup type of overload, whereas the short circuit is a sudden surge of current.

Both types of protection must be considered, but only the latter or "overloading" is classed as "motor running overcurrent protection." The former is considered as short-circuit and ground-fault protection.

21.3 PROTECTION OF THREE-PHASE INDUCTION MOTORS (200 HP MAX.)

The three-phase induction motor comprises the bulk of a designer's application work in an industrial plant. Up to 200 hp, all motors are on a 460-V system unless special conditions exist. Usually protection afforded by the National Electrical Code is adequate, unless special loads of high inertia are assigned. The setting of the branch-circuit overcurrent device will be in accordance with NEC Table 430–152. This is primarily to protect the conductors and controller from short-circuit stresses and temperatures.

The motor running overcurrent protection is usually provided by three thermal heaters located in the motor controller. These are fixed-rated units and the correct one should be installed to meet the allowed overcurrent setting. This is listed in the Code but is generally accepted as 115% of the value listed in NEC Table 430–150. Allowances should be made for motors with special circuit details, such as switched capacitors.

Circuit conductors are rated at 125% of the full-load current given in NEC Table 430–150; therefore, the heater will also protect the conductor by opening at 10% below the minimum conductor rating.

In dual-speed motors the windings provide two different horsepowers; therefore, two different size of thermal overloads will be required, the windings being considered separately.

Unless the motor is extra low speed or has a special load with high inertia, the majority protection will be the minimum as outlined in the code.

21.4 LARGE THREE-PHASE MOTORS (ABOVE 200 HP) (INDUCTION)

Large three-phase motors above 200 hp are rated in the medium-voltage class, that is, 4.16 to 13.8 kV. The fact that the circuits are high voltage means that relaying must be reduced to acceptable low-voltage levels. Due to safety, the clearances and construction of equipment is much more critical. Most high-voltage controllers are in effect an air circuit breaker in series with a CL (current-limiting) fuse and disconnect switch.

This makes everything, including the motor, more expensive than the equivalent in a lower horsepower rating. Here, then, we must consider each high-voltage motor as an individual unit with its own specific problems of application and cost. The first criteria is to establish whether the motor is essential or nonessential to the process. If it is essential, then the basic short-circuit protection will be installed and all other overload devices will actuate alarms rather than initiate shutdown. This will allow the operator time to reduce the possible overload or start a shutdown cycle before shutting down the motor.

If the motor is nonessential, the overload and other protective devices will be set to shut the motor down as fast as possible.

Large motors vary in size, cost, and characteristics; therefore, it is not possible to provide a single scheme for all motors. We will therefore have to discuss the various aspects of protection which can then be used as a guide.

21.5 INRUSH-CURRENT EFFECT

The symmetrical value of the motor inrush (starting) current can be anywhere between 300 to 900% of rated current. The asymmetrical (offset) current can vary up to 600 to 1800%, or approximately 1.8, as much as the symmetrical value. Since the asymmetrical current and consequently the dc component are highest in the first cycle and then gradually fade, the instantaneous trip will react to the dc component, while the inertia in an induction disk relay or thermal element will only recognize the symmetrical current.

The rate of decrease (decrement) of the dc component is a function of the X/R ratio of the circuit and will probably not be fully asymmetrical; therefore, the setting for the instantaneous devices should be around 12 to 15 times rated full-load current.

The setting for the noninstantaneous trips would be based on the normal symmetrical inrush.

21.6 ACCELERATING TIME EFFECT

The accelerating time depends on the inertia of the motor Wk^2 and the load Wk^2. This must be taken into consideration when setting inverse-time overcurrent relays.

Calculation of the accelerating time is fairly simple, providing the Wk^2 loads are known. This is covered in Sec. 10.8; alternately, the motor manufacturer can be contacted for acceleration time.

21.7 SHORT-CIRCUIT PROTECTION

This must be applied to all ungrounded conductors, including the stator winding and the actual controller. One device for each conductor is required. Where protection is a circuit breaker, it is permitted by code to sense the fault by integral or external sensing elements and must disconnect all ungrounded conductors simultaneously. Where protection is by fuses, they shall be arranged with, or also serve as, a disconnecting means. As no condition exists that all ungrounded conductors must be opened, obviously a single fuse could open, leaving the other two intact. This would allow the motor to keep running but provide a reduced output. This will eventually lead to overheating and overloading. Whether the motor is disconnected in time to prevent damage or not depends on the setting of the overload trips. The limiting factor is sometimes the stator and other times the rotor. A more serious single-phase condition will exist when a ground fault on a single-phase line of a primary feed to a star-delta transformer blows the fuse, leaving only two-phase lines feeding the transformer. This then means that the three-phase secondary line will be essentially single-phased with currents in each motor branch circuit of 115, 115, and 230% for the 3 phases. This means that every motor in the plant runs the risk of being burnt out.

21.8 FAULT-CURRENT FEEDBACK

During a fault, all motors will feed back current to the fault. The amount of feedback is an inverse function of the subtransient reactance (X''_d) which is around 15 to 25% for induction motors, 10 to 25% for high-speed synchronous motors, and 25 to 45% for low-speed synchronous motors. During the few cycles while the subtransient reactance is in effect, the feedback currents can be 800 to 1300% of full-load currents for induction motors, 800 to 2000% for high-speed synchronous motors, and 450 to 800% for low-speed synchronous motors. This feedback current may in some cases be enough to trip the instantaneous relays protecting a motor if they are set only marginally high.

21.9 PHASE FAULT

Phase-fault protection can be provided by current-limiting fuses specially designed for motor protection. Alternately, instantaneous overcurrent relays can be used with the setting of 1200 to 1500%. Another alternative is to use an inverse-time overcurrent relay with a timer to prevent operation until the motor is up to speed. This means that low-level faults can be picked up fast with a setting of 400% of rated motor current. Thermal overloads will provide normal overload protection.

21.10 PHASE-TO-GROUND FAULT

A simple method of detecting a phase-to-ground fault is by passing all three-phase conductors through a *window*-type CT. Normal load currents are self-cancelling due to phase shift; however, during a ground fault, *zero-sequence* currents will flow; these are all *in phase* and therefore add together. This will produce an output at the CT. If this output is fed into an instantaneous 0.2/2.0-A overcurrent relay, it will offer sensitive protection and eliminate false tripping due to starting and high inrush currents.

An alternate method is the previously mentioned residual connection with an inverse-time overcurrent relay in the neutral of star-connected CTs. This uses a 0.5/2.0-A relay with a setting of not more than 10% of the maximum ground fault current. If the maximum ground fault current is more than four times the motor rated current, an additional instantaneous trip should be included with a setting of 300 to 1000% rated motor current, depending on inrush and feedback criteria.

21.11 LOW-VOLTAGE PROTECTION

Low-voltage protection in a large motor should be a standard consideration. We are already well aware that torque is reduced by the square of the voltage; by the time magnetic devices drop out at about 65% voltage, torque is reduced to only 43%. If voltage is reduced on starting and it is intended to be across-the-line starting, the rotor could overheat faster than the stator, or even the opposite, depending on the construction and winding connection of the motor.

The low-voltage relay can be combined with a phase-sequence relay and purchased as such. It can also have time-delay functions for transient or dip overrides. The connection can be made as an "alarm only" function, or it can automatically disconnect the motor from the line.

The former (alarm) installation is usually better for continuous-process operations. If the voltage drops to a level where magnetic devices are dropping out, then a major problem exists and motor problems will only be consequential.

21.12 MOTOR PROTECTION AGAINST DAMAGE

By motor protection we mean "trying to limit the amount of damage to a motor by fast shutdown." The general devices which are sensitive to load current must ignore some signals and operate for others; therefore, a gross margin exists. With differential relaying of either the current or percentage scheme, we can instantly sense a change in current distribution within the motor. If current goes in, it must come out; if it does not come out as fast as it went in, it is being diverted internally. This constitutes a reason for shutdown and examination. Winding faults are progressively turn-to-turn, phase-to-phase, and eventually phase-to-ground. If a fault can be caught at the turn-to-turn stage, possibly only a single coil need be replaced. A phase-to-phase fault may require two or more coils (still not detrimental, although there is the possibility of a long downtime); a phase-to-ground fault can slightly, marginally, or heavily damage the stator iron.

The obvious aim then is to prevent the progression to a phase-to-ground fault. Coils are easily replaced in large form-wound motors, but damaged iron can be a serious problem.

This discussion is all leading up to the advisability of applying differential relaying.

For motors of 1500 hp and up and motors above 500 hp at 4.16 kV and higher, differential relaying is definitely recommended. These motors must all have six leads brought out for full differential protection or three leads and the neutral for partial differential protection, the latter only protecting for ground faults. As it is debatable whether turn-to-turn faults will be detected by differential relaying, they would only be confirmed when they change into a phase-to-phase fault. The difference then in partial and full differential protection is the phase-to-phase detection.

Differential relaying then will provide a fast, sensitive protection which is unaffected by any form of inrush or feedback current variations.

21.13 STATOR OVERHEATING

In large motors stator overheating is a much more serious problem than in the smaller motors. Apart from insulation damage, stator overheating can cause frame distortion and, in some cases, bearing damage. In the small motors a bimetallic heater monitors overcurrent and therefore the estimated temperature. In large motors RTDs (resistance-temperature detectors) are installed with the winding in the slot to detect actual hot-spot temperatures. When motors are 1500 hp and over, RTDs are recommended. The Code allows this method of overload protection. The RTDs operate a temperature relay which trips the circuit breaker when a certain temperature is reached; therefore no other protection is required except for short-circuit protection.

Further protection is available in the form of the current-balance relays, which are essentially protection for single-phase conditions. This can also include a phase-sequence combination if desired.

Having introduced the more ideal protection first, we can now consider the usual alternatives.

In motors of 1500 hp and over the overload protection is a choice between the inverse-time overcurrent relay and the thermal replica (motor heating curve) relay.

The thermal-replica-type relay tries to follow the motor heating curve. At light loads and long time overloads it gives best performance. At heavy overloads it tends to be slow. The inverse overcurrent relay works just the opposite, giving the best protection at heavy loads while remaining unsure and therefore not very sensitive at light loads.

Obviously a combination of both gives the best protection, but if that is considered, then the RTDs should also be included for consideration.

Both the replica and the inverse overcurrent relays can be equipped with instantaneous trips for short-circuit protection.

For motors without a service factor the trip should be 115% of rated full-load current. For motors with a service factor the setting should be 125% of full-load current. The latter is in fact the requirement for low-voltage motor conductors.

21.14 ROTOR OVERHEATING

In squirrel-cage rotors it is not economically possible to install detector devices. The devices used for stator overheating detection will in most cases reflect back general overload conditions, but on locked or blocked rotor and single-phase attempted starting problems the current-sensing thermal devices should be used rather than the RTDs. The time lag associated with these on startup may not reflect the rotor heating correctly.

In synchronous motors a field current is supplied to the rotor; therefore, a connection exists to the rotor. By using a replica thermal relay energized by induced field current, protection can be provided if the motor fails to start. A further protection for the rotor is provided by the power-factor relay, which will shut down the motor for an out-of-step condition.

21.15 BEARING TEMPERATURE

Sometimes it is desirable to monitor bearing temperatures. Some motors are equipped with bearings that are "force fed." A small lubrication pump supplies continuous lubrication. A failure could occur in the oil line rather than the auxiliary motor; therefore, the only sure way of preventing overheating or detecting a fault in the lubricating system is by installing an RTD and running the conductors back to a dial thermometer with adjustable trip switch. This switch can be set to operate an alarm or a shutdown when a certain temperature is reached.

The thermometer and switch should be calibrated first to ensure against false operation.

An option to this is the use of the bulb-type sensor connected to a relay at the motor. However, this means running control power out to the motor and also explosionproof housing for the relay if it is in a hazardous area.

21.16 MOTOR PROTECTION SUMMARY

For motors up to 200 hp and 460 V, use standard thermal overloads with circuit breaker or fuse for short-circuit protection.

For motors up to 4.16 kV (high-voltage class) and maximum 2500-hp for induction and synchronous (0.8 PF) and maximum 3000 hp for synchronous (1.0 PF), use the standard high-voltage controller with current-limiting fuse for phase- and ground-fault protection; thermal overloads, time undervoltage, squirrel-cage protection*, power factor* and bearing-temperature detector**. (* synchronous motors, ** optional all motors).

For motors of 3000 hp and larger at all voltages, use circuit-breaker-type starter installations; phase-fault thermal overload and locked-rotor protection by long-time overcurrent induction relay with instantaneous trip; ground-fault protection by use of 0.5/2.0-A instantaneous solenoid current, low-dropout relay; phase sequence and undervoltage by *reverse-phase* relay combination. Current balance should be provided by a *phase-balance* relay. Differential relaying should also be included with *high-speed differential relays.* The stator overheating should be monitored by RTDs and a *temperature relay.* The bearing temperature should be applied if warranted.

An alternate scheme for protection is:

- *Phase fault, thermal overload, and locked rotor.* Use replica-type thermal overload with instantaneous protection. Current balance by use of *phase-balance* relay. Ground Fault by 0.5/2.0 A as in the previous scheme.
- *Undervoltage.* Use short-time low-pickup overvoltage.
- *Differential.* Use optional selection of relays. Bearing temperature as required.

Essential service motors: Use ground-fault protection, differential relaying, current balance, RTDs, bearing temperature, while the thermal overloads and locked rotor currents are arranged to trip during start but alarm during "run" with instantaneous trip for phase fault.

Curve Plotting

Showing the alternate trip curves on a single sheet of log-log paper gives a graphic presentation of where protection is marginal or overlapping.

22 GENERATOR PROTECTION

22.1 GENERATOR PROTECTION

The generator is probably the most important part of an electric system. Without it the rest of the system is useless; therefore, the reliability of the generator is paramount. Fast repair time is also essential; this means that fast shutdown is required and early indication of an impending fault must be recognized.

The economic justification for maximum possible protection must be weighed against the effect on the system of a single generator shutdown. If it is a "swing" generator, the load could possibly be carried by other units until the faulty one is repaired. The problem is that the fault must be a simple one; if it involves damage to iron or requires hard-to-get replacement parts (foreign projects), then the maximum expenditure may still be cheap.

Since the generator requires more sophisticated relaying and the consideration of other factors which do not arise in motor protection, we can do no more than introduce some facets of the problems involved and some approaches to solutions.

It is not possible to get into detailed information without consideration of generator design and operation fundamentals. The average industrial designer will rarely be called on to design protection for generators without the manufacturer's recommendations being available for evaluation; therefore, it becomes a matter of understanding what the manufacturer is recommending rather than making an original selection. This then is what we will consider mostly.

22.2 WINDING PROTECTION (STATOR)

The generator stator winding produces a voltage because it cuts the magnetic field provided by the rotor. If a fault occurs within the winding, opening the main breaker in the three-phase output does nothing except remove the external load current. The fault still exists within the generator.

As long as the field is energized, the generator will be producing an emf (electromotive force) which maintains the fault current. If the field supply is removed, then the flux decay time will dictate the speed with which the current will be reduced in the fault. This is a problem related to winding protection.

Faults in a winding can be considered to follow the process outlined in motors, that is, "turn to turn" first because of the lightest insulation, turning to "phase to phase" because of phase insulation and excess heat from the turn-to-turn fault. The final breakdown to ground is when the heat from the phase-to-phase fault allows a breakdown of insulation to ground. If we accept this process as the probable progression, the detection of these faults should be carried out in that order.

22.3 TURN-TO-TURN FAULT

A turn-to-turn fault is a short circuit between two turns of a coil of a single-phase potential. If each turn is rated at a few volts, for example, 2 V, and the coil has 10 turns, a short between the first and third coils would give 6 V. This may not be enough to cause anything more than a reduction in impedance in that particular phase and would therefore be undetectable unless balanced with the other phases. This is not too practical because of the other disymmetries in the generator. However, most generators use a parallel-circuit winding; each phase has two windings in parallel, and if the parallel circuits are not exactly equal, a small circulating current will exist. In most cases this is reduced by a jumper connecting the two parallel windings together at the halfway point.

We can see that this circulating current will increase as the inequality between parallel circuits increases. We therefore have a means of detecting a short circuit between turns if we monitor this circulating current. This type of relaying scheme should be applied in collaboration with the generator manufacturer. One method of applying a relay is to use a low-burden "very inverse" overcurrent relay with specially designed split-phase current transformers. The circulating current can be considered approximately 1/2% of rated full-load current. A relay of 0.5/2.0-A with an optional 4/16-A instantaneous trip for heavy faults causing unbalance can be utilized, but the winding type and connection, including external leads, must be compatible in allowing correct connection of relays.

22.4 PHASE-TO-PHASE FAULT

The phase-to-phase fault is usually the second-stage condition of a turn-to-turn fault, or it can occur without the turn-to-turn preliminary. The insulation between phases is obviously heavier than turn-to-turn insulation but with the disadvantage that, once a breakdown in insulation occurs, it produces an instant phase-to-phase short circuit, sometimes melting the copper into a molten blob. This requires the fastest detection and instant (as soon as possible) shutdown. As previously mentioned, even when the external load is disconnected, the generator will still try to feed the fault because (1) "the field is still connected" or (2) "the flux is still decaying." Relaying then must detect the fault, dump the load, and open the field and shut down the prime mover.

High-speed differential relaying will detect the fault. The opinion could be made that high-speed relaying is not necessary because of the slow decay of flux; however, we can consider that the high-speed differential can operate within 1 cycle; while the "instantaneous" relays take about 5 cycles. This means that the "shutdown program" can begin 4 or 5 cycles earlier than with non-high-speed relaying. Disconnecting the load circuit breaker is important because of system stability and containing the feedback of fault current. Opening the field circuit fast is not a simple action. The field-breaker and discharge-resistor performances have an effect on the flux rate of decay, as well as the transient voltage generated by flux collapse.

Recommending specific CTs and relays is noncontributing because it is more in the manufacturer's interest to insist on good generator protection, and as such, they will already have schemes worked out to fit the performance of the specific generator. The only additional recommendation would be to go for the high-speed differential rather than the instantaneous slower-speed relaying.

22.5 PHASE-TO-GROUND FAULT

The phase-to-ground fault is the most serious of the faults because of the possible damage to the stator iron (laminated steel core). Most generators are star-connected with a grounded neutral. The neutral may be solid or impedance-grounded, but in actual practice the fault current is usually limited by using reactance grounding on low-voltage generators (below 600 V) and resistance grounding on medium-voltage generators. Where the grounding is done through low resistance (or solid), then differential relaying can be used, protecting about 80% of the winding. Alternately, high-resistance grounding would preclude differential relaying, in which case an alternate scheme must be derived.

When high-resistance grounding is used and the fault current is limited, then a current relay may have trouble distinguishing between third-harmonic currents and fault currents.

One method of generator grounding is to insert a small distribution transformer in the neutral with a resistor connected across the secondary (see Sec. 25.9); this effectively offers a voltage supply during a fault. If a voltage relay is connected across the resistor and it is provided with a filter circuit for reducing third-harmonic content, a better system is offered, rather than just hanging a CT and overcurrent relay on the secondary.

If the transformer-resistor combination is selected to limit the ground current to around 3 A, the damage to the iron will be limited and therefore high speed is not as essential as it would be if it were solidly grounded. Even so, it is good practice to have the generator shut down as fast as possible; therefore this should be taken into consideration when deciding if the relay should sound an alarm or automatically shut down the generator. See Fig. 22.1.

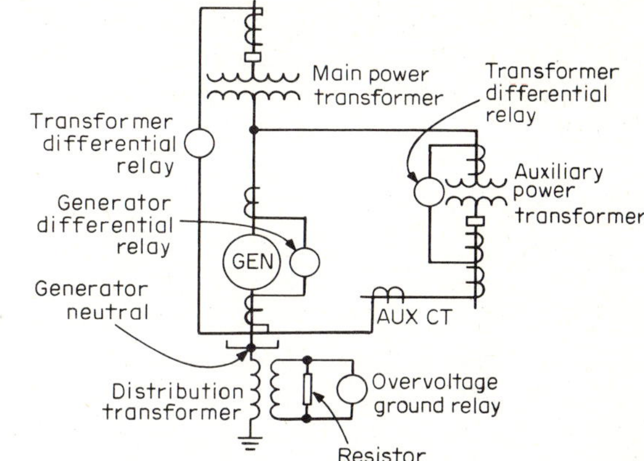

Figure 22.1 Unit generator-transformer protection.

22.6 FIELD GROUND FAULT

The generator field is dc and is an ungrounded circuit; therefore, if one ground occurs, nothing much will happen. If a second ground occurs, however, a portion of the field winding will be short-circuited. This means that the field magnetic flux will become unbalanced. If the short occurred in close proximity, the unbalance could be minimal. If it occurred at two extreme points, a gross unbalance would occur in the magnetic flux. Because the air gap in some machines is small and high-speed turbogenerator shafts are long, distortion can occur, whereby the rotor can rub on the stator, causing major damage.

Again, this problem and selection of relaying should be coordinated with the generator manufacturer. There are ac and dc delaying schemes. The ac scheme uses the shaft to provide a ground signal by picking up current flow through the shaft. This is not recommended and therefore any ac scheme that introduces currents in the shaft of any kind should not be considered.

Shaft currents will normally exist in a generator anyway, because of dissymettries in the flux and because the resulting voltage impressed into the shaft is ac with a high random harmonic content. If the circuit is incomplete through the shaft by insulating one bearing, no current will flow, which eliminates bearing damage. Introducing a current of even marginal amount or accidentally bypassing the insulated bearing with relaying devices offers the possibility of accelerated bearing failure.

Having covered the "don't do," we can now point out that one method of field relaying can be accomplished by using a dc field-protection relay, which works on a balanced-bridge principle. By inserting this relay between the dc field conductors and adjusting the bridge circuit (with a grounded center tap), a balanced condition will give zero current into the grounded conductor. If a sensitive voltmeter is placed in the grounded conductor, a fault on one side of the field will cause an unbalance in the circuit, resulting in a current flow in the grounded conductor.

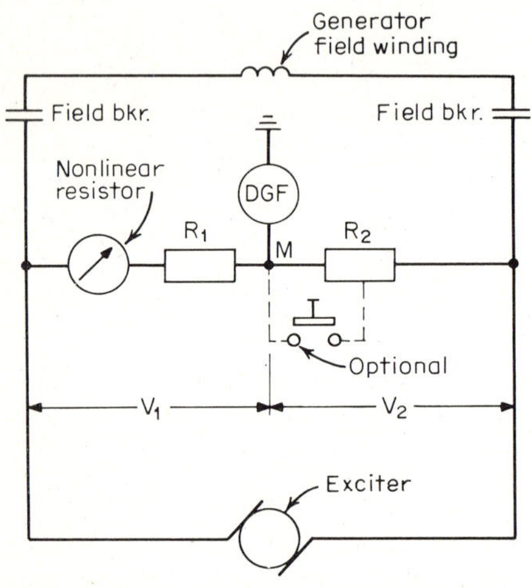

Exciter rating, V	R_1, Ω	R_2, Ω
125	0	45,000
250	5,000	23,000
375	10,000	23,000

Figure 22.2 Field ground protection scheme for a generator.

We now come to the debatable point of whether the relay should operate an alarm or an immediate automatic shutdown. This of course depends on the specific situation but weighing the cost of the extreme damage that can be done with the cost of shutting down and repairing the single failure (which has to be repaired anyway) would lean toward the shutdown. This could be put on a timer which would allow some time to transfer load and operate a proper shutdown but would also remove the responsibility of the operator having to make a decision which may be beyond his job capacity or responsibility. See Fig. 22.2.

22.7 REVERSE-POWER PROTECTION

When a generator prime mover loses its ability to provide enough power to supply the losses in its system, then the system will supply power to the prime mover via the generator. This effect is commonly called *motoring*. Waterwheel generators are exclusively utility-type installations and therefore would not be encountered in industrial plants; however, turbine and combustion-engine generators could have application as standby units or as power-plant units on foreign projects.

Protection against motoring can be provided by a reverse-power relay specially designed for sensitive operation. It will detect reverse power down to about 1.5%. A timer in the relay eliminates false tripping due to transient surges, which can occur during synchronizing operations.

The losses or motoring power for prime movers varies with the type of unit. In order to motor a generator with a turbine prime mover, approximately 3% of the nameplate rating in kW would be required. Diesel engines would require about 25% of nameplate rating. Lightly loaded turbines can sometimes overheat; therefore, in some cases they have overtemperature signalling devices installed. When this is the case, these will act as backup protection for the reverse-power relay.

22.8 NEGATIVE-PHASE-SEQUENCE PROTECTION

Negative-phase sequence is the term used in the method of symmetrical-component analysis. It is in effect a three-phase system of vectors but rotating in the opposite direction to the normal "positive sequence." The generator will produce positive-sequence currents of 60 Hz. A single-phase line-to-line fault would produce negative-sequence currents, and as they rotate in the opposite direction, they will effectively be 120-Hz currents. The generator then will have to produce power to overcome the negative-sequence currents and still maintain its previous output of positive-sequence currents. The ultimate effect is overloading, which shows up as overheating. The guide to overloading is defined as a product of negative-sequence current I_2 squared $(I_2)^2$ and time in seconds (t), or $(I_2)^2t$. When this product is in excess of 30 for turbine-generators and 40 for hydraulic turbine and engine generator sets, damage can be expected and an inspection should be made. If the $(I_2)^2t$ is more than 200% of the 30 and 40 limit, serious damage has probably already occurred.

We see then that line-to-line faults only allow a few seconds before damage can occur. Since the negative-sequence currents decrease with distance, they will be greatest at the fault and will decrease as they approach the generator. This means that the closer the fault to the generator, the less time is allowed for clearing. Line-to-line faults should be limited to under 5 sec. If a generator is fully loaded prior to the fault, the time factor is reduced.

A special negative-sequence time overcurrent relay is available. It is an induction-disk element which will pick up at 65%, or 0.65 per unit, which will allow 70 sec of operation at this low level of negative-sequence current. An alarm which will sense negative-sequence currents as low as 7% and will alert the operator that an unbalanced situation exists can also be included with the relay.

Around this level of unbalance no problem will exist, but it should be monitored to determine whether it clears or gets worse.

22.9 OVERVOLTAGE PROTECTION (GENERATOR OUTPUT)

As far as a generator is concerned, overvoltage can be produced by overspeed and/or a faulty voltage regulator. As both problems are serious enough to warrant instant shutdown, the relaying should be designed to ignore transients, accept some voltage rise within limits, and shut down instantly on large increases. A straight overvoltage relay will provide protection against overspeed due to a faulty governor and faulty regulator. The time-delay setting should be around 10% above normal, while the instantaneous setting should be slightly above the expected transient increase due to load dumping and prior to the regulator correcting the voltage level.

22.10 OVERVOLTAGE PROTECTION (FIELD WINDING)

Overvoltage protection of the field is usually limited to self-excited waterwheel generators, which are a utility-type installation and are usually a predesigned package; therefore, the average industrial designer will not encounter this problem.

22.11 EXCITATION-LOSS PROTECTION

The loss of excitation in a generator will result in the generator operating as an *induction generator.* In order to do this, the machine must "slip" and therefore drop out of synchronism. This can cause oscillating and temporary instability. There is time to sound an alarm and allow a reapplication of the field, providing the system stability was not affected and the time to correct the problem did not exceed a few seconds, for example, 30 to 60.

The problem of whether to have an automatic shutdown or not can be solved as suggested in field ground protection, that is, by installing a timer which allows an alarm but then allows a few seconds for corrective action. After this, it automatically shuts down.

The type of relaying available for this protection has gone beyond the simple dc undercurrent relay and is now accomplished by use of a *directional-distance* relay operating from ac current and potential transformers at the generator. The loss of excitation results in numerous changes to reactive power, power factor, system stability, and real power output. This is explained by means of an *R-X* diagram method of relay analysis, which we will not get involved with at this time. The relay is a *field-loss relay,* and inevitably a discussion of field loss will involve the generator manufacturer, who will also have his own recommendations purely in self-defense against warrantee claims.

22.12 BEARING PROTECTION

Bearings in large generators are usually sleeve-bearing types rather than antifriction bearings. As such the bearing metal is subject to "flowing" at high temperatures.

Various methods are available to measure these temperatures, such as contact-making thermometers, bulb-type thermometers, RTD, (resistance temperature detectors), and thermocouples.

All these options are acceptable, but with the low-mass items like RTDs and thermocouples, they should be protected from cold and incorrect locations which could affect their reading.

22.13 VIBRATION PROTECTION

Vibration can be caused by electric faults as well as mechanical faults; therefore, vibration can also be a "backup" indication of an electrical failure causing unbalanced magnetic forces. The vibration due to the stator going "egg-shaped," or out of round, is caused by unbalanced magnetic forces. Loss of dynamic balance of the rotor can produce vibration along with other possible mechanical faults.

Where the generator unit is a high-speed turbine, vibration recorders with alarm contacts can be provided. With other types of prime movers of low-speed vibration, protection is not usually provided.

22.14 MISCELLANEOUS PROTECTION

Cooling water for bearings can sometimes leak into the bearing oil. An oil-level indicator can give an alarm if the level suddenly increases.

Creep indicators are limited to the waterwheel-type generators and are used to prevent bearing damage. A certain speed is required before a film of oil covers the bearing. If the generator is allowed to slowly "creep," bearing damage could occur due to lack of an oil film. This creep indicator allows the operator to see if the generator rotor is actually stopped.

Potential transformer fuse blowing is a possibility due to aging and transient overvoltages. On large system units a scheme using three-phase *voltage-balance* relays supplied by alternate potential transformers can be used. This will then differentiate between a fuse blowing and relay operation due to low-voltage conditions. The phase voltage-balance relay will prevent the false tripping.

23 TRANSFORMER PROTECTION

23.1 TRANSFORMER CIRCUIT DYNAMICS

A transformer is a very simple static device under normal operating conditions; however, during fault conditions and initial energization the various parameters go through dynamic gyrations. Relaying then must sort out the dynamic variations which seem like a fault from the ones that are actually caused by a fault. The following list gives some of the problems which must be considered for effective relaying.

1. Different voltage levels
2. Tap changing (automatic or manual)
3. Variable primary currents (due to taps)
4. Magnetizing inrush (initial energizing)
5. Current-transformer types
6. Current-transformer accuracy
7. Transformer connections
8. Current-transformer connections
9. Operating speed desired
10. Available money for relaying
11. Transformer spare easily available
12. Transformer spare not readily available
13. Parallel-transformer arrangement
14. Transformer size

23.2 MAGNETIZING INRUSH

The impedance of a transformer is the vector sum of resistance and reactance. The resistance is low, but the reactance is high due to the highly inductive magnetic circuit.

When a transformer is initially energized, the only opposition to the flow of current is the resistance of the winding, which to all intents is negligible. The effect then is the same as a short circuit. This is only for a limited time, and as the core becomes magnetized, the reactance becomes high and therefore the total impedance increases and the current reduces to normal and is termed the exciting current.

This inrush takes a few seconds to die out completely but the initial peak, which can be about 10 times normal current, only lasts for a few cycles on a decreasing scale. To a relay this inrush appears exactly like a fault and therefore must somehow be recognized as inrush current.

Two other factors affect the inrush value. If the transformer is energized at the zero point of the cycle, then the inrush will be minimal. When the voltage begins to rise on the first part of the cycle, it will create magnetic flux in the core. If the previous shutdown left the steel polarized in the same direction, it will contribute to lower inrush; however, if the polarity was reversed, it will have to reverse the polarity before continuing to build up the flux. This all happens so fast that the only significant part is the initial peak inrush effect and the first few cycles rate of decay.

If a transformer is to be paralleled with another transformer, some of the inrush can spill over into the existing transformer if the circuit happens to be closed at full offset of the cycle. The effect would not be as drastic as the normal full inrush but it can occur and must be considered.

23.3 PRIMARY TAPS

The primary taps of a transformer change the voltage level by changing the ratio of turns between the primary and the secondary. As such the effect will be to change the current in the primary and therefore in any primary CTs. This means that any relaying should be set as though the taps were set at midpoint (i.e., normal) and the contemplated rate of change built into the relaying performance expected.

23.4 TRANSFORMER PROTECTION

The transformer lends itself ideally to differential relaying because both incoming and outgoing lines are easily accessible. Unfortunately, differential relaying does not lend itself easily to transformers; this is due to the discrimination between a fault and the inrush current.

A number of problems must be considered when applying transformer protection. First, it should be established what the protection is intended to do and how much money is prepared to be spent to obtain this degree of protection. The protection falls into two categories:

1. The protecting of the transformer because it is an expensive piece of equipment and a failure would require extensive on-site work to repair; alternate power is not available and production loss would be intolerable.
2. The transformer is one of many of the same size and type in the plant. A spare is available and repairs can be done by shipping the transformer back to the factory. Loss of production is limited to the time lost replacing the transformer.

If a fault is going to occur in the transformer, it will most probably occur whether relaying is installed or not. Therefore, repairs must be made. What then is the advantage of relay protection? The assumption must be made that the line (feeder) conductors are adequately protected; therefore a transformer fault will also appear as a fault in the conductors, in which case the circuit breaker or fuses will open the circuit. Clearly, then, the protection afforded a transformer is to limit the amount of damage to the transformer and prevent the plant operation from being radically upset. If the plant distribution is designed for alternate feeds, the protection only has to consider limiting the damage within the transformer. There are alternate ways of doing this.

23.5 TRANSFORMER PROTECTION SCHEMES (ALTERNATES)

First, below 1000 kVA transformer protection is not generally provided beyond the protection offered by the overcurrent protection required by code.

Transformers of 1000 kVA and up warrant consideration of additional protection. This will be judged as outlined in Sec. 23.4. Alternate choices available are:

- Gas-relay (single element); conservator-type liquid filled only.
- Gas-relay (two element); conservator type only.
- Winding temperature device—with actuating contacts—for alarm or tripping.
- Differential relaying (reduced sensitivity and time delay for initial peaks).
- Differential relaying (with harmonic desensitizing coordinated unit).
- Differential relaying (initial energizing desensitizing).
- Differential relaying (with voltage-operated–automatic-tripping suppressor unit).

Whether one or more of these protective devices is used depends of course on whether "everything possible" should be done to limit damage. If a transformer is worth protecting, then the protection added should operate faster than the normal overcurrent protection required by code.

23.6 TRANSFORMER GAS RELAY

The gas relay was described briefly in Sec. 20.21. It is a fairly simple device as far as installation is concerned. Some transformers (liquid filled) are supplied with a conservator. This is a sealed air chamber above the oil level. A single- or dual-element gas relay is available; this senses both a slow rise in pressure and a sudden rise in pressure. The single-element unit is usually the sudden-pressure type. The gas relay is sensitive to faults of a very low level, such as turn-to-turn faults. The speed of response is not consistent and varies with the location of the relay relative to the fault and also the "explosive" nature of the fault. Times for tripping can vary between a half cycle to 30 or 40 cycles.

The gas relay is applicable to transformers of around 5000 kVA and up, especially the utility/service type of transformers. It should not be considered as a "first-line" protection but rather a backup to differential protection.

23.7 TRANSFORMER-WINDING TEMPERATURE DEVICE

This device is more of an overload sensor rather than a fault detector. It measures the top oil temperature but has a compensating device which reflects the hot-spot temperature rather than the oil temperature. This also means that the temperature-rise curve is closely followed by the device. It can be made to operate contacts which can operate an alarm or tripping and cooling device.

This is a fairly inexpensive device and pays for itself by allowing operation up to full thermal capacity.

23.8 TRANSFORMER DIFFERENTIAL RELAYING (REDUCED SENSITIVITY AND TIME DELAY)

This type of differential relaying is the simplest and probably the most economical. We know that differential relaying compares input currents with output currents and therefore dissymmetries in CTs and currents can cause false tripping. By reducing the sensitivity of the relay, this overcomes part of the problem but reduces the protective capability somewhat. The inrush current problem is overcome by a time delay which allows overriding of initial peak currents. This of course cuts out the differential relaying at its most useful time. CTs with multiple taps are used on one side to adjust for the correct ratios.

In all differential relaying on conventionally connected star-delta transformers, the CTs on the star (grounded) side are connected in delta. The

CTs on the delta side must be connected with a star connection and the neutral point grounded. This corrects for the 30° phase shift between the two connections and also prevents zero-sequence currents from operating the relays.

The selection of this type of differential relaying must take into consideration that the protection offered is marginal on the basis of the reduced sensitivity and no protection on inrush.

23.9 TRANSFORMER DIFFERENTIAL PROTECTION (HARMONIC DESENSITIZING)

Harmonics can occur in a transformer both under inrush and fault conditions. During the inrush the second harmonic content will probably be the highest, while during a fault the second harmonic content will be at minimum. There is then a measurable difference between the current during inrush and during a fault. A relay scheme is available which considers these differences. The harmonic content of the inrush wave is used to operate a restraining device, which prevents the differential relay from operating during initial energizing.

The relays are the percentage differential type, which reduces errors caused by unbalanced currents. Also included is an instantaneous-trip unit which operates on the differential current but is set at about 8 to 10 times tap setting, much higher than normal differential operating current. This provides high-speed tripping for heavy faults.

This scheme is probably one of the most ideal. It has a number of good points.

1. Sensitive to small faults in the winding
2. As fast or faster than other relaying in the system
3. Unaffected by inrush
4. Unaffected by CT variable characteristics
5. Can accommodate load-ratio control (taps)
6. High-speed operation for heavy faults

The CTs supplied with this system will have variable taps for correct ratio adjustment. The requirement of the star and delta connections on opposite sides of the main transformer star and delta connections also apply.

23.10 TRANSFORMER DIFFERENTIAL PROTECTION (VOLTAGE-OPERATED TRIPPING SUPPRESSOR)

Percentage differential protection can be applied to a transformer with a tripping suppressor to overcome the problem of inrush current. It is intended primarily for three-winding transformer banks but can be applied to two-winding bank systems. The tripping suppressor is a voltage-sensitive device. It recognizes the fact that a three-phase voltage will be high (full voltage) during inrush, and reduced voltage(s) during a fault.

The tripping suppressor works by opening the three tripping circuits to the differential before the differentials have time to operate. If any of the three voltage-sensing contacts do not open, the differentials will operate. This means that the differentials can instantly detect a fault during energizing, which is one of the most vulnerable periods.

Potential transformers are used to provide a three-phase 120-V 60-Hz voltage. The potential transformers must be energized at the same time as the main transformer; therefore, they should be located on the energizing side within the zone being protected by the differentials. It is usually a delta connection; so line-to-line voltages are used. If it happens to be a star, phase voltages are preferable but only on the basis that it is a lower voltage.

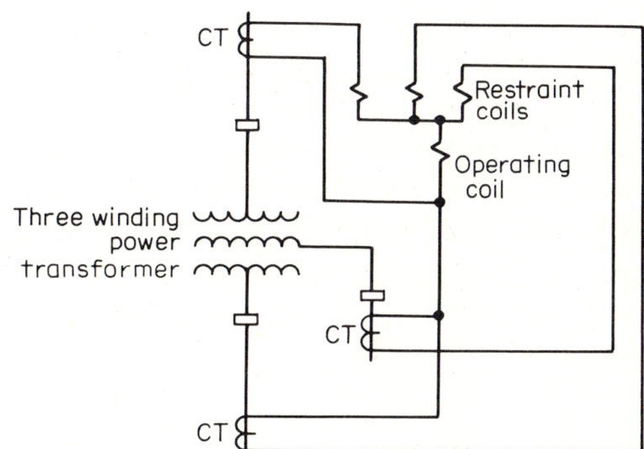

Figure 23.1 Three-winding transformer with differential protection.

The big feature about this system is the instant fault sensing on inrush. This, of course, is offset by the additional cost of the potential transformers and the suppression unit plus more parts, and therefore, probably more maintenance and reduced reliability. See Fig. 23.1.

23.11 TRANSFORMER DIFFERENTIAL PROTECTION (INITIAL DESENSITIZING)

This method of differential relaying is actually an addition to a standard current or percentage-differential protection system. It is a very simple modification and simply uses a resistor in parallel with the operating coil. This in effect raises the pickup current by two or three times. The resistor can be disconnected after the inrush has died out. This can be done by timer or by manual operation. The former is preferred.

This is obviously a cheap method of overcoming the inrush problem, but it also reduces the probability of detecting faults on inrush.

23.12 SUMMARY

With transformer protection "you take your pick and take your chances." The previous methods outlined are some choices, but new devices and techniques, especially in solid-state devices, are constantly making an impact into the power field; therefore, the choice of protection still comes down to the details outlined in Sec. 23.4. Once the importance of the transformer is placed against the scale of values related to that particular project, then it can be decided what degree of protection is required. This can then be weighed against the money available for "extras."

Once it is decided to invest in expensive relaying, the manufacturers should be contacted to obtain the latest devices and modifications applicable.

24 DISTRIBUTION PROTECTION

24.1 BUS PROTECTION

Bus protection is generally limited to large station bus installations. These are utility-company transmission-line stations. The relaying involved is predominantly differential-voltage relays using linear couplers instead of ordinary CTs. As this type of installation and protection is limited to utility companies with their own specific problems, about the only time a designer will encounter this is if his employing company is subcontracting to do utility substation design. In this event the section doing this work is usually separated from the industrial-plant design groups. Relaying is also predesigned by the utility-company engineers along with an issue of a detailed specification. Therefore we will not consider this any further.

24.2 TRANSMISSION-LINE PROTECTION

Transmission lines are high-voltage lines designed to span long distances with minimum of losses. The voltage on these lines can be anywhere from medium voltage, that is, 13 kV, to 700-kV extra-high-voltage (EHV) lines. A good rule of thumb for transmission lines is that 1000 V per mile is acceptable. This means that the 700-kV, EHV line is good for around 700 miles nonstop. This then creates problems of protection. It is difficult to locate and check out a fault in hundreds of miles of desert, mountains, rough country, etc. Special relaying can assist in monitoring these lines.

Once again, this work is designed by utility companies and relay manufacturers' application engineers, and the industrial designer will rarely encounter it. Briefly, however, we will point out that many faults on these lines are transient in nature. Storms, birds, brush, etc., can all cause temporary faults which are usually self-clearing.

The type of relaying used falls into two main types: *distance relaying* and *pilot relaying*. The distance relaying operates by comparing the ratio of voltage to current, which gives impedance (Z) and admittance values ($1/Z$). If resistance is known, reactance X can be determined. These values can be translated into distance. Hence an approximate location of the fault can be determined.

The pilot relaying is in fact a very sophisticated differential-relaying scheme. As such, opposite ends of the line must be interconnected. This of course is out of the question with conventional means; therefore, a *pilot* system is used. This can be either a *wire pilot* or a *carrier pilot.* The first method uses direct-wire connections, that is, telephone line on lease or installed as part of the system. The other and more convenient method for long distance is the *carrier* method. This uses the actual power line as a *carrier* for a signal. The effective distance of the carrier system is only limited by the strength of the carrier transmitter and rate of signal loss.

The carrier system can also be used to carry communication, supervisory, and remote-control signals. In this case the system is set up so that relaying has priority.

As we can guess, these systems can get complex and spending time on analyzing the applications is noncontributing to the industrial designer; therefore, we will not delve any further into the problem.

24.3 SUBTRANSMISSION LINES

Subtransmission lines are generally smaller taps off a main transmission line, the top voltage being about 33 kV. In this voltage range we are considering 30 miles maximum. This means that distance and pilot relaying are probably uneconomical. Again, it is usually a utility company installation not encountered by the industrial designer. In any case, the protection used is similar to the distribution lines which can be encountered in industrial plants.

24.4 DISTRIBUTION-LINE PROTECTION

Distribution lines are in effect miniature transmission lines, the purpose being to supply a block of power to an area some distance away. Along the way taps which feed selected concentrations of load can be made. This type of line is rarely found in an industrial plant, but it can be applicable in industrial-plant operations where the complex might cover large areas such as mining, missile-base installations, explosives storage and manufacture, steel mill operations, and possibly pipeline installations. Foreign projects often have small generating plants with a distribution line supplying a plant with an associated company town.

The protection of distribution lines is accomplished by use of the time overcurrent relays coordinated into a sequential tripping arrangement. It is necessary to do a short-circuit study deriving the minimum fault currents and the maximum fault currents. The pickup of the relays is set to operate on minimum fault current, while the time setting is based on the maximum fault current. This allows adjoining parts of the system to trip before the main part of the system.

The various curves (inverse, very inverse, etc.) have already been covered in previous paragraphs and can be selected to coordinate with fuses or circuit breakers, etc.

The time selection will result in a slower and slower trip time as we progress back from the farthest point of the load to the main substation. In order to "back up" this slow protection, instantaneous trips can be installed which will operate for values of fault current in the primary area.

Directional-current relays can also be utilized where distribution systems form loop systems and interconnecting circuits.

24.5 RECLOSING RELAYS

A distribution line can be considered as the backbone of a small system. Taps are taken off at various points along the line. When a fault occurs somewhere on the system, we need to know a number of things.

1. Where is the fault located?
2. Is it a permanent fault?
3. Is it a transient fault?
4. Should that section be disconnected until a repair crew can be sent out?

If the total length of the distribution line is broken into shorter sections by installing automatic circuit breakers, then a fault can be isolated by opening the circuit breaker ahead of the fault. As the circuit breaker is unattended, it could have opened on a transient fault caused by a bird touching two lines or some other similar condition.

This type of fault is self-clearing; therefore, the circuit breaker is now tripped, requiring someone to check why it tripped and reset it. In all probability, the first approach of a maintenance man would be to try and reclose it to see if the fault was still there. If not, it would remain closed and no further action would be taken. The fault then is examined by re-trying to close the circuit breaker. This then makes a fairly simple operation for a relay to perform. It can in fact be done with timers. In actual fact this type of relay uses a synchronous-motor-driven set of cams which in effect provide fixed time cycles. The cams are adjustable; therefore the time cycle is adjustable.

Records will indicate that around 80% of the breaker trips can be reclosed instantaneously. A further 10% can be reclosed after a short time delay of 15 to 45 sec. A total delay of around 2 minutes will sometimes allow reclosing of another 1 or 2% of faults. This adds up to 92% of the breaker operations being successfully reclosed. We see that the third closing will only pick up

1 or 2% additional reclosures; therefore, the probability of picking up any more on a fourth reclosure is remote.

The available reclosing relays can be programmed for three reclosing operations: (1) instantaneous, (2) after 15 sec, (3) after 45 sec. Modifications can provide more, but as previously pointed out, they probably gain nothing. This is termed *multi-shot* reclosing. If the fault is not cleared after the three "tries," the relay locks the circuit breaker open.

In distribution systems it is usually uneconomical to install circuit breakers at each tap point; fuses are more economical. This leads into another method of *single-shot* reclosing. If the fuse link is sized correctly at the tap point, when a fault occurs on the tap, the circuit breaker will open on "instantaneous" and reclose immediately. If the fault is persistent, the fuse link will "blow." When the recloser tries again the fault will be cleared by the *subline* being disconnected at the fuse cutout. It must be pointed out that reclosers with reliable operating characteristics plus specific fuse coordination is required for the single-shot reclosing system; otherwise the fuse will blow on the first fault before the recloser has a chance to operate. This means that the fuses would require changing when in fact the fault was self-clearing.

24.6 SECTIONALIZER

A sectionalizer is a device similar to a circuit breaker but without a fault-interrupting capability. This makes it a much cheaper device to install. As it has only a no-load interrupting capability, it must operate in conjunction with a recloser. It is controlled by a "counter," which we could (in a vague sort of way) classify as a relay.

As it is a signal-monitoring device, we will include it in this section on protection.

The sectionalizer is used in place of the fused tap points or on the last section of a line replacing the last recloser. When a fault occurs, the recloser opens before the sectionalizer (this means the sectionalizer opens with the fault removed). A counter in the sectionalizer monitors the recloser operations; when two or more reclosure operations occur, the sectionalizer stays open. If the fault was in the line beyond the sectionalizer, the recloser will close a third time and remain in because the fault is now isolated by the open sectionalizer.

24.7 INRUSH CURRENTS

Again we face the problem of inrush currents. When a line is "cold," that is, a new installation or long outage, the startup or energizing of the distribution line may cause the reclosers to suspect a fault. They will therefore go through their protective sequence and lock out. When specifying or dealing with reclosers, check the manufacturer's literature to determine if the recloser has a built-in cold-start feature. If not, some kind of reference should be made to indicate that inrush should be kept to a minimum if possible by dumping automatically started loads and transformers.

Energizing transformers by closing the primary switches individually, rather than the approach of opening "secondaries only" prior to energizing, will reduce inrush.

24.8 AUTOMATIC SYNCHRONIZING

This is a device which belongs in the power station, but as we are not covering power stations, we will introduce it here, the logic being that the distribution line may in fact begin at a small multigenerator unit.

Synchronization of generators can only be accomplished when certain conditions are met. The speed of the incoming machine must exactly match the operating machines. The voltage should be approximately the same as the system and the droop setting on the governor should be correct. This is not a complicated operation, but if a machine is "closed in" by accident or incompetence when significantly "out of phase," damage can be done to the generator and possibly the prime mover. In foreign projects this may be a problem because of language difficulties between construction engineers and "take-over" operators. This possibility can be minimized by installing automatic synchronizing equipment. It should also be installed where generators may operate unattended and phasing in to other lines.

The relay operation is fairly simple. It compares the frequency between the incoming machine and the existing power system. It also compares the voltage. When the two are within predetermined limits, it will close the main breaker. This, however, will not take care of the setting of the governor droop. If these are not set correctly, load swings can cause the generators to motor and trip the main breaker.

24.9 LOAD DUMPING

Some industrial and foreign projects have a mixture of self-generated power and purchased power from utility systems. When the utility system ceases to provide power either through accident or design, it is possible for the plant generators to become overloaded.

If this happened because of a fault on the utility, there would not be time to rearrange loads by selective dumping; therefore, protective relaying can be installed to do this automatically. This relay will sense the slowing up in speed of the prime mover due to its inability to meet the power demand. Since frequency is proportional to speed, a relay can measure the rate of change of frequency from normal. The operating contacts can then be tied into various loads, which can be dumped. These will of course have been preselected.

25 GROUNDING

25.1 GROUNDING

Grounding can be separated into two separate and distinct groups.

1. System and winding grounds
2. Equipment and enclosure grounds

The first type of grounding is associated with problems of circuit function and performance and is essential in system design and equipment application problems.

The second type of grounding deals strictly with safety and accidental grounding of equipment and enclosure which could otherwise be a hazard to personnel. In this chapter we will discuss the aspects of system-grounding problems and offer some solutions.

25.2 SYSTEM GROUNDING

Sooner or later a designer is in the position of having to decide whether to install a system which is grounded or ungrounded. Both systems have been widely used and selected for different reasons.

The two main features of the grounded and ungrounded systems are that a ground on the former will cause an instant shutdown of the affected circuit, while a ground on a nongrounded system will float and will not affect the operation of the circuit unless another ground occurs. At first consideration it would seem that the nongrounded system would be desirable because this means production can be maintained while the fault is being located. Further investigation, however, will show that there are detracting factors from utilizing the nongrounded system.

System grounding must also be considered at the particular voltage level and whether it is primary or secondary grounding.

25.3 DELTA-WINDING CONNECTION

The delta connection is familiar from the discussion on transformer connections (Secs. 8.8 and 8.10). It has no natural neutral point; therefore it is usually used for the nongrounded system. It does in fact have an unintentional grounding through capacitive effect; therefore, when we talk about "grounded" we mean "intentionally" grounded.

The main claim and probably only acceptable feature of the ungrounded system is the ability to maintain operations while a single ground exists. We must now consider the detrimental points of the system.

When a fault occurs from one phase to ground, the voltage stress on insulation is increased by 73%, or 1.73 times, the phase-to-neutral voltage potential existing prior to the fault. In order to eliminate the single-fault, ground indicators must be installed at additional cost. The circuits must then be checked to determine which circuit is faulty. The only way to effectively do this is to open each circuit breaker until the offending circuit is isolated. It is then further required to examine the faulty circuit and determine exactly what is causing the ground. If the ground is in a motor, it may not be detectable until it develops into a phase-to-phase fault. This may then cause more damage than the original fault.

Multiple motor failures can occur due to elevated voltages caused by accidental grounding. Motors can be started accidentally by control circuits being subjected to accidental grounds on one or more phases.

Transient voltages are not limited and exceedingly high voltages can be applied accidentally without any obvious indication of the voltage level. Single line-to-ground faults can become phase-to-phase faults by a second line-to-ground fault. If they are both solid faults, the overload devices will open the circuit, but if one fault is a low-level arcing fault, transient overvoltages can exist and also a low-level fault current, which can cause considerable overheating before being detected by the overload devices.

Maintenance must be expensive if an efficient ungrounded system is to be used. The advantage of nontripping on a single fault has its place in plants where instant shutdown is hazardous because of the stability nature of process gases. Other than this, records can show that lost production due to operating with an ungrounded system is probably slightly higher than with the grounded system, which is actually the reverse to what would be expected.

25.4 GROUNDED DELTA SYSTEM (CORNER DELTA)

The corners of a delta can be considered as potentially neutral and therefore can be grounded. This, however, only grounds two of the phases. It is cheap to install and provides some additional protection over the ungrounded system as far as motor control circuits are concerned. The disadvantages are: it is an unsymmetrical neutral, and it cannot be used as a system for supplying lighting and power at different voltages. The grounded phases must be identified for metering and relaying and the line-to-ground voltage is higher than the conventional grounded system by 73%.

25.5 GROUNDED DELTA SYSTEM (PHASE MIDPOINT)

Grounding at the midpoint of a single phase is essentially providing a single-phase 120/240-V system. It must be identified as the grounded phase when run with other phase conductors. It has some advantage in limiting voltage levels and in detecting and discriminating of line-to-ground faults. As it is limited to single-phase transformer banks and is more of a convenience pickup point for a single-phase three-wire source, it is rarely used by first intent.

25.6 GROUNDED DELTA SYSTEM (ZIGZAG TRANSFORMER)

Sometimes it is desirable to ground a delta system. One of the traditional and recommended methods is by using a grounding transformer. There are two alternate selections, the preferred one of which is the zigzag-connected transformer, the other being a star-delta transformer.

The zigzag transformer consists of six coils wound on a three-phase core, with two coils per leg. The ends of three coils are connected together, giving a neutral point, while the other end of these three coils are connected to the next coil in the adjacent leg, with opposite polarity. See Fig. 25.1.

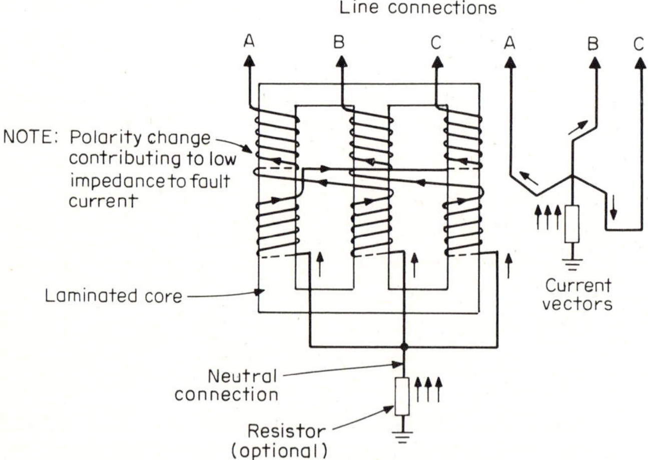

Figure 25.1 Three-phase zigzag grounding transformer.

The zigzag-transformer characteristics are such that it will give high impedance to a three-phase current and low impedance to a ground-fault current. This means that when the transformer is connected across a three-phase line only a small magnetizing current will flow in the transformer, but when a ground fault occurs, a large current will flow.

The direction of flow is from the faulted line to the neutral, up the neutral and dividing into three equal parts in the zigzag transformer. The tendency to equal distribution is by the current in one leg of the core being transferred to an adjacent leg of the core with reversed polarity. This second coil with reverse polarity opposes the flux from the first coil.

The rating of a grounding transformer is usually on a 10-sec basis, although other short-time (60-sec) ratings can be specified. The limited time rating of the transformer means that it will be much smaller than the equivalent "full-time" rated transformer. To estimate the comparative size with a full-rated three-phase transformer use the formula

$$(\text{kV}/1.73)(I_{sc})(0.064) = \text{kVA}$$

An approximate guess or "rule of thumb" for sizing a zigzag transformer is assuming line current as unbalanced neutral current and multiplying by 20 times to obtain a 10-sec rating in amperes. The correct sizing of a zigzag transformer depends on the exact grounding arrangement (i.e. whether solid, resistor, reactor in the neutral, grounding transformer protection, etc.). The specification must give:

1. Grounding transformer (three-phase) (specify service).
2. Voltage: ______ line to line.
3. Liquid-filled (oil) or Askarel.
4. Zigzag type.
5. Frequency.
6. Ohms line to neutral (single-phase) required.
7. Time rating 10 sec (or alternate).
8. Maximum temperature rise 125°C.
9. It must carry ________ A through the neutral lead which will be limited by external (resistor) (reactor).

The above items can be specified fairly simply.

1. *Voltage:* ______ line to line
2. *Current:* ______ maximum neutral (fault) current. Limited by resistor or reactor. In solidly grounded systems, limited by the grounding-transformer impedance.
3. *Time:* ______ 10 sec (or other). Will carry rated current for this time without exceeding 125°C temperature.
4. *Reactance:* of grounding transformer per phase (ohms).

$$X_{GT} = \frac{(X_0/X_1) \times (\text{kV}^2) \times 1000}{\text{kVA}_{sc}}$$

where X_{GT} = grounding transformer reactance (ohms per phase)
X_0 = zero-sequence reactance
X_1 = positive-sequence reactance
kVA_{sc} = system symmetrical three-phase short-circuit kVA.
kV = line-to-line voltage

The quantity X_0/X_1 is for limiting transient overvoltages and for reactance grounding should be 10 or less. For a grounding transformer to be solidly grounded, it should be 10 or less. For a grounding transformer, "resistance grounded," X_0/X, is no limit except if R_0/X_0[1] is less than 2. Then $X_0/X_1 = 10$ or less where R_0 is assessed at three times neutral resistor value.

To calculate the impedance X_{gt}, we need only to decide the value for X_0/X_1. To limit transient overvoltages, we know it must be $(X_0/X_1) = 10$ when considering reactor or solid grounding for transformer neutrals. For low resistance-grounded neutrals we also know that there is no limit except if R_0/X_0 is less than 2, in which case $X_0/X_1 = 10$ or less.

Having to maintain $X_0/X_1 = 10$ or less, we can substitute "10" in the equation, giving:

$$X_{gt} = \frac{10 \times (\text{kV})^2 \times 1000}{\text{kVA}_{sc}}$$

For a 4.16-kV system with 40,000 kVA symmetrical short-circuit kVA, X_{gt} would be:

$$X_{gt} = \frac{10{,}000 \times (4.16)^2}{40{,}000} = 4.33\ \Omega/\text{phase}$$

This then gives the necessary ratings.

1. Voltage is 4.16 V.
2. Amperes is 40,000/(1.73 × 4.16) = 5558 A.
3. Time (10-sec rating).
4. Reactance per phase is 4.33 Ω.

If grounded-neutral lightning arrestors (which will be covered in other chapters) are used, set the ratio $X_0/X_1 = 3$ and modify the previous equation to

$$X_{gt} = \frac{3 \times (\text{kV})^2 \times 1000}{\text{kVA}_{sc}}$$

and for the preceding example would change the X_{gt} to

$$X_{gt} = \frac{3000 \times (4.16)^2}{40{,}000} = 1.3\ \Omega$$

[1] For the ratio R_0/X_0, R_0 is assessed at three times the neutral resistor values.

When using grounding transformers, it is necessary to check that the selected impedance for the grounding transformer allows adequate fault current for operation of fuses, circuit breakers, and relaying.

25.7 GROUNDED DELTA SYSTEM (STAR-DELTA)

An alternate approach to grounding a delta system is by using a star-delta-connected transformer. The neutral point of the star is grounded through a resistor (usually), and the delta must be "closed" to provide a path for the zero-sequence current.

Although this approach is workable, it should be considered as a temporary or "special" installation, with a specific reason for utilizing the star-delta rather than the zigzag grounding method.

25.8 SOLID GROUNDING (TRANSFORMER)

A three-phase transformer in an industrial plant designed for a grounded system will probably be a delta primary and a star-connected secondary. The neutral is usually sized the same size as the line conductors. This is due to a combination of convenience and extra safety. The neutral need only carry the maximum unbalanced load, but if a smaller size is specified, it may not be available on the job site; as the neutral is a short length, it is usually much easier to cut a small piece of line conductor (which is fully rated).

The neutral then is sized based on the continuous rating of the power transformer. When it is solidly grounded, it must also be checked for the short-time rating under short-circuit conditions, that is, line-to-ground fault.

This can be done by using the semiempirical formula (for copper conductors):[2]

$$t = \frac{1}{\left(\frac{I}{CM}\right)^2 (33)} \left[\log_{10} = \frac{(T_2 + 234)}{(T_1 + 234)} \right]$$

where t = time, sec
I = rms current
CM = circular mils
T_1 = initial temperature, °C
T_2 = final temperature, °C

for aluminum conductors substitute 80 for 33 and 228 for 234.

The time t is the time required for the breaker to clear the fault. This can vary from 2 to 8 cycles, the latter time being for large oil circuit breakers of the substation type.

To determine the fault current, it is necessary to do a short-circuit study

[2] See Sec. 33.10 for complete examples.

and determine the line-to-ground fault current. An example of fault current taken at the transformer on a single radial feeder can be shown as follows:

Consider a 1000-kVA transformer, three-phase, 5% Z with 460-V three-phase secondary and the transformer as the sole source of fault current:

1. $\dfrac{1000 \text{ kVA}}{\sqrt{3} \times 0.48} = 1202 \text{ A}$

2. $1202/Z = 1202/0.05 = 24{,}040$ A symmetrical

3. $24{,}040 \times 1.25 = 30{,}050$ A asymmetrical

4. $I_g = \dfrac{3\,E_{1n}}{X_1 + X_2 + X_0}$

5. $X_1 = \dfrac{\%X \times (\text{kV})^2 \times 10}{\text{kVA}} = \dfrac{5 \times (0.48)^2 \times 10}{1000} = 0.0115\ \Omega$

6. $X_2 = X_1 = 0.0115\ \Omega$

7. $X_0 = X_1 = 0.0115\ \Omega$

   (6–7) for transformers $X_1 = X_2 = X_0$

8. $I_g = \dfrac{3(480/1.73)}{0.0115 + 0.0115 + 0.0115} = 24{,}126$ A symmetrical

9. $24{,}126 \times 1.25 = 30{,}158$ A asymmetrical
   The line-to-ground fault current must be more than 25% of the three-phase fault current, so from line 3 we have:

10. $30{,}050 \times 100/30{,}158 = 99.7\%$ of three-phase fault current

To prevent transient overvoltages, the ground-fault current must be more than 25% of the three-phase fault current and generally limited to 100% as maximum.

When lightning arresters of the grounded-neutral type are used, the line-to-ground fault current should be 60% of the three-phase fault current as a minimum, with 100% as a maximum. Figure 25.2 shows four methods where solid grounding could be used, and also where fault current could exceed 100% and therefore should be limited to below 100% three-phase fault. The general criteria for solid grounding is when the system is below 600 V or above 15,000 V (15 kV).

25.9 GENERATOR GROUNDING (LOW VOLTAGE, MAX. 600 V)

When a generator is star-connected, it can be solidly grounded except in a situation where this may cause the ground fault current to exceed the three-phase fault current, that is, 100%. If this occurs, solid grounding should not be used and a change to low-reactance grounding must be considered.

If we compare the three-phase and line-to-ground fault currents, we see

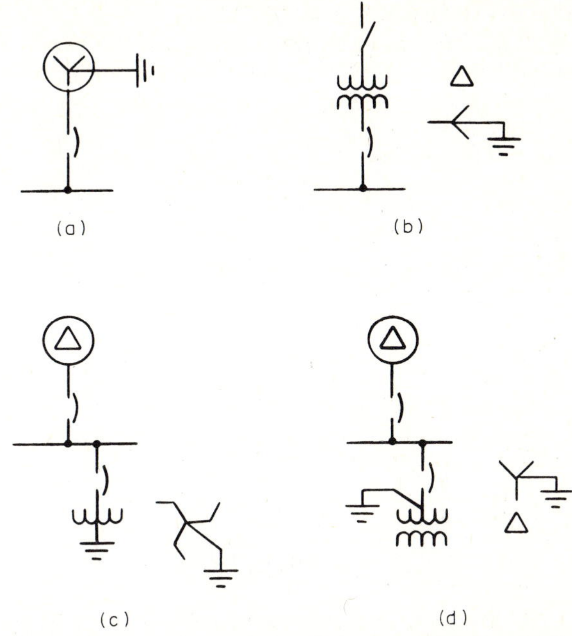

Figure 25.2 Methods of solid grounding generally for less than 600 V or more than 15,000 V. (a) Generator with solid grounding; (b) transformer with solid grounding; (c) delta system with zigzag grounding transformer; (d) delta system with star-delta grounding transformer.

that the three-phase is proportional to the admittance $1/Z$, where Z is usually replaced by X_1, which is the *positive-sequence reactance.*

By contrast, the ground fault current depends on

$$\frac{3}{X_1 + X_2 + X_0}$$

If $X_1 = X_2 = X_0$, the three-phase and ground fault currents should be equal. For example, $1/0.05 = 20$ for three-phase

and $\quad 3/(0.05 + 0.05 + 0.05) = 3/0.15 = 20 \quad$ for ground fault

However, if we change X_0 to 0.02 (2%), we have

$$1/0.05 = 20 \qquad \text{for three-phase}$$

and $\quad 3/(0.05 + 0.05 + 0.02) = 3/0.12 = 25 \quad$ for ground fault

We see that 20 × base kVA will give less short-circuit current than 25 × base kVA as indicated for the ground fault current. In this case then it is necessary to install a reactor to reduce the ground fault current to at least 100% of the three-phase fault current.

For generator reactance grounding the maximum current in any winding must not exceed the three-phase value. This means that the ratio X_0/X_1 must equal 1. To calculate the value of the neutral reactance, we use the following formula:

1. $I_g = \dfrac{3(E/1.73)}{X_1 + X_2 + X_0 + 3X_n}$

This equation can be reduced as follows:

2. I_{sc} (three-phase) $= (E/1.73)/X_1$

3. $I_g = I_{sc}$, then $\dfrac{3(E/1.73)}{X_1 + X_2 + X_0 + 3X_n} = \dfrac{E/1.73}{X_1}$

4. Solving for X_n,

$$X_1 + X_2 + X_0 + 3X_n = \frac{3(E/1.73)X_1}{(E/1.73)} = 3X_1$$

5. If $X_n = \dfrac{3X_1 - X_1 - X_2 - X_0}{3} = \dfrac{2X_1 - X_2 - X_0}{3}$, and

6. If $X_1 = X_2$ and $X_2 = X_d''$, we have $X_n = \dfrac{X_1 - X_0}{3}$

7. We therefore can state $X_n = \dfrac{X_d'' - X_0}{3}$

We must now evaluate the different types of reactances. They are broken into two groups: machine reactances and system reactances. The system reactances are given in their "symmetrical components" designations.[3]

System reactances

- X_1 is positive sequence.
- X_2 is negative sequence.
- X_0 is zero sequence.

Machine (Generator Reactances).

- X_d' is transient reactance.
- X_d'' is subtransient reactance.
- X_{2m} is negative sequence (machine).
- X_{0m} is zero sequence (machine).

If $X_{2m} = X_d''$, use

$$\frac{X_d'' - X_{0m}}{3} = X_n$$

[3] See section on symmetrical components (Chapter 32).

where this is the lowest reactance to limit the machine current to maximum three-phase fault value.

The neutral-ground reactor has two ratings:

1. Impedance value
2. Mechanical and thermal values

There are also two limits between which the reactor must maintain the ground fault current, these are:

1. Maximum current limited to three-phase fault
2. Minimum current must be limited to 25% of three-phase fault current to protect from transient overvoltages

The generator will have three reactances available from the generator manufacturer: X''_d, X'_d, X_{0m}. These will all be presented as a percentage with the generator rating as the base. These must be changed into an "ohms per phase" rating. This is done by using the following equation:

$$X\text{ (ohms)} = \frac{X\% \times (\text{kV})^2 \times 10}{\text{base kVA}}$$

where $X\%$ is generator reactance, kV is line-to-line voltage, and base kVA is generator kVA.

If we are given a generator with the following rating; 750 kVA, 480 V, three-phase, 60 Hz, $X'_d = 23\%$, $X''_d = 13\%$, and $X_{0m} = 7\%$. These would be converted as follows:

$$X'_d = \frac{23\% \times (0.48)^2 \times 10}{750} = 0.0707\ \Omega$$

$$X''_d = \frac{13\% \times (0.48)^2 \times 10}{750} = 0.0399\ \Omega$$

$$X_{0m} = \frac{7\% \times (0.48)^2 \times 10}{750} = 0.0215\ \Omega$$

With the reactances in ohms per phase we can now consider the reactance value by using our previous equation.

$$X_n = \frac{X''_d - X_0}{3}$$

$$X_n = \frac{0.0399 - 0.0215}{3}$$

$$X_n = 0.0061\ \Omega$$

This reactance is in the neutral therefore must always be considered in *series* with the zero-sequence (X_0) reactance. Consider a hypothetical system of two 750-kVA generators and an incoming utility line as shown in Fig. 25.3.

This single line could be a typical system where essential service must be maintained; if the utility goes out, then the generators will maintain essential service power.

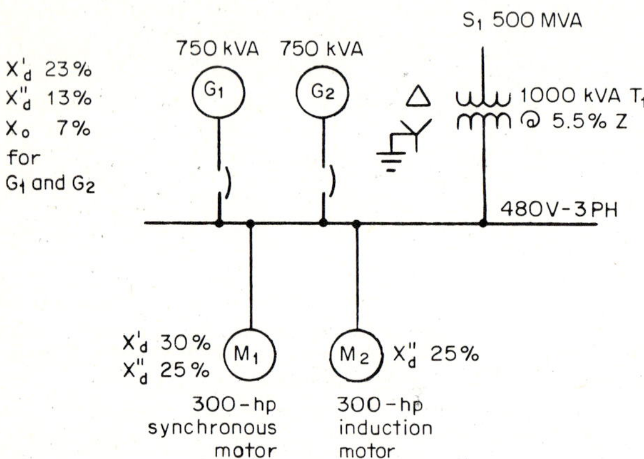

Figure 25.3 Hypothetical single line for short-circuit study.

In order to obtain the ground-current rating of the reactor, it is necessary to find the ground fault current. This is done by making an impedance diagram of all reactances. Because the reactances are positive, negative, and zero sequence, the reactances must be arranged in their individual groups. This is shown in Fig. 25.4.

The next arrangement is only a reshuffling to make it easier to correlate the three individual parallel circuits.

Note that in Fig. 25.4 the load (motor) impedances are shown on the load side. As the load and source impedances are considered to be connected by an infinite bus they can be shown just as easily on the source side. This is done in Fig. 25.5 and the effect is the same as adding the load impedances in parallel to the source impedances.

If we consider Fig. 25.4, we find it is now required to calculate the values of the various reactances. This is done in ohms per phase, and we already have the values for the generators calculated in the earlier exercise.

Generator Reactances

$$\text{G1:}\quad X'_d = 0.0707\ \Omega/\text{phase}$$

$$X''_d = 0.0399\ \Omega/\text{phase}$$

$$X_{0m} = 0.0215\ \Omega/\text{phase}$$

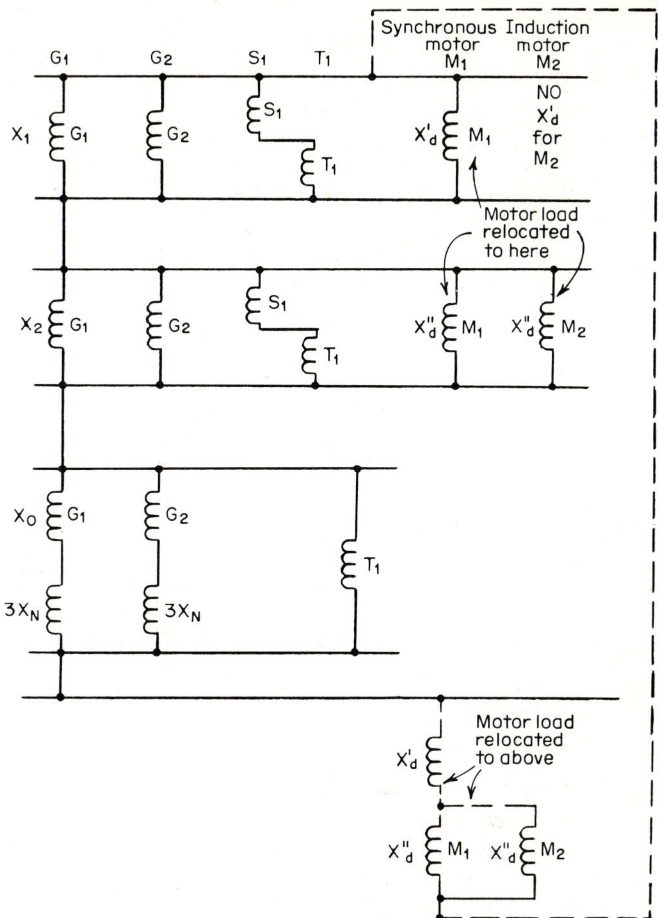

Note: The load is added on the source side; this is a shortcut by considering that all impedances are connected by an infinite bus. So the same effect is obtained by adding the load in parallel with the source.

Figure 25.4 Impedance diagram, first arrangement.

G2: $X'_d = 0.0707\ \Omega/\text{phase}$

$X''_d = 0.0399\ \Omega/\text{phase}$

$X_{0m} = 0.0215\ \Omega/\text{phase}$

Transformer Reactances

T1: $X_1 = \dfrac{5.5\% \times (0.48)^2 \times 10}{1000} = 0.0127\ \Omega/\text{phase}$

$X_2 = 0.0127\ \Omega/\text{phase}$

$X_0 = 0.0127\ \Omega/\text{phase}$

Utility (Source)

$$\text{S1} = \frac{1000 \times 100}{500{,}000} = 0.2\% \text{ and } \frac{0.2\% \times (0.48)^2 \times 10}{1000} = 0.0005\ \Omega/\text{phase}$$

Load (Synchronous Motors)

$$\text{M1:}\quad X'_d = \frac{30\% \times (0.48)^2 \times 10}{300} = 0.23\ \Omega/\text{phase}$$

$$X''_d = \frac{25\% \times (0.48)^2 \times 10}{300} = 0.192\ \Omega/\text{phase}$$

$$X_0 = \text{(not applicable)}$$

For 3X$_n$

$$3X_n = 3\left(\frac{X''_d - X_0}{3}\right) = 3\left(\frac{0.0399 - 0.0215}{3}\right)$$

$$= 3 \times 0.0061$$

$$= 0.0183$$

Load (Induction Motors)

Use only subtransient reactance.

M2: X''_d For 300 hp induction X''_d is approximately the same as in the synchronous motor, and as such, a general rule of thumb is to use 25% if no other information is available or if the load is a multiple of small motors. Therefore, use 0.192 Ω/phase.

With these values of impedance calculated, they are now applied to the reactance as shown on the impedance diagram. Adding reactances in parallel gives us a single reactance:

$$1/X_1 = 1/0.0707 + 1/0.0707 + 1/0.0132 + 1/0.23$$

$$= 14.14 + 14.14 + 75.76 + 4.35$$

$$= 108.39$$

Therefore, $X_1 = 1/108.39 = 0.009\ \Omega$

$$1/X_2 = 1/0.0399 + 1/0.0399 + 1/0.0132 + 1/0.192 + 1/0.192$$

$$= 25.06 + 25.06 + 75.76 + 5.2 + 5.2$$

$$= 136.29$$

Therefore, $X_2 = 1/136.29 = 0.007\ \Omega$

$$\frac{1}{X_0 + 3X_n} \text{ equivalent to } 1/0.0398 + 1/0.0398 + 1/0.0127 \text{ (see Fig. 25.5}a\text{)}$$

$$= 25.12 \quad + 25.12 \quad + 78.74$$
$$= 128.98$$

Therefore $X_0 + 3X_n = 1/128.98 = 0.0078\ \Omega\ (0.007753)$[4]

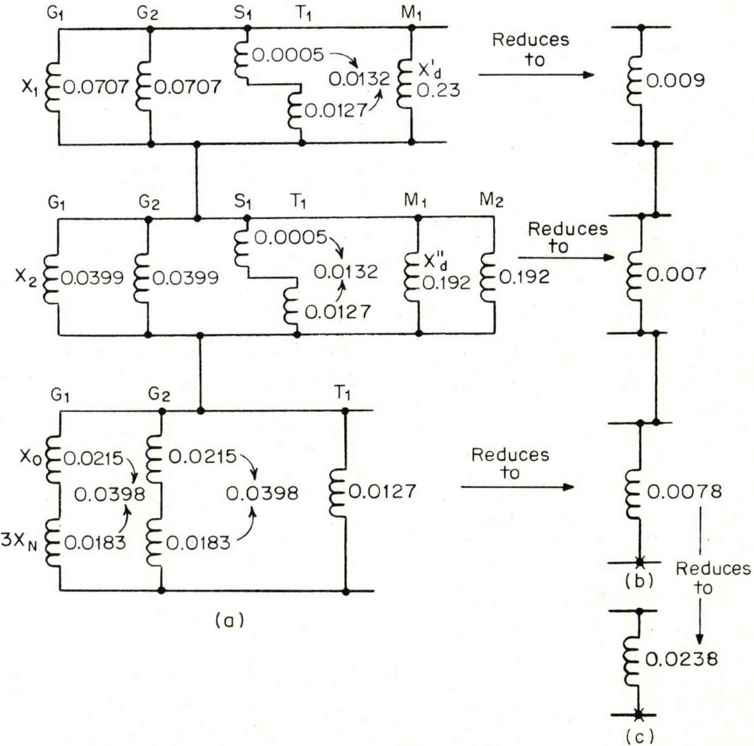

Figure 25.5 (**a**) Basic impedance diagram with values assigned; (**b**) each "group" reduced to single impedance; (**c**) three "group" impedances reduced to a single total impedance.

This now gives the three reactances which are equivalent to the impedance-diagram network. As these are connected in series, they can be added together and divided into "three times the neutral voltage" to give the ground current.

$$I_g = \frac{3(480/1.73)}{0.009 + 0.007 + 0.0078} = \frac{832.37}{0.0238}$$

$$= 34{,}974 \text{ A}$$

[4] See significance in footnote 5 and the last paragraph of Sec. 25.9.

This then gives the total fault current to ground. This, however, must be divided between the three neutrals of the two generators and the transformer. The current will divide inversely proportional to the impedance to ground in each neutral. If we consider the $X_0 + 3X_n$ circuit, we see that we have Fig. 25.6. We see from our previous calculations that the equivalent

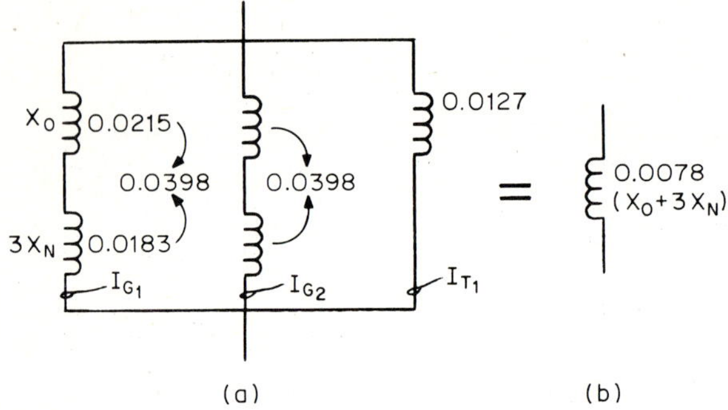

Figure 25.6 Three parallel impedances reduced to single impedance.

single reactance for this circuit is 0.0078 Ω. We must now consider what proportion of the fault current will flow down the transformer neutral. We find this as follows:

$$I_{\mathrm{T1n}} = I_{\mathrm{sc}} \frac{(X_0 + 3X_n)_{\mathrm{total}}}{X_{0\,\mathrm{T1}}} = I_{\mathrm{sc}} \frac{0.0078}{0.0127} = 34{,}974 \times 0.6141$$

$$= 21{,}474 \text{ A}$$

For the generator neutrals we have

$$I_{\mathrm{G1n}} = I_{\mathrm{sc}} \frac{(X_0 + 3X_n)_{\mathrm{total}}}{(X_0 + 3X_n)_{\mathrm{G1}}}$$

$$I_{\mathrm{G1}n} = I_{\mathrm{sc}} \frac{0.0078}{0.0398} = 34{,}974 \times 0.1959 = 6851 \text{ A}$$

$$I_{\mathrm{G2}n} = \text{same as generator 1} = 6851 \text{ A}$$

The three individual currents should total the original of 34,974 A; however, they total 35,179 A. This is a difference of 205 A. If we relate this to the original, or (205 × 100)/34974 = 0.6%, we see that the accuracy of the calculations due to the floating decimal point on calculators and fixed four-place accuracy on reactances gives an error of 0.6%, or less than 1%.[5] This is acceptable for a number of reasons. First, short-circuit calculations are only considered accurate to within about 5%, because of neglecting resistance, contacts, joints, CT impedances, and other factors. Second, slide-rule ac-

[5] By extending $X_0 + 3_n$ (total) to six-figure accuracy, we would get 0.007753, which, if substituted for 0.0078, would give $I_{T1n} = 21{,}350$, $I_{G1n} = 6812$, and $I_{G2n} = 6812$, totaling exactly 34,974.

curacy is usually acceptable, which brings the calculations into two- and three-figure of (marginal) accuracy. Third, the designer must work with the tools available, which is either the slide rule or the electronic calculators with the floating decimal. This means that calculations of the nature we have just completed will rarely "back check," and exactly correspond to the original figures, except in rare instances.

25.10 LOW-RESISTANCE GROUNDING (2.4 TO 13.8 kV)

The degree of "effective grounding" accomplished by a particular scheme is not a precise value. It is a relative value. If the impedance in the neutral is very high, then the system acts similar to an ungrounded system. As the impedance is reduced, it allows more current to flow (fault current). If the impedance is reduced even further, then the more solidly grounded it becomes. If we consider impedance as $Z = \sqrt{R^2 + X^2}$ and $X = 0$, we have $Z = R$; we can therefore consider R (resistance) as impedance.

In low-resistance grounding the intent is to provide a solidly grounded system but to reduce the violent effect of large fault-current damage by limiting the fault current to a lower value.

As the voltage applied to a ground fault is line to neutral, a resistor applied to this circuit would have a line-to-neutral potential when measured across the resistor when the fault occurs. This means that the current in the resistor is inversely proportional to the line-to-neutral voltage. If we have a 4160-V system and 2-Ω resistor, the current would be $(4160/1.73)/2 = 1202$ A. If more than one resistor in parallel is used, the impedance to ground is reduced and the fault current increased accordingly.

With this relationship existing for resistors a resistor can be specified in amperes and voltage. For instance if a 1200-A resistor is required, it is only necessary to specify the 1200-A at 2400-V. The resistance value will be determined by the manufacturer to limit the current to the specified value at the specified voltage.

This method of evaluating resistors can be used for external faults (i.e., not internal in machines). As there are many probabilities involved in a fault occurring in a machine, it is desirable to ground the system, ignoring internal faults, and then, after this is done, reconsider the protection if a fault occurred within a machine. The fault-current magnitude in a machine will be zero at the neutral and maximum at the terminals. Anywhere in between, it will be proportional to the percentage of the winding from the neutral point. If a fault occurred one-third the distance from neutral to terminal the fault current[6] would be $I_{\max_g} \times \frac{1}{3}$. The problem would then be that if the fault current originally was 1200 A, we would now only have 400 A. A CT rated at 1200/5 A would provide a 5-A operating current to a relay. If this were reduced to $5 \times \frac{1}{3} = 1.7$ A, the relay may not operate. For delta-connected machines there is no neutral and therefore the neutral point can be con-

[6] $I_{\max_g}$ = maximum fault current to ground.

sidered a minimum of 50% and maximum of 100% at the terminals. We see then that for delta-connected machines, the problem of partial faults does not pose the same problems of inadequate fault current for relay operation.

To determine the correct size of resistor, a number of points must be considered along with the fact that with reduction in fault current will necessitate relaying rather than relying on the fault current for tripping. These points are listed as follows:

1. Must provide enough fault current for relay operation.
2. Limiting fault current to produce minimum damage.
3. Make single line for ground relaying showing CTs.
4. For star-connected equipment (i.e., motor, transformer, generator) use a CT rated minimum 100% of ground fault current.
5. For delta-connected equipment use a CT rated minimum of 40% of ground fault current.
6. For lines (feeders and tie lines) use a CT rated minimum of 100% of ground fault current.
7. Select a time rating (i.e., usually 10 sec).
8. Select voltage rating (i.e., line-to-neutral voltage).
9. If a grounding bus is used, one resistor dictates the fault current.
10. If multiple grounding resistors are used, then the fault-current total will be the sum of the individual neutral currents.
11. Fault currents should be adequate at around 1000 to 2000 A.
12. Alternately fault currents can be considered as adequate up to 20% of three-phase fault current but with a minimum of 5%.
13. A more appropriate approach is to select the relaying currents required; select the CT and resistor based on this evaluation.
14. Where grounding transformers are used, the resistor rating must be checked for limiting transient overvoltages. The ratio R_0/X_0 should be more than 2; but where it is less than 2, the ratio X_0/X_1 must be *less than 10*, where R_0 is assessed at three times the neutral resistor value.
15. On low-voltage systems which are unusual and not solidly grounded, fault currents should be designed to be around 100% of the three-phase fault current.

25.11 HIGH-RESISTANCE GROUNDING (LOW AND MEDIUM VOLTAGE)

High-resistance grounding should be considered as a special application. The effect of applying high-resistance grounding is that the system acts like an ungrounded system. If a fault occurs, it does not instantly shut down the offending circuit; it sounds an alarm. The fault must then be traced, located, and removed.

The magnitude of fault current flowing in a high-resistance ground should be equal to or more than the charging current, that is,

$$I_{RO}/I_{CO} \geqq 1 \text{ and } X_{CO}/R_0 \geqq 1 \text{ with } I_{RO} = I_N/3$$

$$I_{CO} = I_C/3$$

where I_C is total system charging current and I_N is the neutral current.

This all adds up to the fact that the fault current is very low, on the order of 1 to 10 A. If we make the fault current about 10 A for a 460 V, the resistor would be $R = (460/1.73)/10 = 27.0\ \Omega$. If we use a 30-Ω resistor, the fault current will be 9 A.

A 51G relay in the neutral is generally used to sound an alarm; also, inrush discrimination must be considered, which throws the problem back to being a relaying problem after the resistor has been selected. One method of grounding and relaying is by the use of small distribution transformers. This scheme provides a sensitive method of ground fault protection with ground fault current in the range of 1 to 10 A (considering the charging-current value). Figure 25.7 shows four methods of high-resistance grounding.

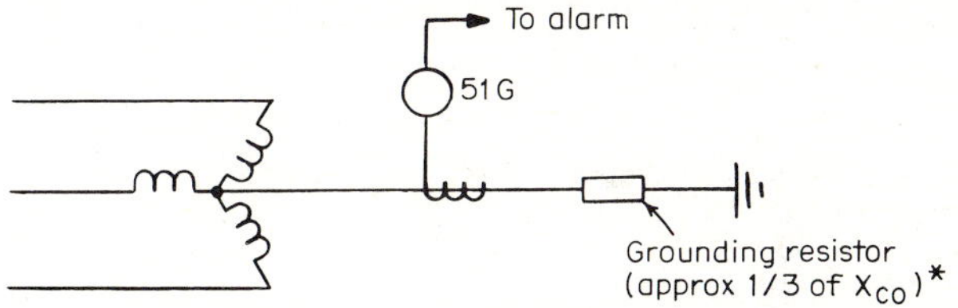

Note: Resistor should limit line-to-ground fault current to less than 0.1% of the 3-phase fault current (25 to 500 Ω for 480-V system; 300 to 10,000 Ω for 2400-V system).

Figure 25.7a Neutral resistor and 51G relay.

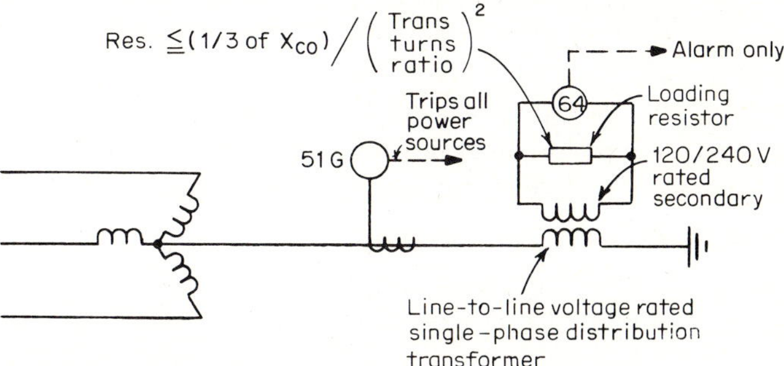

Figure 25.7b Neutral grounding using single-phase distribution transformer and loading resistor with 64 relay and 51G relay for shutdown.

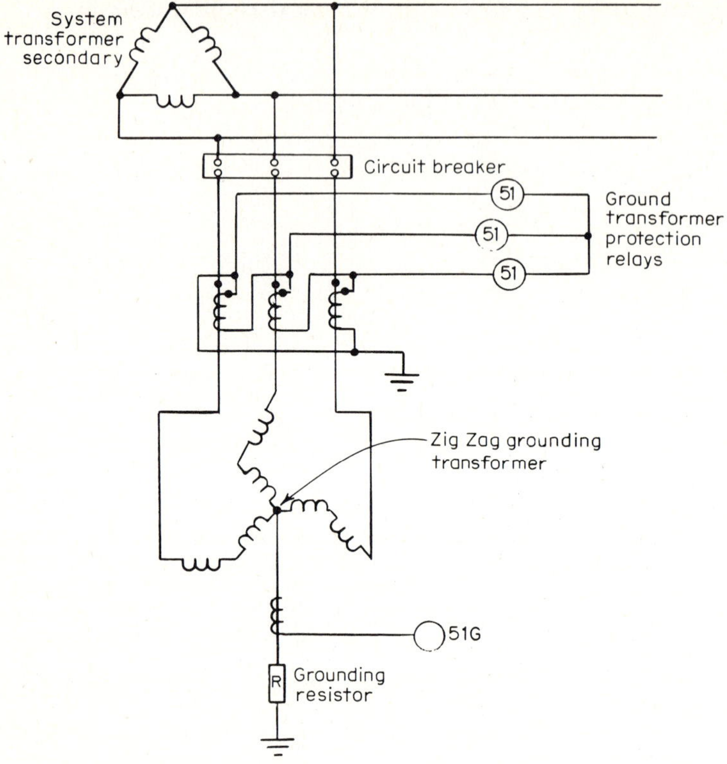

Figure 25.7c Delta system and zigzag grounding transformer with resistor and 51G relay.

All these systems operate an alarm which precludes the instant shutdown which plant engineers avoid and henceforth gamble with. Even though fault currents are low value, they should be removed as fast as possible because they can cause damage due to burning.

In a new design the plant of course does not exist; therefore charging current will not be known in advance, it can only be "guesstimated." Unless this figure is known exactly, the remainder of the calculations are only as good as the guess on the charging current. A guess of 5 A maximum will be fairly close.

To calculate the resistors for direct connection in the neutral of existing star-connected secondaries, the procedure is to select a fault-current level first and then determine the resistor.

1. For 1000 kVA and less at 460 volts
2. Select a 5-A line-to-ground fault current
3. Resistor ohms = (460/1.73)/5 = 53 Ω
4. Watts = $I^2R = 5^2 \times 53 = 1325$ W

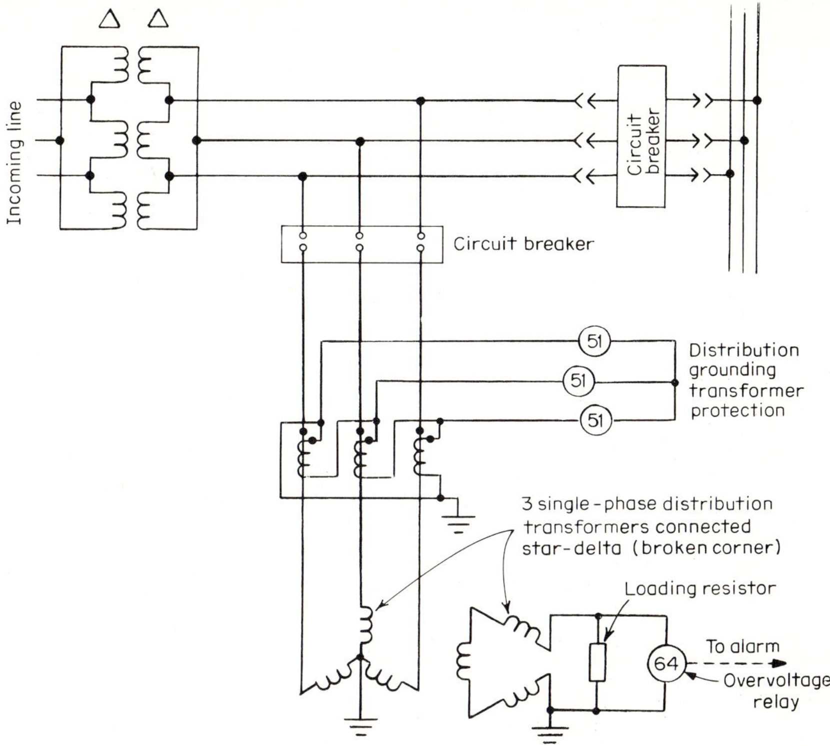

Figure 25.7d Delta system with three distribution transformers, resistor, and 64 relay.

1. For 1500 to 3000 kVA at 460 V
2. Select a 10-A line-to-ground fault current
3. Resistor ohms = (460/1.73)/10 = 27 Ω
4. Watts = $10^2 \times 27 = 2700$ W

For delta-delta systems where a grounding transformer is required, the method of utilizing distribution transformers is a convenient way of grounding. The impedance of the transformer primary acts as the high-resistance ground and the star-connected primary with a solid grounded neutral serves as a grounding transformer. The secondaries are connected in delta with one corner left open. Across this open corner the loading resistor and voltage relay are installed. The calculations for these arrangements require an analysis of the zero-sequence impedance and although not difficult take some time. To preclude this, use Table 25.1 which gives the required information. If the customer requires formal calculations, obviously they will accept and pay for the extra time required. An example is given for a sample procedure of calculation. See Fig. 25.7*d*.

TABLE 25.1 Distribution Transformer Data for High Resistance Grounding

Line-to-ground neutral-fault current	*Dist. transf., number & kVA rating*	*Dist. transf., secondary connections*	*Grounding resistor ohms*	*Watts dissipated in res.*	*Volts across resistor*
2400 VOLTS, DELTA-DELTA SYSTEMS					
5	3–5 kVA	120	6.03	6700	201
10	3–10 kVA	120	3.06	13500	204
15	3–15 kVA	120	2.03	20250	202
2400 VOLTS, DELTA-WYE SYSTEMS					
5	1–15 kVA	240	2.58	6450	129
10	1–25 kVA	240	1.31	13100	131
15	1–37½ kVA	240	0.86	19400	129
480 VOLTS, DELTA-DELTA SYSTEMS					
5	3–3 kVA	120	31.0	1380	207
10	3–3 kVA	120	15.33	2720	204
15	3–3 kVA	120	9.66	3864	193
480 VOLTS, DELTA-WYE SYSTEMS					
5	1–3 kVA	240	12.7	1270	127
10	1–5 kVA	240	6.22	2490	124
15	1–10 kVA	240	4.33	3897	130

TABLE 25.2 Resistor Data for High Resistance Grounding with Resistor in the Neutral

System voltage, V	*Connected load at voltage level, kVA*	*System neutral grounding resistor, Ω*	*Line-to-ground fault current, A*
480	1000 kVA or below	55.4	5 A
	1500 to 3000 kVA	27.7	10 A

Example: High-resistance grounding using three distribution transformers [See Fig. 25.7 (d)]

Criteria: Source is 1,000,000 kVA (1000 MVA Interrupting cap. bkr.); 7500-kVA Δ-Δ transformer; 34.5–2.4 kV and 5% Z motor load; 7500-kVA induction at 2.4 kV.

1. $I_N/I_c \geq 1$ mandatory or $X_{c0}/R_0 \geq 1$.
2. I_c estimated charging current at 7 A.
3. Select 10-A (I_N) neutral current.
4. $I_{R0} = I_N/3 = 10/3 = 3.33$ A.
5. $I_{c0} = I_c/3 = 7/3 = 2.33$ A.
6. Check $10/7 = 1.42$ (ok) (see line 1).
7. 3.33×2.4 kV $= 7.99$ kVA per phase grounding transformer (line 4).
8. Use next standard size 3 at 10 kVA, 2400 to 120 V.
9. X_{t0} is 1.46% distribution-transformer reactance (manufacturers data)
10. R_{t0} is 1.65% distribution-transformer resistance (manufacturers data)
11. $X_{t0} = (0.0146)\,\dfrac{7500\text{ kVA}}{3 \times 10\text{ kVA}}\left(\dfrac{2.4 \times 1.73}{2.4}\right)^2 = 10.92\ \Omega$
12. $R_{t0} = (0.0165)\,\dfrac{7500\text{ kVA}}{3 \times 10\text{ kVA}}\left(\dfrac{2.4 \times 1.73}{2.4}\right)^2 = 12.34\ \Omega$
13. $Z_{R0} = \dfrac{E_{LN}}{I_{R0}} = \dfrac{2400/1.73}{3.33} = 416\ \Omega$ Line 4
14. Base ohms $= \dfrac{(\text{base volts})^2}{\text{base kVA} \times 1000} = \dfrac{(2400)^2}{7500 \times 1000} = 0.768\ \Omega$
15. $Z_{R0} = 416/0.768 = 542$ Lines 13 and 14
16. $R_{R0} = \sqrt{Z_{R0}^2 - X_{t0}^2} - R_{t0}$
17. $R_{R0} = \sqrt{542^2 - 10.92^2} - 12.34 = 530$ Lines 15, 11, and 12
18. $R_{R0} \times$ base ohms $= 530 \times 0.768 = 407$ Line 14 and 17
19. $R_{\text{res}} = (E_{\text{sec.}}/E_{\text{prim.}})^2\, R_{R0}\, 3$ (Criteria and line 17)
20. $R_{\text{res}} = (120/2400)^2\, 407 \times 3 = 3.05\ \Omega$
21. $I = 10/3 = 3.33$ A primary line current
22. Transformer turns ratio $= 2400/120 = 20$
23. $I_{\text{res}} = 3.33 \times 20 = 66.66$ A
24. $V_{\text{res}} = IR = 66.66 \times 3.05 = 203$ V
25. $W_{\text{res}} = I^2R = (66.66)^2\, 3.05 = 13{,}552 = 13.5$ kW
    Use low-pickup voltage relay with high continuous rating. X_1 and X_2 neglected as being insignificant.

where I_N = neutral fault current

I_c = system charging current

I_{R0} = current in zero-sequence series circuit consisting of (X_{t0} and R_{t0}) equivalent ground transformer and R_{R0} equivalent ground resistor

R_0 = zero-sequence resistance

I_{c0} = zero-sequence charging current through X_{c0} (NOTE: parallel to I_{R0})

X_{c0} = zero-sequence equivalent charging current

$I_0 = I_{R0} + I_{c0}$, or $\frac{I_E}{3} = \frac{I_N}{3} + \frac{I_c}{3}$

X_{t0} = zero-sequence equivalent grounding-transformer reactance

R_{t0} = zero-sequence equivalent grounding-transformer resistance

Z_{R0} = zero-sequence impedance of I_{R0} circuit and E_{LN}; that is, $I = E/Z$, hence, $I_{R0} = \frac{E_{LN}}{Z_{R0}}$

R_{R0} = zero-sequence equivalent ground resistor

R_{res} = secondary load resistor ohms

I_{res} = secondary load resistor amperes

kW_{res} = secondary load resistor wattage

To conclude this section on high-resistance grounding, it must be pointed out that some rotating equipment have protective capacitors. These are rated at around 0.5 microfarads (μF) per pole. They will contribute additional current to the charging current. A set of capacitors would add around 0.785 A to the charging current. If there were multiple high-voltage motors with protective capacitors, the charging current would be $3I_{c0} = (V_{L\text{-}N})(2\pi fC) = (1388)(377)(3 \times 0.5)10^6 = 0.785$ A per set of capacitors for a 2400-V system.

The charging current under normal situations will rarely exceed 5 A, but where rotating equipment is protected by capacitors, the relationship of the fault current being higher than the charging current (or equal to) must be carefully considered. For example 10 motors will add 7.85 A to the charging current, if they are protected at the terminals with capacitors.

The application of high-resistance grounding is limited to: continuous-process-type industries where an instant shutdown on the first fault is not desired; conversion of ungrounded systems to grounded with a view to limiting transient overvoltages; systems where three-phase four-wire systems are *not* required and requirements for minimum damage due to fault currents. In all cases however, personnel must be available to trace and remove faults as soon as possible.

25.12 REACTANCE GROUNDING

Reactance grounding is not a generally used method of grounding in industrial plants. Its primary application is to low-voltage generators (600 V or less) for local power. The intent is to reduce fault-current levels to no more than 100% of three-phase fault currents. To avoid transient overvoltages, the minimum ground fault current should be no less than 25% of the three-phase value. The procedure for determining reactor size is given in the Sec. 25.9.

25.13 SYSTEM GROUNDING—GENERAL INFORMATION

The three common basic methods of grounding are *solid*, for below 600 V; low-resistance, for medium voltage (2400 to 13,800 V); and reactance (low), for low-voltage local generators. High-resistance grounding for ungrounded (nearly) operation is usually considered only when special conditions require it; this will take the place of the obsolete ungrounded system.

- Always ground the secondaries of transformers; don't ground the primaries even if it is star-connected primary.
- Ground generators neutrals ensuring that at least one ground is always connected.
- Ground each voltage level, for instance if the incoming line is 100 to 33 kV, ground the secondary (star connection) with a solid-grounded neutral; this steps down to a 33 to 4.16 kV with secondary star connection. Ground the neutral with low-resistance ground. The next step down is from 4.16 to 480 V, with a star-connected secondary that should be grounded solid.
- Don't ground any motors at neutral point of motor; if a ground is required, use grounding transformers.

Where multiple power sources are available in the medium-voltage range, such as generators and incoming power transformers, tie all the neutrals to a common bus and then place a grounding resistor in series with the ground bus.

This ensures that the fault-current level is controlled by the single resistor rather than varying with the number of power sources actually connected. The neutrals should be connected to the neutral bus by circuit breakers. For generators use a circuit-breaker compartment for each generator but only install two circuit breakers. One circuit breaker will be closed; the other will be used for transferring the neutral to another generator in case the "hot" one is taken out of service. This method precludes circulating harmonic zero-sequence currents.

For multiple incoming transformers grounded to a neutral bus, each neutral will be connected through a circuit breaker and all circuit breakers will be closed.

The decision to go to neutral bus should be made when total ground fault current with multiple resistors exceeds 4000 A, or where future additions of power sources are contemplated.

Rate all resistors, reactors, and grounding transformers at 10 sec.

Connect grounding transformers to a system bus through a circuit breaker. This protects the system against a fault in the grounding transformer. If a direct connection is used at the secondary of the transformer, the power transformer circuit breaker must be sized to protect the grounding transformer as well as the power transformer (see Code).

TABLE 25.3 Minimum Ratings of Generators and Power Transformer Banks for Grounding

System short-circuit kVA	*Minimum kVA rating*
1,000,000	7500
500,000	3750
250,000	1750
150,000	1000
100,000	750
50,000	375
25,000	187

NOTES:

1. If a smaller rating is used, system may be subject to transient over voltages during clearing of ground faults.

2. Table assumes 7 percent for power transformer bank reactance or generator zero-sequence reactance.

3. System short-circuit kVA is maximum value possible when generator or bank to be grounded is only source of ground current, all other grounded power sources being out of service. For preliminary estimates use maximum short kVA rating required for circuit breakers on system.

4. Table is based on the criterion that the reactance of the grounded apparatus should be no more than ten times the equivalent three-phase short circuit reactance. For example, a system having 250,000 kVA, three-phase short-circuit duty has a reactance of 100 percent on a 250,000-kVA base. The grounded apparatus may then have a reactance of ten times this or 1000 percent on a 250,000-kVA base. If the apparatus has 7 percent reactance on its own base, then its kVA rating may be:

$$\frac{7}{1000} \times 250{,}000 = 1750 \text{ kVA}$$

TABLE 25.4 Maximum Allowable Reactances of Grounding Transformers

Voltage 3-phase	*Maximum system short-circuit kVA*	*Grounding transformer reactance in ohms per phase*
13.8 kV	150,000	12.7
	250,000	7.6
	500,000	3.80
6900 V	150,000	3.18
	250,000	1.90
	500,000	.95
4160 V	50,000	3.46
	150,000	1.15
	250,000	.69
2400 V	50,000	1.15
	100,000	.58
	150,000	.38

NOTES:

1. Each value of *maximum* allowable grounding transformer reactance in the table above is equal to 10 times the system reactance to three-phase short-circuit current

$$\frac{X_0}{X_1} = 10$$

Higher values of grounding transformer reactance

$$\frac{X_0}{X_1} \text{ greater than } 10$$

may give rise to harmful transient overvoltages in the power system.

2. If a resistor is to be connected between the grounding transformer neutral and ground to limit the ground-fault current, the grounding transformer reactances may be those shown in the table or any *lower* values that may permit more economical designs.

TABLE 25.5 Preferred Rating of Resistors for Neutral Grounding

(Cast-Grid or Stainless Steel Neutral Grounding Resistors)	
System 3-Phase Voltage	— 13,800 — 6,900 — 4,160 2,400 V
Resistor Voltage Ratings	— 8,000 — 4,000 — 2,400 1,380 V
Resistor Ampere Ratings	— 300, 400, 500, 600, 800, 1,000, 1,200, 1,500, 2,000 A
Time Interval Ratings	— 10 seconds, 60 seconds

TABLE 25.6 System Characteristics with Various Grounding Methods

<table>
<tr><th colspan="2"></th><th>Ungrounded</th><th>High-resistance grounding</th><th>Low-resistance grounding</th><th>Solid grounding</th></tr>
<tr><td colspan="6">PROPERTIES DURING FAULTS</td></tr>
<tr><td colspan="2">Current for a phase-to-ground fault in percent of 3-phase fault current.</td><td colspan="2">Less than 0.1%</td><td>5% to 10%</td><td>About 100%</td></tr>
<tr><td colspan="2">Transient overvoltages</td><td>Up to 6 times</td><td colspan="3">Not more than 1½ to 2 times normal</td></tr>
<tr><td colspan="2">Automatic segregation of faulty circuit and equipment.</td><td colspan="2">No</td><td colspan="2">Yes</td></tr>
<tr><td rowspan="2">Circuit outage for various types of system faults</td><td>One ph. to ground</td><td colspan="2">No outage</td><td colspan="2">Outage</td></tr>
<tr><td>Phase-to-phase
Two ph. to ground
Three phase</td><td colspan="4">Outage</td></tr>
<tr><td colspan="2">Multiple Faults</td><td>Many case studies reported showing multiple failures</td><td colspan="3">Report of insignificant number of failures showing multiple outages</td></tr>
</table>

<table>
<tr><th colspan="2">Transformer; winding connection</th><th>Delta</th><th colspan="3">Wye or delta with grounding transformer</th></tr>
<tr><td colspan="2" rowspan="2">Fault Location Method</td><td colspan="2">Have to take part or all of the system out of service or use ground-fault locator to find ground faults</td><td colspan="2">System does not have to be taken out of service because the faulty equipment has been automatically isolated</td></tr>
<tr><td colspan="2">If ground fault is not removed, may lose two circuits due to another ground fault</td><td colspan="2">Ground faults are localized and trip off immediately</td></tr>
<tr><td rowspan="2">First Cost</td><td>Low-voltage system</td><td>Delta-connected substation with ground detector generally costs more than wye</td><td>Slightly higher due to high resistance resistor and ground indicator</td><td>Not generally applied, but would be slightly higher</td><td>Lowest, in that wye and delta transformers cost about the same</td></tr>
<tr><td>Medium-voltage system</td><td>Including ground detector equipment delta is slightly lower in cost</td><td>Somewhat higher due to high resistance grounding equipment</td><td>Somewhat higher due to low resistance grounding equipment</td><td>Wye-connected substation slightly higher than delta</td></tr>
<tr><td colspan="2">Maintenance cost</td><td colspan="2">Takes time and equipment to find grounds</td><td colspan="2">Ground faults are easily located</td></tr>
<tr><td colspan="2">Rating of lightning arresters</td><td colspan="3">Ungrounded neutral type</td><td>Grounded-neutral type</td></tr>
<tr><td colspan="2">Application of grounding method</td><td>Less and less frequently applied</td><td>Applied on low or medium-voltage systems when system not permitted to be tripped for first ground fault</td><td>Applied on medium-voltage systems i.e., 2.4, 4.16, 6.9, or 13.8 KV</td><td>Applied on low-voltage systems i.e., 208, 240, 480, or 600-Y. Some application on small medium-voltage systems</td></tr>
</table>

25.14 LIGHTNING ARRESTERS

Lightning-arrester application is actually a very involved subject if we were to delve into all the aspects involving the theory of lightning strikes, insulation coordination, wave shapes and effects, duration of strikes, hot and cold strikes, low-current and high-current strikes, etc. It is impossible to do justice in a small space such as one paragraph and to go beyond this would involve detailed qualifying information. We will therefore limit the subject to the application of lightning arresters as it affects system neutrals.

First, to obtain some guideline on the severity of lightning and thunderstorms in the area under consideration, use can be made of a map published by the U.S. Weather Bureau. It is called an *isokeraunic map* and gives thunderstorm days per year. This information has limited value because intensity, duration, topography, and other parameters are not taken into consideration on the map. Major manufacturers usually have much more detailed information in the way of technical bulletins which assist in application of lightning arresters.

There are two basic types of lightning arresters. One is the *valve type,* which in various design forms offers a changing nonlinear resistance from the power line to ground. This changing resistance value allows adequate impedance to ground to prevent 60-Hz leakage, but when a lightning strike occurs, the resistance decreases, allowing rapid discharge to ground. The other type of arrestor is the *expulsion type,* which is basically an arc-gap discharge arrangement. By correct design a tube containing multiple gaps in series will allow ionization of the atmosphere in the tube. This in turn offers a low-impedance path to a current. Once the current has peaked and is flowing via the ionization "arc," ionization suppression can be introduced, which will prevent continued ionization due to 60-Hz power.

BIL (Basic Impulse Levels)

To coordinate all equipment with the same protection against a lightning strike, a measurement of the *basic impulse insulation level* is established. This BIL is a basic impulse level for insulation expressed in terms of reference of "impulse crest voltage." Without getting too involved with the analysis of wave shapes, we will point out that transformers, bushings, circuit breakers, etc., have a BIL rating. Unless there is some particular reason to question it, the BIL rating of the equipment when ordered, based on its normal current and voltage rating, is set by the manufacturer, depending on what is felt to be a coordinated insulation system for that class of equipment. There are NEMA standards set for BIL levels which are met or exceeded on all approved equipment. The average ordering of equipment then is generally based on its applied current and voltage ratings, and the BIL levels are usually dictated in the specifications as being NEMA levels or better. If equipment has been used and is being reapplied, the insulation could have deteriorated with age and temperature; therefore, the suggestion is to consider the BIL at approximately 70% of its nameplate rating. In distribution equipment and arrester application the impulse voltage should be limited to 80% of the BIL rating of the equipment.

Arrester Location

Lightning arresters have limited "long-range" protective value. On a distribution line it can be less than a pole span; the approach then should be to locate arresters to protect the equipment (i.e., apparatus) rather than trying to protect the whole line. The secondary backup to the arrester is an efficient recloser and sectionalizer system for rapid restoration of service. It must be considered that lightning strikes are going to take place; the intent is to minimize the long-term effect.

Voltage Class

The voltage rating of the arrester to be applied is determined by the actual line-to-ground voltage of the system. The rating of the arrester (nameplate) is its maximum line-to-ground rating; therefore, the power-system line-to-ground voltage must be less than the arrester rating. For delta or ungrounded wye systems the line-to-ground rating of the arrester must be something above the phase-to-phase voltage.

For the various system grounding methods the following information is the generally accepted application approach: *All the following grounding methods must use the "ungrounded" type lightning arresters.*

- Ungrounded systems
- High-resistance grounding
- Low-resistance grounding
- Ground fault neutralizer
- Distribution transformer with secondary resistor
- High-reactance grounding; limiting fault current from 5% to 25% maximum
- Grounding transformers, low-resistance ground

All the following grounding methods can use the grounded neutral type lightning arresters.

- Solid grounding
- Low-reactance grounding where the reactance limits fault current between a low of 25% to a maximum of 100%, and X_0/X_1 is 3 or less

- Grounding transformer, solidly grounded, and grounding-transformer reactance determined by

$$X_{GT} = \frac{3000 \times (\text{kV})^2}{\text{kVA}_{SC} \text{ symmetrical 3-phase}}$$

where X_0/X_1 is 3 or less

Distribution Transformer Arresters

Pole-type distribution transformers should be protected by arresters which will limit lightning-strike voltage to 50% of the transformer BIL (multiply by 0.70 for used transformers).

For the normal transformers exposed to lightning strikes, a number of factors should be evaluated: the expected life, the desired degree of protection against outage, the type of structure around the transformer, consider connecting the arrester on the line side of the primary fuse. Consider connecting the primary arrester ground to the transformer secondary ground. The grounding of the transformer tank is preferred (bonded to the arrester and transformer neutral), most linemen prefer ungrounded pole-mounted transformer tanks, but this is a continually unsolved problem of what to do.

Pole to Underground Cables

Cables which go underground from a pole installation should have arrester protection at the pole top above the potheads and fairly close to the potheads. The arrester ground should be bonded to the cable sheath near the cable terminal. If cables terminate at poles at both ends, then both ends should be protected. The longer the cable, the more chance of a reflected-wave buildup in voltage; therefore, if the cable is more than 50 ft in length, consideration should be given to protection at both ends of the cable.

Reclosers and Sectionalizers

These devices can be protected by using the conventional arresters mounted on the same crossarm. A single arrester can be applied to the load side or the line side, whichever is deemed more lengthy and exposed. If mounted on the line side, then a reasonable protection is offered, considering that the recloser is in closed operating position. Alternately, if the arrester is applied to the line side and the recloser is open, a strike on the load side could damage the recloser.

The arrester can be located on the load side of the recloser; this would give protection except in the open position with a strike on the line side. If service reliability is paramount, both sides should be protected. The arresters are effectively grounded at the base of the pole with the tank grounding being subject to the same "yes" or "no" as the distribution transformers.

Static Line

For a static line protection a ground wire is mounted on steel *bayonets* above the phase conductors. For effective lightning protection the height of the static line should be such that the preferred angle from the static line to the outer phase conductors is 30° from the vertical; a maximum of 45° should be the extreme limit. This is known as the *Cone of Protection.*

26 SAFETY GROUNDING

26.1 GROUNDING

There are only two reasons why electrical equipment and conductors are connected to ground (earth). The first reason is system grounding where the intentional ground performs a continuous and intended function during normal operation. The second reason is to install a system which only comes into effect if an accidental and unintended voltage is applied to a non-current-carrying part of equipment.

System grounding has already been covered in Chap. 25; therefore, this chapter is concerned only with the accidental or safety grounding. The electrical codes that are in effect for the particular design must be adhered to for minimum requirements, but adhering to the code will not necessarily guarantee a maximum protective effort. This is evidenced by codes continuously being updated, implying that the previous code edition did not offer maximum possible protection. The codes are generally a compromise between maximum protection and reasonable cost. It would be easy for the codes to go overboard with excessive protection, but reason and good judgment should be used. In this chapter we will cover general aspects of grounding which will allow an evaluation and judgment over and above what the codes may require.

26.2 DEFINITION

"Circuits are grounded for the purpose of limiting the voltage upon the circuit which might otherwise occur through exposure to lightning or other voltages higher than that for which the circuit is designed; or to limit the maximum potential to ground due to normal voltage."

By deductive logic we can show that this statement reduces to:

"Circuits are grounded to limit the voltage."

We are concerned then with the potential difference which could be accidentally applied to a person. As we will see, this can mean the difference between being alive or dead.

26.3 PHYSIOLOGICAL EFFECTS

In 1678, Swammerdam, and in 1786, Galvani, showed that when two dissimilar metals are touched to a nerve and muscle a contraction of the muscle takes place. First, we see that the potential difference generated by two dissimilar metals is extremely low and yet muscular contraction could be obtained. The heart is a muscle. The heart functions rhythmically because of a nerve pulse. This provides the heartbeat. If a spurious signal is injected into the heart, this could upset the rhythmic flow of operation of valves and heart components. This leads to a condition known as *ventricular fibrillation.* Once this "out-of-phase" rhythm is established, it is difficult to stop. It is usually necessary to inject another shock to stop the fibrillation and reinstitute the normal rhythm. If fibrillation occurs in the field, or a remote location, the time lapse before medical defibrillation can take place may be prohibitive, resulting in a fatality. Fibrillation then is a most serious result of an electric shock.

The second type of fatality is a result of a *coronary arrest.* This, in nontechnical terms, means the heart stops beating. If we consider that permanent brain damage occurs after only a few minutes, we have a double problem (i.e., heart arrest and brain damage). If the individual is working alone, valuable time is lost. If he is working with another individual who may have had first aid training and trying heart massage or artificial respiration some recovery chance is possible but questionable without immediate expert assistance and correct equipment.

These comments are not medical recommendations in any shape or form, they are only comments on possible situations. They intend to convey the seriousness which accompanies the design of a (safety) grounding system.

The explanation of ventricular fibrillation and all its related aspects are covered in technical papers for those further interested. For the summation on ventricular fibrillation we will make the comment that for 60-Hz currents an excess of around 150 mA (milliamps) should be considered as very dangerous currents. Time is also a factor and therefore we should tie the 150 mA to a maximum of 1-sec duration beyond which it must be considered very dangerous. If we consider an average individual of 500-Ω resistance, we can see that an increase in voltage will give increased current. This means that the time allowed before reaching fibrillation is drastically reduced, that is, 100 V at 0.05 sec and 1000 V at 0.006 sec. All are miniscule time periods.

As far as coronary arrest is concerned, published data[1] indicate that muscle control, that is, the inability to let go of a 60-Hz current-carrying conductor, occurs at around 10 to 15 mA with a stoppage of breathing at around 30

[1] Published data vary, depending on the source, but generally agree when an average range is considered.

mA. From all this we must conclude that any small flow of current can be dangerous. Further, the documented information is assuming, or using experimentally, 100% fit individuals. Many workers are not 100% fit; therefore, they are more susceptible to shock hazards.

This information then creates a background and places the design of a grounding system in its correct perspective.

26.4 EARTH GROUND CHARACTERISTICS

When designing a new plant, it is necessary to determine the condition of the ground with respect to its grounding capabilities. Tests will indicate the resistivity in meter-ohms, foot-ohms, or centimeter-ohms. Sometimes it is difficult to obtain an adequate ground, and drilling is required; a main ground is then established. Some general values for various types of earth are given in Table 26.1.

TABLE 26.1 Approximate Earth Resistance Values (in Meter-Ohms)

Average earth	100
Swampy ground	10–100
Dry earth	1000
Pure slate	10,000,000
Sandstone	100,000,000
Crushed rock	150,000,000
Gravel	100,000,000
Sea water	0.01–1.0

The values in the table are not intended to replace tests which should be conducted. They are intended as a guide at the initial stage in a project when cost estimates and anticipated problems are being considered. If the plant is to be located in a sandstone area, then costs for drilling 200 to 300 ft might be necessary.

The use of driven ground rods is not always sufficient and in most cases is probably marginal if it is for an isolated single item of equipment. If ground rods are used in an attempt to improve the ground conductance, then some factors can be considered.

1. Increased depth provides better conduction.
2. Size (diameter) of ground rod does not significantly change the conductance.

3. Multiple rods improve conduction.
4. The arrangement of multiple rods, that is, square, equilateral triangle, etc., will not significantly change the conductance.
5. Rods added to a ground mat (mesh) (below grade) will only marginally affect its conductance.

We see, then, that the condition of the earth is important and must be tested, even if it is "for the record."

The addition of chemicals to the ground to improve conductance is a debatable practice. Rain and biodegradability of chemicals can change the effectiveness of the chemicals; therefore constant monitoring is necessary.[2] In the days of OSHA and lawsuits this practice could well be attacked by a plaintiff if a fatality occurred. For permanent protection, then, a stable and constant ground should be tried for.

26.5 STRUCTURAL STEEL

Structural steel grounds are only as good as the ground conditions and the web connections of the steel. It is generally good practice to install a buried ground loop to pick up all or at least most of the building steel columns. As columns are generally on 20-ft centers, at least every fourth or fifth column should be picked up. In any case there should be no more than 80 to 100 ft without a tie. If a loop is used, it should be left open at the ends, so that a complete circle is not formed. In some cases a loop can give an antennae effect, increasing the chance of emi (electromagnetic interference) or rfi (radio-frequency interference) if sensitive electronic equipment is being used, such as in aerospace installations. When grounding to structural steel, use a "Cadweld" connection, not a bolted connection. If building steel is to be used for inplant grounding, readings should be taken of the resistance to ground at the ground points if it is the only point of grounding. This again is for the record and also good practice. We can always assume the ground is good, but an assumption can be shown to be incorrect for as many times as it is correct. New techniques in fire prevention have provided an asbestos mixture for coating on some building steel, but its effect on the overall conduction of building steel is not always known.

26.6 GROUND WELLS

Ground well is the recognized term for an artificially constructed ground using ground rods or buried electrodes. Most companies have a standard detail of the preferred method of designing a ground well. It generally consists of a piece of large-diameter soil pipe with a driven ground rod. This is fine if the

[2] An electrolytic ground rod (UL listed) is available which offers a maintenance-free long-life, low-resistance grounding method for systems sensitive to change in ground impedance.

ground well is connected to a ground system, but if it is for an isolated piece of equipment, care should be taken to establish a low enough resistance to ground, that is, less than 25 Ω.

Plates or other configurations can be utilized as buried artificial grounds. The type of material is also important; material which will ultimately erode (like magnesium) should obviously be avoided.

There are various methods of testing ground resistance; all seem to have their problems. A simple method is presented in the previous book[3] also with the recommendations of how and when to test.

26.7 EQUIPMENT ENCLOSURES

All equipment enclosures should be grounded with a properly installed grounding connector. The installation of a piece of conduit with a locknut does not necessarily guarantee a ground during fault conditions. A locknut has points which cut into the metal, ensuring a low-resistance ground connection, but if fault currents are high, the current through these points of contact will become excessively hot, with the possibility of melting the sheet-metal enclosure. There are alternate "hubs" that can be installed in sheet-metal enclosures which provide better contact and current-carrying capability. An alternate to the special hubs is the use of grounding bushings for the smaller-size conduits, that is, around 1 to 1½ in. When the sizes get larger than this, ground clamps around the conduits are preferable for more reliable fault-current carrying. Motor control centers can be ordered with a ground bus to which all incoming conduits can be bonded.

26.8 NONELECTRIC EQUIPMENT

In some cases nonelectric equipment may be in close proximity to electric equipment. Although it is not necessary to ground the nonelectric equipment, it is usually good practice to do so if it is within arm's length. If the nonelectric equipment has a lower impedance to ground than the grounded equipment, the possibility exists that a ground could show up as a difference in potential between the electric equipment and the nonelectric equipment. A bonded ground to the electric equipment will preclude this.

26.9 CABLE CONDUCTORS

The type of conductor used for grounding is optional (i.e., copper or aluminum). Although aluminum is acceptable in nearly all respects, problems exist with connections and terminations. A history of loose connections has gradually become a record of concern with at least one state safety board. This means that the fault-current carrying capability and ground resistance

[3] L. B. Roe, *Practices and Procedures of Industrial Electrical Design,* McGraw-Hill Book Company, New York, 1972.

and continuity can become questionable. One other point that must also be considered is the size of conductor that is adequate to carry the high fault current and still remain within the adequate temperature range. The equation for calculating temperature rise is given as the time required to raise the temperature to "T" for a given conductor size and current value.

The temperature rise time in a copper conductor; heat loss neglected, is:

$$t = \frac{1}{\left(\frac{I}{\text{CM}}\right)^2 (33)} \left(\log 10 \frac{T_2 + 234}{T_1 + 234}\right)$$

where t = time, seconds
I = rms current
CM = circular mils
T_1 = initial temperature, °C
T_2 = final temperature, °C

For aluminum conductors substitute 80 for 33 and 228 for 234.

The size of the conductor may be adequate as far as the size related to the continuous-current rating of the plant, but a check to see that its fault-current-carrying and temperature-rise capability is adequate. See Sec. 33.10 for example calculations.

26.10 RACEWAYS

The ability of a raceway to act as a ground conductor varies with the type of raceway. The various alternates most generally used are:

1. Steel conduit
2. Aluminum conduit
3. Cable tray and ladder
4. Flexible conduit

Steel conduit in smaller sizes has good continuity at the interconnecting bushings; however, in the larger sizes care must be taken to see that bushings, locknuts, etc., are not installed cross-threaded, reducing the fault-current-carrying capabilities. The steel conduit also has reactance characteristics which effectively reduce fault-current levels. If this is taken into account when relays and protective devices are sized, no problem should exist; however, if it is not taken into account, the increased impedance during a fault can lower the fault current, which in turn provides a slow burn until the overcurrent devices eventually disconnect the circuit.

Aluminum conduit is nonmagnetic, meaning that the reactance due to magnetic properties is not present; therefore, the impedance is constant with or without fault-current flow. The impedance is also less than the equivalent steel conduit installation. Although the fault-current reactance parameters may be more stable than the steel conduit, the fault-current-carrying capacity is less; therefore, a check must be made of the expected fault-current magnitude related to the ability of the aluminum conduits to carry the fault current. If it is questionable, a ground conductor may be required to be installed in the conduit with the circuit conductors. However, there is usually no advantage to installing a bonding conductor in 2 in or larger aluminum conduit feeder.

Cable tray and ladder are essentially raceways, although the conductors are usually armored cable. Where approved and enclosed sheet-metal cable tray is used; under certain conditions, nonmechanically protected cables and conductors can be used. Apart from the Code allowance consideration of this type of installation, we are only concerned at this time with the grounding characteristics of this type of system.

One manufacturer of cable tray lists electrical continuity of cable tray as a resistance not exceeding 0.00033 Ω across a connection, this being obtained by passing a 30-A direct current through the connection and measuring the voltage drop 6 in on either side of the joint of the side rails. From this voltage drop the resistance is then computed. The current-carrying capacity of the trays can also be computed by figuring the side rails and relating them to the equivalent copper conductor. The side rail will have a right-angle flange at the top and bottom similar to a channel iron section. To compute the cross-sectional area, we take height plus the two flanges and consider that as L; this must then be multiplied by the thickness of the metal B, giving the cross-sectional area as $L \times B$. To obtain the equivalent circular mils, it is necessary to multiply the cross-sectional area in inches by 2.54×10^6. As this will be related to the equivalent copper conductor, the conductivity of the material should be referenced to the copper as percent conductivity of copper. Hence, if it is a steel tray, an approximation can be found in various handbooks, or the specific conductivity can be obtained from metals handbook if the specific metal is known. For example, using 1.77 microhm-centimeters for copper and 11.9 microhm-centimeters for steel, we have $(1.77/11.9)100 = 14.87\%$ conductivity of copper. So if we multiply the circular mils of the steel area by 14.87%, we will obtain the equivalent current-carrying capacity in a copper conductor.

For example, a 4-in-high side rail with $\frac{3}{4}$-in flanges would have an area of $A = (4 + 2 \times 0.75) \times 0.0598$ (assuming 16 gauge) $= 0.3289$ in². Circular mils $= 0.3289 \times 2.54 \times 10^6 = 835{,}406$ circular mils. The conductivity at 14.87% of copper is $835{,}406 \times 0.1487 = 124{,}224$ circular mils.

This is for one side rail; as there are two side rails, this can be doubled, giving 248,448 circular mils. By checking the tables in the Code, we can determine the equivalent current-carrying capacity. The tray is in "free air"; therefore, it will have a higher current-carrying capacity than the "three conductors in a raceway" rating.

The short-circuit current-carrying and short-time rating can be approximated by applying the formulas for cables to the equivalent copper conductor cable rating. The probability of the tray connections between sections breaking down under heavy fault currents should be considered with regard to installing jumpers. Alternately, the consideration can be made to install a separate ground conductor to lie in the tray with the main current-carrying conductors.

Flexible conduit is essentially an extended coil of wire. Under fault conditions it can have the effect of a current-limiting reactor; therefore, when using flexible conduit to terminate rigid steel conduit to motors or equipment, a copper conductor should be paralleled with the flexible conduit if the connection is longer than a couple of feet.

26.11 BONDING

Any device, equipment, or enclosure which forms a part of a continuous ground system and offers the possibility of poor continuity or high resistance should be bypassed and/or bonded with a jumper of corrosion-resistant material at every point where a possible discontinuity may occur. Typical examples are discontinuous wireway sections with insulated sections for rfi/emi interference, expansion joints and flexible connections, etc. Before doing this, however, a check should be made as to why the insulated section is there in the first place. In the case of large pedestal motors and generators, one pedestal will be insulated to prevent shaft currents from damaging the bearings; this must not be jumpered. The frame, however, can be satisfactorily grounded by a single conductor connected to the base. The same applies to the insulated sections in a tray; the grounding can be so arranged that protection is effective and yet eliminating the closed loop which is undesirable.

One other factor to consider when sensitive electronic equipment is installed and a central main ground is the grounding point. Each piece of equipment should have its own main ground conductor running back to the central ground. Do not connect short pieces to a main single conductor and then run the single conductor back. If short jumpers are used, there is a possibility of setting up an accidental closed loop that could generate a spurious signal, which could be picked up by the electronic equipment. This can be easily confirmed with the manufacturers whether a problem may exist or not.

Grounding to a water pipe is a usual method of picking up a ground. Where this is done, the water pipe should be checked for meters and insulating connections; these must be jumpered by a bonding jumper. Lightning conductors may sometimes come in close proximity to a ground conductor. When this distance is about 6 ft, they should be bonded together.

26.12 PORTABLE EQUIPMENT GROUNDING

Portable equipment can be classed as small, that is, hand-operated and hand-maneuvered (such as electric welders); also, a second category exists of large portable equipment such as electric shovels, mining and earth-moving equipment, and cranes. It goes without saying that the former category of equipment should all be equipped with three-pin plugs for single-phase and four-pin plugs for three-phase portable equipment. The grounding pin on the portable equipment must connect into a correctly grounded terminal in the socket. This is mandatory in any facility that employs people using electric equipment and appliances. The Code and OSHA regulations spell out the details and penalties for using the improper two-pin plug which sometimes comes with small appliances. This should then be a simple procedure to adhere to the rules and yet each year there are many fatalities from using ungrounded hand tools.

Large portable equipment is not as simple to ground as the smaller portable equipment; nevertheless it must be grounded, and effectively. The requirements for grounding large equipment involve the coordination of the many component parts. These are the main substation, a probable pole-line distribution, a smaller substation, and portable switch and receptacle unit (possibly on skids). From here, tough (probably high-voltage) cable will run on the surface of the ground to the equipment. Personnel will constantly come in contact with the equipment frames; therefore, extreme care must be taken when we consider that any voltage over 50 V and currents over 150 mA can be fatal under many conditions.

Any installation of large portable equipment requires a properly engineered scheme which incorporates the grounding; therefore we will recommend here that one of the major manufacturers be contacted for a "packaged" installation properly designed with the correct relaying cables, substations, plugs, etc. The designer/project engineer should spend the time carefully writing the specification for the "package," impressing the safety factor of guaranteed safe grounding. Any fatalities from an incorrectly grounded system will surely involve the engineering company and design engineer. Therefore, unless the designer is an expert on this specific subject, "subcontract the package out to a major manufacturer."[4]

26.13 GROUNDING AND CATHODIC PROTECTION

When two dissimilar metals are installed in close proximity in the earth or even in concrete (6 ft could be considered close), eventually one metal will effectively eat up the other by galvanic action. Whether it does this fast or slow depends on the metals, locations, soil or concrete resistivity, and whether one of the metals is wrapped with a break in the wrapping. The intent in this chapter is to discuss grounding with regard to safety; therefore we do not wish to get into cathodic protection at this time; unfortunately, the two are interrelated. Alternating current from a system neutral would have no contributing effect on corrosion, because when a half cycle removes some ma-

[4] See General Electric Bulletin GET 694, on grounding of large portable machinery for safety.

terial, the other half cycle puts it back. When we consider direct current, however, it is a completely different problem. Each metal has a natural potential when related to that of hydrogen, which is set at 0.00 V. In a table known as the *electromotive series of the metals* hydrogen can be considered as being halfway down the list. The metals above hydrogen will have a negative sign and the metals below the hydrogen will have a positive sign. For iron the natural potential is +0.44 V and for copper it is −0.34 V; the total potential difference is 0.78 V. Whether the signs are positive and negative as outlined or reversed depends on whether the consideration is for current flow or electron flow; regardless of sign, the metals highest in the list will give up metal to metals lower in the list.

The rate at which metal will be removed is a function of current, that is, Faraday's law (mass liberated is proportional to quantity of electricity). This can be summarized as mass $= ZIt$, where Z is a constant called the electrochemical equivalent, I is current in amperes, and t is time in seconds. Assuming the correct electrolyte and iron as the cathode with an electrochemical equivalent of 0.000289, if a current of 2.5 A flows for 10 hours, the mass liberated would be:

$$m = 0.000289 \times 2.5 \times 10 \times 60 \times 60 = 26 \text{ grams}$$

At 454 grams to the lb (16 oz) we have

$$26 \times (16/454) = 0.916 \text{ oz}$$

If we consider pure distilled water as a nonconductor, when we add impurities it becomes a conductor and therefore the equivalent of an electrolyte. In the earth we have moisture and impurities; both are the ingredients of an electrolyte. When two dissimilar metals are placed in the ground, we have a potential (dc). It is only necessary to close the circuit to obtain a current flow and hence a migration of metal. This is generally what happens when a copper grounding system is in the vicinity or interconnected to an underground piping system. To prevent the migration of metal from a pipe, cathodic protection is applied, which essentially is no more than applying a potential (dc) to ensure that the electron flow is into the pipe and not away from it. The design of cathodic-protection systems may involve insulated sections of pipe; this means that any safety grounds may not be continuous. Furthermore, bonding or jumpering of the insulated sections may affect the cathodic-protection system.

It has been fairly well established that corrosion in underground installations is due to galvanic currents from dissimilar metals. The majority of cases are the iron/steel to copper and in some cases aluminum conduit to steel conduit (the aluminum will disintegrate even if installed in concrete); hence it is safer to stay with steel conduit. To show the seriousness of this corrosion problem, consider the fact that 100 mA of current can migrate around 2 lb of iron per year. A further consideration is that if the pipe is wrapped and therefore—to all intents and purposes—insulated, it is only necessary for a stone to make a small cut and the 2 lb of metal will be removed from that spot, obviously leaving a hole. If the pipe were bare and continuous, the 2 lb would be removed from the total surface area, which may be acceptable. To try to design a grounding system with a view to reducing corrosion is not desirable. The first requirement is an effective and safe ground system. When this has been established, the cathodic protection must be designed to balance the incidental bimetallic action plus additional current to offset the copper grounding potential.

26.14 STATIC ELECTRICITY GROUNDING

Static electricity is the term usually applied to the portion of the electrostatic charge phenomenon known as the *disruptive discharge.* This in effect is ionization which we discussed in Sec. 15.2. There was also a brief outline of static electricity in Sec. 4.12. Here we are concerned with the grounding associated with static electricity. Most people are aware of the uncomfortable shock received when walking over a thick carpet with leather- or neoprene-soled shoes and discharging from the knuckles when placing the key in the door. In a situation like this it is just nuisance value; consider, however, the effect of a spark in an area containing explosive fumes. It may or may not be catastrophic. Four conditions are necessary for ignition of an explosive gas due to a static charge.

1. Static must be generated.
2. Accumulation must take place as separate charges.
3. A disruptive discharge must occur with sufficient energy to overcome heat losses.
4. The gas must be within ignitable limits.

These four conditions form a "logic"[5] product, and as such all conditions are mandatory for an ignition (explosion) to occur. If we consider the nonpermissive arrangement of the four conditions, we can state that if any one factor is missing, an ignition (explosion) cannot occur. If we consider each item separately, we can evaluate which items we can control and which items are beyond consistent control. Considering item 1, anywhere friction occurs there is a possibility of static being generated, including the flow of fluids in a pipe; therefore it is virtually impossible to eliminate static electricity. We will leave item 2 until last. Consider item 3; it is virtually impossible to predict the energy level of a disruptive discharge because of multiple and varying factors involved, one of which is the condition of the atmosphere. Item 4 means that the potentially ignitable mixture must be not too rich or too lean, as regards the gas and air mixture. This is impossible to predict except under controlled

[5] See L. B. Roe, *Practices and Procedures of Industrial Electrical Design,* McGraw-Hill Book Company, New York, 1972.

conditions. A gasoline loading platform may seem safe until a cigarette is dropped into a pit or depression, then "ignition."

Considering item 2, we see that it is necessary to build up two separate charges; when the stress between the charges exceeds the dielectric strength of the air (atmosphere) a disruptive discharge will occur. The key to this whole chain of action is the "separate" charges. If a conductor is tied between the two potentially separate charges, no buildup of potential can occur between them, hence no separate charges.

Our main concern with the static discharge is obviously in the hazardous areas, such as truck loading platforms for gasoline, ship unloading, grain handling, spray painting, printing machines (rotary), hospital operating theatres, paper machines, etc. Some areas are more obviously hazardous than others. One problem with bonding at a truck loading platform is that a bonding jumper must be connected to the truck. This act in itself could create a spark. To overcome this problem, a special static discharge unit can be purchased, which is generally used to provide an impedance allowing a slow (few seconds) drain of any charge on the truck, rather than the disruptive discharge that could occur as the crocodile clips are being attached. The device can also be interlocked to prevent pumping unless the ground is in place. For truck with a bottom loading usually the hose itself and its connector are adequate ground. For aircraft fueling all units of the fueling system including the aircraft should be bonded together. When filling barrels with flammable liquids, the barrel should be bonded to the fill pipe.

For blending and mixing operations any containers used should be bonded to the mixer. For other process operations where continuous roller operation spreads glue or a coating which in itself is flammable, special measures must be taken, such as humidity control (i.e., more than 60%).

It is not possible in a single paragraph to cover all possibilities and remedies but recommendations are given by the National Fire Prevention Association (NFPA) for specific conditions; therefore, the engineer must only be aware that a potential problem exists and a solution must be found.

26.15 LIGHTNING GROUNDING

Lightning protection falls into two categories: the basic protection to prevent damage to structures, which could be considered as a safety protection, and protection against lightning strikes injecting an impulse voltage into an electric circuit, which could possibly damage electric insulation and therefore equipment. This latter subject is fairly involved therefore this was covered in a separate section (see Sec. 25.14). As far as buildings and structures are concerned, it should be intended to conduct a lightning strike safely to ground. In an industrial plant where there are platforms, tanks, etc., the steel will act as a conductor. It will also be grounded based on the previously mentioned practice of tying columns, etc., to a common ground loop. For buildings of low profile lightning rods are not generally used. Where the buildings are of exposed profile, and particularly if there are roof projections, such as air conditioning it may well be advisable to consider protection by lightning masts, which offer a cone of protection over lower projections. The rule to remember is that the shortest path possible for lightning ground-conductor circuits is the desired condition. The termination should be to outside ground electrodes with a resistance to ground of less than 25 Ω.

To evaluate the probability of lightning strikes, the use of an isokeraunic map (previously mentioned in Sec. 25.14) will show the areas where the heaviest thunderstorm activity has been recorded. Although it gives the amount of activity in the area, it does not indicate the severity of strikes, etc. It is, however, a starting point from which to pursue further if a critical situation seems to be emerging.

27 MOTOR CONTROL HARDWARE

27.1 MOTOR CONTROL

Motor control defines the system of power and control circuits, and hardware, necessary for the required operation of a motor. This is of course within the limits of the Code and the operating requirements as dictated by the plant process. The basic equipment required is a switch to provide power for the motor, which is termed a *motor starter* and can be a manual or magnetically operated switch. In addition there must be motor protection and conductor short-circuit protection devices in the circuit. The conductors to the motor must be correctly sized. This is the minimum equipment necessary to run a motor. Various additions, modifications, and available hardware make the modern motor control system versatile, compact, interchangeable, and technically simple to maintain. This chapter will deal with the application of the various pieces of hardware for motor control systems. Throughout this chapter we will be considering three-phase alternating-current motors, unless the particular section specifies otherwise.

27.2 MANUAL MOTOR STARTER

The manual motor starter is the basic switch which provides the on/off power control to the motor. It also contains the motor-running overcurrent protection. It does not provide short-circuit protection for the conductors; therefore a safety switch with a motor horsepower rating is required with fuses for the short-circuit protection if the conductors are tapped from a feeder. This type of installation is usually limited to incidental loads, such as vent fans, an air conditioner, or a casually required pump or machine. The size and type of motor is limited to an *across-the-line* start, essentially a low-cost installation. An alternative to the safety switch is of course a circuit already available from a circuit-breaker power panel. It is necessary to review the applicable code for this type of installation, because there are various exceptions and demands that may be desirable or objectionable, requiring consideration of an alternative approach. The manual motor starter should not be confused with the motor starting switch, which does not have overload protection.

Manual motor starters do not provide low-voltage protection and low-voltage release. This is an important consideration, because in the event of a circuit failure the motor would stop, but if the circuit is reenergized, the motor would start up unexpectedly. In this type of installation the motor should be tagged with a warning sign. This type of starter is usually confined to machine tools, fans, pumps, and single conveyors—all of small size—where inrush and starting torque are minimal.

27.3 MAGNETIC MOTOR STARTER

The magnetic motor starter is basically a magnetically operated switch with overload protection as integral components. A solenoid operating an armature closes the main contacts. The motor running protection (overloads) are in series with the main contacts.

The magnetic motor starter should not be confused with a *magnetic contactor*. This unit does not have any overloads and is used for switching lighting circuits, heating loads, or any circuit not requiring the overloads.

The magnetic motor starter is rated in NEMA sizes 00, 0, 1, 2, 3, 4, 5, 6, 7, 8, 9. These range from 2 hp at 460 V for the 00 size, to 1600 hp at 460 V for the size 9. In industrial-plant application the minimum size used is usually the NEMA 1, which is good for 10 hp at 460 V. The maximum size is the NEMA size 5 with a maximum rating of 200 hp at 460 V. Above this size motor starters are nearly always high-voltage rating, that is, 2.4 kV, 4.16 kV, or other voltage systems up to 13.8 kV.

The control of the magnetic motor starter is by external control circuits designed to energize and deenergize the solenoid. For example, the solenoid will only remain energized when power is continuously applied; therefore, the control circuit must provide a *seal-in* circuit which locks in the control-circuit voltage to the solenoid. When this is done (in standard form), it also provides undervoltage protection. If a power (circuit) failure occurs, the solenoid drops out, opening the motor circuit. When power is reapplied, the motor will not restart until the control-circuit "push button" is operated.

The magnetic motor starter does not provide short-circuit protection for the branch-circuit conductors; therefore an additional fused switch (motor hp rated) or circuit breaker must be provided to give completed circuit installations.

The solenoid coils have various voltage ratings and must be specified usually 120 V, although 240-V, 480-V, and 600-V system coils are available.

27.4 COMBINATION MOTOR STARTER

The combination starter is a packaged unit containing a motor starter and disconnecting switch (fused, unfused, circuit breaker, circuit breaker without trip). Generally, the combination motor starter uses the fused switch or the circuit breaker with short-circuit trip, but the short-circuit protection is sometimes already provided and only the disconnecting means, in addition to the automatic/undervoltage protection feature of the magnetic motor starter, is required. The Code of course has a significant bearing on selection of equipment for a particular installation.

27.5 MOTOR CONTROL CENTER

The motor control center is a modular grouping of multiple vertical sections of metal-clad housing. There are various different designs by manufacturers, but essentially the principle of construction is similar in all cases. A single vertical section of the motor control center has a three-phase vertical bus internally mounted. By adding pieces of hardware, various arrangements of different-size starters can be stacked vertically. The motor starters are generally of the combination "circuit breaker/motor starter" type. They are specially designed units with "stabon" connectors which allows them to be "plugged in" to the vertical section of the motor control center. This feature also allows adherence to a Code requirement that, if a motor starter can be locked in the open "unplugged" position, a disconnect is not required within sight of the motor.

These Code requirements, however, should always be checked with the most recent Code and also the code which has governing priority. Never assume that the National Electrical Code has priority over local codes; it does not, unless the local code specifies that this is the case. When the vertical sections required are more than a single section, they are ganged together. Power is supplied to all sections by a horizontal busbar to which are connected all the vertical busbars of the vertical sections. The total motor control center is then powered by a single motor feeder, the size being calculated under the code section for multiple motors, that is, 125% of the largest motor full-load current plus the full-load currents of the other motors. The short-circuit protection for the feeder circuit breaker is 250% of the largest motor full-load current plus the full-load currents of the other motors. In both cases the use of the next highest standard conductor or circuit breaker is selected.

In industrial plants the motor-control-center method of motor control is universally used. When ordering a motor control center, it is necessary to be precise in all details, because there are a number of optional variations offered by individual manufacturers. The following is a list of data that should be precisely selected for the specifications:

- *Voltage:* 460 V (other voltages optional, see catalogs).
- *Phase:* Three phase, three wire or four wire.
- *Frequency:* 60 Hz, optional 50 Hz (see catalog).
- *Horizontal-bus capacity:* 600 A and up (see catalog).
- *Vertical-bus capacity:* 300, or 600, amps generally standard (see catalog).

TABLE 27.1 Motor Control Center NEMA Classification and Wiring Types

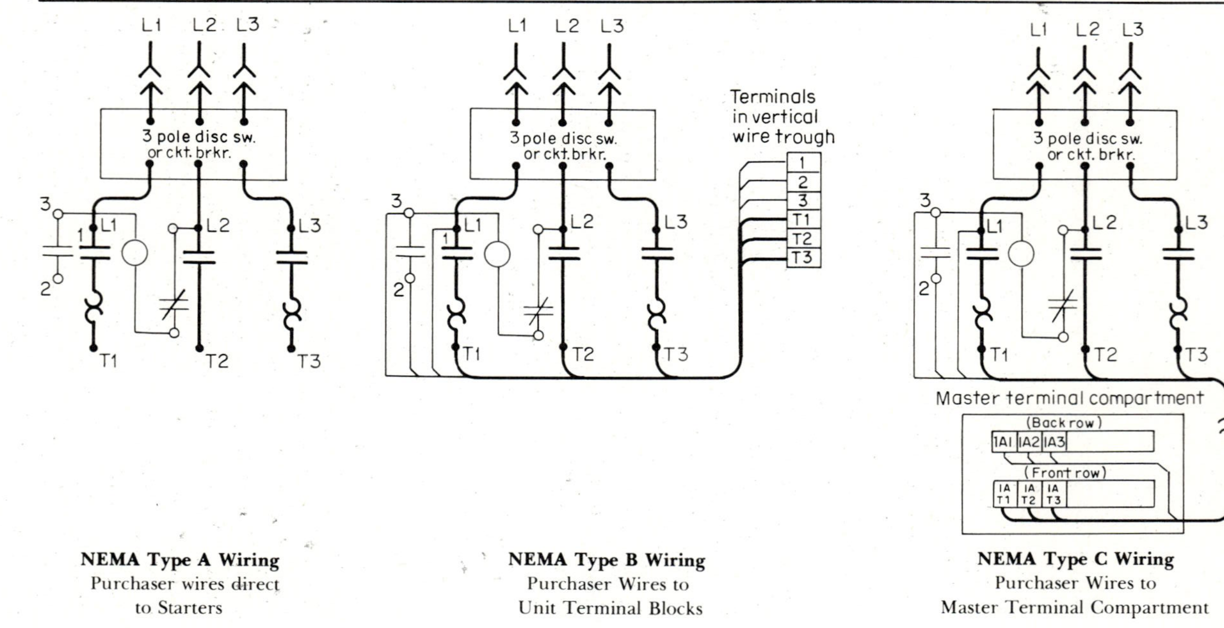

NEMA Type A Wiring
Purchaser wires direct to Starters

NEMA Type B Wiring
Purchaser Wires to Unit Terminal Blocks

NEMA Type C Wiring
Purchaser Wires to Master Terminal Compartment

NEMA CLASSIFICATION AND WIRING TYPES

Description of the NEMA classification and wiring types will be found below:

NEMA Class I wiring should be selected when the control center is essentially nothing more than a mechanical grouping of control units each having independent circuitry. Unit connection diagrams only, without elementary diagrams, are furnished.

NEMA Class II wiring is established for system-type installations where control unit circuitry is special for the application, and involves electrical interlocking and interwiring between various units, and also interlocking provisions to remotely mounted devices. Both elementary and composite connection diagrams of the entire control center, including interlocking, are furnished.

NEMA Type A wiring is the lowest initial cost control centers in which the factory does the least amount of wiring. The purchaser's load and control wires are connected directly on the starter device.

NEMA Type B wiring offers the convenience of clearly identified, factory-wired terminal blocks for purchaser's load and control wires. Terminal blocks are placed either in the vertical wire trough (standard, Form N4) or in the starter unit (optional, Form N3) rather than in a separate compartment. This affords the maximum space in every section for mounting units.

NEMA Type C wiring, as with Type B, also offers the convenience of clearly identified, factory-wired terminal blocks for purchaser's load and control wires. Type C, however, affords added convenience by grouping the terminal blocks in master terminal compartments (one for each control center vertical section) located adjacent to conductor entry areas. The installation is thus quicker and easier.

- *Bus type:* copper or aluminum.
- *Ground bus:* Specify required or not required.
- *Bus bracing:* 22,000, 42,000, or 65,000 A rms symmetrical (varies, see catalogs).
- *Main circuit breaker:* Specify required or not.
- *Main disconnect switch:* Specify required or not.
- *Magnetic motor starter:* Specify combination type with circuit breakers or current-limiting fuses or other. Specify short-circuit rating of short-circuit protection device (i.e., circuit breaker, fuse, or other). Specify starter size, that is, 1, 2, 3, 4, 5, nonreversing, reversing, reduced voltage, single- or multispeed, plug-in type, etc. Check catalog for options.
- *Wiring:* NEMA Class 1, Type A, B, or C
NEMA Class 11, Type B or C } See Table 27.1
- *Enclosure:* NEMA 1, gasketed, etc. check catalog for available options.
- *Metalclad sections:* specify standard 20-in-deep sections or alternate shallower sections or "back-to-back" arrangement. See catalog for alternate arrangements available.
- *Special options:* individual control power transformers for each starter, control-circuit fusing, push buttons, pilot lights, selector switches, auxiliary relays or auxiliary contacts, lighting panels section, etc.

When ordering motor control centers, the ordering will probably be through a purchasing department, but the specification was probably written around the manufacturer's unit that the designer was contemplating using.

The specification then should be specific on all individual details, because the possibility exists that some other manufacturer may supply the motor control center. When this occurs, and before acceptance, the submitted proposal from the manufacturers should be outlined in detail, covering each point in the specification to ensure that it is in fact equal in all respects to the one intended. If an item is not listed, consider that it will not be supplied, rather than assuming it is a standard item and will be supplied.

When the specification is sent out for bid, it is usually accompanied by a drawing showing the arrangement of sections, location of starters, and nameplates required on each starter door.

27.6 THE SWITCHRACK

The term *switchrack* is a colloquial expression used in the petrochemical plant and refinery industry. It is the hazardous area equivalent of a motor control center. Hazardous-area equipment will be covered in another chapter, so here we will only cover the motor-control aspects of the switchrack.

Areas are classified by Class, Group, and Division as outlined in Chapter 5. Predominantly, refinery work is Class 1, Group D, Division 1 and 2, which requires a NEMA 7 enclosure. These motor controllers are the combination type with circuit breaker and magnetic motor starter in a heavy-cast explosionproof enclosure. The switchrack frame consists of prefabricated angle iron (purchased complete or designed by the electrical department). The various explosionproof starters are then mounted on the switchrack frame. The top of the starter contains one or two conduits (power and control) which tie into a common raceway. The various sources of power are all tapped (spliced) to a main feeder (see Code tap regulations); the control is routed to the appropriate place. These conduits are "sealed" with an approved seal at the motor starter hubs. Out of the bottom of the starters the conduit(s) (power and control) are routed to the motor and its HAND/OFF/AUTO switch (or other control); these conduits must also be "sealed" at the motor starter hubs.

Switchracks usually are located in Division 2 areas. This is usually at the top of a tank farm "dyke," which is in close proximity to the location of most of the motors.

The switchracks can be purchased complete by specification similar to a motor control center. This of course requires a drawing of the arrangement desired, sizes, and small single line showing conductor sizes for the line side of the starter plus the feeder. Specify if *main* disconnect is required and, of course, the Class, Group, and division.

Switchracks can also be utilized for NEMA 4 and 9 enclosures, which are watertight, and Class II hazardous locations. A NEMA 4X is for corrosive atmospheres which may not be hazardous but nevertheless require special enclosures which would place them in a switchrack arrangement rather than in the motor control center, which is usually for indoor general-purpose only, although they can be purchased with a special outdoor enclosure.

27.7 HIGH-VOLTAGE MOTOR CONTROLLERS

The high-voltage motor controllers are usually in the 2.4 to 4.16 kV range although higher voltages are also utilized. They are similar to a motor control center in the sense that they are constructed with a sheet-metal enclosure of the general-purpose type. The starters are stacked vertically and vertical sections can be ganged together by a horizontal-bus arrangement.

The controller usually consists of a magnetic-type motor starter with overloads; the branch-circuit short-circuit protection is provided by current-limiting fuses. The disconnect is provided by a switch, mechanically interlocked so it cannot be opened under load. The actual switch design is being acceptably replaced by utilizing the "stabon" connectors associated with the roll-in-type motor starter as the disconnect device.

On the higher-voltage starters and the heavier-horsepower motors the trend is to go to the circuit breaker. The large circuit breakers are automatically (motor) operated and therefore are controllable in the same manner as the magnetic motor starter. The overload protection for the motor is provided by relaying, which in turn operates the circuit breaker. The short-circuit protection is of course offered by the circuit breaker itself and its tripping device(s). These may or may not be stacked depending on type, size, and availability of design from the selected manufacturer.

With these types of starters past performance and trouble-free history and bulk-purchasing contracts sometimes come into the selection of a particular manufacturer's design; so before selecting a specific type, check the customer's specifications and purchasing to see if any desired manufacturer is mandatory or whether it is going for open bid.

The usual information, that is, single-line and elevation-arrangement drawings, short-circuit specifications, etc., must all be carefully included in the specification and bill of material. When proposals are received from the various manufacturers, they should be carefully checked to see that all conditions are spelled out as being complied with. If an item specified is missing from the proposal, assume *it* is omitted intentionally by the supplier and confirm with the manufacturer.

27.8 REVERSING STARTERS

Reversing starters are essentially two single starters installed in a common enclosure with an electrical and mechanical interlock so that only one can be operated at a time (exclusive OR). To reverse a three-phase motor, it is only necessary to reverse two-phase wires; this is essentially what the second starter accomplishes. The enclosure must obviously be larger to accommodate the additional starter; therefore, when laying out a motor control center or a switchrack, ensure that the additional space is allowed for and the starter is spelled out as a reversing starter both on the single-line and the vertical-arrangement drawing.

27.9 REDUCED-VOLTAGE STARTERS

Reduced-voltage starters vary in design and type, each with a difference in characteristics. This was covered in Chapter 12 with regard to performance characteristics. We will, however, review the types of starters generally offered by major manufacturers.

AUTOTRANSFORMER *Advantages:*

Gives highest torque per ampere of line current.

Adjustable taps for reduced voltage.

Acceptable for long acceleration time.

Line current is lower than motor current while starting.

Closed transition (no break) while starting.

Disadvantages:
Low power factor.

More expensive in lower horsepower ratings.

Select as first choice when high starting torque is required and also select if minimum line current is required.

PRIMARY RESISTOR *Advantages:*
Smooth acceleration suitable for frequent starting.

High power factor during starting.

Closed transition starting.

Less expensive than autotransformer in lower horsepower rating.

Available with multiple accelerating points.

Disadvantages:
Low torque, efficiency, resistor gets hot and requires premium additional cost, for resistor to withstand more than 5 sec time.

Starting voltage difficult to adjust to varying conditions.

Select as first choice where smooth starting is required or frequent starting is required.

PART WINDING *Advantages:*
Least expensive reduced-voltage starter.

Closed-transition starting.

Small size.

Applicable to most dual-voltage motors on low voltage.

Disadvantages:
Unsuitable for high-inertia long-duration starting.

Requires special considerations of motor design when used on voltages higher than 240 V.

Unsuitable for frequent starting.

In general this starter would take second choice after the autotransformer or primary resistor starter.

WYE-DELTA *Advantages:*
Cost is less than primary resistor or autotransformer start.

Applicable to long acceleration starting times, with high inertia loads.

High torque efficiency.

Disadvantages:

Starting torque is low ($33\frac{1}{3}\%$).

Requires special type of motor winding.

Is generally open transition during starting.

In general comes as second choice to autotransformer, in some cases (i.e., acceleration), it may be preferable to primary resistor but in general industrial-plant design would not be specified unless as a special request. This is due to having no control over motor winding types.

In summation, the autotransformer is the most generally used reduced-voltage starter, the line current being reduced in proportion to the square of the applied voltage; that is, 80% tap is $(0.8)^2$, or 64%, line current. The 65% and 50% voltage taps would give 42% and 25% line currents, respectively. The starting torque would be the same percentage as the line currents, that is, 64%, 42%, 25%.

Again we must point out that extra space is required by the reduced-voltage starter and the notification is required on the single-line and elevation drawings.

27.10 MULTISPEED STARTERS

Multispeed motors are motors which can be run at different fixed speeds. The consequent-pole motor requires a single winding which is reconnected for another speed. Hence, a consequent pole requires a separate winding for each two speeds. The *separate-winding* multispeed motor uses a single winding for each speed. A variation of the two can be obtained for three speeds and four speeds by using two separate windings but having one or both windings designed for consequent-pole connection. This arrangement offers three separate speeds.

Both types of motor windings offer the option of constant horsepower, constant torque, or variable torque. The starters must be specified and/or selected in accordance with the type of performance required. This may affect the type of starter the manufacturer supplies. The consequent-pole starters usually require a five-pole and three-pole starter, while the two-winding motor only requires two three-pole starters.

The nominal speed of an ac motor is fixed by the frequency of the supply and the number of poles.

$$\text{rpm} = (f \times 60 \times 2)/\text{poles}$$

The horsepower is proportional to $\text{hp} = (T \times \text{rpm})/5250$, where f is frequency, rpm is revolutions per minute, T is torque in lb · ft, and the poles are single poles.

There are some accessories which are optional for multispeed starters. A *compelling relay* is a relay which ensures a specific procedure of operation. These are accelerating relays which require the motor to be started at low speed and accomplish this either automatically or manually, depending on the relay ordered. Another option is the decelerating relay, which dictates lowering of speeds. Therefore, there is a choice of three general-type control relays for speed-compelling operation.

27.11 SINGLE-PHASE FRACTIONAL HORSEPOWER

In process work all small motors should be ordered three-phase. Single-phase motors should only be used for nonessential applications, such as exhaust fans and machine shop tools. With these applications the motor starter is usually a manual switch, which also includes the motor-running overcurrent protection. The short-circuit protection is obtained from the circuit breaker supplying the motor circuit.

For essential service, automatic-controlled service, repetitive stop/start service, continuous process, etc., a three-phase fractional motor should be used. They would probably cost more than the equivalent in single-phase; however, the reliability is superior. By using a standard 460-V three-phase motor starter, the control and sizing of conductors, etc., would make it equivalent to a 10-hp motor. All motors up to 10 hp require the same conductors and starter when the design standard[1] is a minimum size 1; the only variation is in the circuit-breaker trip and motor-running overcurrent protection element.

27.12 DC MOTOR STARTERS

DC motors in industry are always special motors and are usually only used with adjustable speed control. This means that the whole drive system is usually purchased as a package which includes the controller. The responsibility of the electrical department is to review the manufacturer's drawings for any objectionable features. The requirements then become the interpretation of the manufacturer's drawings and a translation into drawings from which the contractor can make an installation. This will involve locating the motor control starters, which are usually predesigned, arranged, and packaged; it is only necessary to find space in a dustfree dry area, usually a special electrical room.

27.13 WOUND-ROTOR STARTERS

The wound-rotor starter falls into the category of special application. Wound-rotor motors in industry are only used with special loads, such as compressors, pumps, fans, and wood chippers. The fact that these are special applications usually means that the manufacturer of the load unit specifies a recom-

[1] Normal minimum size in heavy industrial plant design.

mended drive, or supplies it with the load unit. When it is specified, the specifications are usually presented to the motor manufacturer, who in turn recommends the starter type which will allow the motor to operate within its thermal limits.

If a starter is to be ordered separately, then the information required from the motor manufacturer is as follows: horsepower, voltage, full-load current, locked rotor current, phase, frequency, full-load rotor current per slip ring, open-circuit voltage between slip rings at standstill, and any special features. It is then necessary to select a starter from a manufacturer's catalog for reversing or nonreversing, and attach the motor information for submittal to the starter manufacturer.

27.14 OTHER TYPES OF MOTORS

When large-size motors are involved which are large or have characteristics out of the ordinary, it is usually normal procedure to coordinate the type of starter with the motor manufacturer. For instance in large wind tunnels using 20,000-hp motors, highly specialized problems require consideration. This introduces possible requirements for specialized starters, such as variable frequency, wound-rotor motor auxiliary, and turbine auxiliary including power-surge limitation requirements. In addition the motor manufacturer must confirm that the motor will stand the heat generated from starting-time acceleration.

28 CONTROL HARDWARE

28.1 CONTROLS

Control and instrumentation are usually mentioned in the same breath. They are, however, two distinct and separate areas. Control is the operation and arrangement of switches and magnetic relays so that a signal will initiate a programmed operation of events. Instrumentation is the monitoring of operational parameters. The two have a conjunction when the monitoring system detects a parameter change which requires a change in operational events. The control system then actuates and causes the change in events. This chapter will deal with the conventional hardware associated with control.

28.2 CONTROL RELAYS

The control relay is of course the heart of any control system. There are around 25 different groups of relays such as: general purpose, telephone, miniature, rotary, power, plunger, motor-starting, high voltage, etc., to name a few. This does not include relays which are classed as *protective relaying relays;* these are in a class of their own and are intended for monitoring and protection of the electric system and some component apparatus. For individual groups of relays there exists a complete line of various types with different contacts, coils, enclosures, and mounting arrangements. Couple this with the fact that there are also different manufacturers with variations of the same relay and we find that there is an astounding selection. The first consideration to be made is a review of the customer's specification to see if he has dictated the manufacturer and type(s) of relays to be used; if not, check the standards of the engineering office. If a preferred manufacturer is not dictated, review the various manufacturers' catalogs for diversified range, reliability, cost, reliability of deliveries, and warrantee service.

To specify a relay, it is necessary to first determine the number and type of contacts, that is, normally open or normally closed, or whether the contacts should be "convertible in the field," that is, from normally open to normally closed. With the contacts established, the mounting method must then be decided upon. Should they be the *plug-in* type. In which case plug-in sockets are required at additional cost. Alternately, the relays can be directly mounted onto a panel in a control box. With the contact arrangement and mounting method established, it is only necessary to specify the voltage rating of the relay, that is, 300-V class or 600-V class; the coil voltage, that is, 120 V or other operating voltage between 6 and 600 V; frequency (60 Hz); and contact current-carrying capacity (note that contacts will have different ratings for break, make, continuous, inductive, and dc, for the same contact).

Some control relays have modified action of control. Normally, a general-purpose relay is operated by a solenoid. When power is applied to the solenoid, it actuates. When power is removed, it deactuates. The modified relays can be *latching relays,* which when momentarily energized move into the actuated position; when power is removed, they remain in the actuated position until another pulse reverses the operation and deactuates the relay. The latching mechanism can be mechanical or permanent-magnet type.

Control relays are generally considered as instantaneous in operation even though they are essentially a slow-operating device. For design purposes the contact arrangement (open or closed) is always considered as if the relay was on the shelf in the stockroom.

28.3 TIMING RELAYS

Timing relays are essentially similar to a general-purpose relay except that all or some of the contacts operate after a time delay. There is nothing complicated about timing relays; however, the selection of performance is important. The various types of action involved in the timing device have already been discussed; therefore it is only necessary to determine the time cycle required.

First, the immediate concern is the individual contact(s) and whether it should be time delay on closing or time delay on opening. Second, is power required for the time cycle or will it time out after power is removed? For instance, a relay for voltage dip would remain closed for a predetermined period even if power was "off" due to a lightning strike and recloser operation. Considering a "solid-state" relay, the constant-power supply is required for the timing cycle measurement; therefore, interruption of the power would upset the time cycle. The former relay would use the mechanical dashpot type of relay or a relay with a *RLC* circuit providing slow flux decay in the solenoid. The following points then must be considered for timing relays:

1. *Timing range.* For example, 0.5 to 30 sec, etc.; "specify as required."
2. *Setting accuracy.* That is, 10% of range, etc. If the time cycle is expected to be no more than 30 sec, don't order a 60-sec timer "just to be on the safe side," because the accuracy may be affected.

3. *Repeatability.* This is the ability to keep repeating the exact time cycle as set on the time dial. It is usually specified as a percentage of the setting (i.e., plus or minus 1%, etc.). There are, however, conditions to the repeatability. Factors such as variation in line voltage, temperature, and reset time cycle may change the accuracy; therefore the manufacturer's catalog must be checked for the specifications of the exact relay.
4. *Warmup time.* Sometimes a relay may require a warmup time but most relays are instantaneously operable.
5. *Temperature range.* This is the temperature range at which the relay will still function within the specified accuracy. This is particularly important when using solid-state timing relays.
6. *Housing.* This specifies what the standard housing is good for (e.g., dust, moisture, impact resistance).
7. *Mounting.* This is the method of mounting (i.e., plug-in octal base, plug-in 11-pin base, panel mount, surface mount, etc.).
8. *Voltage.* Operational voltage and ac or dc.
9. *Frequency.* Frequency of the voltage supply.
10. *Cost.* Sometimes a need to know but correct selection has priority.

28.4 CONTACTORS

A contactor is basically an oversize relay. They are generally three- or four-pole normally open contacts. When fitted with overloads, they are called *magnetic motor starters.* When used on lighting loads, they are called *lighting contactors.* They are then a general-purpose heavy-duty magnetic-operated switch. For switching large currents, the control relay would be used to switch the current in the contactor solenoid; this means that by switching a small control relay, large amounts of current can be controlled remotely. The manufacturers' catalogs list the various sizes, ratings, enclosures, etc. The normal specifications of voltage, frequency, etc., are applicable. The contact rating will vary with the type of load (i.e., motor, lighting, heating, etc.).

28.5 PUSH BUTTONS

Push buttons are simply a pair of contacts which open or close when the button is pressed. This is the function; beyond this there is a huge array of designs and types too numerous to mention. Some push buttons are lighted with a light bulb in the button, some buttons are segmented into halves and quarters. Voltage ratings and contact ratings will vary. The type of mounting, enclosure, and housing will all vary. Standard nameplates are available for stop, go, raise, lower, open, close, etc. One point to consider is the amount of use the push button will be getting; ensure an adequately sturdy design for the application intended.

28.6 SELECTOR SWITCHES

Selector switches consist of multiple contacts operated by a knob or lever. They can be two-position, three-position, or multiple-position. Beyond the two- or three-position the basic design changes from a simple device to an arrangement of cams and contacts requiring a contact arrangement/position diagram. The usual approach is to design the control circuit and then specify and write a bill of material for the exact item. The contact/position diagram can be drawn on the bill of material sheet. The manufacturer will then make up the switch cams to conform to the diagram.

Some selector switches are motor-operated by a stepping motor which rotates in fractions of a single rotation. These, of course, are more complex but would be ordered by the same procedure as the hand multistep selector switch.

28.7 PILOT LIGHTS

These are indicating lights which go with the push buttons to form a complete system. The button initiates and the pilot light confirms. The options in design are too numerous to mention. The available voltages are various, and some pilot lights use a small transformer on the pilot-light housing itself to lower the voltage from 120 to 6 V. The purpose of this is to reduce the heat from the bulb, which could damage the plastic lens of the pilot light; therefore, ensure that the type of plastic used as a lens is adequate to sustain the bulb temperature.

28.8 LIMIT SWITCHES

The limit switch is a control device which consists of a switch with an operating arm. When the operating arm is moved, the switch actuates. It is necessary to review the various manufacturers' catalogs to obtain the range of various operating-arm types and contact arrangement of the switches. The operating arms can be: roller type (fixed roller, adjustable roller, micrometer adjustment); rod levers (various lengths and material types); fork levers (with rollers or without rollers at the end of the fork); spring-return, non-spring-return, with neutral position, without neutral position, wobble stick operator; switches (push type, wobble stick, dual push type, plug-in type, two-pole type); enclosures (optional, see manufacturers' catalogs).

When specifying limit switches, consider the angular travel required to operate, torque available, torque required for operating, type of operating arm, contact arrangement, voltage class of switch, contact rating, class of enclosure, mounting details, and contact transfer details. If a motor-operated multiple-rotating-cam limit switch is required, it is necessary to provide a contact/position diagram for contact operation and also a bar chart indicating the degrees of travel a switch should remain open or closed.

28.9 PRESSURE SWITCHES

The pressure switch is a switch specially designed to operate when a change of pressure occurs in a liquid or gas system. The switches can operate on single high pressure, single low pressure, or differential pressure. These are available in standard designs from various manufacturers and are generally ordered and installed by the mechanical department, which is responsible for determining the operating pressures. It is necessary, then, to coordinate with the mechanical department to ensure that the correct electrical rating and contact arrangements are available for circuit design. The consideration when designing a pressure switch into a control circuit is that, if pressure is required in a system before other parts of the system will function, it will be necessary to place a timing relay in the circuit which overrides the low-pressure shutdown during initial startup; otherwise, it will be impossible to start the system. In hazardous areas it is necessary to ensure that the mechanical department ordered the correct enclosure for the class of area.

28.10 FLOW SWITCHES

The flow switch is a switch that operates by a flow of liquid or gas. Similar in effect to the pressure switch, they can be ordered with no flow, low flow, high flow, differential flow, but require more sophistication in design when the flow-detection component is demanded to sense more critical flows. It should be ordered by the mechanical department which is responsible for dictating flow rates, etc. It is necessary then to coordinate with the mechanical department to ensure that the bill of material specifies the correct electrical specifications for the switch portion and the enclosure class. The same also applies to low-flow shutdown switches. In the control circuit it is necessary to provide a time-delay relay which will override the low-flow shutdown on startup.

28.11 OTHER CONTROL DEVICES

There are thousands of various types and designs of control-circuit components and to try to go through the whole list would only be duplicating what manufacturers' catalogs are intended to do. The recommendations then is to have a good catalog library of components available and also a familiarity of what is available, confirm performance record, delivery, and availability; not excluding price; however, price should be the last selection, and also only a consideration between products of exactly equal attributes. A few other components used in control are: mercury switches, proximity switches, photocell switches, magnetic switches, load-cell switches, thermal switches, smoke-detector switches, counters, scanners, transducers, float switches, vacuum switches, foot-operated switches, plugging switches, etc. Everyday new products are being developed which provide more versatility for the control-circuit designer; however, a word of caution is required with new products. Accept advertised claims judiciously. If the product is to be used extensively, obtain the customer's approval to "pioneer" its use. If only a single unit, then consider that it may not perform up to expectations and design the circuit so that the "old proven device" can be replaced without too much problem.

28.12 CONTROL-CIRCUIT TRANSFORMERS

Most control circuits are for 460-V installations and the generally accepted voltage for a control circuit is 120 V. It is therefore necessary to use a transformer off one phase of the three-phase system to provide the control-circuit power. This is done by using a *control power transformer.* These are usually an open-type transformer mounted in the control cabinet with integral fuse protection for the transformer as an option. The ratings of control power transformers are from around 50 to 2000 VA (2 kVA) with primaries rated for 208-, 460-, and 600-V systems, and intermediate voltages.

29 INSTRUMENTATION

29.1 INSTRUMENTATION

Instrumentation is essentially a separate department from the electrical department. There is, however, an obvious overlapping of responsibility for the design of the instrumentation system for an industrial plant. In a large engineering office there is usually a separate instrumentation department with its own group and chief instrumentation engineer. This department is responsible for engineering the instrumentation system, and selecting and ordering the desired instrumentation. It is also the function of the instrumentation department to produce the "instrument portion schematics" and internal interwiring diagrams for the instruments themselves. From this point the electrical department is responsible for providing the raceway installations, instrument interconnecting wiring, and instrument power wiring.

In smaller engineering offices the electrical department will usually have an instrumentation engineer working as an electrical engineer but specialized in instrumentation. In either case the same split in responsibility is allocated.

Therefore, when the electrical department refers to control and instrumentation, it is referring to motor control and interconnecting wiring between instruments that are located and selected by the instrumentation specialists. It is not the intent in a single chapter to try and venture into the instrument engineer's domain; we will, however, cover symbols and terminology used on flow diagrams so that the electrical designer can extract the instrumentation requirements.

29.2 FLOW SHEET INSTRUMENTATION

The "flow" diagram, or flow sheet, correctly termed P&ID (Process and Instrumentation Diagram) should contain all the pertinent information relating to the process flow and instrumentation monitoring and instrumentation-actuated controls. By symbolic presentation the information which pertains to the electrical department only can be extracted.

Standard symbols are only standard as applied to a particular project. There are "standard" symbols issued by the ISA (Instrument Society of America), but it is not necessarily true that these are the ones used on all projects. The first requirement, then, is to be familiar with the symbols as shown for that particular flow diagram. Section 29.3 gives a listing of some selected legends as published by the ISA. These can be used as a guide with the knowledge that alternate symbols will probably be encountered. The electrical interconnections are usually shown by a dashed line. This does not indicate any conductor size, quantity, or rating, it merely means that an electrical interconnection is required between two points. The type, size, and quantity of conductors and raceway must be obtained from the electrical schematics and the instrumentation wiring diagrams and specifications. Whether shielded wire or ordinary control wire is adequate is dictated by the instrumentation department.

29.3 INSTRUMENT FUNCTION IDENTIFICATION

An instrument function (i.e., its intended function) is usually identified by a series of one to five letters. The first letter is the letter that identifies the "measured or initiating" variable. The second letter is a modifier to the first letter. Where a first letter is used with a modifying letter, the two letters in combination should be entered as a symbol constituting a "first" letter. For example, T identifies a "temperature" function but it may also be necessary to identify "differential temperature," identified by "TD." These are considered first letter symbols even though there are two letters in the second example.

The next three letters are further identifying letters. The first one in the group identifies the readout or passive function such as "alarm," indicate, record or print, point (test connection), etc. The second letter in the second group identifies the output function, such as control, switch, transmit, relay or compute, valve, and damper or louvre. The third letter is a modifier (i.e. a letter which has a specially defined meaning for that particular project); as such it must be defined in the legend. Some of the more common abbreviations are: FSL (flow switch low), FAL (flow alarm low), LAH (level alarm high), LAL (level alarm low), LAHH (level alarm very high), LALL (level alarm very low), TDI (temperature-differential indicator), TSL (temperature switch low), LRSH (level recorder switch high), WT (weight transmitter). There is a listing of selected symbols and abbreviations in the Appendix, but it is necessary to use and therefore check the symbols and identification as issued for the specific project. Don't feel self-conscious about asking a stupid question; its easier to fix than a stupid action. Be sure that the symbols you intend to use and follow are correct. It is expensive and error-causing to redo work that should have been correct in the first place.

29.4 INSTRUMENT DEFINITIONS

The ISA "standards" book gives a more comprehensive coverage of definitions; however, we will list a few that are commonly encountered by electrical personnel.

ALARM	A device that signals the existence of an abnormal condition and attracts attention visually or audibly.
BALLOON	A circle (symbol) which denotes an instrument or instrument "tagging." Approximately $\frac{7}{16}$-in. diameter; with an open circle it means "locally mounted," and by definition means an instrument that is neither on nor behind a board; usually located in the vicinity of a *primary element* or a *final control element.*
BEHIND THE BOARD	(1) is within an area that contains the instrument board, and (2) is within or back of the board, or is otherwise not accessible to the operator for his normal use, and (3) is not designated as "local."
BOARD	A structure that has a group of instruments mounted on it and that is chosen to have an individual designation. The board may consist of one or more component panels, cubicles, desks, or racks.
BOARD MOUNTED	A term applied to an instrument that is mounted on a board and that is accessible to the operator for his normal use. The board-mounted instrument is usually identified by the balloon symbol (circle) with a horizontal line inscribed in the circle. If the horizontal line is shown dashed (------), then this indicates a *behind-the-board* mounting.
CONTROL STATION	A manual loading station that also provides switching between manual and automatic control modes of a control loop. It is also known as an auto-manual station and/or an auto selector station. Note that this is an *instrument* control station and should not be confused with an electrical control station.
CONVERTOR	A device that receives information in the form of an instrument signal, alters the form of the information, and sends out a resultant output signal. It is also referred to as a transducer, a

transducer being a device that takes a physical change (i.e., pressure, flow, etc.) and gives an electrical signal output which is proportional (i.e., directly, exponentially, etc.) to the input function. The term transducer is not recommended by the ISA as a descriptive term; however, it is widely used by both electrical and instrument people, including vendors. Therefore the term *transducer* will probably be encountered more often than *convertor*.

FINAL CONTROL ELEMENT — The device that directly changes the value of the manipulated variable of a control loop.

LOOP — A combination of one or more interconnected instruments arranged to measure or control a "process" variable or both.

PILOT LIGHT — A light that indicates a normal condition of a system; not to be confused with an "alarm" light which signals an abnormal condition. The pilot light can also be described as a *monitor light.*

COMPUTING RELAY — A relay that performs one or more calculations or logical functions or both, and sends out one or more resultant output signals. Note that an ordinary magnetic-control-type relay could be considered a computing relay because it (*a*) performs a logic function and (*b*) actually computes in the binary system where 0 and 1 is the complete number system and an open and closed operation is a progression of the relay through the complete number system.

TRANSMITTER — A device that senses a process variable through the medium of a primary element, and that has an output whose steady-state value varies only as a predetermined function of the process variable.

29.5 INSTRUMENT LOOPS

An instrument loop is a combination of one or more interconnected instruments arranged to measure or control a process variable, or both. Having made the technical definition, the practical association of the electrical department with instrument loops is in the *loop diagrams.* These diagrams are a joint effort between the instrument department and the electrical department. There are a number of basic groups of tasks associated with the production of loop diagrams.

First, the size of the sheet on which the diagrams are to be prepared must be established. Usually $8\frac{1}{2}'' \times 11''$ paper is adequate because only one *primary element* is presented on the page, along with the auxiliary elements, terminal blocks, internal panel wiring, field wiring, etc. The elements are shown in schematic form without regard to geographical location.

It is the responsibility of the instrument department to produce these documents and as such they will "rough out" the basic loop component devices the way they intend them to be arranged and interconnected. This information (basic preliminary drawing) is then turned over to the electrical department which in turn ensures that the instrument(s) is located on an electrical plan drawing or "model," or both.

The next step is to design a raceway and terminal box system to accommodate the instrumentation wiring. This is done with the electrical drawings that the contractor uses to install the raceways. To determine the type of wire and the wire fill and also the terminal block numbers for interconnections, it is necessary to show this on the electrical drawings purely as interconnections between two points. These electrical drawings are then used as information sources to complete the loop diagrams. The instrument engineer will have "marked in" the instrument panel wiring and terminal connections; the electrical department will have "marked in" the field wiring and terminal box connections, including equipment connections and type of wire (shielded, twisted, etc.); this then gives a completed picture of the total number of component devices associated with that specific loop. It identifies the routing through the field terminal boxes—the terminal numbers, the wire numbers, and also the instrument numbers. From this loop diagram it becomes a simple matter to troubleshoot and/or modify the design of a single primary-instrument function without having to consider the whole plant instrumentation system.

Sometimes these loop diagrams are omitted completely because it could be considered that the physical installation is made with electrical drawings and instrument location drawings or model; therefore, loop diagrams, would be additional and repeated information. Whether they are omitted or included is purely a project and/or customer decision based on the particular philosophy adopted.

29.6 INSTRUMENT IDENTIFICATION AND TAGGING

The procedure for identifying and tagging an instrument is to use a two-part number. The first part of the *tag number* is the functional identification (this was outlined in Sec. 29.3); the second part of the tag number is the *loop identification.* This loop identification is a continuous block of sequential numbers. Each instrument loop must have its own unique number. A single sequence of numbers shall be used for a single complete project regardless of function identification. For example, don't use a sequence of numbers for flow control and the same sequence for pressure control, relying on the F or P to identify the loop. An additional suffix may be added to the loop number as an additional identifying feature but is rarely used.

A complete tag number would be XXXX–0000X where the X is an identifying letter and the 0 is a number. The whole tag number may be prefixed by a plant number to facilitate warehousing and dispatching for multiplant companies. For example, "5LAHH–0123" would be an instrument belonging to plant 5 and is a "level alarm very high" with instrument loop number 0123. As the drafting procedure dictates that "balloons" will be used, the second (i.e., loop part of the number) is drawn in the balloon directly below the first "functional" part of the number. The sequence of numbers does not necessarily have to be four digits; it can start with the number 1 or 01 or 001, the latter allowing 999 loops.

There are exceptions to both the functional identification and the loop numbers procedure. In cases where there are two parts to the primary element, such as a photocell counting switch, the QX–23 would be the light source, while the QS–23 would be the counting switch. Here the secondary letters can be modified, while the loop remains the same. Alternately, a TE–123A, TE–123B, or TE–123C indicates three single-point temperature indicators with separate manual selector switching HJS–123 with a TI–123 temperature indicator.

The electrical designer should fully understand the symbols and identification numbers used for a particular project.

29.7 CONTROL AND INSTRUMENTATION

There is a definite link between motor control and instrumentation. For instance, cooling water can be on demand by instrumentation (i.e., level, temperature, flow, etc.); however, if the instrumentation indicates lack of cooling water, then an obvious step is to use the same signal to automatically start the water feed pump. It is necessary then for the electrical department to know what instrument signals affect their motors. This is usually termed as "control interlocks" and as a colloquial expression means additional controls to the normal operational controls. For example, two water feed pumps could be independently controlled so that either or both could be used; however, on reviewing the flow sheet, we find that the instrumentation calls for normal operation of a single water feed pump on "low level" and operation of both pumps on a low low (very low) level. This then means that the electrical designer must now modify the control circuits of the two pumps and "interlock" them together so that they will function as dictated by the instrumentation signals, in addition to the conventional controls. This is generally accomplished by a HAND/OFF/AUTOMATIC selector switch.

29.8 LOGIC DIAGRAMS

Some projects generate a set of drawings which are *logic-sequence* drawings. These are not to be confused with control schematics, which are sometimes erroneously referred to as logic diagrams. The logic-sequence drawings are usually made by the process and instrumentation departments.

It is assumed that the reader of this book is familiar with logic mathematics as required in the preface;[1] therefore, we will only consider the "place" of logic diagrams in the overall scheme of things.

First, the process department are the only people that know the sequence of operations of various component parts of the plant equipment. All this process equipment must appear on the P&IDs. The instrument electrical interlocks as shown on the P&ID will not necessarily indicate the total sequence of operation; therefore, additional information is required. In many cases it is obtained by word of mouth, or by operational specifications which describe the process by "Pump 103 starts but pump 102 must be running; if not, then a low-low-level alarm must operate, causing equipment B136 to shutdown and fan F139 to start up." This same set of instructions can be presented in a conventional logic diagram.[1]

Whereas the written specification allows a certain imprecision and the obvious discussion to confirm a sequence with the process engineer; the logic diagram is exact and has only one correct interpretation. If the logic diagrams are incorrect, the electrical controls will be designed correctly from an electrical point of view but incorrectly from a sequence of operations point of view. This leads to the conclusion that electrical control circuits designed from logic diagrams should be fully checked and approved for final issue. Use of preliminary logic diagrams generally leads to work having to be redone; furthermore, each time a control circuit is reworked three things occur:

1. The control circuit begins to appear as if things were added as an afterthought.
2. Errors in the circuit and wire numbers begin to appear.
3. There is a final comment on what a lousy job the electrical department did on the control drawings.

The obvious then to all concerned is to ensure that correct and final instrumentation logic diagrams are used before control-circuit design is started. Changes can always be made by revision.

29.9 CONDUCTOR SELECTION

The field wiring conductors must be selected based on information provided by the instrumentation department. They are the people responsible for knowing how susceptible to interference a particular instrument is. They are generally the only people to have the manufacturer's recommendations for type of conductor to be used with the instrument.

[1] See L. B. Roe, *Practices and Procedures of Industrial Electrical Design*, McGraw-Hill Book Company, New York, 1972.

Alternatively, if the information is not available from the instrumentation department, it is necessary to obtain the manufacturer's name and the model number of the instrument, and contact the manufacturer. Let me repeat, it is easier to ask a stupid question than make a stupid mistake, so don't feel embarrassed about asking for the manufacturer's recommendations. This shows up in a number of ways; wire can be conventional control circuit wire or it can be twisted pairs, shielded, unshielded, one conductor shielded, multiconductor cable, etc.

29.10 THERMOCOUPLES

Thermocouples are very common instrument items in an industrial process plant. A thermocouple is simply a junction of two dissimilar metals which emit a small-voltage signal which varies with temperature of the junction. There is a wide range of types, temperature range, and dissimilar-metal couples. It is necessary to obtain the information from the instrumentation department on what basic types are intended for the project, then correlate the information on wire type, terminals, readouts, etc., associated with the thermocouples. The same thing applies to RTDs (resistance-temperature detectors) and thermistors, both alternatives to the thermocouple device.

29.11 ALARM INDICATORS

The electrical department will be responsible for installing the alarm indicators; these are in addition to the normal alarm-panel display signals and involve audible alarms (i.e., claxons, trumpets, horns, etc.) with the possibility of flashing-light standards. This will generally be specified in the customer's specifications and it is usually the responsibility of the electrical design department to lay out the system with the correct number of audible alarms, amplifiers, and raceways and wiring. The signal to energize the alarms will be dictated either by the specifications or the instrument department as to what will or will not operate an audible signal. This would also be shown on any instrument logic diagrams.

30 EXPLOSION-PROOF EQUIPMENT

30.1 EXPLOSION-PROOF

The term *explosion-proof* requires some defining so that we are able to understand the "physics" of an explosion due to faulty or incorrectly applied equipment. In Chapter 5 we introduced hazardous area classification and a terminology definition for ignition temperatures, etc.; so at this point we will assume that the reader is already familiar with some of the basic general facts and we will not repeat this part of the information except where necessary.

The term *explosion-proof* as applied to a piece of electrical equipment means absolutely nothing unless it is prefixed with the notation **UL Approved.** This of course is applicable only to the United States; in other countries their own recognized testing authority would provide approval. When we use the term *explosion-proof* from now on, it will be considered to have the UL Approved prefix.

For an explosion to occur, three basic requirements are necessary; these were outlined in detail in Chapter 5. Briefly, they are (1) a combustible liquid, vapor, or dust in adequate quantity; (2) the correct air/oxygen mixture; (3) an adequate source of ignitable energy. When an enclosure is designed to be explosion-proof, it must be designed with a number of conditions in mind.

First, since this equipment is assembled and installed by skilled and partially (apprentice) skilled individuals, it must be built so that installation is simple, effective, and capable of maintaining explosion-proof integrity. With this in mind, an explosion-proof enclosure is not constructed to prevent an ignitable mixture from entering because the assumption must be made that a partially adequate or inadequate installation can be made; the intent then is to localize damage. Therefore, the enclosure is designed to contain an explosion without bursting. To allow for a rapid increase of internal pressure it is not constructed airtight. This means that the hot explosive gases are vented into the surrounding atmosphere. By ensuring that the escape vents for the gases are lengthy, it means that by the time the gases reach the outside atmosphere they are cooled sufficiently to prevent ignition of the outside atmosphere, which caused the problem in the first place by seeping into the explosion-proof box. The explosion then is localized and contained within the enclosure. Secondary explosions are usually not forthcoming, because the first ignition source (i.e., the electrical switch) probably opened the short-circuit protective device, deenergizing the circuit. The term *explosion-proof*, then, generally refers to this type of system.

30.2 INTRINSICALLY SAFE EQUIPMENT

Intrinsically safe equipment, like the *explosion-proof* equipment, means absolutely nothing unless approved by the recognized testing authority. Assuming that approval is obtained for the equipment, we can now explain the principle of safety of intrinsically safe equipment.

If we consider the three basic requirements for an explosion, we find that one mandatory requirement is a source of energy with adequate strength to ignite the explosive atmosphere. Intrinsically safe equipment is based on the principle that, if the energy emitted by a spark, arc, etc., is always below the required energy level, then an explosion cannot occur.

This means that special enclosures are not required, because the electric circuits can operate within an explosive atmosphere in complete safety. It must also mean that under fault or failure conditions the energy produced by the electric circuit will be below the energy required for ignition. Here is the problem area, defining what the minimum energy level is which will preclude ignition under "all" situations and conditions in that location. If we consider the small spark used to ignite a kitchen gas stove or the small spark in the electrically ignited cigarette lighters, we can obtain a practical feeling for the situation. Without being melodramatic, it can be shown that sparks, arcs, flames, hot surfaces, etc., can be continually exposed in potentially explosive atmospheres without an explosion occurring; this breeds a sense of complacency until one day an explosion occurs, killing many people.

Energy levels then are difficult things to define, and although manufacturer's publications may list tests, unless the equipment is approved by the recognized testing authority, it is not advisable to use it.

This does not mean that the equipment will not perform adequately; it only means that the acceptance of responsibility and liability for proving that it is intrinsically safe lies with the manufacturer and the recognized testing authorities.

30.3 RECOGNIZED TESTING AUTHORITIES

In the United States the Underwriters Laboratories is the accepted testing authority for explosion-proof electrical equipment. All products approved by them are listed in a "red book" publication. It lists the product by manufacturer and catalog number and the approval given. If the product is not listed in this red book, then it must be presumed that either the red book is out of date, the product is still in test, or approval has not been given.

Generally the customer's specifications are written in such a form as to make a generalized statement that all equipment must be approved by Underwriters Laboratories and/or other possible authorities with the implication that any other authorities that they omitted in the specification should also be included if some unknown authority happens to come along with a ruling.

The obvious conclusion is that the customer is passing the responsibility to the engineering company hired to do the job; this is justified because the customer is not intimately involved in the general design production.

The engineering company must then confirm in their specifications to the contractor what approvals are required for equipment and what substitutions are allowable, if any. They must also inform the manufacturers in the same manner.

In some cases a problem occurs in that an essential and desired piece of equipment is not UL approved, and yet the consensus of opinion is that it is probably safer than the approved equipment due to advanced technology, or it is mandatory to have it or there is no alternate replacement.

In a situation of this nature, a number of options are open. The first step is to notify the customer to see if he will waive the UL approval; the second step is to contact the inspection department of the town which will approve the electrical installation during construction and ask them for a variance for this specific piece of equipment. If this is refused, the customer and his insurance company can consider an acceptance of use. If this is granted, then a second trip to the local authority's electrical inspection department is required; this should all be done with the aid of a technical expert from the company that produces the product along with the files on their tests.

Another possibility is that the city or town where the plant is to be located may have its own testing laboratory, which will give an approval (after testing) for use within its jurisdiction. Many times the results of this testing are acceptable to other states who know of the quality of testing conducted.

The only reason for the manufacturer not to have UL approval is usually that the product is so new that it hasn't been processed through Underwriters Laboratories. If this is the case, Underwriters Laboratories can be contacted for an anticipated date for a ruling on approval, and if the date is not satisfactory, an explanation of the problem and a negotiation for a possible speedup of testing can be evaluated.

The possibility of using non-UL-approved equipment poses a number of problems. First, the electrical inspector may "red tag" it (deny use of). Second, if an accident occurred which was traceable or marginally traceable to this piece of equipment, it would probably be extremely difficult to defend in court of law in the event of a damage suit.

In conclusion, the National Electrical Code and Underwriters Laboratories work in conjunction in the sense that the UL testing is done with a view of approving equipment as required by the National Electrical Code outline for

Class, Division, and Group. Neither the National Electrical Code or the Underwriters Laboratories have enforcement capabilities, but the various inspection authorities that do have enforcement duties invariably use both the NEC and UL as basic criteria for enforcement guides.

30.4 SEALS

A *seal* is a type of fitting which is installed in a conduit system to prevent migration or passage of gases from one location to another. The seal fitting is provided in numerous types and sizes; after installation a compound is poured into the fitting which hardens and is resistant to attack from chemicals and heat and will also withstand pressures from exploding trapped gases.

The National Electrical Code outlines the requirements for the installation (location) of seals. As codes change, it can only be misleading to quote the latest code requirements; however, we can speak in general terms. Basically, in Class 1, Division 1 and 2, seals are required in each raceway entering any enclosure containing an arcing or sparking or high-temperature device. They must also be close, that is, within 18 in. of the enclosure. Any time a conduit passes from a classified area into a nonclassified area it must be sealed at the transition point (see the NEC). In long runs of conduit it is sometimes advisable to place seals periodically, for example, 50 to 100 ft apart, to prevent precompression problems. Short lengths of "sealed" conduit are less likely to burst than long ones, if an explosion occurs within the conduit.

30.5 PRESSURIZING OF CONDUIT AND EQUIPMENT

Utilitizing a pressurized system for the prevention of explosive gases seeping into a system is a method that can be considered. It is, however, generally only considered where special situations exist and unusual conditions are present. The principle of operation is that air is drawn into the system from a nonhazardous area, passing through the hazardous area equipment and conduit(s), and exhausted into a nonhazardous area. A minimum pressure must be maintained, which requires a flow or pressure-switch control, also various interlocks and alarms are necessary to prevent operating arcing or sparking devices without adequate purging and pressure in the system.

One problem with using pressurized equipment in a hazardous area is ensuring that small holes or gaps in equipment don't create a negative pressure by pressurized air flowing past and sucking in explosive gases. A further problem is that during nonoperation of the pressurized system the gases or vapors from the hazardous area must not be allowed to flow into the nonhazardous area via the blowers (fans) or some other part of the pressurizing system.

If the decision is made to go with the pressurized system, then the procedure is to write a specification for a pressurized system, including the equipment to be pressurized, such as motors and control devices, and also the equipment control and instrumentation to provide the pressurization. The added rider being that all the equipment must be approved for pressurized use in a hazardous area and that the total system meet the code of the enforcing authority. It will probably be the case that there will only be a single area where pressurizing is necessary; therefore, it can usually be packaged in a single specification as outlined.

30.6 NATIONAL ELECTRICAL CODE SECTION 500

The National Electrical Code outlines the requirements for installations in hazardous areas. However, the code does change; also, even though most states, cities, counties, etc., adopt the basic principles of the National Electrical Code, they may have their own variations; therefore, ensure that an installation is designed to the requirements of the "enforcing authority's code." As the code is written in semilegal outline without any design pointers toward intent, then assistance from helpful code digests published by major explosion-proof equipment manufacturers can be referred to. These digests pinpoint the obvious areas of concern in design and also the approved products that meet the code requirements.

30.7 OIL TANKER TERMINALS

Oil tanker terminals are for the transshipment of product between oil tanker ships and the shore-based bulk-loading facilities. As the NEC is written mainly for onshore installations, there is a certain undefined area between requirements up to the dock, which the code outlines; then there is the area and condition existing where an off-loading ship is attached to the dock and therefore becomes an extension of the dock. Furthermore, the ship may be from another country, introducing "international standards" of safety.

A guiding code for practices relating to the loading, discharge, and related operations at bulk oil tanker terminals is a book published by the International Oil Tanker Terminal Safety Group (I.O.T.T.S.G.), which was formed in 1966. The publication has the obvious title of "International Oil Tanker and Terminal Safety Guide." Rather than repeat the recommendations of this excellent book, we will point out some of the main chapters.

CHAPTER 1 Properties and Hazards of Petroleum: Personnel Protection Equipment.

CHAPTER 2 The Evolution and Dispersal of Hydrocarbon Gas on Tankers.

CHAPTER 3 Communications before Arrival of Tanker: Precautions for Mooring.

CHAPTER 4 Precautions and Preparations for Cargo Handling and Ballasting.

CHAPTER 5 Cargo and Ballast Handling.

CHAPTER 6 Gas Freeing and Cleaning of Ships Cargo Tanks.

CHAPTER 7 Terminal Bulk Cargo Handling Facilities.

CHAPTER 8 Handling of Bulk Liquified Petroleum Gas (LPG) and Liquified Natural Gas.

CHAPTER 9 Packed Petroleum Cargo.

CHAPTER 10 Static Electricity: Earthing, Bonding and Insulating Techniques; Cathodic Protection.

CHAPTER 11 Electrical Equipment and Installations in Classified Areas.

CHAPTER 12 Ship and Shore Communications and Communications Equipment.

CHAPTER 13 Fire Fighting and Emergency Procedures.

The publication also points out that for similar operations its contents are compatible with the recommendations contained in the "Tanker Safety Guide (Petroleum)" issued by the International Chamber of Shipping. This of course leads once again to the comment that these code guides and publications have no enforcing authority. Enforcement is always in the jurisdiction of the actual inspection department of the locality; the problem of course is that when dealing with a ship and a dock the harbor authorities usually have jurisdiction; therefore, on a docking installation it is necessary to confirm with both harbor and city officials as to where enforcement begins and finishes for inspection and design criteria.

30.8 EXPLOSION-PROOF MOTORS

A motor approved for operation in a classified area must have the correct approvals for that area marked on the nameplate. It is not sufficient for the electrical designer to assume that because a motor is a TEFC (totally enclosed fan-cooled) type it can be used in an explosion-proof area; it cannot. There are conditions however in classified areas where a general-purpose motor of the squirrel-cage type can be used such as Class 1, Division 2 locations. Here however the code allows this. If it is a Class 1, Division 1 location, then the motor must be approved for it. In the event of a failure, repairs to an approved explosion-proof motor must be made by a company with the necessary authorization to repair explosion-proof equipment; otherwise, the equipment approval will probably be void.

We are once again faced with what can be done and what should be done. It is no more difficult to repair or rewind an explosion-proof motor than the equivalent TEFC motor; therefore the tendency is for a company to consider repairing the motor in their own shop without the explosion-proof repair approval. If, after this motor was replaced in service, an explosion occurred, resulting in injury and/or fatalities, it would be a difficult point to defend in a legal suit and an obvious attack point by the plaintiff's expert witness.

If a motor is to be used in a Class 1, Division 2 location outdoors, the obvious approach is to the TEFC (Totally Enclosed Fan Cooled); however, this may not be the best choice. When a motor is shut down, under the right conditions it can draw outside air into the motor, which presents two possibilities: (1) the motor will collect moisture that it has drawn in from the outside atmosphere; (2) the outside atmosphere can contain contaminants which may or may not be explosive. The alternative to the TEFC motor in a semi-hazardous area is the drip-proof enclosure with an encapsulated winding.

This approach prevents the remote possibility of explosive vapors being sucked into a motor due to differential pressures between the inside and outside.

30.9 EXPLOSION-PROOF MOTOR CONTROL

There is nothing unique about explosion-proof motor control equipment. It is basically general-purpose motor starters and control components mounted into explosion-proof enclosures. The only unique part is that switchracks must be built instead of the normal motor control center. See Sec. 27.6.

Due to the higher cost of explosion-proof enclosures the design layout should try and locate as much motor control equipment as possible in general-purposes areas. This decision has to be a compromise between the savings on explosion-proof equipment and the added cost of running longer branch circuits.

There is no fixed rule regarding this; it is just a matter of judgment and decision, however, if a group of pumps are located in a tank farm area, then the switchrack is usually located at the top of the dyke nearby. The switchrack is then supplied by a single feeder.

30.10 EXPLOSION-PROOF LIGHTING

Explosion-proof lighting fixtures are expensive and the trend is away from the many small incandescent lighting fixtures to the larger-output mercury-vapor fixtures. The procedure for calculating lighting levels, outputs, and fixture quantity as well as point-to-point lighting calculations was outlined in the previous book[1] and would serve no purpose to repeat the exercises. The Code is very explicit with regard to the type of lighting fixtures that can be used in the Class 1, Division 1 and Division 2 areas. The Class 1, Division 1 areas require "approved" explosion-proof fixtures, while the Class 1, Division 2 areas will accept vaportight fixtures, provided that lamp temperatures do not exceed 80% of the ignition temperature of the gas or vapor involved. The

[1] L. B. Roe, *Practices and Procedures of Industrial Electrical Design*, McGraw-Hill Book Company, New York, 1972.

code must be carefully perused and the manufacturer's catalogs must be correctly interpreted to ensure that lighting fixtures which appear in a catalog picture to be explosion-proof are not in fact "vaportight." As with everything else, read the manufacturer's specifications for the exact lighting fixture you intend to order. The manufacturer will also supply the curves for a fixture light output.

30.11 EXPLOSION-PROOF RECEPTACLES

Receptacles are an obvious arcing device and as such are a specially engineered product. Arcing at terminals must be prevented; the approach to this is varied. One approach is to ensure that the contact legs of the plug break contact while still in the cylindrical chamber guides. The chamber should be long (deep) enough to ensure cooling of any gases which may escape around the legs. Another approach is to interlock the receptacle with the circuit disconnect switch so that the circuit is deenergized when the plug is withdrawn. As in all hazardous-area products the plugs must be approved for the specific hazardous service.

30.12 JUNCTION BOXES

Junction boxes are available in explosion-proof types. The Code does not require mandatory use of explosion-proof boxes in Class 1, Division 2 areas, except as dictated for special conditions. In practice, however, all boxes and fittings for a hazardous-area project are usually explosion-proof. This is not because of a disregard for the customer's money but is more of a problem of inspectors' opinions, warehousing, and disbursement of equipment.

On a large project there are hundreds of fittings and boxes; the electrician and warehouseman must be able to recognize a fitting approved for Class 1, Division 1, and a similar fitting or box approved for Class 1, Division 2, only. Time is expensive, and if the wrong fitting or box is installed in the wrong area, the differential cost of the Class 1, Division 1, and Class 1, Division 2, fitting or box is small compared to the cost of warehouse sorting and correcting wrong installations. Generally the customer specifications will outline the type of fittings and boxes to be used throughout the project; if not, the philosophy of using Class 1, Division 1, approved fittings throughout hazardous areas should be confirmed with the customer. In cases where a model is used instead of detailed drawings, the problem becomes more acute because individual fittings and boxes are not generally shown and called out in detail; this is left to the contractor, in which case the "contractor" specification must be the guiding factor.

The same thing applies to the Class 2 and Class 3 equipment; it should be approved for the specific service.

30.13 OTHER

Selecting explosion-proof equipment requires a familiarity with a catalog. A good approach is to be completely familiar with one manufacturer's range. Make the selection from the catalog with which you are familiar; after selection a comparison can be made with other manufacturers for price and delivery. Most times (except on government projects requiring special procedures) the specifications are written on an "or equal" basis. Therefore, the equipment would be specified as the manufacturers you are familiar with and are sure that they have an approved "red book" line. The contractor will then come back and ask if another manufacturer's equipment can be substituted in place of the one specified. The engineer must then examine the specifications for the requested substitute and confirm that it is equal and therefore allowed to be substituted.

Many times a product may be equal in published manufacturers' brochures with regard to approvals, but may not be equal on a history of past performance (maintenance, reliability, etc.). Deliveries are also a problem. Explosion-proof equipment is not mass-produced and stocked like the sheet-metal general-purpose equipment; therefore, speed of delivery is many times the deciding factor but beware of broken promises of delivery. The salesman may be overenthusiastic; therefore, if and when a proposal is requested, the quotation of delivery should be from the factory on the written proposal and not on the word of the salesman. It is extremely costly to have a project stopped because of the nondelivery of some particular items, which is even more critical if the items are routine, such as junction boxes and fittings. A major piece of equipment can be worked around, but routine items are essential.

31 SECONDARY DISTRIBUTION AND LIGHTING PANELS

31.1 SECONDARY DISTRIBUTION

Secondary distribution is concerned with feeding the many small areas of concentrated and miscellaneous individual low-voltage (600 V max.) loads. In the early chapters we covered the basic primary distribution methods available such as radial and secondary selective. In this chapter we will deal with the available components and approaches to secondary distribution.

We will consider the different types of panels, circuit breakers, loads, and also their contributing value to short-circuit loading. Again we will not deal with specifics, as covered in the earlier book[1] or by prior experience. We will however "point the way" to possible advantages or disadvantages of equipment and the applications.

31.2 POWER SOURCES

The sources of low-voltage power are the unit-substation low-voltage circuit-breaker metal-clad lineup. This is generally supplied as part of the primary equipment, even though it is low voltage. This is due to the purchasing of a package-type unit substation which includes the low-voltage switchgear.

These circuit breakers are usually the air circuit-breaker types, which are very rugged in construction and have high continuous-current ratings. They have high short-circuit ratings; however, the improvement in the molded-case circuit breakers also allows good short-circuit ratings. The advantage of the air circuit breakers is their rugged construction and ability to take abuse that the molded-case circuit breaker could not tolerate. Also they can be controlled by protective relaying, whereas the molded-case circuit breaker must have a fixed trip unless accessories are purchased. Here then is the source of main feeders to supply blocks of power to various plant areas.

[1] L. B. Roe, *Practices and Procedures of Industrial Electrical Design*, McGraw-Hill Book Company, New York, 1972.

If a plant is well designed to begin with, these secondary power sources will be strategically located throughout the plant in sizes of around 500-kVA, 750-kVA, or 1000-kVA three-phase four-wire 460-V (nominal) unit substations. The impedance of the transformers which must be known for the short-circuit calculations is around 5 to 7%; the impedances on the nameplate will probably vary slightly, that is, 5.5%, 5.7%, etc., for the same-size unit substation. For short-circuit calculations this variation is insignificant and the same-size substations, for example, 1000 kVA, could all be assigned an average value of 5.5%, which is considered standard range. For the substation to have a higher impedance than this would indicate that the available short-circuit current was high and that a "special" order for a higher-impedance (current-limiting) transformer was decided upon. If it is a new project with high short-circuit availability, then the option of selecting a special higher-impedance transformer is open. If the plant is large enough that a considerable number of transformers (i.e., at least more than six) is required, then a spare should be ordered. If it is decided that no spare transformer should be carried, then staying with the standard-impedance transformer should be considered and the problem of high short-circuit current should be solved some other way. This then provides the major sources of low-voltage power. The switchgear is usually fitted with an ammeter and a voltmeter as secondary metering; this is of course ordered as part of the unit.

31.3 MOTOR-CONTROL-CENTER (MCC)

The motor control center is the major power-distribution user in an industrial plant. There are two approaches to the installation and feeding of a motor control center. The basic philosophy should be worked out with the plant operating people (customer) whether motor control centers should be centralized or decentralized. If the project is a continuous-process machine such as a paper machine, where most of the motors are centralized, in the event of a problem all the motor control centers should be located in the one room so that the chief operator can rapidly inspect and make alternate evaluations and decisions and possibly keep the machine in limited production.

If the plant is in a process plant with widely diversified areas, then usually all the controls are brought back to a central operating panel where operators can evaluate all systems by alarm panels and complex instrumentation. In a situation like this the primary view to location selection is a point near the center of the main motor loads while still retaining the general-purpose classification. This means shorter branch circuits and therefore less labor and material cost for multiple branch-circuit installations but slightly higher cost for the feeder installation.

For the centralized location, a short piece of three-phase metal-clad bus can be used to connect to the air circuit breaker feeding the motor control center; in the latter "diversified areas" example, it would require a conduit and wire feeder with the necessary voltage-drop calculations. One approach in the early stages is to obtain a plot-plan print and circle the areas with the concentrated motor loads, then consider the location of the load centers compared to the closest unit substation.

Furthermore, keep in mind that above 500 MCM, conductors become more difficult to work with and if long runs are contemplated, multiple 500 MCM conductors may be required along with the possible voltage-drop problems; therefore a careful logistic study should be made on the locations of the motor control centers. In some cases, the engineer has no choice; the customer's preliminary plot plan may have already designated the location for the motor control center(s).

31.4 MOTOR-LOAD ESTIMATION

In order to evaluate motor-control-center loads, substation loads, etc., consider that the main loading is usually from motors. It is essential then that a preliminary single line and plot plan are available. A preliminary motor list is also necessary. A single line is not concerned with geographical location; its function is load analysis; therefore a motor control center can be given an arbitrary designation as MCC "A" and similarly for the other MCCs. With a combination of motor list and plot plan each motor can be located approximately and temporarily assigned a MCC. When all motors have been assigned, the horsepowers are totaled and 1 kVA assigned to each horsepower. For a total of 400 hp of miscellaneous motors, we would assign a kVA equivalent loading of 400 kVA. If the unit substation was rated at 500 kVA, then this would be a good point to stop further loading. The remaining 100 kVA will probably be assigned to lighting and miscellaneous loads via circuit breakers located in the motor control center and used as small miscellaneous feeders.

In this previous statement we have assigned 500 kVA to the unit substation; at this point in the design this is not usually "fixed." If we find that the motor load in that area is around 600 hp (600 kVA), we may decide to "up" the rating of the transformer to a 750-kVA unit. This can only be done, however, by keeping in mind the philosophy established for primary distribution and interchangability of transformers if only a single spare is to be carried. This may dictate shifting some load to another MCC in another area at the expense of longer branch circuits.

Inevitably, motor loads will grow both in quantity and horsepower as the project begins to firm up; rarely do the loads decrease. With this in mind, never load up the unit substation to capacity in the early part of a project; using only 80% of the rated capacity allows 20% spare for additional unforeseen loads during initial project design and also a thankful chief engineer when the plant is in operation.

The inevitable comment arises where, for example, 500 hp (connected) are to be applied to a 500-kVA unit-substation transformer: "It's OK because we have diversity." This then opens up a whole range of definitions of:

(1) connected load, (2) demand, (3) maximum demand, (4) maximum diversified demand, (5) coincident demand, (6) noncoincident demand, (7) diversified demand, (8) utilization factor, (9) demand factor, (10) load factor, (11) diversity factor.

Without getting into the various definitions (which can be a study in itself), the intent of the statement is: "All the motors will not be operating at once, therefore the transformer won't be fully loaded." This is not necessarily true and is not acceptable to inspection authorities and utility companies. In order to design for an acceptable higher connected load than the transformer can carry, loads must be "interlocked" so that they cannot possibly run together. Alternately, if the plant is a reproduction of an existing plant and recorders (charts) can show the load cycle, the authorities will consider a connected overload exceeding plant capacity but don't gamble on a favorable ruling in advance. Check and be sure.

Later, when the plant is in operation and the loads have been determined from ammeters, transformer temperatures, etc., it is possible to add more load; however, in the early stages don't rely on "diversity."

31.5 LIGHTING-LOAD ESTIMATION

Lighting-load estimation is fairly simple; however it is still only an estimate and not a substitute for design calculations. The rule of thumb is that incandescent lighting requires 5 W per square foot for 50 fc of lighting level. So, if only 10 fc (level) are required, then this would only require 1 W per square foot. For mercury vapor an estimated 2 W per square foot would provide around 50 fc. The same figure can be used for fluorescent lighting. Remember that we are only estimating electrical loading and not how many fixtures heights, locations, etc.; therefore it is advantageous to overestimate rather than underestimate.

31.6 POWER PANELS

Power panels are small panels containing three-phase power at 460, 240, or 208 V. The power panels contain molded-case circuit breakers of three-pole and sometimes two-pole type. The intent of a power panel is to supply small power loads of a non-process-type, such as vent fans, heaters, laboratory equipment, and maintenance shop tools.

The feeder for these power panels can be obtained from a circuit breaker in a motor control center, providing it is not too large a panel. If the panel is a large floor-standing unit, then it may be necessary to provide a feeder from one of the air circuit breakers.

When we use the term "small" power panel, we are using it in the sense that a power panel in an industrial plant is an auxiliary panel and a supplement to the motor control center and is only used as a convenient method of providing power to incidental loads that are not normally considered "process loads." There is a good reason for this. Process and production are the only reasons for the plant's existence; therefore everything in the design should be considered in the light of separating essential production equipment from nonessential plant-operating equipment. The maintenance personnel responsible for production equipment may not be the same personnel that are responsible for building and plant facility maintenance.

The training of the production equipment maintenance people is important so that they can immediately locate, identify, and correct a production problem. By having nonessential equipment on auxiliary power panels the plant maintenance people who are not trained on production equipment can calmly carry on with their work without a nervous production chief wondering what they are doing.

With this in mind, large power panels which are in a sense "nearly" small motor control centers are slightly out of place in an industrial plant. If a large one is required, then a motor control center should be considered because loads are either motor control, lighting, or special type. The motor control center can have a lighting panel included and special loads can be served with motor starters or circuit breakers.

If a plant has a special self-contained building which in itself might be doing special manufacturing, and a small power supply is required, then the large floor-standing power panel would be an obvious design solution.

31.7 LIGHTING PANELS

Lighting panels are circuit-breaker panels identified as lighting panels because only "lighting loads" are supplied from them. Panels as selected from catalogs can be used as power panels or lighting panels. The identification on the design drawings will discriminate between the two. The purpose of this is to separate lighting from miscellaneous loads for easier control. To go to a panel and turn off the circuit breakers, knowing it is only lighting, is a lot easier than opening circuit breakers of unknown loads whose identification tags may or may not be accurate. Turning off the circuit for a local sump pump may not be disastrous, but it is nice to avoid it.

Lighting panels usually have 120-V single-pole circuit breakers with a maximum allowable of 42 circuits. The panels can be single-phase, that is, two busbars at 240 V with a neutral busbar. The 120 V is obtained from a single circuit breaker and a neutral connection. For a 240-V single-phase circuit it is only necessary to use two adjacent circuit breakers. Alternately a lighting panel can be three phase, 120/208 V, four wire. Here the panel is equipped with three busbars and a neutral bar providing three-phase 208-V power; however, by using single-pole circuit breakers and the neutral connection, 120 V are obtained.

A further variation in the lighting panel is the use of a panel containing three-phase circuit breakers providing 208-V, 240-V, or 460-V three-phase power. These circuit breakers then supply lighting at the higher voltage levels; this is usually done through a lighting contactor, which is similar to a motor starter except it does not have overloads.

The lighting contactor can then be controlled by an ordinary light switch. In most industrial plants the contactors are considered a redundant item on the basis that it is easy to switch the lighting by the circuit breaker. Where remote control of lighting is required, however, contactors must be used.

31.8 WIREWAYS

Wireways are sheet-metal troughs; beyond that short statement there are many variations in manufacturers' designs which are acceptable and unacceptable, depending on the state and the inspecting authorities. The wireway has two alternate functions; on the one hand it can be considered purely as a mechanical support, in which case only self-protected conductors can be installed, such as armored cable. On the other hand, a wireway can be considered a raceway for installation of nonmechanically protected conductors. Here comes the problem. Some inspection authorities take the stand that if unprotected conductors are to be used, then the wireway must be totally enclosed on four sides without holes and approved as a wireway for the installation of nonmechanically protected conductors.

This means that the practice of using the expanded metal basket and tray for installation of ordinary TW, TWH, etc., is open to rejection (red tag). It is most important, then, to get a specific ruling or confirmation from the local inspecting authorities on the type of wireway what you intend to use to determine if it is acceptable.

An alternate companion to the wireway is the *ladder*. This is basically a mechanical support for armored cable installations. It is constructed of sidewalls and rungs; hence the term ladder.

There are optional fittings available for bends, offsets, dropouts, etc., and the various manufacturers each have their own design range and type. The materials used are both steel and aluminum, giving an option for corrosive areas. Continuity and short-circuit current-carrying capability must also be evaluated. Maximum wire fill is outlined in the Code.

31.9 BUSWAYS

Busway as used in industrial plants is generally termed *plug-in* busway. A busway consists of a three-phase three-wire or four-wire arrangement of busbar in a metal-clad enclosure in sectionalized lengths of around 10 ft as standard. A ground bus is available as an option. Busbar material can be either aluminum or copper.

When a plug-in section of busway is installed, optional methods of tapping off are available. Circuit breakers, fused switches, and cable tap boxes can all be conveniently mounted (plug in). This means that a busway can be installed in the center of an area and equipment can be connected later as locations dictate. This is particularly suitable where machine-shop equipment, aircraft assembly equipment, etc., may have to be periodically moved to accommodate new layouts of production. The circuit breakers and plug-in devices are all intended to be operable from the floor.

31.10 RACEWAYS

We now come to the predominant method of industrial-plant electrical wiring methods. This is the "rigid conduit" installation. This is by far the most usual method of wiring. The only decision to make with this type of installation is whether steel or aluminum should be used. In potentially corrosive areas, such as encountered in paper mills, aluminum should be considered; if it is, then the attendant evaluation of fault current, via the aluminum instead of steel must be made. The aluminum will not generate the same magnetic flux as the steel; therefore, the reactance values will be different. Conditions where steel and aluminum may have an accidental electrolyte (liquid) should be avoided due to electrolytic action taking place and eventually destroying the aluminum. This precludes installation of steel and aluminum together in concrete. Concrete can act as an electrolyte and many an installation has been destroyed by aluminum being installed in the same slab as steel. A record of installations with spacing of 10 ft between aluminum and steel conduit in concrete slab have shown a loss of the aluminum conduit after a few years.

31.11 OTHER OPTIONS

There are other methods of installing wiring, such as mineral insulated, and there are other products and accessories that all contribute to providing a wide range of products and choices to meet a particular need. But basically, most of the products will be the ones previously outlined for industrial installations.

Such things as uninterruptible power sources, emergency generators, slab heating, and pipeline heating all come under the category of accessories, in the sense that they would be written up as a packaged specification and manufacturers would submit proposals on what was available and the price and delivery details of the products.

32 SYMMETRICAL COMPONENTS

32.1 SYMMETRICAL COMPONENTS: USE AND TERMINOLOGY

Symmetrical components is the description of a method of procedure for analyzing an unbalanced polyphase system of vectors (phasors). The vectors can represent voltages, currents, or impedances. Before we progress, it will be assumed that the reader will be familiar with trigonometry and vector analysis at least up to the level as presented in the earlier book[1]; without this there will be a distinct disadvantage in understanding the symmetrical components. Manipulation of polar and cartesian vectors is mandatory; therefore a review should be made before progressing further, if the reader is a little rusty in the mathematical manipulations.

Considering a three-phase system only, if we take a voltmeter and measure the voltages between phases A and B, phases B and C, and phases C and A, we will probably get three slightly different voltages. For example, consider differences between A and B (240 V), B and C (248 V), and C and A (232 V). In a three-phase system of balanced voltages, the vectors are 120° degrees apart; but how do we determine the displacement angles? We know that a three-phase system can be represented as a closed-delta system. We also know that the total of the three angles in a delta must equal two right angles, or 180° degrees. By using the cosine law we can calculate the three angles associated with the voltages. If we consider *ABC* as the angles and *abc* as the sides with side *a* opposite to angle *A*, etc. We can write the cosine law as $c^2 = a^2 + b^2 - 2ab \cos C$. We can represent side *c* (240), side *a* (248), and side *b* (232). See Fig. 32.1*a*.

[1] L. B. Roe, *Practices and Procedures of Industrial Electrical Design*, McGraw-Hill Book Company, New York, 1972.

Finding angle C, we have

$$\cos^{-1} C = \frac{a^2 + b^2 - c^2}{2ab}$$

$$= \frac{(248)^2 + (232)^2 - (240)^2}{2 \times 248 \times 232}$$

$$= 0.50 \text{ gives a } 60^\circ \text{ angle}$$

To find angle B, we set up the cosine law with b as the subject:

$$b^2 = a^2 + c^2 - 2ac \cos B$$

rearranged, this gives:

$$\cos^{-1} B = \frac{a^2 + c^2 - b^2}{2ac}$$

$$= \frac{(248)^2 + (240)^2 - (232)^2}{2 \times 248 \times 240}$$

$$= 0.54, \text{ giving a } 58^\circ \text{ angle}$$

To find angle A, we know that a closed triangle has a total of 180° for the three angles; therefore we have $A = 180^\circ - 60^\circ - 58^\circ = 62^\circ$. In Figure 32.1 we show the closed triangle and also the equivalent representation shown on coordinate axis.

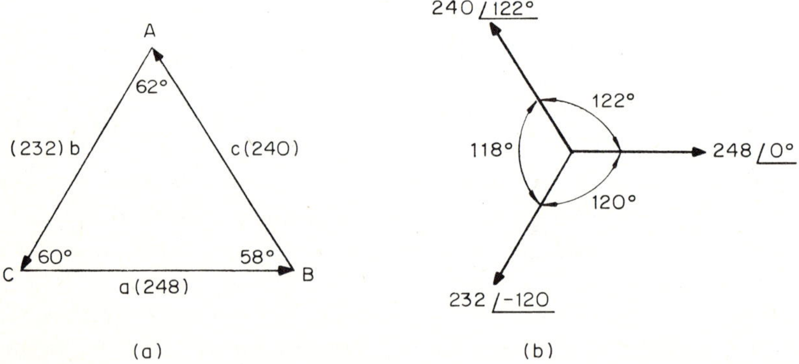

Figure 32.1 (*a*) Closed triangle of vectors; (*b*) vectors shown on coordinate axis.

If we show vector CB on the horizontal axis, it has the value of side a (248) volts so we set it at angle 0°, giving a polar vector of $248\underline{/0^\circ}$. Vector BA, side c (240 Volts) has a relative angle of $180^\circ - 58^\circ$ (angle B), giving 122° and a polar vector of $240\underline{/122^\circ}$. The third vector AC, side b, is rotated backwards with reference to the zero axis; therefore we have $180^\circ - 60^\circ$ (angle C) $= -120^\circ$, giving a polar vector of $232\underline{/-120^\circ}$.

This then brings us to the "original vector" presentation, which will be shown in the style of Fig. 32.1*b* for symmetrical-component analysis.

The method of symmetrical components is based on Fortescue's theorem. Applied to a three-phase system, it states that any unbalanced three-phase system of vectors can be resolved into three balanced systems of vectors. These are known as: (1) positive-sequence system, (2) negative-sequence system, (3) zero-sequence system.

The positive-sequence system is represented by a balanced system of vectors having the "same" phase sequence (phase rotation) as the original unbalanced system. The negative-sequence system is represented by a balanced system of vectors having the "opposite" phase sequence to the original system. The zero-sequence system is represented by "three single vectors" which are equal in magnitude and angular displacement, (i.e., in phase) from the reference axis. As an example, Fig. 32.2 shows the four basic relationships of the symmetrical components.

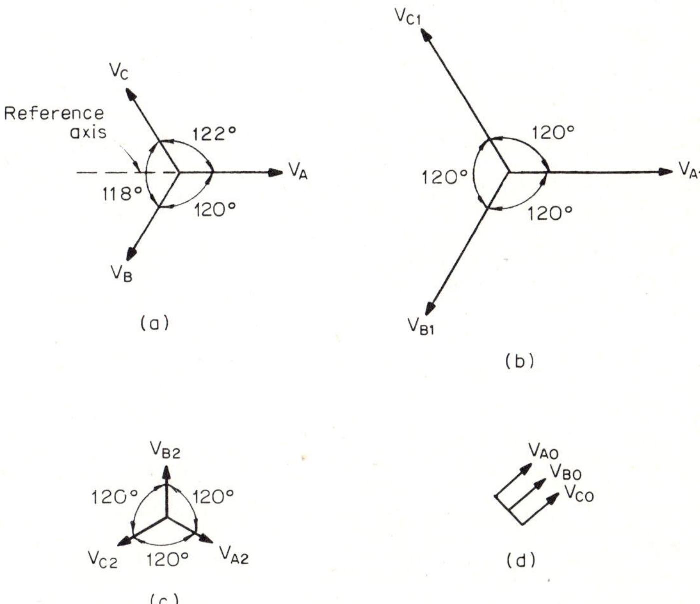

Figure 32.2 Three-phase vectors for symmetrical component analysis. (*a*) Original vector; (*b*) positive-sequence vector; (*c*) negative-sequence vector; (*d*) zero-sequence vector.

Note that the positive and negative system vectors (that is, V_{a1}, V_{c1}, etc.) are exactly 120° apart. As we are dealing with balanced three-phase systems, we can introduce an operator similar to the "j" operator; it will be an "a" operator. It will rotate a vector through 120°; also (a^2) will rotate a vector through 240°. The rotation of the "a" operator is always in the positive (i.e., counterclockwise direction); this means that a^2 is equivalent to 120° in the "negative" direction. The single subscript[2] notation gives the phase and a number (1, 2, or 0) for positive, negative, and zero sequence, respectively. If we were considering voltages for positive sequence, we would have:

$V_{a1} = V_{a1}$ (angle referred to reference point, for example, horizontal axis)

$$V_{b1} = a^2 V_{a1} = V_{a1}\underline{/-120^\circ}$$

$$V_{c1} = aV_{a1} = V_{a1}\underline{/-240^\circ}$$

Also remember that phase rotation is defined by assuming that the vectors actually rotate under a fixed point and the standard accepted rotation is counterclockwise, this means that at standstill the vectors are marked in alphabetical sequence in a clockwise direction. See Fig. 32.2*b* (positive sequence).

Using the single-subscript notation again, we will define the negative-sequence vectors as V_{a2}, V_{b2}, V_{c2}, and the respective displacements as:

$$V_{a2} = V_{a2}$$

$$V_{b2} = aV_{a2} = V_{a2}\underline{/-240^\circ}$$

$$V_{c2} = a^2 V_{a2} = V_{a2}\underline{/-120^\circ}$$

The zero-sequence-system vectors, V_{a0}, V_{b0}, C_{c0}, are all equal in length and angular displacement; therefore they can all be shown as equal:

$$V_{a0} = V_{a0}$$

$$V_{b0} = V_{a0}$$

$$V_{c0} = V_{a0}$$

We have used voltage vectors for purposes of identification, but current vectors I_{a1}, I_{b1}, I_{c1}, and I_{a2}, I_{b2}, I_{c2}, and I_{a0}, I_{b0}, I_{c0}, can be applied just as simply.

32.2 SYMMETRICAL COMPONENTS: VECTOR COMPOSITION

A single vector in the original unbalanced system is broken down into three parts; therefore, these three parts when combined should reproduce the original vector. If this is true, we have:

[2] Single subscript indicates phase a; double subscript gives phase a, b, indicating which direction the circuit is being analyzed. The numbers 1, 2, 0 are not then considered as "subscripts."

$$V_a = V_{a1} + V_{b2} + V_{c0}$$

$$V_b = V_{b1} + V_{b2} + V_{b0}$$

$$V_c = V_{c1} + V_{c2} + V_{c0}$$

If we apply the operator a to the three vectors we have:

$$V_a = V_{a1} + V_{a2} + V_{a0}$$

$$V_b = a^2V_{a1} + aV_{a2} + V_{a0}$$

$$V_c = aV_{a1} + a^2V_{a2} + V_{a0}$$

By reading the columns vertically, we see that each vector is displaced by 120° by the application of the operator a except for the zero sequence which by now we know are all in phase.

32.3 DERIVING V_{a1}, V_{b1}, AND V_{c1} VECTORS

Before evaluating the vectors let us consider operator a and its multiples. As a is 120°, then a^3 is 360° or one full rotation; therefore, we can make $a^3 = 1$, meaning that a^4 is $1a$, or simply a. With this in mind, we can write the following equation $(1 + a + a^2) = (1 + a^2 + a) = 0$.

Now the intent is to apply this arrangement to the last three equations in the last paragraph. We see, however, that only two equations have the operator a; therefore, we will apply only to these. Taking equation V_b, we see that we must multiply a^2V_{a1} by a to give a^3V_{a1}, which equals V_{a1}. We must, however, multiply both sides of the equation; therefore we have:

$$(a)V_b = (a)a^2V_{a1} + (a)aV_{a2} + (a)V_{a0}$$

then

$$aV_b = V_{a1} + a^2V_{a2} + aV_{a0}$$

To do the same thing to Phase c we must multiply through by a^2 to obtain the same arrangement in the equation:

$$a^2V_c = V_{a1} + aV_{a2} + a^2V_{a0}$$

We can combine the first parts, giving $V_a + aV_b + a^2V_c$; if we regroup the three equations, we now have:

$$V_a = V_{a1} + V_{a2} + V_{a0}$$

$$aV_b = V_{a1} + a^2V_{a2} + aV_{a0}$$

$$a^2V_c = V_{a1} + aV_{a2} + a^2V_{a0}$$

If we add all three equations together, factor the a, and solve for V_{a1}, we have:

$$V_a + aV_b + a^2V_c = 3V_{a1} + V_{a2}(1 + a^2 + a) + V_{a0}(1 + a + a^2)$$

Replacing the a on the right part of the equation gives

$$3V_{a1} + V_{a2}(0) + V_{a0}(0)$$

As $(1 + a + a^2)$ is equal to zero, we have

$$Va + aV_b + a^2V_c = 3V_{a1} + 0 + 0$$

and by cross-multiplying, we have

$$\tfrac{1}{3}(V_a + aV_b + a^2V_c) = V_{a1}$$

Applying the commutative law and replacing a with the angle we have the polar representation of:

$$V_{a1} = \tfrac{1}{3}(V_a + V_b\underline{/120^\circ} + V_c\underline{/240^\circ}$$

which can be stated as "V_{a1} is a vector one-third as large as the vector obtained by adding V_a, $V_b\underline{/120^\circ}$, and $V_c\underline{/240^\circ}$. If we apply this to the three vectors in Sec. 32.1 and Fig. 33.1*b*, we have $V_a = 248\underline{/0^\circ}$, $V_b = 232\underline{/-120^\circ}$, and $V_c = 240\underline{/122^\circ}$. Solving for V_{a1}, we have the following:

Va **Vb** **Vc**

$$\tfrac{1}{3}(248\underline{/0^\circ} + a232\underline{/-120} + a^2240\underline{/122^\circ})$$

$$\tfrac{1}{3}(248\underline{/0^\circ} + 232\underline{/0} + 240\underline{/2^\circ})$$

Expanding the equation, we have

$$\tfrac{1}{3}(248\underline{/0^\circ}) + \tfrac{1}{3}(232\underline{/0^\circ}) + \tfrac{1}{3}(240\underline{/2^\circ})$$

Changing to complex numbers (cartesian form),

$$\tfrac{1}{3}(248\underline{/0^\circ}) = 82.67\underline{/0^\circ} = 82.67 + j0$$

$$\tfrac{1}{3}(232\underline{/0^\circ}) = 77.33\underline{/0^\circ} = 77.33 + j0$$

$$\tfrac{1}{3}(240\underline{/2^\circ}) = 80\underline{/2^\circ} = \underline{79.95 + j2.79}$$

$$V_{a1} = \underline{239.95 + j2.79}$$

in polar form $V_{a1} = 239.97\underline{/0^\circ}$; as it is a balanced system of vectors, V_{b1} and V_{c1} will be the same, except 120° apart.

$$V_{a1} = 239.97\underline{/0^\circ} \qquad V_{b1} = 239.97\underline{/-120} \qquad V_{c1} = 239.97\underline{/120^\circ}$$

32.4 DERIVING V_{a2}, V_{b2}, AND V_{c2}

The method of deriving the negative-sequence values is essentially the same as deriving the positive; therefore we will not go through another complete example. We will, however, point out the differences.

Using the three equations at the end of Sec. 32.2, which can be considered the basic equations, we must again arrange them so that the second part of the equation will eliminate the V_{a1} and V_{a0} terms, by the use of the a operator. The last two equations are the ones of concern; we will show the operation of multiplying out by using parentheses on the a operator:

$$(a^2)V_b = (a^2)a^2V_{a1} + (a^2)aV_{a2} + (a^2)V_{a0}$$
$$= aV_{a1} + V_{a2} + a^2V_{a0}$$

and by multiplying phase c by a, we derive

$$aV_c = a^2V_{a1} + V_{a2} + aV_{a0}$$

Adding phase a, b, and c equations gives the same arrangement as for V_{a1}, with the exception that the operators of the second terms are reversed.

$$V_{a2} = \tfrac{1}{3}(V_a + a^2V_b + aV_c) = \tfrac{1}{3}(V_a + V_b\underline{/240^\circ} + V_c\underline{/120^\circ})$$

This can be stated as follows: The negative-sequence vector is one-third the magnitude of the three original vectors with vector V_b rotated 240° and vector V_c rotated 120°, both in the positive direction.

Using the original three vectors, the negative sequence would be:

$$\begin{array}{ccc} \mathbf{V}_a & \mathbf{V}_b & \mathbf{V}_c \end{array}$$
$$\tfrac{1}{3}(248\underline{/0^\circ} + a^2 232\underline{/-120^\circ} + a240\underline{/122^\circ})$$

$$\tfrac{1}{3}(248\underline{/0^\circ} + 232\underline{/120^\circ} + 240\underline{/242^\circ})$$

Expanding the equation, we have

$$82.67\underline{/0^\circ} + 77.33\underline{/120^\circ} + 80\underline{/242^\circ}$$

Changing to cartesian form, we have:

$$\begin{array}{lr} & 82.67 + j\ 0.00 \\ & -38.67 + j66.97 \\ & -37.56 - j70.63 \\ \hline V_{a2} & +\ 6.44 - j\ 3.66 \end{array}$$

in polar form, we have:

$$V_{a2} = 7.41\underline{/-29^\circ}$$

Note that the plus sign represents the cosine function and the minus sign the sine function; the only quadrant which matches the (+) cosine and (−) sine is the fourth quadrant, hence $\underline{/-29^\circ}$.

32.5 DERIVING V_{a0}, V_{b0}, AND V_{c0}

The three basic equations for V_a, V_b, and V_c when added together give the following, with the operators factored separately:

$$V_a + V_b + V_c = V_{a1}(1 + a^2 + a) - V_{a2}(1 + a + a^2) + 3V_{a0}$$

The V_{a1} and V_{a2} terms drop out because the operators are equal to zero. By cross-multiplying and using the commutative law, we get the equation for the zero-sequence component.

$$V_{a0} = \tfrac{1}{3}(V_a + V_b + V_c)$$

Using the earlier vectors again, we have to determine a vector one-third the magnitude of the sum of the original three vectors. If the sum of the three vectors adds to zero, no zero-sequence voltages or currents can exist.

$$\begin{array}{ccc} \mathbf{V}_a & \mathbf{V}_b & \mathbf{V}_c \\ \tfrac{1}{3}(248\underline{/0^\circ} + & 232\underline{/-120} + & 240\underline{/122^\circ}) \end{array}$$

In cartesian form and expanded, we have:

$$\begin{array}{rr} & 82.67 + j\ 0.00 \\ & -38.67 - j66.97 \\ & -42.39 + j67.84 \\ \hline V_{a0} = V_{b0} = V_{c0} = & +\ 1.61 + j00.87 \end{array}$$

in polar form, we have

$$V_{a0} = V_{b0} = V_{c0} = 1.83\underline{/29^\circ}$$

32.6 RECOMBINATION OF SYMMETRICAL COMPONENTS

In order to confirm the individual symmetrical components it is only necessary to use the expression $V_a = (V_{a1} + V_{a2} + V_{a0})$, and if our arithmetic was correct and pocket calculator working correctly, we should be able to derive the original vector V_a from the symmetrical components we have just worked out.

$V_a = 248\underline{/0^\circ}$ (original Vector)

Symmetrical Components

$$\begin{array}{lcr} V_{a1} = 239.97\underline{/0^\circ} & = & 239.97 + j0 \\ V_{a2} = 7.41\underline{/-29^\circ} & = & 6.48 - j3.59 \\ V_{a0} = 1.83\underline{/29^\circ} & = & 1.60 + j0.88 \\ \hline & & 248.05 - j2.71 \end{array}$$

Sum of V_{a1}, V_{a2}, V_{a3}

The difference between the original vector of $248\angle 0°$ and the resulting vector of $248.08\angle >0° <1°$ is the result of using a pocket calculator with a floating decimal rather than the fixed decimal. The figures, however, are accurate to less than $\frac{1}{4}$ of 1%.

32.7 SUMMATION: SYMMETRICAL COMPONENTS

This very brief introduction into symmetrical components is not intended to teach symmetrical components. There are many excellent books and standard texts available for that. This was purely an introduction to the terminology so that when we are talking about positive-, negative-, and zero-sequence components during short-circuit studies, the reader will have some idea of what the terms mean. It will also be obvious that to work with symmetrical components, one should not be bothered with wondering how to change a vector from a polar to cartesian form; hence, a refresher or reference to the previous book.[3]

In addition, whether zero-sequence "currents" can flow or not depends on the particular arrangement and connection of equipment. Zero-sequence currents cannot flow in any three-phase three-wire systems. This means a delta- or ungrounded-wye system. In contrast, a three-phase four-wire system can carry zero-sequence currents, and furthermore, the neutral return current will be three times as large as the individual zero-sequence component current. See Fig. 32.2*d*, that is, three currents in phase for zero-sequence currents.

It is not probable that the average industrial project will require extensive work with symmetrical components; therefore unless an individual is particularly interested in this branch of analytical methods, there is no need to delve further. The criteria in industry is reasonably fast production of construction design with standardized materials and methods. The use of symmetrical components isn't exactly fast but without it some problems would be very laborious and maybe nearly impossible.

[3] L. B. Roe, *Practices and Procedures of Industrial Electrical Design*, McGraw-Hill Book Company, New York, 1972.

33 SHORT CIRCUITS

33.1 SHORT CIRCUITS

When we talk of a *short circuit* in a power system we are generally thinking in terms of how much damage will be done to equipment and what would be the loss of production. The short circuit itself is something abstract that may or may not happen and if it did it could occur anywhere in the system. The equipment used in a power system should be short-circuit proof. By this we mean that it will operate as intended during a short circuit without permanent damage; this includes wire and cable.

There are a number of different methods of calculating short-circuit currents and probably all are good methods. The method(s) we will present here are selected on the premise that they will be acceptable to most customers as formal calculations, and they are fairly simple in that they are not overly involved with complex mathematics nor are they too time-consuming. In the earlier book[1] we introduced the short-circuit study, so once again we are going to assume that the reader has some initial familiarity at least with the terminology of short-circuit studies.

33.2 THE PERCENTAGE METHOD

The percentage method of figuring short circuits is one of the most common and most widely understood methods. Any individual using any other method will necessarily be familiar with the percentage method, even if he prefers some other method. The routine is fairly simple and involves five stages:

1. Make a single line showing transformers, motors, generators, circuit breakers, switchgear, fuses, motor control centers, wire and cable, etc.
2. Identify equipment, make listing, change all impedances to a common percentage base, that is, 1000 or 10,000 kVA, or other optional base.

[1] L. B. Roe, *Practices and Procedures of Industrial Electrical Design*, McGraw-Hill Book Company, New York, 1972.

3. Make an impedance diagram, replacing all transformers, rotating equipment, wire and cables, etc., with an electronic resistor or inductance symbol and percentage value. Locate faults A, B, C, etc., with X.

4. Rearrange the impedance diagram to solve for first fault and combine impedances; reducing to single impedance.

5. Calculate the momentary and interrupting short-circuit currents, in kVA and/or amperes.

This then is the basic approach. The term *percentage method* refers to the procedure of representing "ohms impedance" as a percentage impedance; for example,

$$\%\text{ ohms impedance} = \frac{(\text{ohms impedance})(\text{base kVA})}{(\text{kV})^2 \times 10}$$

Manufacturers publish tables indicating the percentage impedances of various equipments. The terms *impedance* and *reactance* although not mathematically equal are used interchangeably in short-circuit calculations. This is due to the fact that in most cases the resistance portion of the impedance $r \pm jx$ is neglected. Only in low-voltage wire and cables is it generally necessary to include the resistance into the calculations.

Again in the interests of accepted or usual practice, we will use the term reactance rather than impedance for the short-circuit calculations.

33.3 MULTIPLIERS

The multipliers are a range of numbers between 1.0 and 1.6 which are used to compensate for the asymmetrical variance in short-circuit current wave. To try to explain this simply is difficult, but we will attempt it.

For a fixed impedance an increase in voltage will give an increase in current. In an alternating-current sine wave, the voltage wave passes through a zero point and begins to increase until it reaches a maximum at peak; it then begins to reduce. If a short circuit occurs at the peak, then the voltage is on a downward trend and will tend to reduce the magnitude of the short-circuit current when considering instantaneous values; however, if the short circuit occurred somewhere on the zero-to-peak rise portion of the wave, it would tend to increase the current magnitude. These of course are instantaneous values at "instants" along the first half cycle of a wave. We are of course interested in the continuous effect over a number of complete cycles. In essence then we are saying that there is a remote chance that the short circuit might just occur at the right time so that the current wave will be symmetrical with the voltage wave and therefore suddenly change into a nice level wave. This could happen but a horse player would "lose his shirt" betting on it.

Oscillograms will show that short circuits will nearly always be asymmetrical (offset) during the first few cycles; it will also show that the asymmetry (offset) is maximum at the instant the short circuit occurs. This "offset" difference between the symmetrical wave around the neutral axis and the amount of distortion due to the short circuit occurring at an "offset creating period" produces an additional current wave. This shows up as a unidirectional current rather than an alternating-current wave and therefore is termed the *dc component.* As the oscillogram will show, the offset is maximum at the instant the short circuit occurs; therefore, the dc component will immediately begin to decay with time. This rate of decay, as with any inductive circuit is a function of the ratio of reactance to resistance X/R ratio. With low resistance (i.e., high ratio), it takes a long time to decay. Conversely, with high resistance (i.e., low ratio), it decays very rapidly.

A summation of all the mathematics, probabilities, experience, and studies have resulted in a simple multiplier that can be applied to the short-circuit "symmetrical" value and will give the probable expected maximum asymmetrical current. In general, 1.6 is used on all systems above 5 kV and any systems of 5 kV which have generators applied. A 1.4 multiplier can be used on most industrial plants which have a conventional 5-kV primary system, either through a transformer from a single radial feeder or a direct 5-kV line. For 600 V and below, a multiplier of 1.25 is the accepted normal. Table 33.1 (pages 318 and 319) gives various multipliers for use in different situations.

33.4 MOMENTARY RATING

The momentary rating of circuit-opening equipment could be called the "instantaneous" rating, referring to the instant the short circuit occurred. Considering a circuit breaker, at the instant a short circuit occurs, mechanical stresses from electromagnetic forces will try to force open contacts, latching mechanisms, bend conductors, and explode the shell. These, among other things, will try and tear the circuit breaker apart. As these forces are a function of the square of the current (I^2), we see that a short circuit of 20 times normal will produce stresses of 400 times normal in the circuit breaker. The momentary rating then is the rating of maximum current that the circuit breaker is able to withstand without sustaining any permanent damage. This value must not be exceeded for obvious reasons.

The next obvious question is how to calculate for the momentary rating. As the momentary rating is at the instant the short circuit occurs, the impedance diagram is set up to include all equipment which will contribute to short-circuit current. We can figure the symmetrical current (i.e., the steady-state short-circuit current), but the problem is that the rotating equipment will tend to act as generators and therefore feed a voltage into the fault, consequently increasing the fault current further. Therefore, all motors and generators must be included using the subtransient reactance $X''d$. In addition, when the calculation is completed, the correct multiplier must be used on the answer to give the asymmetrical current.

33.5 INTERRUPTING RATING

The interrupting rating of a circuit-opening device is its ability to open a circuit under short-circuit conditions without damage to itself. On the one hand, if a circuit breaker opens extremely fast after the fault occurs, it will be opening part of the dc component as well as the symmetrical current. Alternatively, if it is slower on opening, the dc component will probably have decayed and only the symmetrical current needs to be opened. Most circuit breakers fall into this latter category. The impedance diagram then is slightly different for the interrupting duty than for the momentary duty. All induction motors can be omitted, but generators must be included using the subtransient reactance, and all synchronous motors must be included, but using the "transient" reactance instead of the subtransient. When the calculation is complete, it is not necessary to use the multiplier because the dc component is assumed to have decayed by this time.

In very large power systems, that is, 500 MVA and up, the X/R ratio is probably high; therefore, the dc component will probably take longer to decay, in which case a multiplier of 1.1 should be used to compensate.

33.6 ROTATING-EQUIPMENT REACTANCES

The reactances in rotating equipment are effective in the following order:

1. Subtransient reactance $X''d$
2. Transient reactance $X'd$
3. Synchronous reactance Xd

The subtransient appears at the instant the short circuit occurs and is effective for the first few cycles. For small motors of less than 600 V a value of around 25% subtransient reactance should be used. Also, instead of showing all small motors, they can be lumped together with a total connected kVA equivalent to the connected horsepower. Many times the total motor load is not known; in this case use the kVA of the transformer supplying the motors as the motor kVA.

For motors above 600 V use 20% for induction motors and 15% for synchronous-motor subtransient reactances. For generators it is necessary to obtain the information from the manufacturer. See Tables 33.2 and 33.3.

Transient reactance becomes effective following the subtransient period. It is in effect during the interrupting of the circuit and therefore must be included for synchronous motors for interrupting-duty calculations. The value to use for the transient reactance for synchronous motors is 25% for motors above 600 V and 33% for the smaller motors below 600 V.

The generator subtransient reactance lasts longer than the equivalent motor reactance; therefore, the subtransient period of the generator will

TABLE 33.1 Condensed Table of Multiplying Factors and Rotating-machine Reactances
To Be Used for Calculating Short-circuit Currents for Circuit-breaker, Fuse, and Motor-starter Applications

				Rotating machine reactances to use		
Classification	*Circuit voltage*	*Location in system*	*Multi-plying factor*	*Generators, synchronous converters, synchronous condensers, frequency changers*	*Synchronous motors*	*Induction motors*
POWER CIRCUIT BREAKERS						
				Interrupting duty		
Eight cycle or slower (general case)	Above 600 volts	Any place where symmetrical short-circuit kvA is less than 500 MVA	1.0	Subtransient	Transient	Neglect
Five cycle	Above 600 volts		1.1	Subtransient	Transient	Neglect
				Momentary duty		
General case	Above 600 volts	Near generating station	1.6	Subtransient	Subtransient	Subtransient
Less than 5 kV	601 to 5,000 volts	Remote from generating station (X/R ratio less than 10)	1.5	Subtransient	Subtransient	Subtransient
HIGH-VOLTAGE FUSES						
				Three-phase kVA interrupting duty		
All types, including all current-limiting fuses	Above 600 volts	Anywhere in system	1.0	Subtransient	Transient	Neglect
				Maximum rms ampere interrupting duty		
All types, including all current-limiting fuses	Above 600 volts	Anywhere in system	1.6	Subtransient	Subtransient	Subtransient
Non-current-limiting types only	601 to 15,000 volts	Remote from generating station (X/R ratio less than 4)	1.2	Subtransient	Subtransient	Subtransient

HIGH-VOLTAGE FUSED MOTOR STARTERS

				Three-phase kVA interrupting duty		
All horsepower ratings	2,400 and 4,160 wye, volts	Anywhere in system	1.0	Subtransient	Transient	Neglect
				Maximum rms ampere interrupting duty		
All horsepower ratings	2,400 and 4,160 wye, volts	Anywhere in system	1.6	Subtransient	Subtransient	Subtransient

HIGH-VOLTAGE MOTOR STARTERS

				Interrupting duty		
Circuit breaker or contactor type	601 to 5,000 volts	Anywhere in system	1.0	Subtransient	Transient	Neglect
				Momentary duty		
Circuit breaker or contactor type	601 to 5,000 volts	Anywhere in system	1.6	Subtransient	Subtransient	Subtransient
Circuit breaker or contactor type	601 to 5,000 volts	Remote from generating station (X/R ratio less than 10)	1.5	Subtransient	Subtransient	Subtransient

APPARATUS, 600 VOLTS AND BELOW

				Interrupting or momentary duty		
Air circuit breakers or breaker-contactor combination motor starters	600 volts and below	Anywhere in system	1.25	Subtransient	Subtransient	Subtransient
Low-voltage fuses or fused combination motor starters	600 volts and below	Anywhere in system	1.25	Subtransient	Subtransient	Subtransient

spill over into the time period of the transient reactance of the synchronous motor. This must also be included with the transient reactances.

The synchronous reactance is not effective for a number of seconds, by which time the circuit-opening devices have operated; therefore it will not be considered in short-circuit calculating procedures.

33.7 THREE-PHASE SHORT CIRCUIT

The three-phase short circuit is generally the largest magnitude of fault current; therefore in general a single calculation for three-phase faults will suffice. The following example(s) will give the simple routines involved. The first example is fairly straightforward, while in the second example we have a situation with two sources and a tie breaker. In this case a delta-star transformation is necessary. It is not difficult but does require some care to prevent mistakes.

The key to a short-circuit study is careful arrangement of the single-line

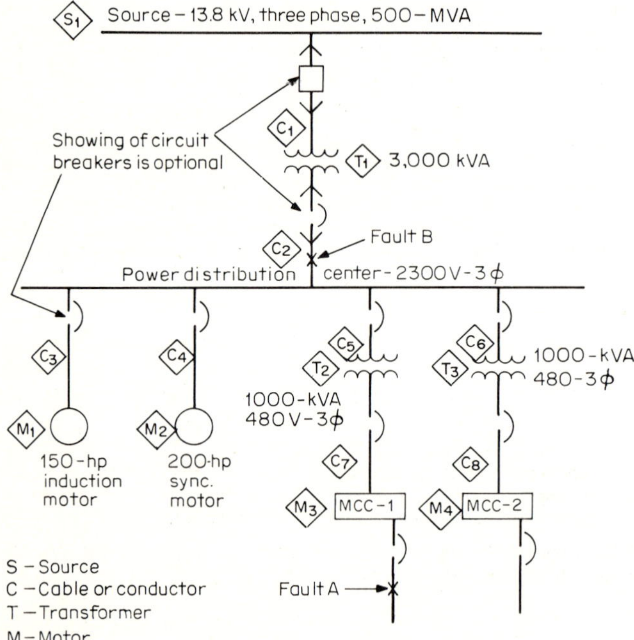

Figure 33.1 Single-line identification of reactances.

and impedance diagrams to ensure that nothing has been omitted and that the arrangement is correct. See Figs. 33.1 to 33.5.

With the arrangement of the impedance diagram it is now necessary to plug in the reactance values; these of course are obtained from the listing previously made. Section 33.8 will list the procedures for calculating the various reactances.

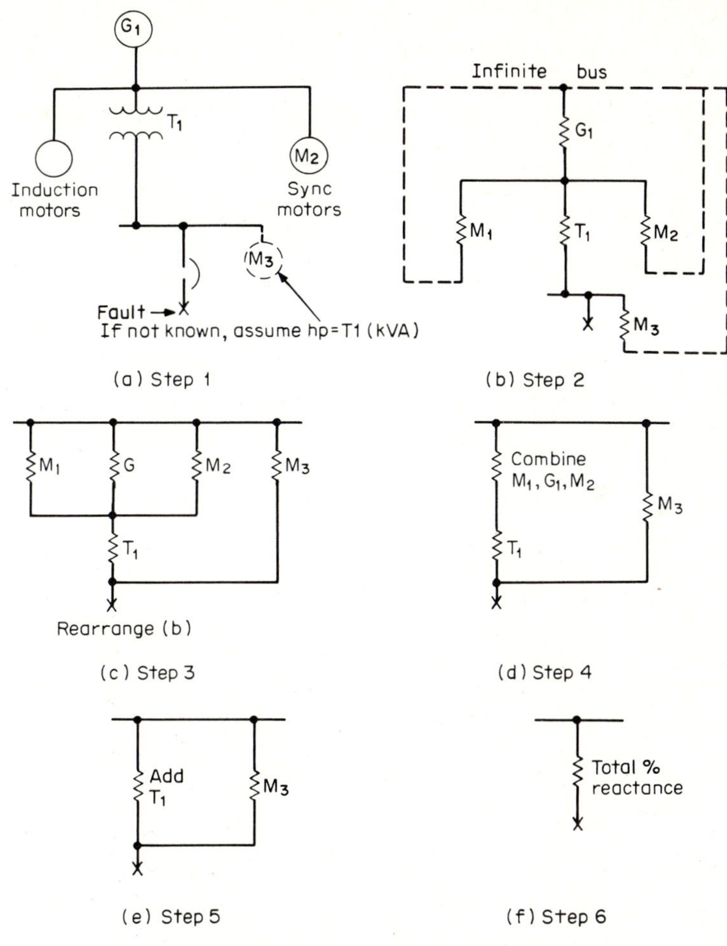

Figure 33.2 Impedance diagram, Example 1. Neglect cables for example only. Calculation is for monetary rating.

33.8 COMMON BASE REACTANCES

Before we can change reactances to a common base, it is first necessary to select a base unit. This base unit is a base kVA and any convenient number can be selected. Usually it is 1000 kVA or 10,000 kVA, purely because they are nice round numbers. The larger the base kVA selected, the larger the

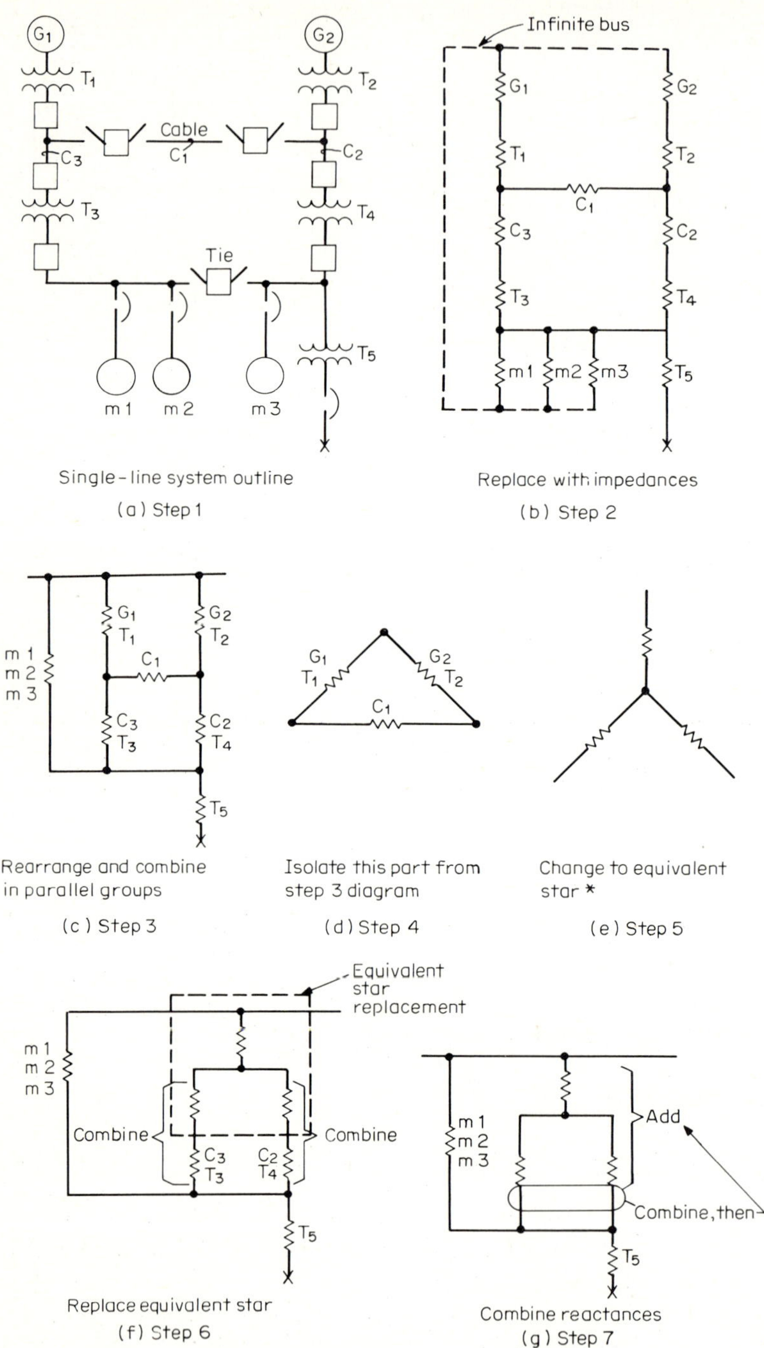

Figure 33.3 Impedance diagram, Example 2; example with tie breaker closed.

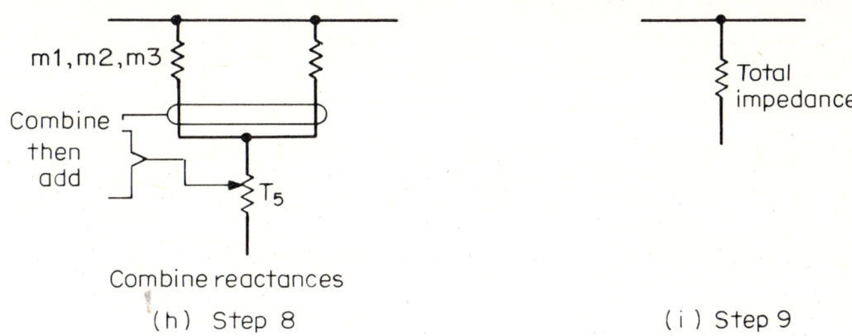

*See Fig. 33.4 for star-delta conversion

Figure 33.3 (Continued)

The star-delta conversion method is accomplished by the use of the following formulas:

$$B = \frac{ab + ac + bc}{b} \qquad b = \frac{CA}{A + B + C}$$

$$C = \frac{ab + ac + bc}{c} \qquad c = \frac{AB}{A + B + C}$$

$$A = \frac{ab + ac + bc}{a} \qquad a = \frac{BC}{A + B + C}$$

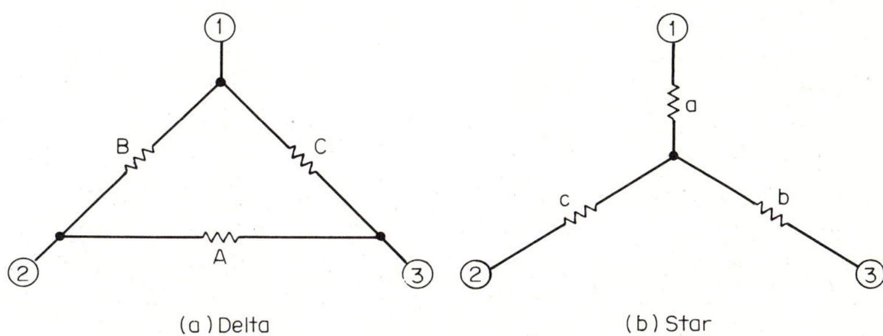

We see then that if we assign the numbers 1, 2, and 3 to the corners of a delta, we can solve for a, b, and c. This produces the star connection with corresponding 1, 2, and 3 connections.

Figure 33.4 Star-delta conversion numbering method.

reactance percentage value. The equation to use for percentage reactance on a common base is:

$$\%X = \frac{\text{(base kVA) (\% reactance)}}{\text{Equipment kVA}}$$

For example, selecting a 3000-kVA transformer with 6.75% impedance and a 10,000-kVA base would give:

$$\frac{10{,}000 \times 6.75\%}{3{,}000} = 83.3\%$$

For wire and cable the published tables usually give figures in ohms per 1000 ft or 100 ft for resistance, reactance, and impedance. It also gives different

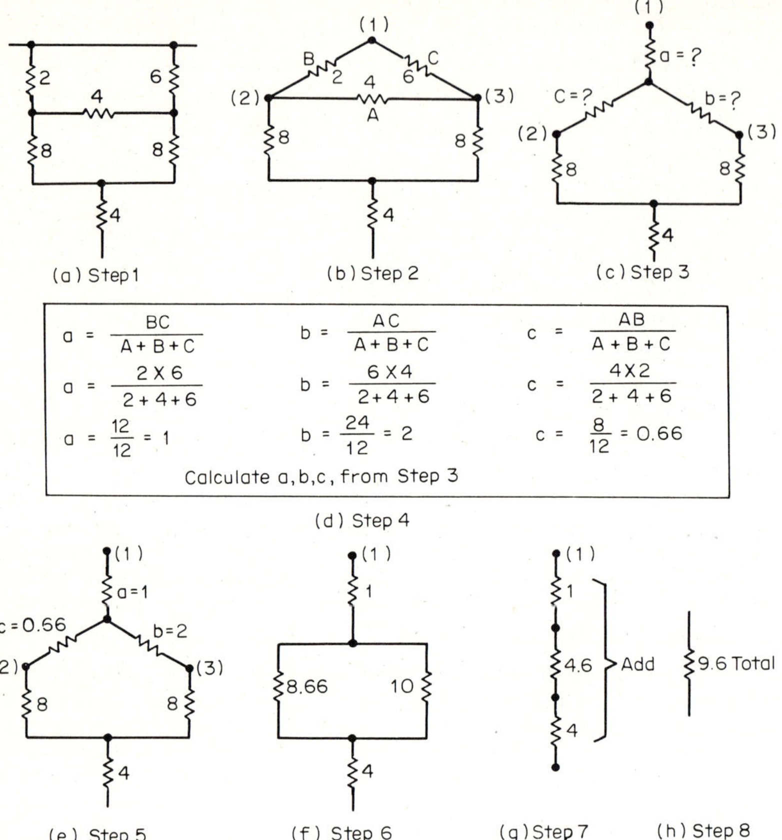

Figure 33.5 Star-delta conversion application, Example 3.

tables for three conductors in magnetic or nonmagnetic duct, and also armored-cable installations and other variations. The first criteria then is to ensure that the correct information is available. If we consider an example of three single-conductor cables in magnetic duct with a size of No. 8, the resistance is given as 0.0779 Ω, the reactance is 0.00638, and as $r \pm jx$ is impedance, $\sqrt{(0.0779)^2 + (0.00638)^2}$ gives 0.0782 Ω. All values are per 100-ft unit length. To relate this to a percentage base, we use the following approach:

$$\%X = \frac{\text{(ohms reactance) (base kVA)}}{(\text{kV})^2 \times 10}$$

Considering only the conductor reactance of 0.00638 and base kVA of 10,000 kVA and a 4.16 kV system, we would have:

$$\%X = \frac{(0.00638)\ (10{,}000)}{(4.16)^2 \times 10}$$

$$= 0.368\% \text{ per 100 ft}$$

$$= 0.00368\% \text{ per 1 ft}$$

Two considerations are now left; one is to determine the length of cable run and multiply by the 0.00368%; the other is to decide whether to include the resistance in the calculations. In the smaller-size cables the resistance is high compared to the reactance but on the other hand the smaller cables are not generally used on the main feeders on which the short-circuit study is made. Consider the reactance of a 300-MCM conductor in the same class: the resistance is 0.00520 and the reactance is 0.00519. In the preceding example the resistance was nearly 10 times more than the reactance, while the latter gives resistance and reactance being nearly equal.

Including resistance for cables will give a higher impedance and therefore limit the fault current more; however, we are generally trying to ascertain what the rating of a circuit breaker or piece of switchgear should be. Therefore if we use only reactance, we will be in a "worse condition" situation. If the fault current is too high for the equipment, another look at the whole study is necessary, and an inclusion of all reactances and possible significant resistances to determine if a marginal situation exists or if it is necessary to go to the next higher fault-current rating.

Obtaining the reactance for the utility source is fairly simple. There are two sources of information for the utility-company short circuit. The first and obvious is the utility company itself. They will state that "there is 500,000 kVA available" or some other kVA level. To change this to a percentage on the selected base, it is only necessary to divide into the base kVA and multiply by 100. For example, on a 10,000-kVA base, with 500,000 kVA available, the percentage reactance would be:

$$\% = \frac{10{,}000 \times 100}{500{,}000}$$

$$= 2\% \text{ source impedance}$$

In some cases the information is not available from the utility company, in which case use the rating of the incoming circuit breaker device in kVA and follow the preceding method. For example, if the circuit breaker was rated at 32,000 A on a 34.5-kV system, the kVA rating would be:

$$34.5 \times 32{,}000 \times 1.73 = 1{,}909{,}920 \text{ kVA}$$

On a 10,000-kVA base it would be

$$\% = \frac{10{,}000 \times 100}{1{,}909{,}920}$$

$$= 0.523\%$$

This equivalent impedance can be arranged as an extension of the main substation-transformer impedance. This means that the source impedance, the main transformer, and the main transformer secondary bus or cable to the secondary breaker can all be shown as connected in series and therefore will be arithmetically added and shown as a single impedance in the second step.

A similar routine is applied to any generators, except that the generator subtransient reactance is required either from the manufacturer, or from published tables, providing the correct model is selected. This is then calculated to the correct base, and also the generator conductors to the first breaker; they can then be shown as two reactances in series.

33.9 PER UNIT IMPEDANCES

Some times calculations and reactances are represented by the per unit method. The method simply means that the calculations for reactances to a unit base are left in decimal form rather than being multiplied by 100. Conversely, the per unit figure is the percentage figure divided by 100. For example, 35% is equivalent to 0.35 per unit. The symbol for percent is (%) and the symbol for per unit is (o/1) or sometimes (pu). There are reasons for preferring to work with per unit values rather than percentages, but there are also reasons for working with the percentage units. One reason is that probably more people are familiar with it than any other; also, it is easier to keep track of the all-too-elusive decimal point.

33.10 CONDUCTOR HEATING UNDER SHORT CIRCUIT

When a short circuit occurs, the rise in current is fast. The heating effect on a conductor is a function of I^2R. The resistance of a conductor remains constant (except for a minor change due to heat); therefore, the rise in temperature can be contributed to the I^2 portion. In order to determine if a conductor is adequately sized, it is necessary to check it for continuous rating and the short-circuit rating. It may be possible that a small size is adequate for the continuous duty, but a much larger size is necessary for short-circuit duty. The current rise, and therefore the temperature rise, is limited by the maximum short-circuit current available and also the opening time of the circuit breaker, which can be anywhere from 3 to 8 cycles. Therefore, the opening time of the protective device is significant. The empirical basic equation for heating of a conductor is given as a time function. In other words, the equation states that it will take a time of t seconds for a copper conductor of an area CM (circular mils) to rise to a temperature of T_2 (Celsius[1]) from an ambient of T_1 (Celsius) when subjected to a current of I amperes (rms). The two constants 33 and 234 are for copper; these should be substituted by 80 and 228, respectively, for aluminum. The criteria for this example is as follows.

- Current I is 10,000 A.
- Conductor is 500,000 CM area.
- Ambient temperature T_1 is 40°C. Final temperature T_2 is 130°C (40° + 90° rise).

[1] Celsius is the metric name for the centigrade scale.

In the following examples we will solve for the unknown t seconds first. We will then run through the exercise of solving for the other four variables, which should of course check with the given criteria. Although the mathematics are not complicated, the reason for presenting completed problems for each variable is that it offers a time-saver and only requires a "plugging in" of numbers to solve for any variable. The temperature rise is considered to be in the conductor only with no losses contributed by the sheath or conduction; hence the calculations are conservative.

Solve for time t

1.1. $t = \dfrac{1}{\left(\dfrac{I}{\mathrm{CM}}\right)^2 (33)} \left[\log_{10} \dfrac{(T_2 + 234)}{(T_1 + 234)}\right]$ *Basic equation*

1.2. $t = \dfrac{1}{\left(\dfrac{10{,}000}{500{,}000}\right)^2 33} \left[\log_{10} \dfrac{(130 + 234)}{(40 + 234)}\right]$ *Substitute criteria*

1.3. $t = \dfrac{1}{0.0132} \left[\log_{10} \dfrac{364}{274}\right]$ *Simplify*

1.4. $t = 75.757 \times \log_{10} 1.328.$ *Simplify*

1.5. $t = 75.757 \times 0.123.$ *Simplify*

1.6. $t = 9.318$ seconds. *Resultant*

Solve for I amperes

2.1. $t = \dfrac{1}{\left(\dfrac{I}{\mathrm{CM}}\right)^2 (33)} \left[\log_{10} \dfrac{(T_2 + 234)}{(T_1 + 234)}\right]$ *Basic equation*

2.2. $\left(\dfrac{I}{\mathrm{CM}}\right)^2 = \dfrac{1}{t(33)} \left[\log_{10} \dfrac{(T_2 + 234)}{(T_1 + 234)}\right]$ *Cross-multiply*

2.3. $\dfrac{I}{\mathrm{CM}} = \sqrt{\dfrac{1}{t(33)} \left[\log_{10} \dfrac{(T_2 + 234)}{(T_1 + 234)}\right]}$ *Square root of both sides*

2.4. $I = \mathrm{CM} \sqrt{\dfrac{1}{t(33)} \left[\log_{10} \dfrac{(T_2 + 234)}{(T_1 + 234)}\right]}$ *Cross-multiply*

2.5. $I = 500{,}000 \sqrt{\dfrac{1}{9.318 \times 33} \times 0.123}$ *Lines 1.5 and 1.6, and criteria*

2.6. $I = 500{,}000 \sqrt{\dfrac{0.123}{9.318 \times 33}}$ *Simplify*

2.7. $I = 500{,}000 \times 0.02$ *Simplify*

2.8. $I = 10{,}000$ A *Checks with criteria*

Solve for Area in CM (circular mils)

3.1. $\frac{I}{\mathrm{CM}} = \sqrt{\frac{1}{t(33)}\left[\log_{10}\frac{(T_2+234)}{(T_1+234)}\right]}$

3.2. $\frac{I}{\mathrm{CM}} = \sqrt{a}$ — *Substitute (a)*

3.3. $\mathrm{CM} = \frac{I}{\sqrt{a}}$ — *Cross-multiply, and commutative*

3.4. $\mathrm{CM} = \frac{I}{\sqrt{\frac{1}{t(33)}\left[\log_{10}\frac{(T_2+234)}{(T_1+234)}\right]}}$ — *Replacement for (a)*

3.5. $\mathrm{CM} = \frac{10{,}000}{0.02}$ — *Lines 2.7 and 2.8*

3.6. $\mathrm{CM} = 500{,}000$ — *Checks with criteria*

Solve for Temperature T_2

4.1. $t = \frac{1}{\left(\frac{I}{\mathrm{CM}}\right)^2 33}\left[\log_{10}\frac{(T_2+234)}{(T_1+234)}\right]$ — *Basic equation*

4.2. $t\left(\frac{I}{\mathrm{CM}}\right)^2 33 = \left[\log_{10}\frac{(T_2+234)}{(T_1+234)}\right]$ — *Cross-multiply*

4.3. $t\left(\frac{I}{\mathrm{CM}}\right)^2 33 = \log_{10}(T_2+234) - \log_{10}(T_1+234)$ — *Separate T_1 and T_2*

4.4. $t\left(\frac{I}{\mathrm{CM}}\right)^2 33 + \log_{10}(T_1+234) = \log_{10}(T_2+234)$ — *Isolate T_2*

4.5. $a = t\left(\frac{I}{\mathrm{CM}}\right)^2 33 + \log_{10}(T_1+234)$ — *Separation of equality and sub (a)*

4.6. $a = \log_{10}(T_2+234)$ — *Line 4.4 separa[tion] of equality*

4.7. $\log_{10} x = a$ — *Axiom*

4.8. $10^a = x \therefore 10^a = (T_2+234)$ — *Axiom and line 4.6*

4.9. $a = \log_{10} x$ and antilog of $\log_{10} x = a$ — *Axiom*

4.10. antilog $a = (T_2+234)$ — *Line 4.6*

4.11. antilog $a - 234 = T_2$ — *Isolate T_2*

4.12. antilog $\left[9.318\left(\frac{10{,}000}{500{,}000}\right)^2 33 + \log_{10}(40+234)\right] - 234 = T_2$ — *Replace (a) line 4.5*

4.13. antilog $[9.318 \times 0.0132 + 2.4378] - 234 = T_2$ — *Simplify*

4.14. antilog $(2.5608 - 234) = T_2$ — *Simplify*

4.15. $T_2 = 364 - 234 = 130°\text{C}$ *Find antilog*

Solution checks with criteria.

Solve for Temperature T_1

5.1. $t\left(\frac{I}{\text{CM}}\right)^2 33 = \log_{10}(T_2 + 234) - \log_{10}(T_1 + 234)$	*Line 4.3*
5.2. $t\left(\frac{I}{\text{CM}}\right)^2 33 - \log_{10}(T_2 + 234) = -\log_{10}(T_1 + 234)$	*Isolate* T_1
5.3. $9.318 \times 0.0132 - \log_{10}(130 + 234) = -\log_{10}(T_1 - 234)$	*Sub from Part 4.1.*
5.4. $0.1229 - 2.5611 = -\log_{10}(T_1 + 234)$	*Simplify*
5.5. $2.4382 = \log_{10}(T_1 + 234)$	*Simplify and divide by (−1)*
5.6. $a = \log_{10} x = \log_{10}(T_1 + 234)$	*Sub* (a)
5.7. $10^a = x = T_1 + 234$	*Axiom*
5.8. antilog $a = T_1 + 234$	*Lines 4.8 and 4.9.*
5.9. antilog $a - 234 = T_1$	
5.10. antilog $2.4382 - 234 = T_1$	*Replacement from line 5.5.*
5.11. $274 - 234 = 40°\text{C}$	*Find antilog and solve.*

Solution checks with criteria.

The previous examples are arbitrary figures selected purely for demonstrating the mathematical routines as applied to copper conductors.

For actual temperature rise, the temperature limit of the conductor is of course related to the ambient and the type of conductor; therefore these figures must be selected based on the actual project specifications. It is also obvious that in this day of the pocket calculator with the floating decimal, although it is better than the slide rule, a back check on figures will rarely give you what you started out with, hence the variance in our examples. The figures, however, are good enough for design of industrial power circuits.

33.11 UNBALANCED SHORT CIRCUITS

Unbalanced short circuits occur when a fault develops between phases (line to line). Variations on this are the "line to line to ground," the "single open line," and "single line to ground." These faults all have other variations like "line to line to ground through an impedance," etc. The message then is that this is a field of study warranting a better than average familiarity with symmetrical components to derive solutions and further more understanding of the solution and knowing what to do with it when you have it. We will therefore not introduce these types of faults except for the ground fault, which has already been covered in an earlier chapter.

33.12 LINE-TO-GROUND FAULT

The line-to-ground fault belongs in the category of the preceding paragraph; however, an understanding of this is mandatory for the design of electrical power systems; therefore we introduced it earlier as part of the calculations necessary for system grounding. Electrical engineers tend to lump short circuits into one group (set) with the statement "can you do short-circuit studies." This is really incorrect, short-circuit studies do not build an industrial plant, they confirm that it is a safe design. An electrical design falls into three groups (sets).

1. Power system
2. Grounding system
3. System performance (stability)

When designing a power system, one of the concluding exercises is a short-circuit study which is a "three-phase" fault study. When designing a three-phase system, and a grounded system is required, it is necessary to confirm short-circuit currents to ground and therefore a "line-to-ground" short-circuit study is required. If a system study is required, then other types of faults are considered and their effects analyzed. This is the reasoning for including the line-to-ground fault examples in the chapter on system grounding.

33.13 SUMMATION

To conclude this chapter on short circuits, we will point out that short-circuit calculations, when completed, provide the electrical designer with a number. This number is probably not an accurate value, it is only accurate to the extent that circuit devices were included and the correct resistance and reactances were used to represent the devices. In low-voltage systems resistance plays a big part in lowering fault currents. Contacts, bus bars, current transformers, disconnect switches, bus taps, etc., are all parts not usually included, and the calculation is generally very simple with regard to including minimum components. This will give a higher than actual fault current; therefore in a borderline situation it may be necessary to redo the calculation but including all items as well as the resistance.

This then is one action related to evaluating the number given by the calculation. The other action is in relating the number to available equipment. In all probability the equipment is selected first and the short-circuit calculation is "run" to confirm that the rating of the selected equipment is adequate. As long as the rating of the equipment is higher than the number given in the short-circuit calculation, safety is generally assured. In fact a safety margin will exist because of the simplified approach to the calculations. For example, motor contribution is generally accepted as being equivalent to the kVA of the transformer for a 460-V system and 50 to 60% of the transformer kVA for the 240- or 208-V classes. The probability is that the diversity of operation means that not all these motors will be running at the same time; therefore the fault will probably have a lower momentary rating than expected. The system, however, must be designed for the "maximum probable"; therefore the full allocation should be included.

As far as positive-, negative-, and zero-sequence values are concerned, Tables 33.2 to 33.8 list some values along with various formulas and useful information.

TABLE 33.2 Reactances Based on kVA of Connected Motors

Item	*Motor ratings and connections*	*Subtransient reactance X''_d, percent*	*Transient reactance X'_d, percent*
1	600 volts or less – induction	28*	
2	600 volts or less – synchronous (items 1 and 2 include motor leads)	21*	29
3	600 volts or less – induction	34*	
4	600 volts or less – synchronous (items 3 and 4 include motor leads and stepdown transformers)	27*	35
5	Motors above 600 volts – induction	20	
6	Motors above 600 volts – synchronous	15	25
7	Motors above 600 volts – induction	26	
8	Motors above 600 volts – synchronous (items 7 and 8 include stepdown transformers)	21	31

* Based on AIEE Standard No. 20.

NOTE: Large induction motors will have reactances of approximately 15 to 25 percent (on own kVA base) with a 20 percent reactance as most common.

TABLE 33.3 Approximate Reactances of 60-Hz Synchronous Machines (Percent values on machine kVA rating)

Machines	X''_d		X'_d	
	Range	*Mean*	*Range*	*Mean*
Salient-pole generators (without amortisseur):				
12 poles or less	15–35	25		
14 poles or more	25–45	35		
Salient-pole generators[a] (with amortisseur):			Not used in normal short-circuit calculations	
12 poles or less	10–25	18		
14 poles or more	10–35	24		
Synchronous condensers	18–35	27		
Synchronous converters:[b]				
600 volts dc	17–22	20		
250 volts dc	28–38	33		
Synchronous motors:[c]				
6 pole	10–20	15	15–30	23
8–14 pole	15–25	20	20–40	30
16 pole or more	25–45	30	25–60	40

[a] Nearly all salient-pole generators built by General Electric Company since 1935 have amortisseur windings.

[b] Add transformer reactance:

For compound-wound converters add 12 percent.
For shunt-wound converters add 7 percent.

[c] These data are useful for estimating reactances of individual large motors of several hundred or several thousand horsepower.

TABLE 33.4 Approximate Impedance of 60-Hz Power Transformers (Above 500 kVA)

Insulation class, kV		*Impedance at kVA base equal to 55°C rating of largest capacity winding for*	
High voltage	*Low voltage*	*Self-cooled or water-cooled rating, percent*	*Forced-oil cooled rating, percent*
15 or lower	15 or lower	5½	6¾
25	15 or lower	5½	8¼
34.5	15 or lower	6	9
46.0	15 or lower	6½	9¾
69.0	15 or lower	7	10½
92.0	15 or lower	7½	11¼
115.0	15 or lower	8	12
138.0	15 or lower	8½	12¾

For high-voltage insulation classes intermediate of those given, use the impedance of the next higher listed insulation class.

For transformers with a load-ratio control add 0.5 percent to the values listed above except in those cases in which a lower impedance has been specified.

The percent resistance on the base given above ranges from 1.0 down to 0.06.

TABLE 33.5 Approximate Reactance of Load-center-type Transformers, 60 Hz (Three-phase)

kVA range	*15-kV maximum primary voltage 600-volt maximum secondary voltage percent reactance on own kVA base**
112½–150	3.0
225–500	5.0
750–2000	5.5

* Percent resistance on own kVA base is approximately 1.5 percent for 150 kVA and below and varies from approximately 1 down to 0.8 percent on ratings above 150 kVA.

TABLE 33.6 Approximate Resistance, Reactance, and Impedance of Single-phase Distribution Transformers

	High voltage: 2400/4160Y volts and 2400/4800/8320Y volts Low voltage: 120/240, 240/480, 600 volts – 60 Hz			*High voltage: 7200/12,470Y volts Low voltage: 120/240, 240/480, 600 volts – 60 Hz*		
kVA	***Percent R***	***Percent X***	***Percent Z***	***Percent R***	***Percent X***	***Percent Z***
3 5	1.7	1.5	2.3	2.2	1.7	2.8
10 15 25	1.5	1.7	2.3	1.6	1.6	2.3
37½ 50	1.3	2.2	2.6	1.3	2.0	2.4
75 100	1.2	2.3	2.6	1.2	3.5	3.7
167	1.1	3.8	4.0	1.0	3.6	3.7
250 333 500	1.0	4.7	4.8	1.0	5.1	5.2

TABLE 33.7 Correction Factors for Nonmagnetic Ducts. Three-conductor Cables (Determine correct Z from corrected values of X and R. No correction is required for interlocked armor.)

Factor for correcting reactances, all sizes of cable	*Factors for correcting resistances*	
	No. 14 to No. 00 Awg	*No. 0000 Awg to 750 MCM*
0.87	1.0	0.98

TABLE 33.8 Percent Reactance of Typical Three-Phase Cable Circuits (Percent Reactance of 1000 circuit feet on a 1000-kVA Base)

System voltage	*230*	*460*	*575*	*2,400*	*4,160*	*6,900*	*13,800*
CABLE SIZE, NO. 4 TO 1 AWG							
Three single-conductor cables in iron conduit	98.3	24.6	15.74	1.075	0.358		
Three-conductor cable in iron conduit or interlocked armored cable	71.8	18	11.5	0.669	0.222	0.11	0.0276
Three-conductor cable in non-magnetic duct	58.5	14.7	9.4	0.581	0.194	0.0955	0.024
CABLE SIZE, NO. 1/0 TO NO. 4/0 AWG							
Three single-conductor cables in iron conduit	92.5	23.2	14.85	0.955	0.318		
Three-conductor cable in iron conduit or interlocked armored cable	68	17.1	10.9	0.6	0.2	0.0943	0.0237
Three-conductor cable in non-magnetic duct	54.8	13.72	8.8	0.52	0.173	0.0818	0.0205
CABLE SIZE, 250 TO 750 MCM							
Three single-conductor cables in iron conduit	85	21.3	13.63	0.868	0.289		
Three-conductor cable in iron conduit or interlocked armored cable	61.4	15.4	9.85	0.538	0.179	0.0796	0.02
Three-conductor cable in non-magnetic duct	51	12.8	8.19	0.477	0.159	0.07	0.0176

For single-phase circuits multiply values by 2.

APPENDIX

TABLE A.1 Motor-branch-circuit Data – 460-volt Three-phase AC

Horse-power	*Full-load amp*	*Starter NEMA size*	*Circuit breaker*		*Fuse size*	*Power control*		*Three control*	*Three power*
			Frame size	*Trip size*					
½	1.0	1	100	15	15	1*		No. 12	No. 12
¾	1.4	1	100	15	15	1*		No. 12	No. 12
1	1.8	1	100	15	15	1*		No. 12	No. 12
1½	2.6	1	100	15	15	1*		No. 12	No. 12
2	3.4	1	100	15	15	1*		No. 12	No. 12
3	4.8	1	100	15	15	1*		No. 12	No. 12
5	7.6	1	100	15	20	1*		No. 12	No. 12
7½	11.0	1	100	20	30	1*		No. 12	No. 12
10	14.0	1	100	30	40	1*		No. 12	No. 12
15	21	2	100	40	60	1		No. 12	No. 10
20	27	2	100	50	70	1		No. 12	No. 8
25	34	2	100	70	90	1		No. 12	No. 8
30	40	3	100	70	100	1¼		No. 12	No. 6
40	52	3	100	100	150	1½		No. 12	No. 4
50	65	3	225	100	175	1¼	¾	No. 12	No. 2
60	77	4	225	125	200	1¼	¾	No. 12	No. 2
75	96	4	225	150	250	1½	¾	No. 12	No. 1
100	124	4	225	200	350	2	¾	No. 12	No.2/0
125	156	5	400	300	400	2	¾	No. 12	No.3/0
150	180	5	400	400	450	2½	¾	No. 12	No.4/0
200	240	5	600	500	600	3	¾	No. 12	350 MCM
Table 430–150 ↑		Motor starter	Short-circuit protection based on Table 430–152			Table 4 conduit size, in.		Table 310–12 75°C RHW or THW	

*¾ in. allowed if three No. 14 controls are used instead of No. 12.

1. 50 hp and up requires separate conduit for control.

2. Do not use TW unless specified.

3. Notes 8 and 10 to Tables 310–12 to 310–15 and Exception 1 – Reference 300–3e exempts derating due to motor control conductors.

TABLE A.2 Properties of Conductors

Size, AWG or MCM	Area, circular mils	Concentric-lay stranded conductors		Bare conductors		Dc resistance, ohms/M ft at 25°C (77°F)		
						Copper		
		No. wires	Diam. each wire, in.	Diam., in.	Area,* sq. in.	Bare cond.	Tinned cond.	Alumi-num
18	1,620	Solid	0.0403	0.0403	0.0013	6.51	6.79	10.7
16	2,580	Solid	0.0508	0.0508	0.0020	4.10	4.26	6.74
14	4,110	Solid	0.0641	0.0641	0.0032	2.57	2.68	4.22
12	6,530	Solid	0.0808	0.0808	0.0051	1.62	1.68	2.66
10	10,380	Solid	0.1019	0.1019	0.0081	1.018	1.06	1.67
8	16,510	Solid	0.1285	0.1285	0.0130	0.6404	0.659	1.05
6	26,240	7	0.0612	0.184	0.027	0.410	0.427	0.674
4	41,740	7	0.0772	0.232	0.042	0.259	0.269	0.424
3	52,620	7	0.0867	0.260	0.053	0.205	0.213	0.336
2	66,360	7	0.0974	0.292	0.067	0.162	0.169	0.266
1	83,690	19	0.0664	0.332	0.087	0.129	0.134	0.211
0	105,600	19	0.0745	0.372	0.109	0.102	0.106	0.168
00	133,100	19	0.0837	0.418	0.137	0.0811	0.0843	0.133
000	167,800	19	0.0940	0.470	0.173	0.0642	0.0668	0.105
0,000	211,600	19	0.1055	0.528	0.219	0.0509	0.0525	0.0836
250	250,000	37	0.0822	0.575	0.260	0.0431	0.0449	0.0708
300	300,000	37	0.0900	0.630	0.312	0.0360	0.0374	0.0590
300	350,000	37	0.0973	0.681	0.364	0.0308	0.0320	0.0505
400	400,000	37	0.1040	0.728	0.416	0.0270	0.0278	0.0442
500	500,000	37	0.1162	0.813	0.519	0.0216	0.0222	0.0354
600	600,000	61	0.0992	0.893	0.626	0.0180	0.0187	0.0295
700	700,000	61	0.1071	0.964	0.730	0.0154	0.0159	0.0253
750	750,000	61	0.1109	0.998	0.782	0.0144	0.0148	0.0236
800	800,000	61	0.1145	1.030	0.833	0.0135	0.0139	0.0221
900	900,000	61	0.1215	1.090	0.933	0.0120	0.0123	0.0197
1,000	1,000,000	61	0.1280	1.150	1.039	0.0108	0.0111	0.0177
1,250	1,250,000	91	0.1172	1.289	1.305	0.00863	0.00888	0.0142
1,500	1,500,000	91	0.1284	1.410	1.561	0.00719	0.00740	0.0118
1,750	1,750,000	127	0.1174	1.526	1.829	0.00616	0.00634	0.0101
2,000	2,000,000	127	0.1255	1.630	2.087	0.00539	0.00555	0.00885

* Area given is that of a circle having a diameter equal to the overall diameter of a stranded conductor.

The values given in the table are those given in Handbook 100 of the National Bureau of Standards except that those shown in the eighth column are those given in Specification B33 of the American Society for Testing and Materials, and those shown in the ninth column are those given in Standard No. S-19-81 of the Insulated Power Cable Engineers Association and Standard No. WC3-1964 of the National Electrical Manufacturers Association.

The resistance values given in the last three columns are applicable only to direct current. When conductors larger than No. 4/0 are used with alternating current, the multiplying factors in Table 9, Chapter 9, National Electrical Code, should be used to compensate for skin effect.

TABLE A.3 Transformer Data

THREE-PHASE TRANSFORMER, FULL-LOAD CURRENTS

	Line-to-line volts											
kva	***208***	***240***	***480***	***2,400***	***4,160***	***4,800***	***7,200***	***8,320***	***12,000***	***12,470***	***13,200***	***14,400***
9	25.0	21.7	10.8	2.17	1.25	1.08	.72	.63	.43	.42	.39	.36
15	41.6	36.1	18.0	3.61	2.08	1.80	1.20	1.04	.72	.69	.66	.60
30	83.3	72.2	36.1	7.22	4.17	3.61	2.41	2.08	1.44	1.39	1.31	1.20
45	125	108	54.1	10.8	6.25	5.41	3.61	3.13	2.17	2.08	1.97	1.80
75	208	180	90.2	18.0	10.4	9.02	6.01	5.21	3.61	3.48	3.28	3.01
112½	312	271	135	27.1	15.6	13.5	9.02	7.81	5.41	5.21	4.92	4.51
150	416	361	180	36.1	20.8	18.0	12.0	10.4	7.22	6.95	6.56	6.01
225	625	541	271	54.1	31.3	27.1	18.0	15.6	10.8	10.4	9.84	9.02
300	833	722	361	72.2	41.7	36.1	24.1	20.8	14.4	13.9	13.1	12.0
500	1,388	1,203	601	120	69.4	60.1	40.1	34.8	24.1	23.2	21.9	20.1
750	2,082	1,804	902	180	104	90.2	60.1	52.1	36.1	34.7	32.8	30.1
1,000	2,776	2,406	1,203	241	139	120	80.2	69.4	48.1	46.3	43.7	40.1
1,500	4,164	3,608	1,804	361	208	180	120.3	104	72.2	69.4	65.6	60.1
2,000	5,552	4,811	2,406	481	278	240	160.4	138.8	96.2	92.6	87.4	

SINGLE-PHASE TRANSFORMER, FULL-LOAD CURRENTS

	Line volts									
kvA	**120**	**240**	**480**	**2,400**	**4,160**	**4,800**	**7,200**	**7,620**	**12,000**	**14,400**
3	25.0	12.5	6.3	1.25	.72	.63	.42	.39	.25	.21
5	41.7	20.8	10.4	2.08	1.20	1.04	.69	.66	.42	.35
10	83.3	41.7	20.8	4.17	2.40	2.08	1.39	1.31	.83	.69
15	125	62.5	31.3	6.25	3.61	3.13	2.08	1.97	1.25	1.04
25	208	104	52.1	10.4	6.01	5.21	3.47	3.28	2.08	1.74
37½	313	156	78.1	15.6	9.01	7.81	5.21	4.92	3.13	2.60
50	417	208	104	20.8	12.0	10.4	6.94	6.56	4.17	3.47
75	625	313	156	31.3	18.0	15.6	10.4	9.84	6.25	5.21
100	833	417	208	41.7	24.0	20.8	13.9	13.1	8.33	6.94
167	1,392	696	348	69.6	40.1	34.8	23.2	21.9	13.9	11.6
250	2,083	1,042	521	104	60.1	52.1	34.7	32.8	20.8	17.4
333	2,775	1,388	694	139	80.0	69.4	46.3	43.7	27.7	23.1
500	4,167	2,083	1,042	208	120	104	69.4	65.6	41.7	34.7

TABLE A.4 American Standard Device Function Numbers

1. Master element
2. Time-delay starting, or closing, relay
3. Checking, or interlocking, relay
4. Master contactor
5. Stopping device
6. Starting circuit breaker
7. Anode circuit breaker
8. Control power disconnecting device
9. Reversing device
10. Unit sequence switch
11. Reserved for future application
12. Overspeed device
13. Synchronous-speed device
14. Underspeed device
15. Speed, or frequency, matching device
16. Reserved for future application
17. Shunting, or discharge, switch
18. Accelerating, or decelerating, device
19. Starting-to-running transition contactor
20. Electrically operated valve
21. Distance relay
22. Equalizer circuit breaker

35. Brush-operating, or slip-ring short-circuiting, device
36. Polarity device
37. Undercurrent, or underpower, relay
38. Bearing protective device
39. Mechanical condition monitor
40. Field relay
41. Field circuit breaker
42. Running circuit breaker
43. Manual transfer, or selector, device
44. Unit sequence starting relay
45. Atmospheric condition monitor
46. Reverse-phase, or phase-balance, current relay
47. Phase-sequence voltage relay
48. Incomplete sequence relay
49. Machine, or transformer, thermal relay
50. Instantaneous overcurrent, or rate-of-rise, relay
51. AC time overcurrent relay
52. AC circuit breaker
53. Exciter, or dc generator, relay
54. High-speed dc circuit breaker
55. Power-factor relay

66. Notching, or jogging, device
67. AC directional overcurrent relay
68. Blocking relay
69. Permissive control device
70. Electrically operated rheostat
71. Liquid or gas level relay
72. DC circuit breaker
73. Load-resistor contactor
74. Alarm relay
75. Position changing mechanism
76. DC overcurrent relay
77. Pulse transmitter
78. Phase angle measuring, or out-of-step protective, relay
79. AC reclosing relay
80. Liquid or gas flow relay
81. Frequency relay
82. DC reclosing relay
83. Automatic selective control, or transfer, relay
84. Operating mechanism
85. Carrier, or pilot-wire, receiver relay
86. Locking-out relay
87. Differential protective relay
88. Auxiliary motor, or motor generator

23. Temperature control device
24. Reserved for future application
25. Synchronizing, or synchronism-check, device
26. Apparatus thermal device
27. Undervoltage relay
28. Flame detector
29. Isolating contactor
30. Annunciator relay
31. Separate excitation device
32. Directional power relay
33. Position switch
34. Motor-operated sequence switch

56. Field application relay
57. Short-circuiting, or grounding, device
58. Power rectifier misfire relay
59. Overvoltage relay
60. Voltage balance relay
61. Current balance relay
62. Time-delay stopping, or opening, relay
63. Liquid or gas pressure, level, or flow relay
64. Ground protective relay
65. Governor

89. Line switch
90. Regulating device
91. Voltage directional relay
92. Voltage and power directional relay
93. Field changing contactor
94. Tripping, or trip-free, relay

95.–99. Used only for specific applications on individual installations where none of the assigned numbered functions from 1 to 94 are suitable

NOTE: Alternate names such as *relay, contactor, circuit breaker, switch,* or *device* may be used for any function where applicable.

NOTE: Suffix letters are used with device function numbers for various purposes; for instance, suffix *N* is generally used if the device is connected in the secondary neutral of current transformers, and suffixes *X, Y,* and *Z* are used to denote separate auxiliary devices.

TABLE A.5 Natural Trigonometric Functions

Angle	Sin	Tan	Cot	Cos	Deg
0	0.0000	0.0000	∞	1.0000	90
1	0.0175	0.0175	57.2900	0.9998	89
2	0.0349	0.0349	28.6363	0.9994	88
3	0.0523	0.0524	19.0811	0.9986	87
4	0.0698	0.0699	14.3007	0.9976	86
5	0.0872	0.0875	11.4300	0.9962	85
6	0.1045	0.1051	9.5144	0.9945	84
7	0.1219	0.1228	8.1443	0.9925	83
8	0.1392	0.1405	7.1154	0.9903	82
9	0.1564	0.1584	6.3138	0.9877	81
10	0.1736	0.1763	5.6713	0.9848	80
11	0.1908	0.1944	5.1446	0.9816	79
12	0.2079	0.2126	4.7046	0.9781	78
13	0.2250	0.2309	4.3315	0.9744	77
14	0.2419	0.2493	4.0108	0.9703	76
15	0.2588	0.2679	3.7321	0.9659	75
16	0.2756	0.2867	3.4874	0.9613	74
17	0.2924	0.3057	3.2709	0.9563	73
18	0.3090	0.3249	3.0777	0.9511	72
19	0.3256	0.3443	2.9042	0.9455	71
20	0.3420	0.3640	2.7475	0.9397	70
21	0.3584	0.3839	2.6051	0.9336	69
22	0.3746	0.4040	2.4751	0.9272	68
23	0.3907	0.4245	2.3559	0.9205	67
24	0.4067	0.4452	2.2460	0.9135	66
25	0.4226	0.4663	2.1445	0.9063	65
26	0.4384	0.4877	2.0503	0.8988	64
27	0.4540	0.5095	1.9626	0.8910	63
28	0.4695	0.5317	1.8807	0.8829	62
29	0.4848	0.5543	1.8040	0.8746	61
30	0.5000	0.5774	1.7321	0.8660	60
31	0.5150	0.6009	1.6643	0.8572	59
32	0.5299	0.6249	1.6003	0.8480	58
33	0.5446	0.6494	1.5399	0.8387	57
34	0.5592	0.6745	1.4826	0.8290	56
35	0.5736	0.7002	1.4281	0.8192	55
36	0.5878	0.7265	1.3764	0.8090	54
37	0.6018	0.7536	1.3270	0.7986	53
38	0.6157	0.7813	1.2799	0.7880	52
39	0.6293	0.8098	1.2349	0.7771	51
40	0.6428	0.8391	1.1918	0.7660	50
41	0.6561	0.8693	1.1504	0.7547	49
42	0.6691	0.9004	1.1106	0.7431	48
43	0.6820	0.9325	1.0724	0.7314	47
44	0.6947	0.9657	1.0355	0.7193	46
45	0.7071	1.0000	1.0000	0.7071	45
Deg	**Cos**	**Cot**	**Tan**	**Sin**	**Angle**

TABLE A.6 Temperature Conversion
Degrees Celsius to Degrees Fahrenheit

C	*F*	*C*	*F*	*C*	*F*	*C*	*F*	*C*	*F*	*C*	*F*
−40	−40.0	+5	+41.0		+104.0	+175	+347	+350	+662	+750	+1382
−38	−36.4	6	42.8	41	105.8	180	356	355	671	800	1472
−36	−32.8	7	44.6	42	107.6	185	365	360	680	850	1562
−34	−29.2	8	46.4	43	109.4	190	374	365	689	900	1652
−32	−25.6	9	48.2	44	111.2	195	383	370	698	950	1742
−30	−22.0	10	50.0	45	113.0	200	392	375	707	1000	1832
−28	−18.4	11	51.8	46	114.8	205	401	380	716	1050	1922
−26	−14.8	12	53.6	47	116.6	210	410	385	725	1100	2012
−24	−11.2	13	55.4	48	118.4	215	419	390	734	1150	2102
−22	− 7.6	14	57.2	49	120.2	220	428	395	743	1200	2192
−20	− 4.0	15	59.0	50	122.0	225	437	400	752	1250	2282
−19	− 2.2	16	60.8	55	131.0	230	446	405	761	1300	2372
−18	− 0.4	17	62.6	60	140.0	235	455	410	770	1350	2462
−17	+ 1.4	18	64.4	65	149.0	240	464	415	779	1400	2552
−16	3.2	19	66.2	70	158.0	245	473	420	788	1450	2642
−15	5.0	20	68.0	75	167.0	250	482	425	797	1500	2732
−14	6.8	21	69.8	80	176.0	255	491	430	806	1550	2822
−13	8.6	22	71.6	85	185.0	260	500	435	815	1600	2912
−12	10.4	23	73.4	90	194.0	265	509	440	824	1650	3002
−11	12.2	24	75.2	95	203.0	270	518	445	833	1700	3092
−10	14.0	25	77.0	100	212.0	275	527	450	842	1750	3182
− 9	15.8	26	78.8	105	221.0	280	536	455	851	1800	3272
− 8	17.6	27	80.6	110	230.0	285	545	460	860	1850	3362
− 7	19.4	28	82.4	115	239.0	290	554	465	869	1900	3452
− 6	21.2	29	84.2	120	248.0	295	563	470	878	1950	3542
− 5	23.0	30	86.0	125	257.0	300	572	475	887	2000	3632
− 4	24.8	31	87.8	130	266.0	305	581	480	896	2050	3722
− 3	26.6	32	89.6	135	275.0	310	590	485	905	2100	3812
− 2	28.4	33	91.4	140	284.0	315	599	490	914	2150	3902
− 1	30.2	34	93.2	145	293.0	320	608	495	923	2200	3992
0	32.0	35	95.0	150	302.0	325	617	500	932	2250	4082
+ 1	33.8	36	96.8	155	311.0	330	626	550	1022	2300	4172
2	35.6	37	98.6	160	320.0	335	635	600	1112	2350	4262
3	37.4	38	100.4	165	329.0	340	644	650	1202	2400	4352
4	39.2	39	102.2	170	338.0	345	653	700	1292	2450	4442

Table of Values for Interpolation in the Above Table

Degrees Celsius	1	2	3	4	5	6	7	8	9
Degrees Fahrenheit	1.8	3.6	5.4	7.2	9.0	10.8	12.6	14.4	16.2

INDEX